Communications in Computer and Information Science   **2116**

Rationale

The CCIS series is devoted to the publication of proceedings of computer science conferences. Its aim is to efficiently disseminate original research results in informatics in printed and electronic form. While the focus is on publication of peer-reviewed full papers presenting mature work, inclusion of reviewed short papers reporting on work in progress is welcome, too. Besides globally relevant meetings with internationally representative program committees guaranteeing a strict peer-reviewing and paper selection process, conferences run by societies or of high regional or national relevance are also considered for publication.

Topics

The topical scope of CCIS spans the entire spectrum of informatics ranging from foundational topics in the theory of computing to information and communications science and technology and a broad variety of interdisciplinary application fields.

Information for Volume Editors and Authors

Publication in CCIS is free of charge. No royalties are paid, however, we offer registered conference participants temporary free access to the online version of the conference proceedings on SpringerLink (http://link.springer.com) by means of an http referrer from the conference website and/or a number of complimentary printed copies, as specified in the official acceptance email of the event.

CCIS proceedings can be published in time for distribution at conferences or as post-proceedings, and delivered in the form of printed books and/or electronically as USBs and/or e-content licenses for accessing proceedings at SpringerLink. Furthermore, CCIS proceedings are included in the CCIS electronic book series hosted in the SpringerLink digital library at http://link.springer.com/bookseries/7899. Conferences publishing in CCIS are allowed to use Online Conference Service (OCS) for managing the whole proceedings lifecycle (from submission and reviewing to preparing for publication) free of charge.

Publication process

The language of publication is exclusively English. Authors publishing in CCIS have to sign the Springer CCIS copyright transfer form, however, they are free to use their material published in CCIS for substantially changed, more elaborate subsequent publications elsewhere. For the preparation of the camera-ready papers/files, authors have to strictly adhere to the Springer CCIS Authors' Instructions and are strongly encouraged to use the CCIS LaTeX style files or templates.

Abstracting/Indexing

CCIS is abstracted/indexed in DBLP, Google Scholar, EI-Compendex, Mathematical Reviews, SCImago, Scopus. CCIS volumes are also submitted for the inclusion in ISI Proceedings.

How to start

To start the evaluation of your proposal for inclusion in the CCIS series, please send an e-mail to ccis@springer.com.

Constantine Stephanidis · Margherita Antona ·
Stavroula Ntoa · Gavriel Salvendy
Editors

HCI International 2024 Posters

26th International Conference
on Human-Computer Interaction, HCII 2024
Washington, DC, USA, June 29 – July 4, 2024
Proceedings, Part III

 Springer

Editors
Constantine Stephanidis
University of Crete and Foundation for
Research and Technology - Hellas (FORTH)
Heraklion, Crete, Greece

Margherita Antona
Foundation for Research
and Technology – Hellas (FORTH)
Heraklion, Crete, Greece

Stavroula Ntoa
Foundation for Research
and Technology – Hellas (FORTH)
Heraklion, Crete, Greece

Gavriel Salvendy
University of Central Florida
Orlando, FL, USA

ISSN 1865-0929 ISSN 1865-0937 (electronic)
Communications in Computer and Information Science
ISBN 978-3-031-61949-6 ISBN 978-3-031-61950-2 (eBook)
https://doi.org/10.1007/978-3-031-61950-2

This Springer imprint is published by the registered company Springer Nature Switzerland AG
The registered company address is: Gewerbestrasse 11, 6330 Cham, Switzerland

If disposing of this product, please recycle the paper.

Foreword

This year we celebrate 40 years since the establishment of the HCI International (HCII) Conference, which has been a hub for presenting groundbreaking research and novel ideas and collaboration for people from all over the world.

The HCII conference was founded in 1984 by Prof. Gavriel Salvendy (Purdue University, USA, Tsinghua University, P.R. China, and University of Central Florida, USA) and the first event of the series, "1st USA-Japan Conference on Human-Computer Interaction", was held in Honolulu, Hawaii, USA, 18–20 August. Since then, HCI International is held jointly with several Thematic Areas and Affiliated Conferences, with each one under the auspices of a distinguished international Program Board and under one management and one registration. Twenty-six HCI International Conferences have been organized so far (every two years until 2013, and annually thereafter).

Over the years, this conference has served as a platform for scholars, researchers, industry experts and students to exchange ideas, connect, and address challenges in the ever-evolving HCI field. Throughout these 40 years, the conference has evolved itself, adapting to new technologies and emerging trends, while staying committed to its core mission of advancing knowledge and driving change.

As we celebrate this milestone anniversary, we reflect on the contributions of its founding members and appreciate the commitment of its current and past Affiliated Conference Program Board Chairs and members. We are also thankful to all past conference attendees who have shaped this community into what it is today.

The 26th International Conference on Human-Computer Interaction, HCI International 2024 (HCII 2024), was held as a 'hybrid' event at the Washington Hilton Hotel, Washington, DC, USA, during 29 June – 4 July 2024. It incorporated the 21 thematic areas and affiliated conferences listed below.

A total of 5108 individuals from academia, research institutes, industry, and government agencies from 85 countries submitted contributions, and 1271 papers and 309 posters were included in the volumes of the proceedings that were published just before the start of the conference, these are listed below. The contributions thoroughly cover the entire field of human-computer interaction, addressing major advances in knowledge and effective use of computers in a variety of application areas. These papers provide academics, researchers, engineers, scientists, practitioners and students with state-of-the-art information on the most recent advances in HCI.

The HCI International (HCII) conference also offers the option of presenting 'Late Breaking Work', and this applies both for papers and posters, with corresponding volumes of proceedings that will be published after the conference. Full papers will be included in the 'HCII 2024 - Late Breaking Papers' volumes of the proceedings to be published in the Springer LNCS series, while 'Poster Extended Abstracts' will be included as short research papers in the 'HCII 2024 - Late Breaking Posters' volumes to be published in the Springer CCIS series.

I would like to thank the Program Board Chairs and the members of the Program Boards of all thematic areas and affiliated conferences for their contribution towards the high scientific quality and overall success of the HCI International 2024 conference. Their manifold support in terms of paper reviewing (single-blind review process, with a minimum of two reviews per submission), session organization and their willingness to act as goodwill ambassadors for the conference is most highly appreciated.

This conference would not have been possible without the continuous and unwavering support and advice of Gavriel Salvendy, founder, General Chair Emeritus, and Scientific Advisor. For his outstanding efforts, I would like to express my sincere appreciation to Abbas Moallem, Communications Chair and Editor of HCI International News.

July 2024   Constantine Stephanidis

HCI International 2024 Thematic Areas and Affiliated Conferences

- HCI: Human-Computer Interaction Thematic Area
- HIMI: Human Interface and the Management of Information Thematic Area
- EPCE: 21st International Conference on Engineering Psychology and Cognitive Ergonomics
- AC: 18th International Conference on Augmented Cognition
- UAHCI: 18th International Conference on Universal Access in Human-Computer Interaction
- CCD: 16th International Conference on Cross-Cultural Design
- SCSM: 16th International Conference on Social Computing and Social Media
- VAMR: 16th International Conference on Virtual, Augmented and Mixed Reality
- DHM: 15th International Conference on Digital Human Modeling & Applications in Health, Safety, Ergonomics & Risk Management
- DUXU: 13th International Conference on Design, User Experience and Usability
- C&C: 12th International Conference on Culture and Computing
- DAPI: 12th International Conference on Distributed, Ambient and Pervasive Interactions
- HCIBGO: 11th International Conference on HCI in Business, Government and Organizations
- LCT: 11th International Conference on Learning and Collaboration Technologies
- ITAP: 10th International Conference on Human Aspects of IT for the Aged Population
- AIS: 6th International Conference on Adaptive Instructional Systems
- HCI-CPT: 6th International Conference on HCI for Cybersecurity, Privacy and Trust
- HCI-Games: 6th International Conference on HCI in Games
- MobiTAS: 6th International Conference on HCI in Mobility, Transport and Automotive Systems
- AI-HCI: 5th International Conference on Artificial Intelligence in HCI
- MOBILE: 5th International Conference on Human-Centered Design, Operation and Evaluation of Mobile Communications

List of Conference Proceedings Volumes Appearing Before the Conference

1. LNCS 14684, Human-Computer Interaction: Part I, edited by Masaaki Kurosu and Ayako Hashizume
2. LNCS 14685, Human-Computer Interaction: Part II, edited by Masaaki Kurosu and Ayako Hashizume
3. LNCS 14686, Human-Computer Interaction: Part III, edited by Masaaki Kurosu and Ayako Hashizume
4. LNCS 14687, Human-Computer Interaction: Part IV, edited by Masaaki Kurosu and Ayako Hashizume
5. LNCS 14688, Human-Computer Interaction: Part V, edited by Masaaki Kurosu and Ayako Hashizume
6. LNCS 14689, Human Interface and the Management of Information: Part I, edited by Hirohiko Mori and Yumi Asahi
7. LNCS 14690, Human Interface and the Management of Information: Part II, edited by Hirohiko Mori and Yumi Asahi
8. LNCS 14691, Human Interface and the Management of Information: Part III, edited by Hirohiko Mori and Yumi Asahi
9. LNAI 14692, Engineering Psychology and Cognitive Ergonomics: Part I, edited by Don Harris and Wen-Chin Li
10. LNAI 14693, Engineering Psychology and Cognitive Ergonomics: Part II, edited by Don Harris and Wen-Chin Li
11. LNAI 14694, Augmented Cognition, Part I, edited by Dylan D. Schmorrow and Cali M. Fidopiastis
12. LNAI 14695, Augmented Cognition, Part II, edited by Dylan D. Schmorrow and Cali M. Fidopiastis
13. LNCS 14696, Universal Access in Human-Computer Interaction: Part I, edited by Margherita Antona and Constantine Stephanidis
14. LNCS 14697, Universal Access in Human-Computer Interaction: Part II, edited by Margherita Antona and Constantine Stephanidis
15. LNCS 14698, Universal Access in Human-Computer Interaction: Part III, edited by Margherita Antona and Constantine Stephanidis
16. LNCS 14699, Cross-Cultural Design: Part I, edited by Pei-Luen Patrick Rau
17. LNCS 14700, Cross-Cultural Design: Part II, edited by Pei-Luen Patrick Rau
18. LNCS 14701, Cross-Cultural Design: Part III, edited by Pei-Luen Patrick Rau
19. LNCS 14702, Cross-Cultural Design: Part IV, edited by Pei-Luen Patrick Rau
20. LNCS 14703, Social Computing and Social Media: Part I, edited by Adela Coman and Simona Vasilache
21. LNCS 14704, Social Computing and Social Media: Part II, edited by Adela Coman and Simona Vasilache
22. LNCS 14705, Social Computing and Social Media: Part III, edited by Adela Coman and Simona Vasilache

47. LNCS 14730, HCI in Games: Part I, edited by Xiaowen Fang
48. LNCS 14731, HCI in Games: Part II, edited by Xiaowen Fang
49. LNCS 14732, HCI in Mobility, Transport and Automotive Systems: Part I, edited by Heidi Krömker
50. LNCS 14733, HCI in Mobility, Transport and Automotive Systems: Part II, edited by Heidi Krömker
51. LNAI 14734, Artificial Intelligence in HCI: Part I, edited by Helmut Degen and Stavroula Ntoa
52. LNAI 14735, Artificial Intelligence in HCI: Part II, edited by Helmut Degen and Stavroula Ntoa
53. LNAI 14736, Artificial Intelligence in HCI: Part III, edited by Helmut Degen and Stavroula Ntoa
54. LNCS 14737, Design, Operation and Evaluation of Mobile Communications: Part I, edited by June Wei and George Margetis
55. LNCS 14738, Design, Operation and Evaluation of Mobile Communications: Part II, edited by June Wei and George Margetis
56. CCIS 2114, HCI International 2024 Posters - Part I, edited by Constantine Stephanidis, Margherita Antona, Stavroula Ntoa and Gavriel Salvendy
57. CCIS 2115, HCI International 2024 Posters - Part II, edited by Constantine Stephanidis, Margherita Antona, Stavroula Ntoa and Gavriel Salvendy
58. CCIS 2116, HCI International 2024 Posters - Part III, edited by Constantine Stephanidis, Margherita Antona, Stavroula Ntoa and Gavriel Salvendy
59. CCIS 2117, HCI International 2024 Posters - Part IV, edited by Constantine Stephanidis, Margherita Antona, Stavroula Ntoa and Gavriel Salvendy
60. CCIS 2118, HCI International 2024 Posters - Part V, edited by Constantine Stephanidis, Margherita Antona, Stavroula Ntoa and Gavriel Salvendy
61. CCIS 2119, HCI International 2024 Posters - Part VI, edited by Constantine Stephanidis, Margherita Antona, Stavroula Ntoa and Gavriel Salvendy
62. CCIS 2120, HCI International 2024 Posters - Part VII, edited by Constantine Stephanidis, Margherita Antona, Stavroula Ntoa and Gavriel Salvendy

https://2024.hci.international/proceedings

Preface

Preliminary scientific results, professional news, or work in progress, described in the form of short research papers (4–11 pages long), constitute a popular submission type among the International Conference on Human-Computer Interaction (HCII) participants. Extended abstracts are particularly suited for reporting ongoing work, which can benefit from a visual presentation, and are presented during the conference in the form of posters. The latter allow a focus on novel ideas and are appropriate for presenting project results in a simple, concise, and visually appealing manner. At the same time, they are also suitable for attracting feedback from an international community of HCI academics, researchers, and practitioners. Poster submissions span the wide range of topics of all HCII thematic areas and affiliated conferences.

Seven volumes of the HCII 2024 proceedings are dedicated to this year's poster extended abstracts, in the form of short research papers, focusing on the following topics:

- Volume I: HCI Design Theories, Methods, Tools and Case Studies; User Experience Evaluation Methods and Case Studies; Emotions in HCI; Human Robot Interaction
- Volume II: Inclusive Designs and Applications; Aging and Technology
- Volume III: eXtended Reality and the Metaverse; Interacting with Cultural Heritage, Art and Creativity
- Volume IV: HCI in Learning and Education; HCI in Games
- Volume V: HCI in Business and Marketing; HCI in Mobility and Automated Driving; HCI in Psychotherapy and Mental Health
- Volume VI: Interacting with the Web, Social Media and Digital Services; Interaction in the Museum; HCI in Healthcare
- Volume VII: AI Algorithms and Tools in HCI; Interacting with Large Language Models and Generative AI; Interacting in Intelligent Environments; HCI in Complex Industrial Environments

Poster extended abstracts were accepted for publication in these volumes following a minimum of two single-blind reviews from the members of the HCII 2024 international Program Boards, i.e., the program committees of the constituent events. We would like to thank all of them for their invaluable contribution, support, and efforts.

July 2024

Constantine Stephanidis
Margherita Antona
Stavroula Ntoa
Gavriel Salvendy

26th International Conference on Human-Computer Interaction (HCII 2024)

The full list with the Program Board Chairs and the members of the Program Boards of all thematic areas and affiliated conferences of HCII 2024 is available online at:

http://www.hci.international/board-members-2024.php

HCI International 2025 Conference

The 27th International Conference on Human-Computer Interaction, HCI International 2025, will be held jointly with the affiliated conferences at the Swedish Exhibition & Congress Centre and Gothia Towers Hotel, Gothenburg, Sweden, June 22–27, 2025. It will cover a broad spectrum of themes related to Human-Computer Interaction, including theoretical issues, methods, tools, processes, and case studies in HCI design, as well as novel interaction techniques, interfaces, and applications. The proceedings will be published by Springer. More information will become available on the conference website: https://2025.hci.international/.

General Chair
Prof. Constantine Stephanidis
University of Crete and ICS-FORTH
Heraklion, Crete, Greece
Email: general_chair@2025.hci.international

https://2025.hci.international/

Contents – Part III

Interacting with Cultural Heritage, Art and Creativity

eXtended Reality and the Metaverse

Unraveling the Meta Quest 3: An Out-of-Box Experience of the Future of Mixed Reality Headsets

Michelle Aros[✉], Colton L. Tyger, and Barbara S. Chaparro

Embry-Riddle Aeronautical University, Daytona Beach, FL 32119, USA
arosm1@my.erau.edu

Abstract. The application of Augmented Reality (AR) and Virtual Reality (VR) to industrial settings, military, manufacturing, and education continues to increase as more affordable devices and applications become available (Bottani & Vignali, 2019; Ahir et al., 2020). As such, it is necessary to understand a user's first impressions of these products as it demonstrates a product's ease of use, learnability, and acceptance. An Out-of-Box Experience (OOBE) is a method that assesses user perceptions of product unboxing, setup, and first-time usage. This study will report the results of an Out-of-Box Experience for the Meta Quest 3 among novice users. The Meta Quest 3 is unique in that it has both AR and VR capabilities so users can be immersed within their own environment or in a completely virtual world. This poster will display summary results from six first-time users as they unboxed and used the headset for the first time. Key findings regarding the delights and frustrations of each stage of the process will be displayed along with recommendations for improvement based on human factors principles. In addition, results from the Net Promoter Score and the System Usability Scale will also be discussed as they relate to the users' OOBE experience.

Keywords: Extended Reality · Mixed Reality headset · First Impressions · Out-of-box Experience · User Experience

1 Introduction

The rapid advancement of technology in recent years has brought about a shift in the way individuals interact with digital environments, particularly within the realms of Augmented Reality (AR) and Virtual Reality (VR). These immersive technologies, collectively referred to as Mixed Reality (MR), blend elements of the physical and virtual worlds to create novel experiences across various domains such as industrial settings, military operations, manufacturing, and education [1, 2]. The adoption of MR devices and applications continues to grow rapidly, driven in part by the increasing affordability and accessibility of these technologies. As MR becomes more prevalent, industries are making use of its capabilities to foster groundbreaking levels of innovation and productivity, such as in construction, engineering, and architecture [3].

C. Stephanidis et al. (Eds.): HCII 2024, CCIS 2116, pp. 3–8, 2024.
https://doi.org/10.1007/978-3-031-61950-2_1

Essential to the adoption and success of MR products is the user experience, particularly during the initial stages of interaction. An often-overlooked aspect of user experience is the Out-of-Box Experience (OOBE), which encompasses users' perceptions and interactions during product unboxing, setup, and first-time usage [4]. The OOBE serves as a critical determinant of a product's ease of use, learnability, and overall acceptance among users [5]. Positive OOBEs not only enhance user satisfaction but also contribute to positive word-of-mouth and product advocacy, driving adoption and retention. Conversely, a negative OOBE can lead to user frustration, dissatisfaction, and eventual product abandonment, underscoring the importance of a seamless and intuitive initial user experience.

In this context, understanding and evaluating the OOBE of MR devices are important, given their unique capabilities and complexities. The Meta Quest 3, for instance, stands out as a multifaceted MR headset that offers both AR and VR functionalities, enabling users to immerse themselves in a blend of their physical environment and virtual worlds. Assessing the OOBE of such devices among novice users provides valuable insights into the challenges and opportunities associated with MR adoption, shedding light on areas for improvement and optimization. This study aims to investigate the OOBE of the Meta Quest 3 among a cohort of first-time users ranging in experience with a VR headset, to elucidate key factors influencing their initial impressions and experiences. By examining users' delights and frustrations across various stages of the OOBE process, along with incorporating measures such as the Net Promoter Score (NPS) and the System Usability Scale (SUS), this research seeks to inform iterative design aimed at enhancing the user experience of novel technologies through a human factors approach [6, 7].

2   First Impressions

The initial encounter with the Meta Quest 3 sets the tone for users' overall experience and perception of the product. In this stage of the OOBE, first-time users reported a myriad of delights and frustrations. Delights involved several aspects that contributed to a positive initial impression. Notably, users expressed satisfaction with the compact size of the headset, highlighting its size compared to previous generations of VR devices. This compactness not only contributed to portability but also aligned with users' preferences for sleek and unobtrusive hardware. Users mentioned during the study, "It's so small, I really thought it was gonna be like a computer box." Moreover, users found the aesthetics of the headset and its packaging visually appealing. The aesthetically appealing colors adorning the box and the white of the headset itself were noted as eye-catching and attractive, enhancing the overall impressions. Additionally, the design of the packaging conveyed a sense of sustainability, with users appreciating the use of eco-friendly materials and minimalist packaging.

However, alongside these delights, users encountered certain frustrations that interfered with their initial impressions of the Meta Quest 3. Among these was the perceived weight of the headset, which exceeded users' expectations and posed a challenge to prolonged usage. Despite its compact size, the Meta Quest 3 exhibited a noticeable heft, leading some users to express concerns regarding comfort and wearability over extended periods. Furthermore, users reported feelings of unease and hesitation upon encountering the cameras on the headset. While these cameras serve essential functions, their prominent appearance on the exterior of the device elicited apprehension among some users.

Overall, the first impressions of the Meta Quest 3 encompassed a range of delights and frustrations that shaped users' initial experiences and perceptions of the device. While aspects such as compactness, aesthetic appeal, and sustainability contributed to positive impressions, challenges such as weight and visual design elements posed significant hurdles to user satisfaction.

3 Unboxing

The unboxing stage represents a pivotal moment in users' interactions with a product, shaping their initial impressions and setting the stage for subsequent experiences. Upon unboxing the Meta Quest 3, users encountered a mix of delights and frustrations that influenced their perceptions of the device and its packaging. Delights during this stage centered around the organization and presentation of the headset within its packaging. Users remarked on the neat and compact arrangement of the headset components within the small container, appreciating the efficiency of space utilization and the attention to detail in packaging design. One user commented, "I thought it was organized well. Yeah, it's exciting like unwrapping a bouquet of flowers."

However, amidst these delights, users also encountered certain frustrations that detracted from their unboxing experience. The process of separating the box from its sleeve, some users found cumbersome and unnecessary. One user expressed frustration, stating, "I have to take apart the box from the sleeve, and it's a little annoying, why is the sleeve extra material?" This sentiment emphasized the importance of minimizing

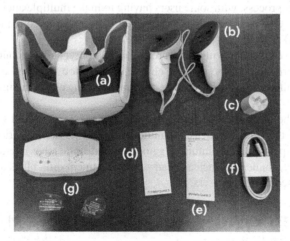

Fig. 1. Photo depicting all elements found within the Meta Quest 3 box. (a) Meta Quest 3 headset. (b) Controllers. (c) Power adapter. (d) Welcome guide. (e) Safety and Warranty Guide. (f) Charging cable. (g) Other protective packaging to cover the lenses.

unnecessary components to enhance user convenience. Additionally, users encountered challenges in locating and accessing the box containing the charging components, which was hidden within the packaging. The lack of clear instructions or intuitive design elements hindered users' ability to navigate the packaging effortlessly, detracting from the overall unboxing experience (Fig. 1).

Thus, the unboxing stage of the Meta Quest 3 comprised both delights and frustrations that influenced users' initial impressions of the device and its packaging. While aspects such as organization and compactness elicited positive feedback, challenges such as cumbersome packaging and hidden components presented hurdles to user satisfaction.

4   Use Case 1: Using Controllers to Play a Game

The first use case stage marks the transition from unboxing to active engagement with the Meta Quest 3 and its controllers. During this phase, users encountered a spectrum of delights and frustrations that shaped their initial experiences interacting with the device. *First Encounters* is a preloaded application that scans the user's physical environment and incorporates it into an interactive game chasing aliens. Delights were evident in users' interaction with many expressing satisfactions with the intuitive controls and immersive gameplay. One user remarked, "The game controls were intuitive, and the game's interaction with the real environment was enjoyable," demonstrating the smooth integration of virtual and physical elements.

However, users also encountered frustrations that impeded their enjoyment and usability of the Meta Quest 3. Foremost among these was the challenge of adjusting the head strap for the best comfort and fit. Users reported discomfort and pressure on their face and cheeks, attributing it to improper adjustment of the head strap. One user stated, "The headset is starting to hurt my face as well as my cheeks because I didn't adjust it right." Similarly, users expressed frustration with the complexity and duration of the adjustment process, with some users having to make multiple attempts to achieve a satisfactory fit. One user expressed, "This takes way too long, so many adjustments, like 6 times I had to change it."

In addition to challenges with hardware adjustment, users also encountered difficulties with the instructions of the game itself, which were too brief and disappeared too quickly. This limited exposure hinders their overall learning curve and immersion in the game experience.

Ultimately, the first use case stage of the Meta Quest 3 showcased various delights and frustrations that influenced users' initial impressions and experiences with the device. While aspects such as intuitive gameplay and immersive interactions elicited positive feedback, challenges such as head strap adjustment difficulties and insufficient instructions caused issues for users.

5   Use Case 2: Using Hand Tracking to Learn How to Play the Piano

The second use case stage aided with further exploration of the Meta Quest 3's hand-tracking capabilities, as they attempted to play the game *PianoVision. PianoVision* is an application that allows users to use all ten fingers using a Mixed Reality keyboard to learn how to play the piano. During this phase, users experienced several more delights and frustrations that influenced their perception of the device's usability. Delights were evident in users' interactions with the game, particularly surrounding hand-tracking and interactive feedback. Many users expressed satisfaction with the hand-tracking capabilities, noting that multiple fingers were accurately detected during gameplay. Additionally, users appreciated the immersive feedback provided by the game, such as the illumination of piano keys when pressed, enhancing the sense of engagement. One user remarked, "Choosing a song and going through [the app] went well," spotlighting the smooth navigation within the application.

However, alongside these delights, users also commented on their frustrations that decreased their immersion during gameplay. The main frustration was with the inconsistency in key inputs with users experiencing intermittent responsiveness and reliability issues. Some users reported frustration with key presses failing to register input consistently, leading to disruptions. One user stated, "Every time I tried to click a key it would only work for a bit and then it wouldn't work," emphasizing the lack of consistent and reliable performance. Furthermore, users encountered challenges with the piano setup and adjustment process, which proved to be less user-friendly than anticipated. Difficulty in making adjustments detracted from the overall user experience, making it difficult to fully immerse themselves in the game. Additionally, users expressed disappointment with the overall performance of the game, citing suboptimal responsiveness as a significant detractor from their enjoyment and engagement.

Overall, the second use case stage of the Meta Quest 3 included a mix of delights and frustrations that influenced users' perceptions of the device's functionality and usability. While aspects such as hand-tracking and interactive feedback were a delight, challenges such as inconsistent key inputs, setup difficulties, and disappointing game performance became major frustrations for users.

6 Post Study Assessment

Following the use cases, the NPS and SUS provided further insights into participants' experience and perceived usability of the Quest 3. Promoters, representing advocates of the product, included 3 users. Conversely, detractors, representing dissatisfied users likely to discourage the product, included 2 users. One user fell into the passive category, indicating a neutral stance toward recommending the product. Although a small sample, it did appear that previous VR experience contributed to the recommendation of the product. The SUS, on the other hand, provided insights into overall perceived usability. The results revealed varying perceptions of usability among participants, with scores ranging from 5 to 92.5 out of a possible 100. Recognizing the outlier of 5, their biggest issue was the inability to correctly fit the headset to their small head and inexperience with VR. The user was not able to fit the head strap around their head size correctly and had to conform to the headset sliding off their face throughout the study.

7 Conclusions

In summary, this study provides valuable insights into the first impressions and user perceptions of the Meta Quest 3, a Mixed Reality (MR) device. Key recommendations emerged from the study, aimed at enhancing user satisfaction and optimizing the overall user experience. In terms of packaging, eliminating the external sleeve and clearly labeling the charger component box are recommended to streamline the unboxing process. For hardware improvements, participants suggested implementing an easier-to-adjust head strap designed to accommodate various head sizes and reduce the visibility of cameras on the device's front. Furthermore, enhancing game experiences entails providing better adjustment tools for the *PianoVision* game, increasing hand-tracking sensitivity, and incorporating comprehensive game instructions to facilitate smoother gameplay. These recommendations call attention to the importance of iterative design refinement and user-centric enhancements to foster positive user engagement with MR and other novel technologies.

References

1. Ahir, K., Govani, K., Gajera, R., et al.: Application on virtual reality for enhanced education learning, military training and sports. Augment. Hum. Res. **5**, 7 (2020). https://doi.org/10.1007/s41133-019-0025-2
2. Bottani, E., Vignali, G.: Augmented reality technology in the manufacturing industry: a review of the last decade. IISE Trans. **51**(3), 284–310 (2019)
3. Dunston, P.S., Wang, X.: Mixed reality-based visualization interfaces for architecture, engineering, and construction industry. J. Constr. Eng. Manag. **131**(12), 1301–1309 (2005)
4. Kowalski, L.A.: Designing the out-of-the-box experience: a case study. In: STC Proceedings, Society for Technical Communication (2001)
5. Serif, T., Ghinea, G.: HMD versus PDA: a comparative study of the user out-of-box experience. Pers. Ubiquit. Comput. **9**(4), 238–249 (2005)
6. Reichheld, F.F.: The one number you need to grow. Harv. Bus. Rev. **81**(12), 46–55 (2003)
7. Brooke, J.: SUS-a quick and dirty usability scale. Usabil. Eval. Ind. **189**(194), 4–7 (1996)

Exploring the Influences of Virtual Reality Experiences from the Perspective of Children's Cognition

Zijie Ding, Yan Gan[⊠], and Yukun Xia

Huazhong University of Science and Technology, Wuhan 430074, Hubei, China
1203240266@qq.com

Abstract. VR (Virtual reality) technology is the technology of computer-generated environment, and its immersive and intelligent interaction make it widely used in children's education, entertainment and sports and rehabilitation therapy in recent years. From the perspective of children's cognition, this study proposed research hypotheses based on relevant literature to explore the relationship between various influencing factors of VR experience. In the specific research process, 159 valid sample questionnaires were collected for children aged 4 to 12, and the data were analyzed by SPSS and AMOS tools. The results showed that when providing children's VR experience, special attention should be paid to the quality of system elements and the stimulation of use motivation, and the influence of design factors should also be considered. This study further discusses the differences of design optimization analysis under different motivations. The study found that children pay more attention to the immersion and depth of VR experience when they pursue distracting experiences; In the pursuit of entertainment and relaxation, they pay more attention to fun and playability. When social interaction is the purpose of experience, children pay more attention to interactivity and immersive feeling. The pursuit of a sense of accomplishment, on the other hand, focuses more on complex interaction mechanisms and interesting scenarios and character elements. Therefore, future VR experience research can focus on these design recommendations, so as to effectively enhance children's enjoyment of VR experiences.

Keywords: Children's cognition · virtual reality · AMOS model · Influencing factors

1 Background

1.1 A Subsection Sample

Due to the swift advancement of science and technology, virtual reality (VR) technology has progressively integrated into people's daily lives as a novel interactive mode. Currently, there is an increasing focus on studying user experience and perception in the field of VR. Several researchers have conducted extensive investigations into users'

C. Stephanidis et al. (Eds.): HCII 2024, CCIS 2116, pp. 9–21, 2024.
https://doi.org/10.1007/978-3-031-61950-2_2

perception, emotion, attention, memory, and other characteristics within virtual reality (VR) environments [1, 2]. Their primary focus has been on examining the impact and enhancement of various design features on the overall VR experience [3]. Recently, there has been a noticeable shift in the development of virtual reality (VR) towards a focus on content [4]. The ongoing progress of virtual reality (VR) technology presents the potential for increasingly immersive experiences.

Nevertheless, the existing studies on virtual reality (VR) mostly concentrate on adults and provide minimal consideration to the cognitive traits and requirements of children. This neglect concerns regarding the appropriateness of content, educational aspects, as well as safety and health implications [5]. Furthermore, the VR experience is predominantly utilized by a large number of children and adolescents. It is imperative to investigate the aspects that influence their cognitive viewpoint in order to acquire more specific and focused outcomes. The cognitive viewpoint offers a theoretical foundation for the design of virtual reality (VR), which is more favorable for the future advancement of VR.

2 Research Hypothesis Model from Children's Cognitive Perspective

2.1 Children's Cognitive Perspective

According to Swiss psychologist Jean Piaget [7], children go through four primary stages as they develop: the sensorimotor stage, preoperational stage, concrete operational stage, and formal operational stage. The pre-operational stage, which occurs between the ages of 2 and 6, is characterized by the ability to use words to express ideas. However, children in this period tend to be self-centered and have limited understanding of complex concepts. These children possess a restricted cognitive capacity, but they do have a fundamental level of expression. Children between the ages of 4 and 6 are classified as being in the kindergarten education stage and can be utilized as secondary research subjects in this study. The specific operational period, which occurs between the ages of 7 and 12, pertains to the cognitive ability to solve problems based on specific experiential thinking and comprehend the concept of reversibility. These youngsters possess fundamental cognitive skills for object recognition and are typically at the primary school level of development. These children possess a greater level of familiarity and expertise with virtual reality (VR), making them suitable as the primary subjects for study.

2.2 Factors that Affect VR Experience

VR experience denotes a fully immersive encounter facilitated by virtual reality technology, enabling users to engage with either the physical or virtual realm as if they were there in a fictional setting [8]. Prior research has predominantly focused on examining the influence of virtual reality (VR) on the cognitive abilities of adults. These studies have identified and consolidated the key aspects that determine the VR experience, namely immersion, presence, agency, and the interplay between VR experience and these factors [9–11]. Furthermore, the emotional aspects of consumers are crucial considerations to consider while evaluating [12, 13]. This research examines additional aspects that impact children's cognition, as illustrated in Fig. 1, from a cognitive perspective.

Immersion. The level of immersion in a virtual reality (VR) experience is mostly determined by the user, but it is also influenced by objective elements such as the technical specifications of the VR system and the duration of the user's experience. Thus, a moderate duration of experience will likewise influence the user's immersion.

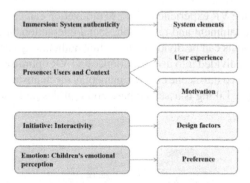

Fig. 1. VR experience factor extraction

Presence. This is a metric that quantifies the level of user involvement and interaction in virtual reality (VR), and it is based on subjective factors [9]. The impact of the VR experience varies depending on the individual user and their subjective interpretation. Users' desire for virtual reality (VR) and their previous encounters with VR will impact their impression of the VR experience [16]. Additionally, children and adults require distinct virtual surroundings in order to create a satisfactory feeling of realism [17]. Hence, the VR experience of children is influenced by their preferences, past experiences, motives, and attitudes towards VR. According to Reinhard E. K et al., user motivation and system quality have a major impact on the flow experience in virtual reality (VR) games. The determinants of presence are intricate and unique, necessitating differentiation across users of varying ages and cognitive capacities.

Activity. Refers to the interactive nature of virtual reality (VR) technologies. Users have the option to select their preferred method of interaction with virtual reality (VR) and can promptly deliver responses to minimize cognitive dissonance [10]. The quality of activity is contingent upon the suitable level and manner of engagement, with a particular emphasis on investigating the influence of different aspects of virtual reality (VR) design on the user experience, in order to enhance the efficacy of VR performance.

Emotion. Relates to the user's affective response and subjective perception of the virtual reality encounter. The emotional experiences of users can be influenced by immersion, presence, and agency. Virtual reality (VR) has the ability to successfully manage children's emotions, and children exhibit greater emotional sensitivity compared to adults [5]. Immersive virtual reality (VR) experiences have a positive impact on the development of children's self-awareness.

2.3 Research Hypothesis Model

To investigate the subjective and objective factors influencing children's virtual reality (VR) experience and to enhance their preference for VR, a hypothesis model (see Fig. 1) is developed. This model encompasses five dependent variables: use motivation, system factors, user experience, design factors, and liking. The primary objectives of this study are to examine design variables and determine preferences. Design variables can be examined to determine ways to enhance interactivity, while liking measures the emotional impact of the VR experience. The use motivation can be categorized into distraction, seeking entertainment and relaxation, social interaction, and achievement [18, 20]. The system elements can be divided into picture authenticity and VR duration. The user experience can be divided into user experience and VR optimism. Lastly, the design factors can be categorized into scene content, gameplay mechanism, character modeling, and background music. Liking is assessed based on four design factors (Fig. 2).

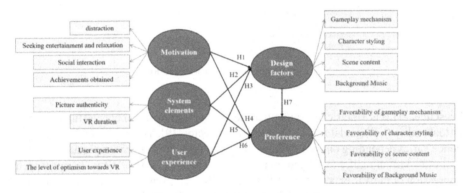

Fig. 2. Research hypothesis model

This study thoroughly examines the function and relationship of design components in various usage motivations, such as VR content, interaction, and experience feedback, in order to present constructive suggestions. Additionally, it puts up 16 hypotheses (refer to Table 2) based on the findings (Table 1).

Table 1. Hypothesis content between children's use motivation and design factors.

No.	Hypothetical content
H8	Mechanic play has a significant positive effect on motivation (distraction)
H9	Role modeling has a significant positive effect on motivation (distraction)
H10	Scene content has a significant positive effect on motivation (distraction)
H11	Background music has a significant positive effect on motivation (distraction)

(continued)

Table 1. (*continued*)

No.	Hypothetical content
H12	Mechanic play has a significant positive effect on motivation (seeking entertainment and relaxation)
H13	Role modeling has a significant positive effect on motivation (seeking entertainment and relaxation)
H14	Scene content has a significant positive effect on motivation (seeking entertainment and relaxation)
H15	Background music has a significant positive effect on motivation (seeking entertainment and relaxation)
H16	Mechanic play has a significant positive effect on motivation (social interaction)
H17	Role modeling has a significant positive effect on motivation (social interaction)
H18	Scene content has a significant positive effect on motivation (social interaction)
H19	Background music has a significant positive effect on motivation (social interaction)
H20	Mechanic play has a significant positive effect on usage motivation (achievement)
H21	Role modeling has a significant positive effect on motivation (achievement)
H22	Scene content has a significant positive effect on motivation (achievement)
H23	Background music has a significant positive effect on usage motivation (achievement)

3   Analysis of Research Results

3.1   Research Method

The research subjects consisted of children between the ages of 4 and 12. A total of 159 valid questionnaires were acquired through the utilization of both online and offline questionnaires, as well as the collection of research data. Out of the total, 82 individuals (51.6%) were males, while 77 individuals (48.4%) were girls. Additionally, 38 individuals (23.9%) were between the ages of 4 and 6, while 121 individuals (76.1%) were between the ages of 7 and 12. The valid questionnaire data was processed and analyzed using IBM SPSS Statistics 26.0 and IBM SPSS Amos 26.0 in this study.

3.2   Model Reliability and Validity Test

Firstly, the internal consistency of each dimension was examined using the clonal Baring coefficient reliability test. The results indicate that all of the scale coefficients fall within the range of 0.75–1 and are greater than 0.6, suggesting that the measurement model exhibits favorable detection outcomes.

Subsequently, the CFA model underwent a fit test, yielding a CMIN/DF (Chi-square degree of freedom ratio) value of 2.319, falling within the acceptable range of 1–3. Additionally, the RMSEA (root mean square error) was calculated to be 0.071, which is considered satisfactory as it is below the threshold of 0.08. Furthermore, the test results for IFI, TLI, and CFI all above the satisfactory threshold of 0.8. Hence, the exhaustive analysis findings of this study demonstrate that the CFA model of the research outcomes exhibits a strong fit.

3.3 Hypothesis Model Test Results

Once Amos had passed the aforementioned tests, it was employed to evaluate the model hypothesis put forward in this study. The test results for the parameter are displayed in Table 3. The significance test of parameters should satisfy the condition C.R. > 2 and P < 0.05, while the rationality test of parameters should satisfy the condition S.E. > 0, which aligns with the standard range.

The study found that system factors had a strong positive effect on design factors ($\beta = 0.772$, p < 0.001), suggesting that the use of a VR system can enhance the effectiveness of design by creating a more immersive experience. The study did not confirm the existence of a significant link ($\beta = -0.208$, p > 0.05) between user experience and design elements. This suggests that children's cognitive perception does not have an impact on the effectiveness of virtual reality. The utilization of motivation was a substantial and favorable predictor of design factors ($\beta = 450$,p < 0.001), suggesting that a stronger utilization of motivation had a greater impact on design aspects. The study found a strong positive correlation between system elements and the liking degree of children ($\beta = 0.985$, p < 0.01). This suggests that as the VR system becomes more immersive, children tend to have a higher like degree. The route association between user experience and liking ($\beta = -0.326$, p > 0.05) was not confirmed, suggesting that there was no direct correlation between user experience and liking. The level of incentive to use had a strong positive impact on like ($\beta = 0.907$, p < 0.01), demonstrating that motivation to use directly influenced liking. The design features had a strong positive impact on like ($\beta = 0.815$, p < 0.01), suggesting that when the design components in virtual reality were aligned with children's cognitive abilities, their liking increased.

Table 2. Test values of model parameters and validation of research hypotheses.

Model path				Estimate	S.E.	C.R.	P	Result
H1	Design factor	<—	System element	.772	.122	7.873	***	Set up
H2	Design factor	<—	User experience	−.208	.403	−1.288	.198	false
H3	Design factor	<—	Use motive	.450	.054	6.941	***	Set up
H4	Liking degree	<—	System element	.985	.520	2.368	**	Set up
H5	Liking degree	<—	User experience	−.326	.751	−1.082	.279	false
H6	Liking degree	<—	Use motive	.907	.197	3.843	***	Set up
H7	Liking degree	<—	Design factor	.815	.486	4.239	***	Set up

Note: *** means P < 0.001; ** means P < 0.01; * indicates P < 0.05.

3.4 Influence Effect Analysis

Figure 3 demonstrates that the design factor serves as the independent variable, with the system factor ($\beta = 0.77$) and use motivation ($\beta = 0.45$) having the highest and second highest total effect values, respectively. These findings suggest that the design of virtual reality (VR) experiences for children has a notable influence on the authenticity and duration of the experience. Additionally, the stability of system elements and the quality of the VR environment play a crucial role in shaping children's perception and overall experience. This finding suggests that although children's individual motives may contribute to their engagement in virtual reality (VR) experiences, it is crucial to prioritize the quality of the system's equipment and environment to guarantee a superior experience for them.

When preference was considered as the independent variable, the overall effect values of other components were as follows, ranked from highest to lowest: system factor ($\beta = 0.99$), usage motive ($\beta = 0.91$), and design factor ($\beta = 0.81$). This indicates that children's preference for VR experience is mostly influenced by the system aspects, which could be strongly correlated with the system's user-friendliness, picture quality, and the available material. The second factor is the utilization of motivation, specifically referring to the innate drive and enthusiasm that youngsters have towards engaging in virtual reality activities. These findings indicate that design features have a very minor impact on preference, but they remain one of the significant factors that influence children's views towards VR experiences, such as gameplay, interactivity, and user interface design.

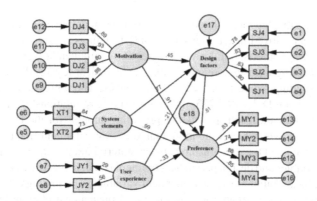

Fig. 3. Model hypothesis verification and path coefficient

Therefore, these discoveries emphasize the importance of prioritizing the excellence of system components and the drive to utilize them when creating and providing virtual reality experiences for children. Additionally, it is crucial to consider the impact of design aspects. Considering these aspects collectively can enhance a child's virtual reality (VR) experience and augment their level of involvement and happiness.

3.5 Multiple Regression Analysis

The association between children's use motivation and design elements was further examined using multiple regression analysis. The obtained results successfully passed the test. Firstly, by considering distraction (DJ1) as the independent variable and design parameters (gameplay mechanics, character modeling, scene content, background music) as the dependent variables, the obtained results are as follows:

Table 3. Regression model coefficient and significance test table of distraction (DJ1) and design factors

model	Unnormalized coefficient		Standardization coefficient			B has a 95.0% confidence interval	
	B	Standard error	Beta	t	significance	floor	Upper limit
(constant)	0.359	0.247		1.453	0.048	−0.129	0.848
SJ1	0.091	0.104	0.091	0.878	0.382	−0.114	0.297
SJ2	0.208	0.086	0.207	2.417	0.017	0.038	0.378
SJ3	0.286	0.117	0.279	2.446	0.016	0.055	0.517
SJ4	0.233	0.101	0.23	2.321	0.022	0.035	0.432

Table 4 shows that the regression coefficient of role modeling on DJ1 (distraction) is 0.208, showing a positive impact. The statistical test findings are significant ($p < 0.05$), validating the H9 hypothesis. Similarly, the regression coefficient of scene content to DJ1 was 0.286, indicating a positive relationship. The statistical test result was significant ($p < 0.05$), providing support for the H10 hypothesis. The regression coefficient for background music on DJ1 was 0.233, indicating a positive relationship. The statistical test yielded a significant result ($p < 0.05$), providing support for the H11 hypothesis. The remaining P-values, which were more than 0.05, were not confirmed.

The study examined the relationship between entertainment and relaxation (DJ2) as independent variables and design parameters (gameplay mechanics, character modeling, scene content, background music) as dependent variables. The findings are as follows:

Table 5 shows that the regression coefficient of mechanical play on DJ2 (seeking entertainment and relaxation) is 0.323, which is positive. This indicates that mechanical play has a positive effect on DJ2. The statistical test result is significant ($p < 0.05$), providing support for the H12 hypothesis. The regression coefficient for the relationship between role modeling and DJ2 was 0.206, indicating a positive association. The statistical test yielded a significant result ($p < 0.05$), providing support for the H14 hypothesis. The regression coefficient of background music on DJ2 was 0.283, indicating a positive relationship. The statistical test result was significant ($p < 0.05$), providing support for the H15 hypothesis. The remaining P-values, which were more than 0.05, were not confirmed.

Table 4. Regression model coefficients and significance tests for recreation and relaxation seeking (DJ2) and design factors

model	Unnormalized coefficient		Standardization coefficient			B has a 95.0% confidence interval	
	B	Standard error	Beta	t	significance	floor	Upper limit
(constant)	1.151	0.204		5.638	0.000	0.747	1.554
SJ1	0.323	0.083	0.339	3.9	0.000	0.159	0.486
SJ2	0.206	0.092	0.215	2.242	0.026	0.024	0.387
SJ3	−0.04	0.094	−0.041	−0.42	0.675	−0.225	0.146
SJ4	0.283	0.082	0.303	3.456	0.001	0.121	0.445

Taking social interaction (DJ3) as the independent variable and design factors (game-play mechanics, character modeling, scene content, background music) as the dependent variable, the results are as follows:

Table 5. Regression model coefficient and significance test table of social interaction (DJ3) and design factors

model	Unnormalized coefficient		Standardization coefficient			B has a 95.0% confidence interval	
	B	Standard error	Beta	t	significance	floor	Upper limit
(constant)	0.668	0.248		2.693	0.008	0.178	1.158
SJ1	0.239	0.101	0.243	2.375	0.019	0.04	0.437
SJ2	0.126	0.111	0.127	1.127	0.262	−0.095	0.346
SJ3	0.236	0.114	0.237	2.062	0.041	0.01	0.462
SJ4	0.058	0.099	0.06	0.582	0.561	−0.139	0.254

Table 6 shows that the regression coefficient of mechanistic play on DJ3 (social contact) is 0.239, showing a positive impact. The statistical test result is significant (p < 0.05), validating the H16 hypothesis. The regression coefficient between the scenario content and DJ3 was 0.236, indicating a positive relationship. The statistical test yielded a significant result (p < 0.05), providing support for the H18 hypothesis. The remaining P-values, which were more than 0.05, were not confirmed.

Using achievement (DJ4) as the independent variable and design elements (gameplay mechanics, character modeling, scene content, background music) as the dependent variable, the following results were obtained:

Table 7 shows that the regression coefficient of mechanical play on DJ3 (achievement) is 0.252, suggesting a positive relationship. This means that mechanical play has

Table 6. Regression model coefficients and significance test tables for achievement (DJ4) and design factors

model	Unnormalized coefficient		Standardization coefficient			B has a 95.0% confidence interval	
	B	Standard error	Beta	t	significance	floor	Upper limit
(constant)	1.026	0.226		4.534	0.000	0.579	1.473
SJ1	0.252	0.092	0.257	2.752	0.007	0.071	0.434
SJ2	0.2	0.102	0.204	1.972	0.049	0.000	0.401
SJ3	0.183	0.091	0.19	2.015	0.046	0.004	0.362
SJ4	0.118	0.104	0.119	1.134	0.258	−0.088	0.324

a positive impact on DJ3. The statistical test result is significant ($p < 0.05$), providing support for the H20 theory. The regression coefficient for the influence of role modeling on DJ3 was 0.2, indicating a positive relationship. The statistical test yielded a significant result ($p < 0.05$), providing support for the H21 hypothesis. The regression coefficient for the scenario content on DJ3 was 0.183, indicating a positive relationship. The statistical test yielded a significant result ($p < 0.05$), providing support for the H22 hypothesis. The remaining P-values, which were more than 0.05, were not confirmed.

Table 7. Results of research hypothesis verification

No.	content	result	No.	content	result
H9	SJ2 <—DJ1	valid	H16	SJ1 <—DJ3	valid
H10	SJ3 <—DJ1	valid	H18	SJ3 <—DJ3	valid
H11	SJ4 <—DJ1	valid	H20	SJ1 <—DJ4	valid
H12	SJ1 <—DJ2	valid	H21	SJ2 <—DJ4	valid
H14	SJ3 <—DJ2	valid	H22	SJ3 <—DJ4	valid

The verification results of H8–23 are presented in Table 8, as indicated by the preceding analysis. Out of the hypotheses tested on children's use motivation and design aspects, 62.5% were found to be successful. Specifically, SJ3 (scene content) has a notable and favorable influence on various usage motivations, making the individualized evaluation of scene content a primary factor. Varying usage motivations provide incongruous outcomes, indicating that youngsters had diverse requirements and desires when engaging with virtual reality. The verification results can offer comprehensive assistance for the scene's requirements, subsequently determining the optimization direction for both common and personalized design.

4   VR Experience Design Optimization Suggestions

This study centers on the diverse motives of children in utilizing virtual reality (VR) based on the analysis results. Additionally, it provides optimization recommendations to enhance the VR experience.

Distraction and Exploration. Children seek immersion and depth in VR experiences for distraction. To enhance this, improve character modeling, scene content, and background music for better engagement. Simplify gameplay mechanics to reduce interaction complexity.

Entertainment and Relaxation. When it comes to entertainment, give priority to activities that are enjoyable and engaging. Improve the attractiveness of gameplay, expand the ways players can interact (including using multiple senses and motion recognition), and make sure the characters' behavior matches popular animation styles. Align the background music with the experience to enhance the overall quality.

Social Interaction. Emphasize interactive and immersive virtual reality (VR) experiences designed for engaging in social interactions. Highlight collaborative interactions by incorporating novel components, and integrate extended reality (XR) aspects with scene content to enhance engagement.

Achievement and Learning. To cultivate a feeling of fulfillment, incorporate intricate interaction mechanisms to stimulate cognitive capabilities. Implement incentive structures and ranking systems to enhance motivation. Ensure that the character modeling and scene content are designed to align with the cognitive abilities of youngsters, in order to provide them with valuable feedback on their accomplishments.

5   Conclusion

This study empirically verifies a proposed model of characteristics that impact virtual reality (VR) experiences using statistical software tools such as SPSS and AMOS. The findings suggest that there is no true correlation between user experience, design characteristics, and liking. However, there are substantial correlations between other factors. This underscores the importance of focusing on the excellence of system components and the encouragement of user drive when offering virtual reality (VR) encounters for youngsters, while also taking into account the impact of design aspects.

This study conducts a thorough examination of the relationship between usage motivation and design elements using multiple regression analysis in SPSS, in order to offer more constructive ideas. The findings indicate that children prioritize immersion and depth in virtual reality (VR) experiences when seeking distraction, enjoyment, and engaging gameplay for entertainment and relaxation. They also prioritize interactivity and immersion for social interaction, and complex interaction mechanisms and intriguing scenarios for a sense of achievement.

Therefore, further investigation into virtual reality (VR) experiences has the potential to significantly improve children's enjoyment and contentment by optimizing the design viewpoint using these findings.

References

1. Cadet, L.B., Chainay, H.: Memory of virtual experiences: role of immersion, emotion and sense of presence. Int. J. Hum.-Comput. Stud. **144**, 102506 (2020). https://doi.org/10.1016/j.ijhcs.2020.102506
2. Kim, S.J., Laine, T.H., Suk, H.J.: Presence effects in virtual reality based on user characteristics: attention, enjoyment, and memory. Electronics **10**, 1051 (2021). https://doi.org/10.3390/electronics10091051
3. Alexiou, A., Schippers, M.C.: Digital game elements, user experience and learning: a conceptual framework. Educ. Inf. Technol. **23**, 2545–2567 (2018). https://doi.org/10.1007/s10639-018-9730-6
4. Che, X., Ma, S., Yu, Q., et al.: An event-based user experience evaluation method for virtual reality applications. In: 2019 IEEE SmartWorld, Ubiquitous Intelligence & Computing, Advanced & Trusted Computing, Scalable Computing & Communications, Cloud & Big Data Computing, Internet of People and Smart City Innovation (SmartWorld/SCALCOM/UIC/ATC/CBDCom/IOP/SCI). IEEE (2019). https://doi.org/10.1109/SmartWorld-UIC-ATC-SCALCOM-IOP-SCI.2019.00164
5. Cadet, L.B., Reynaud, E., Chainay, H.: Memory for a virtual reality experience in children and adults according to image quality, emotion, and sense of presence. VirtualReality **26**, 55–75 (2022). https://doi.org/10.1007/s10055-021-00537-y
6. Mulder, H,, Oudgenoeg-Paz, O., Hellendoorn, A., et al.: How children learn to discover their environment: an embodied dynamic systems perspective on the development of spatial cognition. Neuropsychol. Space: Spatial Func. Hum. Brain 309–360 (2017)
7. Franinovic, K.: Amplified Movements: An Inactive Approach to Sound in Interaction Design. Springer. Vienna (2024). https://doi.org/10.1007/978-3-211-78891-2_26
8. Takahashi, Y., Murata, A.: Change of equilibrium under the influence of VR experience. In: IEEE International Workshop on Robot & Human Interactive Communication. IEEE (2001). https://doi.org/10.1109/ROMAN.2001.981977
9. Theingi, S., Leopold, I., Ola, T., et al.: Virtual reality as a non-pharmacological adjunct to reduce the use of analgesics in hospitals. J. Cogn. Enhan. **6**, 108–113 (2021). https://doi.org/10.1007/s41465-021-00212-9
10. Xu, X., Kang, J., Yan, L.: Understanding embodied immersion in technology-enabled embodied learning environments. J. Comput. Assist. Learn. (2021). https://doi.org/10.1111/jcal.12594
11. Jung, S., Lindeman, R.W.: Perspective: does realism improve presence in VR? Suggesting a model and metric for VR experience evaluation (2021). https://doi.org/10.3389/frvir.2021.693327
12. Lottridge, D., Chignell, M., Yasumura, M.: Identifying emotion through implicit and explicit measures: cultural differences, cognitive load, and immersion. IEEE Trans. Affect. Comput. **3**, 199–210 (2011). https://doi.org/10.1109/T-AFFC.2011.36
13. Gasselseder, H.P.: Dynamic music and immersion in the action-adventure an empirical investigation. In: Audio Mostly: A Conference on Interaction with Sound. ACM (2014). https://doi.org/10.1145/2636879.2636908
14. Anthes, C., García-Hernández, R.J., Wiedemann, M., Kranzlmüller, D.: State of the art of virtual reality technology. In: 2016 IEEE Aerospace Conference, Big Sky, MT, USA, pp. 1–19 (2016). https://doi.org/10.1109/AERO.2016.7500674
15. Wang, D., Wang, X., Zheng, Q., et al.: How interaction paradigms affect user experience and perceived interactivity in virtual reality environment (2020). https://doi.org/10.1007/978-3-030-49695-1_15

16. Shin, D.: Empathy and embodied experience in virtual environment: to what extent can virtual reality stimulate empathy and embodied experience? Comput. Hum. Behav. **78**, 64–73 (2018). https://doi.org/10.1016/j.chb.2017.09.012

17. Won, A.S., Bailey, J., Bailenson, J., Tataru, C., Yoon, I.A., Golianu, B.: Immersive virtual reality for pediatric pain. Children **4**, 52 (2017). https://doi.org/10.3390/children4070052

18. Kunz, R.E., Zabel, C., Telkmann, V.: Content-, system-, and hardware-related effects on the experience of flow in VR gaming. J. Media Econ. **34**(4), 213–242 (2022). https://doi.org/10.1080/08997764.2022.2149159

19. Li, L., Li, M., Pan, D.: Immersive narrative design in VR game. Highl. Sci. Eng. Technol. **49**, 509–519 (2023). https://doi.org/10.54097/hset.v49i.8603

20. Herodotou, C., Winters, N., Kambouri, M.: An iterative, multidisciplinary approach to studying digital play motivation: the model of game motivation. Games Cult. **10**(3), 249–268 (2015). https://doi.org/10.1177/1555412014557633

Selection in Stride: Comparing Button- and Head-Based Augmented Reality Interaction During Locomotion

Aaron L. Gardony[1,2]($\boxtimes$), Kana Okano[2], Andrew B. Whitig[2], and Marisa Smith[2]

[1] U.S. Army Combat Capabilities Development Command (DEVCOM) Soldier Center, Natick, MA, USA
`aaron.gardony.civ@army.mil`
[2] Center for Applied Brain and Cognitive Sciences (CABCS), Medford, MA, USA

Abstract. Military users of augmented reality (AR) head-mounted displays must interact with their heads-up displays (HUDs) effectively and while on the move. Yet, there is a paucity of human-computer interaction (HCI) studies investigating AR multimodal interfaces (MMIs) and interaction methods during locomotion. We conducted a mixed methods study comparing stationary and ambulatory button- and head-based AR interaction methods. Utilizing a within-participants design, Soldier participants completed a simple task sequence in an AR HUD while walking on an omnidirectional treadmill and standing still using both a chest-mounted controller alone (C) and a head-gaze cursor with button input for selection (C + HG). Quantitative task performance analysis revealed faster time-on-task for the C + HG method when stationary. However, when walking, the C method generally surpassed the C + HG method. Careful analysis of selection and head-gaze hovering inputs reflected participants' difficulty in stabilizing their head while walking which led to inaccuracies in menu icon selection and necessitated additional selection input. Moreover, several participants reported difficulty with stabilizing their head-gaze as well as greater preference for and better success using the C method to perform the task sequence while walking. Taken together, these findings support the idea that while head-gaze is a promising AR interaction method in relatively stationary contexts, the fact that it requires good head stability for reliable interaction negatively impacts task performance and user experience during locomotion. This study brings attention to the challenges of MMIs in ambulatory AR usage contexts and the need for more research in this area.

Keywords: Augmented Reality · Interaction Methods · Locomotion · Military

1 Introduction

In the coming years, Soldiers will increasingly rely on Augmented Reality (AR) head-mounted displays (HMDs) to support military operations in challenging and austere environments. To effectively navigate and control their many embedded capabilities, Soldiers will need optimized user interfaces and user experience (UI/UX). The present

C. Stephanidis et al. (Eds.): HCII 2024, CCIS 2116, pp. 22–32, 2024.
https://doi.org/10.1007/978-3-031-61950-2_3

study describes novel methodologies and emerging findings surrounding a critical knowledge gap of Soldier AR human-computer interaction (HCI): How different interaction methods impact task performance and UX when using an AR HMD during dynamic locomotion.

Emerging military AR HMDs, such as the U.S. Army's Integrated Visual Augmentation System (IVAS), use button-based inputs for user interaction [1] which are ruggedized, time-tested, and reliable. Yet, commercial mixed reality (XR) HMDs include head tracking, hand tracking, gaze tracking, and gesture control for user input. Pairing these interaction methods with button-based input can yield user-friendly multimodal AR interfaces (MMIs) [2, 3] with enhanced UX compared to unimodal ones [4, 5]. For example, the recently released Apple Vision Pro XR headset combines gaze input with a simple pinch gesture to enable intuitive cursor-like interaction.

Yet, intuitive MMIs may not fully satisfy Soldier users' unique needs and constraints. For example, MMIs often incorporate speech commands [6] but voice recognition system performance is severely degraded in loud and auditorily-dynamic combat environments [7]. Gestures, including pointing, tapping, and arm movements, are challenging to accurately classify in the field [8], physically effortful [4, 9], and conflict with Soldiers' need to maintain manual control of their weapon at all times [10]. Gaze tracking accuracy degrades during walking [11] and eye tracking technology typically uses emissive infrared (IR) light, which raises light security concerns [12]. Gaze-based interaction can also lead to eyestrain during prolonged use [13]. In contrast, head orientation can be accurately derived from inertial measurement units (IMUs) embedded within the AR HMD's hardware [14] with little to no battlefield signature. Head pointing (or head-gaze) has been demonstrated to provide a stable and precise hands-free interaction modality [15–18] that represents the current state-of-the-art for AR interaction [19] and a good candidate for integration into military AR HMDs.

Importantly, Soldiers are expected to interact with AR while on the move, such as during locomotion (walking) toward an objective or during active combat. Walking while using XR HMDs alters gait parameters, such as by slowing walking velocity and lowering stability [20], and thus could influence UX during AR interaction. Recent work has begun to examine how AR HMD UIs can be altered to support interaction during walking [21] or how locomotion itself can be leveraged as an input modality [22], but to date no work has directly and systematically compared how different interaction methods impact AR UX while walking vs stationary.

In the present study, we investigated button- and head-gaze-based interaction methods during locomotion and while stationary. Soldiers performed a sequence of simple tasks in an AR heads-up display (HUD) interface using either a chest-mounted controller alone or in combination with head-gaze. Critically, Soldiers used both interaction methods while standing still and walking on an omnidirectional treadmill, allowing an A-B comparison during stationary and ambulatory AR interaction. To evaluate task performance and UX, we employed a mixed methods approach, collecting quantitative data, including time-on-task, input counts, and walking data gathered from the treadmill, as well as qualitative Soldier feedback and surveys.

2 Method

2.1 Participants

The study was approved by the DEVCOM Armaments Center and Tufts University Institutional Review Boards. 23 active-duty U.S. Army Soldiers provided written informed consent and participated in the study. In total, 15 participants ($M_{age} = 20.7$, $SD = 2.7$, all male) were included in the final dataset.

2.2 Materials

We implemented a military-styled HUD application on a Microsoft Hololens 2 (HL2) AR HMD which included a compass indicator and four corner menu icons. Controller input was implemented with a chest-mounted Bluetooth Xbox controller affixed to a tactical vest. The HUD application logged several quantitative metrics, including time-on-task, button presses, UI states, and continuous head-gaze at 30 Hz. The interface implemented two interaction methods: Controller Only (C) and Controller + Head-Gaze (C + HG). For the C method, participants performed all user input with the controller's buttons such as, the D-pad for HUD navigation and mode changes and button presses for selection. For the C + HG method, participants activated head-gaze interaction with a button hold which locked the HUD in place, unlinking HUD from the user's head orientation. They then positioned a cursor via head rotation to highlight interface elements for selection, selecting them with a button press. To track locomotion we used the Infinadeck omnidirectional treadmill [23]. We developed a software application to collect walking speed data from the treadmill using Unity [24] and Infinadeck's Unity plugin to characterize how the two AR interaction methods impact locomotion.

2.3 Experimental Design and Procedure

We employed a 2 × 2 fully factorial within-participants design, crossing walking condition (stationary vs walking) with interaction method (C vs C + HG). Participants always completed the stationary interaction blocks first followed by the walking blocks. This ensured participants were familiar with the AR task before walking on the omnidirectional treadmill. The order participants used each interaction method was counterbalanced within each walking condition block. The study lasted approximately 1.5 h. Upon arrival, the participant completed a demographics questionnaire and watched a three-minute tutorial video explaining the HUD and two interaction methods used in the experiment. The researcher then briefed the participant on the goals of the study, assisted them with donning the tactical vest, Xbox controller, and tracking belt used with the treadmill, and explained the button mappings. Next, the participant completed HL2 eye tracking calibration to calibrate its display. The researcher then launched the HUD application and verbally guided the participant through a prescribed task sequence using both the C and C + HG methods. The task sequence and its corresponding controls for each interaction method are depicted in Fig. 1. The task sequence involved: (1) toggling the visibility of the HUD, (2) unlocking it (i.e., making it interactable), (3C) entering menu navigation (menu nav) or (3H) head-gaze interaction mode, (4C/4H) selecting the Media menu icon and then (5) returning to the main HUD, (6C/6H) selecting the Map icon and then (7) returning to the main HUD, (8C) deactivating menu nav or (8H) head-gaze interaction mode, and (9) locking the HUD.

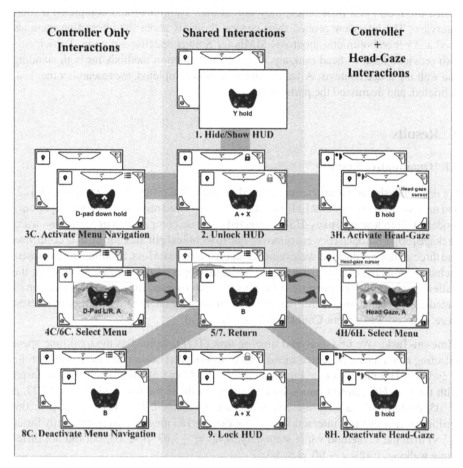

Fig. 1. AR HUD task sequence for the Controller Only (C) and Controller + Head-Gaze (C + HG) conditions. The task sequence involved an identical sequence with unique and shared interactions. Note: the controller is depicted for illustrative purposes and was not visible in the HUD.

Following guided practice, the researcher began the stationary blocks, verbally guiding the participant through the task sequence and confirming their completion at each step. After the participant finished the first sequence, they completed the System Usability Scale (SUS) [25] and the NASA Task Load Index (NASA-TLX) [26] to assess their experience with the interaction method they just used. They then repeated the sequence using the other interaction method. Following the stationary block, the participant began the walking block. Here, participants started walking on the treadmill in a single direction at casual walking pace (~2 mph). Once this pace was established, the researcher began the task sequence, and the participant completed it as before. Upon completion, the participant safely came to a stop and the researcher disabled the treadmill. As before, the participant then completed the SUS and NASA-TLX. They then repeated the task sequence while walking using the other interaction method. After the participant completed the fourth and final block, they doffed their equipment and completed a short interview. The interview probed their general thoughts about the interaction methods used and general opinions about AR MMIs for Soldier-specific use cases. Participants also provided head-to-head rankings of the two interaction methods for both standing and walking usage contexts. After the interview was completed, the researcher thanked, debriefed, and dismissed the participant.

3   Results

3.1   Quantitative Results

For data analysis and visualization, we used the statistical programming language R [27] and the *lmer* [28] and *ggplot2* [29] packages. We employed mixed effects intercepts-only models with follow-up Tukey-HSD-corrected pairwise comparisons using the *emmeans* package [30]. Five datasets were removed due to technical glitches during data collection and three additional datasets were removed due to partial data loss, resulting in 15 datasets included for analysis. One participant erroneously opened the map menu twice in the stationary phase; for the purposes of analysis, we considered the extra map selection as a media menu selection for this participant. Our primary quantitative metrics of interest were Time-on-Task, Input Count, and Walking Speed.

Time-on-Task. We first analyzed time-on-task (TOT), defined as the total time spent selecting menu icons. Note that menu selection depended on unique interactions for the C and C + HG methods (see Fig. 1, steps 3C/4C/6C and 3H/4H/6H). TOT was faster with the C + HG interaction method compared to the C method, $F(1, 42) = 10.27$, $p < .05$. Additionally, a marginal 2-way interaction emerged, $F(1, 42) = 3.75$, $p = .06$. Drilling deeper into this interaction, TOT for the C + HG method was significantly faster (~5 s) than the C method while stationary, $t(42) = -3.63$, $p < .05$, but did not differ while walking, $t(42) = -.90$, $p > .05$.

Input Count. We next investigated the number of discrete user inputs across interaction methods. Specifically, we investigated two metrics: button press frequency, or the number of discrete button presses, and *head-gaze hover (HGH) frequency*, or the number of instances when the head-gaze cursor hovered over a selectable menu icon.

We first examined the frequencies of common button presses between the interaction methods and found that they were generally similar apart from selection input (i.e. A-button presses). Analysis of selection input (SI) frequency revealed higher frequency for the C + HG interaction method compared to the C method, $F(1, 42) = 6.67$, $p < .05$, and the higher frequency during walking vs while stationary, $F(1, 42) = 13.52$, $p < .05$. These main effects were qualified by a 2-way interaction, $F(1, 42) = 7.50$, $p < .05$. Drilling deeper into this interaction, both main effects appeared to be driven by high

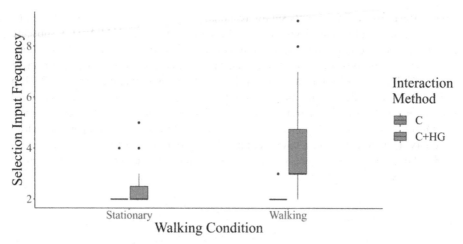

Fig. 2. Selection input (SI) frequency by walking condition and interaction method. *Note: The (SI) distribution appears as a flat line for the C interaction method due to the small variance in SIs. One outlier (walking, C + HG SI frequency = 13) was removed from the plot for clarity.*

SI counts with the C + HG method compared to the C method while walking, $t(42) = 4.54, p < .05$ (see Fig. 2).

Looking directly at the C + HG method, we next investigated HGH frequency for the two menu icons embedded in the task sequence. HGH frequency was higher while walking compared to while stationary, $t(14) = 3.43, p < .05$.

Walking Speed. There was no significant difference in overall walking speed between the two interaction methods, $t(14) = -1.67, p > .05$. We also compared walking speeds within half-second windows before an input (button press or HGH) to walking speeds at other times in the task sequence. This analysis yielded no significant differences for either interaction method, $t_C(14) = -.18, p > .05; t_{C+HG}(14) = -.96, p > .05$.

3.2 Qualitative Results

Interview Feedback. 8/15 participants (53%) reported difficulty with the C + HG method while walking. 7/15 participants (47%) specifically relayed difficulties with hovering over the icons due to sensitivity of the tracker to head bob. Some participants reported head-gaze was useful because it was silent and hands-free while others reported they thought head-gaze would be useful as an emergency option if an alternative inter-action, such as eye-tracking, were degraded or denied in combat. Yet, some also felt that the controller added equipment burden that could present a disadvantage when carrying objects or during combat.

Lastly, participants reported their binary preference for each interaction method in stationary and ambulatory usage contexts. In stationary contexts, participants (8/15, 53%) slightly preferred the C method over the C + HG method, while in ambulatory contexts, participants (13/15, 87%) overwhelmingly preferred the C method.

Survey Responses. Participants survey responses were broadly consistent with sentiments expressed in the interviews (see Fig. 3). Most of the mean NASA-TLX subscale scores were near zero and did not differ significantly between the interaction methods and walking conditions, all p's > .05, except the performance subscale. Participants rated the C + HG method's performance lower than the C method overall, $t(14) = -2.04$, p < .05. SUS scores did not significantly differ between the interaction methods but did differ between the walking conditions for every SUS item, all p's < .05, except ease of use. Overall, participants responded more favorably while walking compared to while stationary. However, this may have stemmed from the novelty of the omnidirectional treadmill or a learning effect because the walking condition was always completed after the stationary condition.

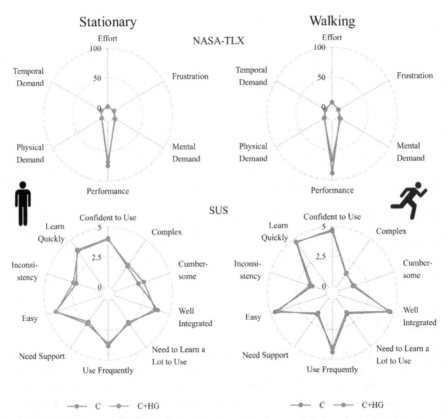

Fig. 3. NASA-TLX and SUS responses by interaction method and walking condition.

4 Discussion

The present study directly compared button- and head-based interaction methods while Soldier users stood still and walked, yielding insights into the strengths, weaknesses, and tradeoffs of these interaction methods for ambulatory AR use. First, participants completed AR menu selection faster when using the Controller + Head-Gaze (C + HG) method vs the Controller Only (C) method while standing still. This aligns with previous head-gaze interface studies demonstrating their potential for stationary AR applications [15–19]. However, time-on-task (TOT) did not differ between the two methods while walking, suggesting the C + HG method's strength, its intuitive cursor-like interaction, did not extend to ambulatory usage contexts. Indeed, other quantitative metrics confirmed challenges with the C + HG method. First, participants made a high number of selection inputs (i.e. A-button presses) using the C + HG method while walking. They also tended to hover the head-gaze cursor over the selectable menu icons more frequently while walking vs stationary. Taken together, these findings suggest that participants had difficulty stabilizing their head to hover the head-gaze cursor, leading to inaccuracies in icon selection and necessitating additional selection input.

Participants' qualitative feedback supported this interpretation. Around half of participants reported difficulty using the C + HG method while walking and noted difficulty specifically with hovering the head-gaze cursor. Moreover, participants both strongly preferred the C method over the C + HG method and reported better success using it while walking. Together, the quantitative and qualitative data suggest that while head-gaze is a promising AR interaction method in relatively stationary contexts, because it requires good head stability it is not well-suited for AR interaction during locomotion.

A few limitations of the present study should be considered alongside its insights. First, walking on a treadmill is qualitatively different from walking in the real world. In the present study, we did not observe differences in walking speed between interaction methods. In real-world locomotion, shifting visual attention to interacting with an AR interface carries the risk of bumping into or tripping over obstacles. It is possible that differences between the interaction methods, such as slowing of pace during interaction, could emerge during immersive virtual or real-world locomotion. Second, the task sequence employed in the present study was brief and comprised simple actions. Our findings may not generalize to more complex and/or longer duration AR actions that require sustained and high number of inputs (e.g., typing, gaming, etc.). Lastly, to ensure safety, the walking condition was always completed after the stationary condition so participants could become familiar with the AR interface before walking on the treadmill. However, this may have led to order effects. In addition, participants universally considered the omnidirectional treadmill a novel and interesting technology which may have colored their perception and assessments of the interaction methods.

Two implications for HCI research on AR MMIs are evident from the present study's findings. First, HCI researchers should continue to investigate AR interaction methods with diverse user groups. Military personnel will use AR in high-stakes contexts which in turn shapes their attitudes toward MMIs, such as prioritizing reliability of interaction methods and their generalizability across a range of operational contexts and missions. While head-gaze interfaces are considered current state-of-the-art in the extant literature, their reduced usability during locomotion contributed heavily to Soldiers' preference for button-based input. Future research should continue to explore military users' needs for AR systems because, as the present study's findings show, they can diverge from the civilian populations' that have been garnered from academic HCI research. Second, the present study demonstrates the need for research to develop and evaluate novel "walking user interfaces" [31] to compensate for the reduced input performance that occurs during locomotion. For head-gaze, this may involve smoothing the gaze cursor trajectory to reduce jittering due to head bob or by implementing interaction methods that go beyond pointing, such as by leveraging smooth pursuit [32], large head-gesture movements [33], or marking menus [34].

Acknowledgements. We thank Daniel Grover for assistance in developing the walking speed data collection software. We also thank Jessica Armstrong for assistance with data collection.

Funding Statement. This work was conducted by the DEVCOM SC Cognitive Science and Applications Branch and was supported by the Measuring and Advancing Soldier Tactical Readiness and Effectiveness (MASTR-E) Program and the Center for Applied Brain and Cognitive Sciences under a cooperative agreement (W911QY-19-2-0003) with Tufts University during the period of February 2022 to March 2024.

Disclosure of Interests. The authors have no competing interests to declare that are relevant to the content of this article.

Disclaimers. The views expressed in this article are solely those of the authors and do not reflect the official policies or positions of the Department of Army, the Department of Defense, or any other department or agency of the U.S. Government. The primary author prepared this work as part of their official duties as an employee of the United States Government. Pursuant to Sect. 105 of the Copyright Act of 1976, this work is not entitled to domestic copyright protection under U.S. law. The citation of trade names in this report does not constitute official product endorsement or approval. The companies providing software and technology (Infinadeck and Pison Technology Inc.) to support this effort did not contribute to the preparation of this report.

References

1. Soldier, P.E.O.: PEO Soldier | Portfolio - PM IVAS - Integrated Visual Augmentation System (IVAS). https://www.peosoldier.army.mil/Equipment/Equipment-Portfolio/Project-Manager-Soldier-Warrior-Portfolio/Integrated-Visual-Augmentation-System/
2. Hornbæk, K., Mottelson, A., Knibbe, J., Vogel, D.: What do we mean by "interaction"? An analysis of 35 years of CHI. ACM Trans. Comput.-Hum. Interact. **26**, 1–30 (2019). https://doi.org/10.1145/3325285
3. Azofeifa, J.D., Noguez, J., Ruiz, S., Molina-Espinosa, J.M., Magana, A.J., Benes, B.: Systematic review of multimodal human-computer interaction. Informatics **9**, 1–13 (2022). https://doi.org/10.3390/informatics9010013
4. Lazaro, M.J., Lee, J., Chun, J., Yun, M.H., Kim, S.: Multimodal interaction: input-output modality combinations for identification tasks in augmented reality. Appl. Ergon. **105**, 103842 (2022). https://doi.org/10.1016/j.apergo.2022.103842
5. Turk, M.: Multimodal interaction: a review. Pattern Recogn. Lett. **36**, 189–195 (2014). https://doi.org/10.1016/j.patrec.2013.07.003

6. Ismail, A.W., Billinghurst, M., Sunar, M.S.: Vision-based technique and issues for multimodal interaction in augmented reality. In: Proceedings of the 8th International Symposium on Visual Information Communication and Interaction, pp. 75–82. Association for Computing Machinery, New York (2015)

7. Li, S., Yerebakan, M.O., Luo, Y., Amaba, B., Swope, W., Hu, B.: The effect of different occupational background noises on voice recognition accuracy. J. Comput. Inf. Sci. Eng. **22** (2022). https://doi.org/10.1115/1.4053521

8. Wu, S., Li, Z., Li, S., Liu, Q., Wu, W.: An overview of gesture recognition. In: Varadarajan, V., Lin, J.C.-W., Lorenz, P. (eds.) International Conference on Computer Application and Information Security (ICCAIS 2022), p. 1260926 (2023)

9. Boring, S., Jurmu, M., Butz, A.: Scroll, tilt or move it: using mobile phones to continuously control pointers on large public displays. In: Proceedings of the 21st Annual Conference of the Australian Computer-Human Interaction Special Interest Group: Design: Open 24/7, pp. 161–168. Association for Computing Machinery, New York (2009)

10. Department of the Army: Rifle and carbine training circular (TC 3-22.9). Army Publishing Directorate, Washington, D.C. (2016)

11. Kapp, S., Barz, M., Mukhametov, S., Sonntag, D., Kuhn, J.: ARETT: augmented reality eye tracking toolkit for head mounted displays. Sensors **21**, 2234 (2021). https://doi.org/10.3390/s21062234

12. Gardony, A.L., Lindeman, R.W., Brunyé, T.T.: Eye-tracking for human-centered mixed reality: promises and challenges. In: Kress, B.C., Peroz, C. (eds.) Optical Architectures for Displays and Sensing in Augmented, Virtual, and Mixed Reality (AR, VR, MR), p. 113100T. SPIE (2020)

13. Hirzle, T., Cordts, M., Rukzio, E., Bulling, A.: A survey of digital eye strain in gaze-based interactive systems. In: ACM Symposium on Eye Tracking Research and Applications. Association for Computing Machinery, New York (2020)

14. Callahan-Flintoft, C., Jensen, E., Naeem, J., Nonte, M.W., Madison, A.M., Ries, A.J.: A comparison of head movement classification methods. Sensors **24**, 1260 (2024). https://doi.org/10.3390/s24041260

15. Bates, R., Istance, H.O.: Why are eye mice unpopular? a detailed comparison of head and eye controlled assistive technology pointing devices. Univ. Access Inf. Soc. **2**, 280–290 (2003). https://doi.org/10.1007/s10209-003-0053-y

16. Bernardos, A.M., Gómez, D., Casar, J.R.: A comparison of head pose and deictic pointing interaction methods for smart environments. Int. J. Hum.-Comput. Interact. **32**, 325–351 (2016). https://doi.org/10.1080/10447318.2016.1142054

17. Jalaliniya, S., Mardanbeigi, D., Pederson, T., Hansen, D.W.: Head and eye movement as pointing modalities for eyewear computers. In: 2014 11th International Conference on Wearable and Implantable Body Sensor Networks Workshops, pp. 50–53 (2014)

18. Hansen, J.P., Rajanna, V., MacKenzie, I.S., Bækgaard, P.: A Fitts' law study of click and dwell interaction by gaze, head and mouse with a head-mounted display. In: Proceedings of the Workshop on Communication by Gaze Interaction. Association for Computing Machinery, New York (2018)

19. Kytö, M., Ens, B., Piumsomboon, T., Lee, G.A., Billinghurst, M.: Pinpointing: precise head- and eye-based target selection for augmented reality. In: Proceedings of the 2018 CHI Conference on Human Factors in Computing Systems, pp. 1–14. Association for Computing Machinery, New York (2018)

20. Kuber, P.M., Rashedi, E.: Alterations in physical demands during virtual/augmented reality-based tasks: a systematic review. Ann. Biomed. Eng. **51**, 1910–1932 (2023). https://doi.org/10.1007/s10439-023-03292-0

21. Lages, W.S., Bowman, D.A.: Walking with adaptive augmented reality workspaces: design and usage patterns. In: Proceedings of the 24th International Conference on Intelligent User Interfaces, pp. 356–366. Association for Computing Machinery, New York (2019)

22. Müller, F., Schmitz, M., Schmitt, D., Günther, S., Funk, M., Mühlhäuser, M.: Walk the line: leveraging lateral shifts of the walking path as an input modality for head-mounted displays. In: Proceedings of the 2020 CHI Conference on Human Factors in Computing Systems, pp. 1–15. Association for Computing Machinery, New York (2020)

23. Infinadeck: The Only True Omnidirectional Treadmill | VR Treadmill. https://www.infina deck.com/

24. Unity. https://unity.com/

25. Brooke, J.: SUS: a quick and dirty usability scale. Usabil. Eval. Ind. **189**, 4–7 (1995)

26. Hart, S.G., Staveland, L.E.: Development of NASA-TLX (Task Load Index): Results of empirical and theoretical research. In: Hancock, P.A., Meshkati, N. (eds.) Advances in Psychology, pp. 139–183. North-Holland (1988)

27. R Core Team: R: A Language and Environment for Statistical Computing (2022). https://www.r-project.org/

28. Bates, D., Mächler, M., Bolker, B., Walker, S.: fitting linear mixed-effects models using lme4. J. Stat. Softw. **67**, 1–48 (2015). https://doi.org/10.18637/jss.v067.i01

29. Wickham, H.: Ggplot2: Elegant Graphics for Data Analysis. Springer-Verlag, New York (2016)

30. Lenth, R.: emmeans: Estimated Marginal Means, aka Least-Squares Means (2023). https://cran.r-project.org/package=emmeans

31. Kane, S.K., Wobbrock, J.O., Smith, I.E.: Getting off the treadmill: evaluating walking user interfaces for mobile devices in public spaces. In: Proceedings of the 10th International Conference on Human Computer Interaction with Mobile Devices and Services, pp. 109–118. ACM, Amsterdam (2008)

32. Esteves, A., Verweij, D., Suraiya, L., Islam, R., Lee, Y., Oakley, I.: SmoothMoves: smooth pursuits head movements for augmented reality. In: Proceedings of the 30th Annual ACM Symposium on User Interface Software and Technology, pp. 167–178. ACM, Québec City (2017)

33. Shi, R., Zhu, N., Liang, H.-N., Zhao, S.: Exploring head-based mode-switching in virtual reality. In: 2021 IEEE International Symposium on Mixed and Augmented Reality (ISMAR), pp. 118–127 (2021)

34. Kim, T., Ham, A., Ahn, S., Lee, G.: Lattice menu: a low-error gaze-based marking menu utilizing target-assisted gaze gestures on a lattice of visual anchors. In: Proceedings of the 2022 CHI Conference on Human Factors in Computing Systems. Association for Computing Machinery, New York (2022)

Investigating How Interaction with Physical Objects Within Virtual Environments Affects Knowledge Acquisition and Recall

Ryan Garrett, Justin Gast, Spencer Henry, Kalli Mellili, Seung Hyuk Jang, Markus Santoso, and Angelos Barmpoutis$^{(\boxtimes)}$ (ID)

Digital Worlds Institute, University of Florida, Gainesville, FL 32611, USA
{rgarrett,justin.gast,spencer.henry,kmelilli}@ufl.edu,
{hyuk,markus,angelos}@digitalworlds.ufl.edu

Abstract. This paper introduces a small-scale study that examines the utilization of a simple physical object as the primary interactive tool in a gamified educational virtual reality (VR) application. The study aims to evaluate the impact of passive haptics on the learning process within VR environments. The findings suggest that incorporating passive haptic interfaces in VR has the potential to enhance the learning experience and overall outcomes. Specifically, the results indicate that participants exhibited increased confidence when using a physical object (a jar) rather than traditional VR controllers. This confidence led to more accurate interactions, such as pouring liquids, and contributed to an enhanced sense of immersion. Additionally, results from recall tests suggest that participants demonstrated improved memory retention when knowledge was acquired through the haptic VR experience.

Keywords: Virtual Reality · Tactile and haptic interaction · Passive Haptics · User Perception

1 Introduction

The use of passive haptics in virtual reality (VR) environments has been shown to improve procedural learning across various application domains such as first responders training, kayaking, and others [3,4]. Studies have shown that introducing haptic interfaces in VR can positively affect user experience [1], enhance simulations [7,8], and improve performance in various forms of training [4,5], ranging from medical procedures [6], to music conducting training [2].

In this paper we want to go one step further and quantify the effect of passive haptics on knowledge acquisition and recall, extending our laboratory's previous research projects on the use of low-cost passive haptics in VR [2,3]. We developed a specialized virtual reality application for learning various chemical compounds and their components. Participants engaged in activities that involved precise mixing and proportioning of chemical components to form targeted compounds (see Fig. 1). Employing an A-B test framework, participants

Fig. 1. Illustration of the user interaction using the physical jar. Components of the virtual environment are superimposed to show the alignment between the virtual and the real world.

were randomly assigned to two identical virtual reality environments, differing only in the substitution of the VR controller with a physical jar.

Pre- and post-study surveys were administered to gauge user perceptions regarding interaction accuracy and realism, as well as their ability to recall acquired knowledge (specifically, the list of components) from their virtual experience. Statistical analyses, including chi-square tests, were performed on the collected data, with detailed results outlined in this paper.

Two key findings emerged from the study: (a) the presence of the physical jar significantly heightened perceived interaction accuracy, particularly in precise liquid pouring tasks, and (b) users exhibited improvement in knowledge recall when the knowledge was acquired using the physical jar as opposed to a conventional VR controller. These results establish a compelling correlation between the integration of passive haptic objects in VR and knowledge acquisition and recall. Despite the study's small size, which limits the conclusiveness of the results, the findings clearly indicate that the use of passive haptic interfaces in VR can improve the learning experience and outcomes, and this project lays the groundwork for a larger-scale research study in the future.

The rest of the paper is organized as follows: Sect. 2 describes the VR application that was developed for the purposes of this study, Sect. 3 presents the details of the user study protocol, and Sec. 4 discusses in detail the results collected from the pilot study.

Fig. 2. Screen capture of the virtual environment showing the jars with the constituents (right), the recipe book (center), and the mixing cauldron (left).

2   Methods

A novel virtual reality application for Oculus Quest 2 headset was developed in Unity 3D for the needs of this project. The purpose of this application was to simulate a small-scale training process, during which the users obtain new procedural knowledge. More specifically, in this virtual experience the users had to complete a series of procedural tasks that involved mixing various components to create six specific compounds: Aluminum Iodine (3 constituents), Caesium (2 constituents), Thermite (2 constituents), Golden Rain (4 constituents), Luminol (4 constituents), and Belousov (6 constituents). The process was gamified by representing all constituents as liquids that had to be poured in the right quantities into a cauldron and mixed together to create the compound. For example, to create thermite the users had to mix together two constituents: aluminum and iron oxide (rust). A recipe book that appeared in front of the users provided the list of the constituents and the appropriate quantities for each compound. Figure 2, shows a screen captured view of the developed gamified application.

The main object of interaction was a jar that the user was holding continuously throughout the virtual experience. The content of the jar could change interactively into one of the available constituents from each recipe. To facilitate testing the main hypothesis of our project, a passive haptic version of the jar was designed using a real jar that was half filled with water. One of the VR controllers was rigidly attached to the jar using a 3D printed attachment as shown in Fig. 3, so that the jar is tracked in real time. The other VR controller was normally held on the other hand (as shown in Fig. 1), and was used for typical user interactions, such as making selections in VR, and was visualized in VR as a wand to match with the rest of the gamification elements.

The same VR application but without a physical jar was used as the control case. In that version, the user was holding the VR controller instead of the real jar, but it was visualized as a virtual jar identical to the one shown in the test

Fig. 3. Picture of the haptic jar with the VR controller using a 3D printed attachment.

case version. Therefore, the only difference between the test and control versions was the presence or absence of the physical jar respectively, which was the only variable in our study.

3   User Study

A pilot study was designed to investigate how the use of passive haptics in educational VR applications could affect learning outcomes. Starting with this broad topic in mind, a small-scale experiment was designed using the generalizable VR application that was presented in Sect. 2. More specifically, the VR application was used as a training platform that exposed users to new knowledge through an interactive experiential learning session.

The research study was structured as a randomized controlled trial (RCT) employing a crossover design. Within this framework, every participant underwent both the test condition (real jar version) and the control condition (traditional VR controller version), with the sequence randomly determined. This methodology aims to reduce the impact of individual variations and potential biases, enabling a more comprehensive evaluation of the intervention's efficacy, within the limits of the pilot nature of our study.

The study was approved by the University of Florida institutional review board (IRB protocol 17379, approval date: February 8, 2023). A total of 12 individuals participated in this study in the period between February 27, 2023 and April 19, 2023. The subjects' ages ranged from 18 to 34, with eight falling into the 18 to 24 age group and four into the 25 to 34 category. Among the participants, six had used VR a few times before the study, while three reported using VR frequently, and another three had never used VR prior to the study. None of the subjects were familiar with the specific training content of the VR application, ensuring equal exposure to new knowledge for all participants during the study.

In the beginning of the study session, the order of the two experiences (test and control) was randomly chosen. The session started with a pre-test questionnaire covering demographics questions, followed by the first VR experience. After that, a post-test questionnaire was administered with multiple choice questions about the first VR experience. The questions were expressed in the form of statements such as "It was easy to pour precise liquid amounts" with five possible answers ranging from "strongly agree" to "strongly disagree". Then, the subject had the second VR experience followed by another post-test questionnaire with the same set of questions as before. The session concluded with an exit survey that included A-B questions comparing the two experiences, a recall test assessing the acquired knowledge, and other open-ended feedback questions.

4   Results

As this study was conducted in a pilot capacity with a small participant pool, the conclusions drawn from the data analysis are largely suggestive rather than conclusive. Data analysis employed Chi-squared test statistics or Fisher's exact test in instances where the former's assumptions were not satisfied. Furthermore, to address the issue of low expected frequency counts in the corresponding contingency tables, the responses were grouped into broader categories, by merging 'weak' and 'strong' agreement or disagreement levels accordingly.

Table 1. Results from post-condition questionnaires

Scale	χ^2	p	Direction
Jar was lighter than expected	15.5	<0.001	Control
Jar was heavier than expected	12.0	<0.001	Test
Wand was lighter than expected	0.2	NS	N/A
Wand was heavier than expected	1.7	NS	N/A
Felt the liquid inside the jar	11.0	<0.001	Test
Jar was intuitive to use	2.2	NS	N/A
Easy to pour precise amounts	4.9	<0.05	Control

Table 1 presents the analysis of the data collected from the two post-test surveys. Each statement in the survey was assessed using a set of two complementary hypotheses: the null hypothesis stating no perceived difference between the two conditions (haptic VR vs. traditional VR), and an alternative hypothesis suggesting a difference. When the statistical test yielded a small p-value, indicating significance, the null hypothesis was rejected, which implied evidence of a significant difference between the two conditions. For example the virtual wand, which was operated by a VR controller in both VR experiences, was not perceived differently (lighter or heavier) across the two VR experiences. This is indicated by a low χ^2 value, which corresponds to a non-significant (NS) finding in Table 1. Statistical significance was found regarding the perception of the jar across the two VR experiences: it was perceived as lighter than expected in the control case and heavier than expected in the test case. Similarly, users were able to feel the liquid inside the jar in the test case, as anticipated. One of the most intriguing statistically significant findings reported in Table 1 is that users found it easier to pour liquids in precise amounts in the control case (real jar) compared to the test case (VR controller).

Table 2. Results from post-test comparative questionnaire

Scale	%
Was more immersive	91.66%
Was more appropriate	77.27%
Teaches how to judge measurements	70.83%
Was more enjoyable	66.66%
Was clear how to operate	66.66%
Easier to remember ingredients	62.50%
I felt dizzier or nauseated	54.16%

Table 2 summarizes the results from the A-B comparative questions included in the exit survey. To avoid any confusion with the order of the two VR experiences, all responses in this table are reported with respect to the test case (real jar). According to the collected data, the users felt that the haptic VR experience was more immersive, more appropriate for this type of interaction, and that it better taught how to judge measurements, which is in agreement with the last statistically significant finding reported in Table 1. Furthermore, nearly two-thirds of the subjects found the VR experience with the real jar more enjoyable, clearer to operate, and easier to remember the ingredients.

Finally, Table 3 presents the results from the recall test administered as part of the exit survey. The table compares the results based on the first experience (control or test case). For example, Aluminum Iodine was presented in this gamified experience as the result of a reaction between three components. Recall was measured using the formula $recall = n_{present} - n_{absent}$, which counts how many of the correct components were identified by the subject minus the number of components missing from their response. In the previous example, the maximum possible score was 3 if all three components were correctly identified, and the smallest possible score was -3 if none of the components were identified. According to the first row of Table 3, subjects who started with the control experience

Table 3. Results from the recall test

Compound	Components	Control Recall	Test Recall	Δ Recall	%
Aluminum Iodine	3	1.00	2.00	1.00	33.3%
Caesium	2	−0.40	0.33	0.73	36.6%
Thermite	2	−0.80	−0.83	−0.03	−1.6%
Golden Rain	4	0.80	1.50	0.70	17.5%
Luminol	4	1.20	2.16	0.96	24.1%
Belousov	6	0.00	4.00	4.00	66.6%
Mean	3.5	0.30	1.52	1.22	29.4%
Median	3.5	0.40	1.75	0.85	28.7%
Std. Dev.	1.5	0.81	1.65	1.40	22.7%

(VR controller) identified, on average, 1 out of the 3 components, while subjects who had the test experience first (real jar) identified, on average, 2 out of three components, representing a 33.3% increase.

By observing the mean and median differences, it is evident that participants who acquired the knowledge with the real jar in their first experience demonstrated approximately 29% better recall than those who acquired the knowledge with the conventional VR experience. This finding indicates that the presence of passive haptics in virtual reality can positively affect knowledge acquisition and recall. Furthermore, it suggests that the modality (haptic or conventional VR) of the first experience during which new knowledge is acquired plays a significant role.

5   Conclusions

In conclusion, this paper presented a small-scale study that employed a simple physical object as the primary interaction tool in a gamified educational VR application. The study aimed to evaluate the impact of passive haptics on the learning process in virtual reality. The findings revealed that participants exhibited greater confidence when operating the physical tool (in our case, a jar), enabling them to pour liquids more accurately and enhancing their overall sense of immersion. Additionally, recall tests indicated that participants demonstrated improved memory retention when knowledge was acquired through the haptic VR experience initially. While the study's small size limits the conclusiveness of the results, they clearly suggest that the incorporation of passive haptic interfaces in VR can significantly enhance the learning experience and outcomes in various ways.

Acknowledgments. This project was funded in part by the Digital Worlds Institute faculty development fund to M. Santoso and A. Barmpoutis. We would also like to thank the volunteers for agreeing to participate in this study.

Disclosure of Interests. The authors have no competing interests to declare that are relevant to the content of this article.

References

1. Azmandian, M., Hancock, M., Benko, H., Ofek, E., Wilson, A.D.: Haptic retargeting: dynamic repurposing of passive haptics for enhanced virtual reality experiences. In: Proceedings of the 2016 CHI Conference on Human Factors in Computing Systems, pp. 1968–1979 (2016)
2. Barmpoutis, A., et al.: Assessing the role of virtual reality with passive haptics in music conductor education: a pilot study. In: Chen, J.Y.C., Fragomeni, G. (eds.) Proceedings of the 2020 Human-Computer Interaction International Conference, vol. 12190, pp. 275–285 (2020)
3. Barmpoutis, A., et al.: Virtual kayaking: a study on the effect of low-cost passive haptics on the user experience while exercising. In: Stephanidis, C., Antona, M. (eds.) HCII 2020. CCIS, vol. 1225, pp. 147–155. Springer, Cham (2020). https://doi.org/10.1007/978-3-030-50729-9_20
4. Calandra, D., De Lorenzis, F., Cannavò, A., Lamberti, F.: Immersive virtual reality and passive haptic interfaces to improve procedural learning in a formal training course for first responders. Virtual Real. **27**(2), 985–1012 (2023)
5. Franzluebbers, A., Johnsen, K.: Performance benefits of high-fidelity passive haptic feedback in virtual reality training. In: Proceedings of the 2018 ACM Symposium on Spatial User Interaction, pp. 16–24, October 2018
6. Fucentese, S.F., Rahm, S., Wieser, K., Spillmann, J., Harders, M., Koch, P.P.: Evaluation of a virtual-reality-based simulator using passive haptic feedback for knee arthroscopy. Knee Surg. Sports Traumatol. Arthrosc. **23**, 1077–1085 (2015)
7. Joyce, R.D., Robinson, S.: Passive haptics to enhance virtual reality simulations. In: AIAA Modeling and Simulation Technologies Conference, p. 1313 (2017)
8. Kim, D., Kim, Y., Jo, D.: Exploring the effect of virtual environments on passive haptic perception. Appl. Sci. **13**(1), 299 (2022)

Generative AI Tool Pipeline for Creating Artificial Historical Characters for Cultural Heritage XR

Jan Gemeinhardt⬡, Michael Zöllner⁽✉⁾ ⬡, and Celina Jahn⁽✉⁾ ⬡

Hof University, Alfons-Goppel-Platz 1, 95028 Hof, Germany
jan.gemeinhardt.2@iisys.de, michael.zoellner@hof-university.de

Abstract. In our project, we aimed to create historically authentic and vivid virtual representations of historic personalities that are connected to the regional Fichtelgebirge (Bavaria, Germany) to support the storytelling of our immersive XR applications. We are describing the tools in detail, the process of the tool chain and the resulting media. Next, we are discussing the challenges in media production like historical correctness and the consultation of historians. In order to create visual reproducibility we are explaining the detailed text prompts, their limitations and how to cope with resulting errors of the human physiognomy. Finally, we are briefly describing the application of the animated and talking generated historic characters in an immersive interactive WebXR environment. The XR experience is presented in web browsers on smartphones, tablets and XR headsets and the underlying software is based on the open-source framework Aframe. Our paper will describe the process, the results and the limitations in detail. Furthermore, we will provide a flow chart of the tool pipeline with visual examples of these aspects. The animations and voices of the historic characters will be demonstrated in videos of the XR application.

Keywords: Generative AI · Cultural Heritage · Extended Reality (XR)

1 Introduction

During the last years we saw a large amount of new creative tools based on Generative AI. Text-to-image models like OpenAI's Dall-E [10], Stable Diffusion [4] and Midjourney [7] are generating synthetic images in variable styles from text prompts. Stable Video Diffusion [3] creates short animations from text or images. Generative Text-to-Voice is publicly available via online-platforms like ElevenLabs [2]. With these tools at hand, a single artist today is able to create the workflow of a whole team. In this paper we introduce a Generative AI tool pipeline designed to facilitate the creation of historically accurate characters for cultural heritage and extended reality (XR) applications, that enables the creation of historic characters for the usage in cultural heritage and extended reality (XR), by combining separately available machine learning solutions.

Our motivation is to bring historical figures authentically to life, letting animated AI portraits tell stories in our WebXR Application. With the Generative AI Pipeline

C. Stephanidis et al. (Eds.): HCII 2024, CCIS 2116, pp. 41–46, 2024.
https://doi.org/10.1007/978-3-031-61950-2_5

Toolchain, we also aim to ensure reciprocity for the creation of all the other historical personalities.

Additionally, we seek to digitize museum experiences by integrating generative characters into a XR application, making classical historical content like 2D imagery and text more engaging and accessible to contemporary audiences. Through these efforts, we want to bridge the gap between past and present, preserving cultural heritage while telling our stories with today's digital age possibilities.

2   Related Work

During the last years we saw several related work regarding AI Generated Characters.

The 'Living Memories: AI-Generated Characters as Digital Mementos' explores the concept of digital mementos and living memories, showcasing technologies such as an interactive conversational agent which is used to preserve and interact with the departed to create meaningful connections with historical characters [8].

The website MyHeritage's deep learning feature Deep Nostalgia [6] revives the dead by adding ambient facial expressions to historic portraits.

In educational settings, AI characters can democratize learning experiences, from classroom delivery to engagement at cultural sites or in nature, offering immersive encounters with historical, modern-day, or fictional figures. With advanced algorithms, the generated characters can bring to life the experiences of scientists, historical figures, or artists, enriching educational content with personalized narratives and insights from that time [9].

3   Generative AI Tool Pipeline

3.1   The AI Toolchain

The creation of historically accurate characters involved a multi-step approach, beginning with the enhancement of the original historic upper body portraits. Further steps involved the removal of unwanted elements such as background objects and adding generative details to compensate for missing or obscured features, such as the hair in Queen Luise's original portrait.

The second step involved utilizing text-to-image AI capabilities provided by the tool 'gencraft.com' [5]. However, the success of this approach was only partially successful upon the precision and clarity of the provided text prompts. Despite detailed text descriptions, the resulting images often fell short of our expectations due to their unsatisfactory appearance and overly modern aesthetic, which did not align with the original portraits. Despite our best efforts to articulate the desired characteristics, the generated images failed to capture the essence of historical accuracy we sought. This discrepancy presented a challenge in achieving the intended fidelity to historical representations within our project.

Continuing the pipeline, we used Adobe's Photoshop's [1] AI feature to augment the generated images by creating new poses and seamlessly integrating objects into the characters' hands. This step proved crucial, as it addressed a limitation of scenario.com and allowed us to generate input images that better aligned with our desired outcomes. By refining the poses beforehand, we ensured that the subsequent training of models on 'www.scenario.com' [11] yielded more accurate and historically faithful results.

FIRST PROMPT:

"A full body portrait, white, bright, Elizabethan, smiling, nature, red dress, pearl necklace, hiking in a needle tree forest"

INPUT IMAGERY:
See Fig. 1.

Fig. 1. Input Imagery to create the historical character 'Queen Luise von Preussen'.

NEGATIVE PROMPT:
white, white dress

SECOND (REFINED) PROMPT:

"sitting on a granite rock, holding a piece of paper, writing, red dress, red, fully red dress"

Another aspect of our pipeline was the generation of speaking text and voices to imbue the characters with lifelike attributes. To achieve this, we first utilized AI-generated voices tailored to the characteristics of the historical personalities. These voices were then incorporated into the creation of speaking portrait videos, thereby enriching the immersive experience for users. This comprehensive approach not only enhanced the realism of the characters but also contributed to the overall authenticity of the historical narratives portrayed in our project (Fig. 2).

3.2 Challenges and Limitations

Despite the capabilities of Generative AI tools, several challenges and limitations persist. Ensuring historical correctness and consulting with historic experts were taken into considerations, especially as inaccuracies can detract from the authenticity in our virtual

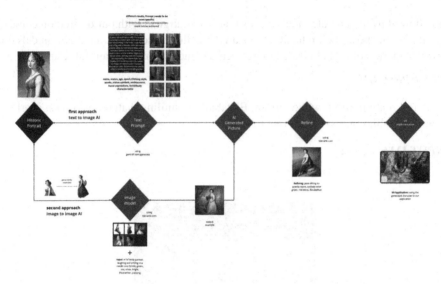

Fig. 2. The AI Pipeline Toolchain used to create the historical character 'Queen Luise von Preussen'.

XR Application. Further limitations showed up in generating human physiology of the characters, such as hand gestures and specific wanted body poses, which have not yet been a characteristic in the input imagery.

To overcome the challenges, it was necessary to work closely with historical experts and maintain historical accuracy. Regarding the body poses, we were able to use Photoshop's generative expanding functionality to expand the lower body and other objects in the portrait imagery with text prompts, which opened new opportunities in generating the content.

4   Usage in Our XR-Application

Before the generated portrait video of the historical character could be integrated into the XR application, it needed further processing. The background first had to be removed using keying in video editing software, allowing the speaking character to be embedded alone without any background. For our purposes, an Alpha Channel Export with the video codec format. webm was necessary to enable the videos to be played in XR later via click events (Fig. 3).

Fig. 3. The historical character 'Queen Luise von Preussen' in a WebXR Application setting.

5   Conclusion and Future Work

In this paper, a Generative AI tool pipeline for the creation of historically accurate characters for cultural heritage and extended reality (XR) applications was introduced. Leveraging state-of-the-art AI models, such as text-to-image and text-to-voice, we aimed to bring historical figures to life in an immersive XR environment. Our motivation centered on authentically portraying the historical characters and allowing audiences to engage with their stories from a personal and historical correct perspective.

Despite the challenges and limitations encountered, including ensuring historical correctness and addressing inaccuracies in human physiology generation, our pipeline demonstrated good results. By working closely with historical experts and utilizing software tools like Photoshop, we were able to overcome the posing obstacles and were able to produce more variety in the representations of historical personalities.

Looking ahead, future work could focus on further enhancing the reproducibility of our approach for other historical characters within the XR application. This involves refining the tool pipeline to accommodate a wider range of historical figures and scenarios, as well as improving the accuracy and fidelity of generated content. Additionally, continued collaboration with historians and interdisciplinary experts will be essential in ensuring the ongoing authenticity and relevance of our XR experiences.

References

1. AI photo editing with Photoshop - online & desktop. Adobe. https://www.adobe.com/uk/products/photoshop/ai.html. Accessed 20 Mar 2024
2. AI Voice Generator & Text to Speech. https://elevenlabs.io/. Accessed 20 Mar 2024
3. Blattmann, A., et al.: Stable video diffusion: scaling latent video diffusion models to large datasets. arXiv (2023)
4. Esser, P., et al.: Scaling rectified flow transformers for high-resolution image synthesis. arXiv (2024)
5. Gencraft - AI Art Image and Video Generator. https://gencraft.com/. Accessed 20 Mar 2024

6. Kopelman, S., Frosh, P.: The "algorithmic as if": computational resurrection and the animation of the dead in Deep Nostalgia. New Media Soc. (2023). https://doi.org/10.1177/146144482 31210268
7. Midjourney. https://www.midjourney.com/website. Accessed 20 Mar 2024
8. Pataranutaporn, P., et al.: Living memories: AI-generated characters as digital mementos. In: Proceedings of the 28th International Conference on Intelligent User Interfaces, New York, NY, USA, March 2023, pp. 889–901 (2023)
9. Pataranutaporn, P., et al.: AI-generated characters for supporting personalized learning and well-being. Nat. Mach. Intell. **3**, 1013–1022 (2021). https://doi.org/10.1038/s42256-021-004 17-9
10. Ramesh, A., Dhariwal, P., Nichol, A., Chu, C., Chen, M.: Hierarchical text-conditional image generation with CLIP latents. arXiv (2022)
11. Scenario: AI-generated game assets. https://www.scenario.com/. Accessed 20 Mar 2024

Force Characteristics to Reproduce Writing Pressure Introduction of Writing Task Characteristics into Virtual Reality

Manabu Ishihara[✉]

National Institute of Technology, Tokyo College, Hachioji, Tokyo 193-0997, Japan
ishihara@m.ieice.org

Abstract. In this study, we used a force-sensing device to measure the threshold and subjective equivalence points of tactile perception of frictional force. We were able to determine the correlation with the actual tactile sensation by measuring the correlation between the friction force presented by the force-sensing device and the value set by the PHANToM. When friction is presented by a force sensing device, it is observed that a force above approximately 0.3 [N] is the value at which the user can determine the difference.

The PHANToM DeskTop used in this study is a pen-type force-sensing device, and the force sensation is presented through the hand that holds the pen. Therefore, it is not a surface sensation felt only through direct contact with the skin on the hand, but a deep sensory characteristic that is felt by the entire hand. This method can also be applied to the paper-mediated systems. In the future, we aim to analyze the sensory characteristics of devices other than the pen-type and to verify the differences and compatibility of the sensory characteristics presented by those devices.

Keywords: Virtual reality · force-sensing device · vertical drag force

1 Introduction

Virtual reality technology has been rapidly developing in recent years and is being employed in various fields such as simulation and medicine. Further development is also expected in this field with the increasing popularity of touch-panel devices due to the growing demand for interfaces that provide a sense of touch. Additionally, there is an increasing requirement for tactile interfaces that can provide actual sensory characteristics, such as those provided in virtual reality environments. However, the expressions of force and tactile sensation vary physiologically [1], and these expressions are sometimes sensed by the entire hand [2, 3] For example, when writing on Japanese paper, we can feel the friction of the paper and the sliding of the brush.

In this study, we have simulated this frictional sensation [4] using a pen-type force-sensing device called PHANToM DeskTop, and have also investigated the threshold, point of subjective equivalence (PSE), and sensory characteristics of tactile perception.

C. Stephanidis et al. (Eds.): HCII 2024, CCIS 2116, pp. 47–57, 2024.
https://doi.org/10.1007/978-3-031-61950-2_6

Furthermore, we measured the friction force generated by this device and applied it to the experimental results as a friction coefficient while considering the vertical drag force.

2 System Configuration

2.1 Basic Concepts of Force Sensing Displays Basic Concepts of Force Sensing Displays

A force-sensing display is a device that presents a sense of force to the user by acquiring the positional information of the input, such as the tip of a pen in the case of a pen-type device. When the user operates the force-sensing display, the three-dimensional position information is transmitted to the computer. Subsequently, the computer performs physical operations using the position information and a model of the virtual space, and transfers this information to the force-sensing display as a three-dimensional force and direction vector. The force-sensing display then provides the user with a sensation of force. This process is repeated at a high speed, providing the user with the sensation of actually touching the model in the virtual space.

2.2 Hardware Configuration

A force-sensing display called the PHANToM DeskTop E Device from Sensable Technologies was used for this experiment. Section 2.2.1 presents the details of the device. The control computer has an Intel®Core™i5-4430 CPU @3.00 GHz with 8.00 GB of RAM. A digital force gauge (DPS-5, IMADA CORPORATION was used to measure the frictional force.

The PHANToM DeskTop comprises a 3–6 DOF position sensor and feedback mechanism. It is a force-sensing device that enables a user to manipulate objects within a virtual space on a PC to obtain a high-precision force sensation. Figure 1 depicts the appearance of the PHANToM used in this study. Figure 1(b) illustrates the PHANToM Omni and (a) depicts the PHANToM DeskTop. Table 1 lists the detailed specifications of PHANToM.

(a)PHANToM DeskTop   (b)PHANToM Omni

Fig. 1. Appearance of PHANToM Device.

Table 1. PHANToM Specifications.

	Omni	DeskTop
workspace	6.4W x 4.8H x 2.8D [inches]. 160W x 120H x 70D [mm]	6.4W x 4.8H x 4.8D [inches]. 160W x 120H x 120D [mm] (mm)
Positional resolution	450 [dpi]. 0.055 [mm]	1100 [dpi]. 0.023 [mm]
Mechanical friction resistance	1 [oz.]. 0.26 [N]	0.23 [oz.] 0.06 [N]
Maximum presentation power (Maximum continuous presentation power)	0.75 (0.2) [lbf] 3.3 (0.88) [N].	1.8 (0.4) [lbf]. 7.9 (1.75) [N].
stiffness	X axis>7.3[lbs./in.] 1.26 [N/mm] Y axis>13.4[lbs./in.] 2.31[N/mm] Z axis>5.9[lbs./in.] 1.02 [N/mm]	X axis>10.8[lbs./in.]1.86 [N/mm] Y axis>13.6[lbs./in.]2.35 [N/mm] Z axis>8.6[lbs./in.] 1.48 [N/mm]
inertia	<0.101 [lbm]. <45g	<0.101 [lbm]. <45g
Position sensing	x,y,z(digital encorders) Pitch,roll,yaw(±5%)	x,y,z(digital encorders) Pitch,roll,yaw(±3%)

2.3 Software Configuration

The application used in this study was developed using OpenHaptics™ from Sensable Technologies.

The HLAPI toolkit v3.0 [5, 6] was used. Microsoft Visual Studio 2015 Express was used as the development environment for this application.

3 Experimental Investigation of the Coefficient of Presented Friction

3.1 Objectives of the Experiment

In a typical experimental system, the presented stimulus (frictional force) does not take into account the vertical drag force. However, based on the operation of the PHANToM and the observations made during the experiment, it is empirically observed that there appears to be a reciprocal sensation between the force of pushing against the plane in the virtual space and the resistance due to friction. Consequently, we have considered the possibility that the coefficient of friction presented by the PHANToM may vary from the value that can be set within PHANToM, which is considered as the coefficient of friction.

The reference of the control program OpenHaptics™ toolkit v3.0 does not explain this phenomenon, and there is no detailed description of the parameters for the friction sensation presentation. There is only a statement that "0 indicates no presentation and 1 indicates the maximum value that can be presented by the machine." To determine the relationship between these settings and the actual presentation values, we analyzed the actual friction coefficients presented by PHANToM in this study.

Target Stimuli. The stimuli presented in this experiment were expressed based on the coefficient of friction in the PHANToM. However, the reference for the function used to represent the friction was "the maximum force that can be presented by the device used is 1, and the minimum force is 0." If this is considered as the reference, Table 1 shows that the friction force is the product of the maximum force of 7.9 [N] of the PHANToM DeskTop and is a value between 1 and 0 set in the application. Therefore, even with the same coefficient setting, the PHANToM DeskTop (maximum presentation force of 7.9 [N]) and PHANToM Omni (maximum presentation force of 3.3 [N]) exhibited different friction forces.

Psychophysics. Psychophysics is a branch of psychology that helps in understanding the characteristics of the senses. The two main terms of psychophysics used in this experiment are described below:

(a) Point of subjective equivalence (PSE). The PSE is defined as a point that feels psychologically equal to an arbitrary reference point on a scale used to measure a physical quantity, and is defined as the point where the probability function, Pr, and the physical quantities, x and a can be given as:

$$\Pr(x > a) + \Pr(x < a) = a \tag{1}$$

$$\Pr(x > a) = \Pr(x < a) = \frac{1}{2} \tag{2}$$

Here, x represents the PSE, such that:

$$\Pr(PSE > a) = \Pr(PSE < a) = \frac{1}{2} \tag{3}$$

The following is a summary of the results.

(b) Just noticeable difference (JND). The discrimination threshold or just noticeable difference (JND) is defined as the smallest stimulus difference that can be perceived when the same stimulus type is varied.

It is calculated based on the discrimination probability $\Pr(x > a)$ set for the threshold. Since the discrimination probability changes continuously with x, the difference between the smallest distinguishable stimulus values is determined according to the discrimination probability set for the threshold.

The discrimination probability used to determine the JND is 0.75 for the constant method, which was determined by Fechner (Fechner, G. T.) [7]. Essentially,

$$\Pr(x_{0.75} < a) = 0.75 \tag{4}$$

where the stimulus value, $x_{0.75}$, is the upper discrimination threshold, and

$$Pr(x_{0.25} < a) = 0.25 \tag{5}$$

where $x_{0.25}$ is the lower discrimination threshold. Farmagne determined the JND as follows:

$$JND = \frac{x_{0.75} - x_{0.25}}{2} \tag{6}$$

The psychometric function is said to be well represented by a normal distribution [8]. Essentially, the psychometric function can be expressed as follows:

$$Pr(\xi(a) > a) \approx \int_{-\infty}^{\xi(a)} \Phi(x, \mu, \sigma)dx \tag{7}$$

where $\Phi(x; \mu, \sigma)$ represents the probability density function of a normal distribution with μ denoting the mean and σ denoting the standard deviation. The hypothesis that the distribution is normal is called the phygamma hypothesis.

3.2 Experimental Methods

Each experiment was performed simultaneously on a single subject. The subject was seated in front of the PHANToM and asked to hold it as if holding a pen. The subjects were instructed to hold the pen in the same way to ensure that there would be no differences in the way they held the device.

We fixed a part of the arm of the PHANToM such that the subject could operate the PHANToM, as shown in Fig. 2. A weight was suspended from the pen-nib of the PHANToM and connected to a force gauge by using a thread. The subject was able to feel the frictional sensation by pulling the tip of the pen at a constant velocity while operating the PHANToM, similar to the experiment described in friction, and the frictional force was measured with a force gauge. The weight of the suspended weight is 0.2 [kg], and 0.271 [kg] including 0.029 [kg] of the device used to fix the arm and 0.042 [kg] of the pen-nib part. Figure 3 shows an example of a display screen for this experiment.

The coefficient of friction was derived by calculating the vertical drag force from the weight based on the correlation between the set value in PHANToM and the friction force measured using the force gauge. Figure 2 presents a schematic diagram of the measurement method. The measurement was performed by changing the value that can be set on the PHANToM side from 0.0 to 1.0 in intervals of 0.1. In deriving these values, we referred to the PHANToM specifications provided in the Sensable OpenHaptics™API REFERENCE MANUAL, which states that the machine can set a minimum value of "0" and a maximum value of "1".

The maximum and minimum values of the measurement results were excluded to account for measurement errors; therefore, the actual measurement results were used 10 times in the calculations for each set value. The minimum value of 0.0 is the value of the set value, which does not present any result and may not measure the correct value;

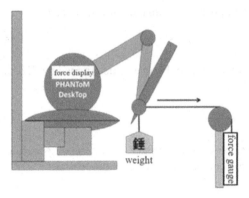
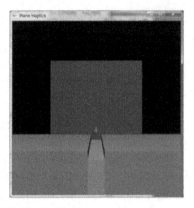

Fig. 2. Experimental analysis of friction coefficient.   **Fig. 3.** Application run screen for friction coefficient analysis experiment.

the maximum value of 1.0 is the maximum force that PHANToM can provide, which may cause the device to break down.

Based on the measurement results, the values that were actually handled by the force sensing device were examined by applying the formula "friction force = coefficient of friction x vertical drag force" to the friction.

One of the two stimuli presented was the standard stimulus (represented as SS), which in this experiment was set at 4.0 [N]. The other stimulus was the comparative stimulus (represented as CS), which comprised seven types of stimuli including one that was 4.0 [N], which was equivalent to SS, by varying the number of large and small stimuli in three steps at equal intervals around the standard stimulus. Six types of intervals were prepared, such as ± 1.0 [N] and ± 0.4 [N]. Table 2 presents the stimuli used in the experiment [4]. Each subject was asked to make 10 judgments between the seven types of stimuli and the CS, with one type of interval per subject. Approximately 10 subjects were tested at each interval. Based on these results, we estimated the frictional sensation threshold by using the maximum likelihood method.

Table 2. Parameters for the experiment

pattern	stimulus difference	Comparative stimulus CS						
		$sadist_1$	$sadist_2$	$sadist_3$	$sadist_4$	$sadist_5$	$sadist_6$	$sadist_7$
A	±1.0	1.0	2.0	3.0	4.0	5.0	6.0	7.0
B	±0.8	1.6	2.4	3.2	4.0	4.8	5.6	6.4
C	±0.6	2.2	2.8	3.4	4.0	4.6	5.2	5.8
D	±0.5	2.5	3.0	3.5	4.0	4.5	5.0	5.5
E	±0.4	2.8	3.2	3.6	4.0	4.4	4.8	5.2
f	±0.2	3.4	3.6	3.8	4.0	4.2	4.4	4.6

Table 3 shows the measured results of several frequency distributions from a to f.

Table 3 presents the parameter values where, μ denotes the mean, σ denotes the variance, c denotes the criterion of judgment, and $Z_{0.75}$ denotes the normal deviation for which the cumulative probability is 0.75 in a normal distribution. Additionally, $\mu + Z_{0.75}$ and $\mu\text{-}Z_{0.75}$ represent the upper and lower discrimination thresholds, respectively.

Table 3. (a) Frequency distribution of Pattern C. and Parameter values for Pattern C.

comparative stimulus	Number of decisions		
	$S_4 <S_i$	$S =S_{4i}$	$S_4 >S_i$
sadist$_1$	0	10	40
sadist$_2$	0	16	34
sadist$_3$	3	19	28
sadist$_4$	19	19	12
sadist$_5$	40	5	5
sadist$_6$	50	0	0
sadist$_7$	49	1	0

average mu	decentralization sigma	Criteria for Judgment c
3.696	0.783	0.432

discrimination threshold $Z_{0.75}$	upper discrimination threshold $\mu+Z_{0.75}$	sub-dialectal threshold $\mu\text{-}Z_{0.75}$
0.528	4.224	3.168

(b)Frequency distribution of Pattern E. and Parameter values for Pattern E.

comparative stimulus	Number of decisions		
	$S_4 <S_i$	$S =S_{4i}$	$S_4 >S_i$
sadist$_1$	4	5	41
sadist$_2$	8	10	32
sadist$_3$	13	8	29
sadist$_4$	27	9	14
sadist$_5$	37	9	4
sadist$_6$	46	3	1
sadist$_7$	50	0	0

average mu	decentralization sigma	Criteria for Judgment c
3.720	0.674	0.185

discrimination threshold $Z_{0.75}$	upper discrimination threshold $\mu+Z_{0.75}$	sub-dialectal threshold $\mu\text{-}Z_{0.75}$
0.455	4.175	3.265

3.3 Experimental Results

Table 4 presents the measurement results. As explained earlier, the set values were those that could be set on the PHANToM side, and the measurement results were averaged by excluding the maximum and minimum values from the force gauge measurement results. The friction coefficients were derived from these values and weights.

Figure 4 depicts a graph of these results. These results demonstrated that the correlation between the setpoint and friction coefficient was not linear; thus, an approximation was made [9].

A comparison of the approximations with the measurement results demonstrated that the approximations were accurate because the approximate curves were within the

Table 4. Frictional forces presented by PHANToM

(a)	0.9	0.8	0.7	0.6	0.5	0.4	0.3	0.2	0.1
(b)	0.1650	0.1450	0.1213	0.1163	0.0963	0.0838	0.0738	0.0763	0.063
(c)	0.0135	0.0175	0.0188	0.0133	0.0142	0.0072	0.0258	0.0503	0.0249
(d)	0.06189	0.05439	0.04548	0.04360	0.03610	0.03141	0.02766	0.02860	0.02344

(a) set value (e.g. of a function, parameter, etc.) (b) Average value of measurement results [N]
(c) Standard deviation σ. (d) Derived coefficient of friction

measurement error range. The actual equation obtained by the approximation is given
as follows:

$$M = 0.042p^2 + 0.0045p + 0.0236 \qquad (8)$$

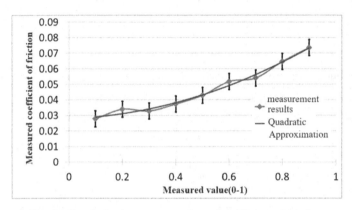

Fig. 4. Correlation between setpoint and coefficient of friction.

Where M is denotes the actual friction coefficient value, and p is denotes a value
between 0.0 and 1.0, which that can be set on the PHANToM side. In the experiment
described above, the product of p and the maximum value of 7.9, which that can be
presented by the PHANToM DeskTop, was PHANToM DeskTop is used as the parameter
F'/ 7.9, which is the maximum value that can be presented by the PHANToM DeskTop.
Therefore, by setting p = F'/7.9 the actual friction coefficient presented in the experiment
can be used as a parameter.

The conversion Eq. (8) obtained in vertical drag force is mapped to the measurement
results of Harada et al.'s study [4]. The results of the friction coefficient study by Harada
et al. are shown in Figs. 5 and 7. Figure 6 and 8 shows some of the transformation results.

These results demonstrate that although the approximate shape of the probability
distribution chart did not change significantly before and after the transformation, the
sharpness of the distribution was increased. It was also observed that the human judgment
was blunted when the interval between the stimulus values was less than 0.4 [N] for the
frictional force, both before and after the transformation.

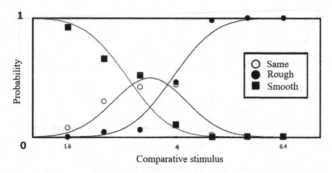

Fig. 5. Probability distribution diagram for dynamic friction experiment in Pattern C.

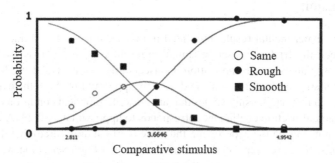

Fig. 6. Pattern C after conversion.

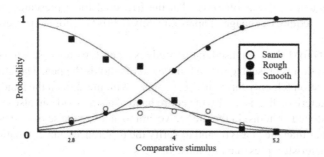

Fig. 7. Probability distribution diagram for dynamic friction experiment in Pattern E.

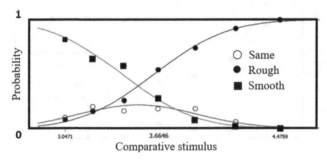

Fig. 8. Pattern E after conversion.

4 Conclusion

Based on the experimental results presented in this section, we determined the correlation between the friction sensation actually presented by the PHANToM DeskTop and the setting values in the application. Consequently, we analyzed the human sensory characteristics of the force-sensing device by applying Eq. (8) to the experimental results obtained in Sect. 3, using values that are closer to practical conditions. Applying Eq. (8), the actual friction coefficient corresponds to approximately 0.23. According to our observations during the experiment, the force (vertical drag force) that the subjects exerted against the force-sensing device to search for friction sensation was approximately 1.5 [N] [10]. This is close to the general writing pressure of normal subjects, and there was no significant difference observed in writing pressure, even in the virtual space. Consequently, it was observed that the frictional force presented by the force sensing device requires a change of approximately 0.3 [N] or more to perceive a change in the friction.

The PHANToM DeskTop used in this study is a pen-type force-sensing device, and the force sensation is presented through the hand that holds the pen. Therefore, it is not a surface sensation felt only through direct contact with the skin on the hand, but a deep sensory characteristic that is felt by the entire hand. This method can also be applied to the paper-mediated systems. In the future, we aim to analyze the sensory characteristics of devices other than the pen-type and to verify the differences and compatibility of the sensory characteristics presented by those devices.

Acknowledgments. This work was supported by JSPS KAKENHI Grant Number 21K12186.

References

1. Hoshimiya, N.: Seitai Kougaku, Shoukoudo, p. 197, February 1980. (in Japanese)
2. Ishihara, M.: Empirical study regarding representing roughness with haptic devices. In: Proceedings of the 2013 IEEE 2nd GCCE, pp. 491–493, October 2013
3. Ishihara, M.: Haptic display of representing roughness. In: Stephanidis, C. (ed.) HCI 2014. CCIS, vol. 434, pp. 590–595. Springer, Cham (2014). https://doi.org/10.1007/978-3-319-07857-1_104

4. Harada, Y., et al.: Experiment of representing roughness with haptic devices. In: Proceedings of the ROBOMECH2015 in Kyoto, 2A1-U01, June 2015. (in Japanese)
5. Sensable OpenHaptics™ programmer's guide
6. Sensable OpenHaptics™API reference manual
7. Link, S.W.: The Wave Theory of Difference and Similarity. Lawrence Erlbaum Associates, Hillsdale (1992)
8. Luce, R.D., Galanter, E.: Handbook of Mathematical Psychology. Wiley, New York (1963)
9. Masuyama, M.: Jikken Koushiki no Motomekata, Takeuchi Shoten Sinsya, p. 26 (1978). (in Japanese)
10. Shindo, K., et al.: An analysis of writing patterns in writer's cramp patients using a simple writing pressure gauge. Jpn. J. Rehabil. Med. **41**(5), 296–301 (2004). (in Japanese)

The Optokinetic Nystagmus as a Physiological Indicator of Cybersickness – A Vergence-Based Evaluation

Judith Josupeit[1]([⊠]) [iD] and Leonore Greim[2] [iD]

[1] Engineering Psychology and Applied Cognitive Research, TU Dresden, Dresden, Germany
judith.josupeit@tu-dresden.de
[2] TU Chemnitz, Chemnitz, Germany

Abstract. The application of virtual reality (VR) is increasing steadily. However, cybersickness - a diffuse set of symptoms like discomfort and nausea - remains an accessibility problem for VR. The eye movement hypothesis stresses the role of the optokinetic nystagmus (OKN), a distinct eye movement pattern for gaze stabilizing in moving scenes, in the genesis of cybersickness symptoms. Thus, we postulate a time lag between OKN and cybersickness onset, as well as an explorative approach for using the OKN as a diagnostic criterion. For the study, 70 subjects were exposed to two VR environments in a randomized order. One of the VR environments aimed at achieving a naturalistic VR use case scenario while the other used an optokinetic drum in VR for inducing the OKN. Each participant rated cybersickness Pre/Post-VR on a symptom questionnaire and during VR on a single-item questionnaire every two min. To reduce the error probability in velocity-based eye event coding we applied a 3-dimensional vergence-based algorithm for the pre-processing of the eye-tracking data. The results show that cybersickness was successfully induced in both VR environments but with different main symptom facets. However, there was a negative correlation between the frequency of occurrence of OKN and upcoming reported cybersickness. None of the OKN parameters served as diagnostic predictors for cybersickness. We discuss methodological limitations regarding the applicability of physiological indicators for predicting cybersickness and the advantages of openness.

Keywords: Virtual Reality · Eye-Tracking · Cybersickness · Optokinetic Nystagmus · Vergence · Pupil Labs · Open Source

1 Introduction

The use of virtual reality (VR) allows not only controllable but also naturalistic visual input, which makes VR applications a valuable asset for research, industry, education, and leisure. Advantages include the cost-efficiency of virtual prototypes and an augmented adherence of users through the system's immanent gamification [1].

While some users experience VR applications as intended, it is estimated that the majority of VR users (60% to 95%) experience cybersickness with varying intensity (5%

C. Stephanidis et al. (Eds.): HCII 2024, CCIS 2116, pp. 58–66, 2024.
https://doi.org/10.1007/978-3-031-61950-2_7

to 13% have to discontinue) [2]. Cybersickness manifests in symptoms ranging from general discomfort to dizziness, headaches, or nausea [3, 4]. To increase the accessibility of VR, the working mechanisms of cybersickness need to be understood.

Among the cybersickness theories, the eye movement hypothesis [5] focuses on the optokinetic nystagmus (OKN). Following the theory, the OKN not only stabilizes the gaze in moving scenes but also coincidentally stimulates the vagus nerve—which innervates the intestines and is crucial for bodily self-calibration [6, 7]. Thus, not only nausea but also balance impairments become explainable. The OKN comprises a slow phase (smooth pursuit eye movements following the moving object) and a fast phase (a saccade in the opposite direction of the movement), resulting in a distinctive sawtooth pattern. For discomfort induced by physical motion correlations between the symptom severity and the frequency of the OKN have been reported [8].

This study aims to convey the findings of physical motion to VR. In line with previous research, a temporal dependency between OKN frequency in a given interval and the upcoming cybersickness rating is hypothesized. In addition to previous research, we test the diagnostic validity of the OKN onset and offset without any visual stimulation present (optokinetic after-nystagmus – OKAN) [9] for predicting cybersickness not only in the virtual optokinetic drum, which induces the OKN, but also in a naturalistic VR application representing well-established applications.

To sample the eye events while striving for high transparency, a Pupil Labs add-on eye tracker, for which software and algorithms are available on GitHub, was deployed. For labeling the eye events, the velocity information from the raw data is required. Instead of trigonometric calculations known from fix-base eye trackers, which would have been prone to measuring inaccuracies, we applied a three-dimensional vergence-based algorithm [10]. In contrast to depth perception in the physical world that couples accommodation and vergence information, in VR vergence exclusively is a valid eye metric for depth perception [11].

2 Methods

2.1 Participants

In total, the sample consisted of 70 participants, of which three had to be excluded due to severe symptoms. Additionally, six data sets were excluded due to technical difficulties, as well as two due to low confidence in the gaze data during the calibration. This left 59 complete data sets for the analysis. Of these, 33 subjects reported their gender as female, 25 as male, and one as non-binary. Their age ranged from 18 to 38 years ($M = 28.81$ years, $SD = 4.36$). The study gained approval from the local ethics committee (SR-EK-315072020).

2.2 Materials

A custom-built computer with an Intel Core i7-9700K processor and an NVIDIA GeForce RTX 2070 graphic controller rendered the VR applications. An HTC Vive was used as VR-Headset (HTC 2018). As room-scale VR is allowed for the naturalistic

VR, the infrared lighthouses (emitters) were installed diagonally across the lab. The HTC Vive was featured with the Pupil Labs Eye-Tracking Add-On lenses with a sampling rate of 120 Hz (Pupil Labs, Berlin, max sampling rate 200 Hz). Additionally, because the connector cable of the eye tracker limits the range of movement the height and distance to the computer were adjusted by a wheeled lectern.

The VR application was made with Unity (v2018.4.25) and the assets Steam VR and Winridge City were applied. The locomotion through the controller required custom key bindings. Moreover, some of the 3D-game objects were created with Blender (v2.90). All Pupil Labs software and plugins can be found on GitHub [12, 13]. To actuate the eye tracker through Unity the Pupil Core Apps (v2.4) and the Unity Developer Plugin hmd.eyes (v 1.3) were required; all gaze tracking components were adjusted to the experimental setup. The Unity event file sampled with 60 Hz all information necessary for synchronizing the arbitrary Pupil Labs timestamps with the Unix epoch system time.

Additionally, demographic questions were collected via LimeSurvey. To monitor the well-being of the participants before, during, and after the VR exposure cybersickness questionnaires were deployed [14, 15]. The multi-dimensionality of the construct was respected in baseline and post-VR assessments with a symptom questionnaire (VRSQ). During the VR exposure, a less-intrusive single-item questionnaire (MISC) assessed cybersickness.

2.3 Procedures

After signing an informed consent, the visual acuity of the participant was tested [16, 17]. If the visual acuity was considered sufficient, the HTC Vive was fit. Participants were randomly assigned to start either with the VR optokinetic drum (D) that provoked the OKN or the naturalistic VR city (C). Before the main application was displayed, the cybersickness questionnaires were administered and the eye tracker was calibrated in a neutral grey VR environment.

After successful calibration, the VR application was shown. For the D, participants sat on a chair to prevent injuries from falling, in case of severe vertigo. The D contained vertical black and white stripes, and constantly rotated with 1 rad/s. The VR exposure lasted 7 min before the grey room was presented to measure the OKAN and post-VR cybersickness.

For the C, room-scale VR was allowed. However, the participant mostly moved around virtually with the magic carpet locomotion. This means a continuous longitudinal acceleration was implemented when the trackpad was touched with a maximum speed of 7 rad/s. For gamification, the participant was tasked with collecting checkpoints by virtually walking through them. After 10 min, the grey room was displayed again and OKAN and cybersickness post-VR were measured.

In both environments, the participant's well-being was checked every 2 min with the single-item cybersickness questionnaire [15]. Then, the HTC Vive was removed, and after a short break (10 min), the respective other application was displayed. After the second application participants received compensation and were dismissed. The experimental sessions took 45 min to 1 h per participant in total.

2.4 Design and Measures

A within-subjects design with the randomized factor application order was used. Cybersickness was assessed as a dependent variable with the VRSQ and MISC. To control for effects not related to cybersickness, baseline corrected cybersickness ratings are used [18][1]. As an additional dependent variable, the OKN was deployed.

The eye-tracking raw data were exported from the Pupil Core App. Using Python (v 3.10.8), the velocity information was extracted. Further data processing and all analysis were carried out using R (v 4.3.0). For the OKN, smooth pursuit eye movements were coupled with the rotation of the D at 57.3°/s (with a margin of 45 to 65°/s), and saccades were defined as accelerations over 4000°/s^2 [19]. Raw gaze data had to have a confidence of at least 0.6 to be included in the preprocessing. Additionally, for the velocity-dependent eye events, a sampling rate of 120 Hz was set as a minimum requirement. This means whenever the arithmetic mean of three Δ-timestamps was higher than the sampling rate, these data were excluded. For the regression models the following OKN metrics were preprocessed: OKN onset (OKN_{Start}) and OKN offset (OKAN), additionally for the temporal connection of the OKN with the upcoming cybersickness rating a sampling rate corrected event count was employed (OKN_{Freq}).

3 Results

The descriptive results for cybersickness are presented in Fig. 1. The comparison of baseline and post-VR by application shows an increase in reported cybersickness in both applications[1]. Through visual inspection, it becomes apparent that symptoms vary depending on the application: Items that belong to the subscale of oculomotor symptoms were more pronounced in the D, while in the C disorientation was the predominant subscale. The error bars and outliers indicate that cybersickness data are right-skewed and descriptively higher in the D compared to the C.

Before applying inference statistics multivariate normality was checked. A Mardia's test (VRSQ: skewness = 2144.308, $p < .001$ kurtosis = 49.214, $p < .001$/MISC: skewness = 722.30, $p < .001$ kurtosis = 28.202, $p < .001$) and univariate Anderson-Darling-Test (all $p < .001$) indicated that neither multivariate nor univariate normality could be confirmed. Thus, non-parametric estimators were applied.

The first hypothesis postulated a temporal dependency between the OKN_{Freq} in a given interval and the upcoming cybersickness rating and was tested with a linear panel model with feasible generalized least squares estimators (FGLS) to account for the heteroscedasticity of the data. The model contained the OKN_{Freq} split into the 4 cybersickness assessment intervals during the D rotation as the predictor and the baseline corrected cybersickness ratings (Δ-MISC) as regressands. The factor subject was

---

[1] To test the effect of the VR application on cybersickness, non-parametric longitudinal analyses were run with the assessment time for the symptom questionnaire ($VRSQ_{Total\ Score\ raw}$ ATS(2.8,59) = 58.47, $p < .001$) and single-item questionnaire (MISC ATS(2.8,59) = 58.47, $p < .001$) as a within-factor, before applying baseline correction to the data. As a significant main effect of time was found, sequential post-hoc contrasts were run ($VRSQ_{Total\ Score\ raw}$ all $\hat{p} < .001$; in both applications only for the $MISC_{Baseline\ vs.\ Min\ 2}$ $\hat{p} < .001$).

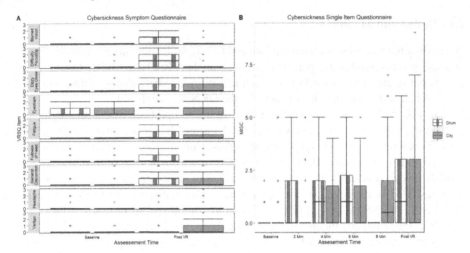

Fig. 1. Boxplots of cybersickness ratings by application in dependency of the assessment time. A) Items from the symptom questionnaire B) Single-item questionnaire. For the assessment of 8 min of VR exposure, only C data are available.

included in the model as a random effect, whereas the effect of time was included as a within-effect, taking the variability of the cybersickness ratings into account. A borderline significant effect of the OKN_{Freq} on the upcoming cybersickness rating was found ($R2 = .017$, $F(1,203) = 3.472$, $p = .064$.). The following Table 1 gives an overview of the coefficients.

Table 1. FGLS estimator of the linear panel regression.

	B	SE	t	p
Y: MISC				
X: OKN_{Freq}	−0.0027	<0.001	−1.863	.006

The diagnostic validity of the OKNStart, OKNFreq, and OKAN for baseline corrected cybersickness ratings in both environments (VRSQTotal score raw) was tested with a Spearman's rank correlation. The correlation coefficients can be found in Fig. 2. Only the correlation of the symptom questionnaires reached significance ($r = .443$, $p < .001$). As in the regression model, the correlation of the global OKNFreq and the symptom questionnaire in the D environment reached borderline significance ($r = -.276$, $p = .075$)

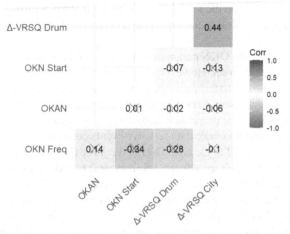

Fig. 2. Correlation coefficients of the Spearman's rank correlation. Non-significant results are marked with an X.

4 Discussion

This study tested whether the eye movement hypothesis as well as its prospective validity in a naturalistic environment applies in VR while striving for high transparency by using open-source software and open data. Cybersickness was induced by both VR environments. However, the symptom facets were different—more oculomotor symptoms in the D, while more disorientation in the C. For the gaze data, only the negative correlation between the OKN_{Freq} and the cybersickness questionnaires applied in the D reached borderline significance.

The different symptom facets are partly explainable by the different tasks and setups. Hence, the universality of physiological indicators for predicting cybersickness is highly debatable when scenarios are fundamentally different. As the symptom facets are environment-dependent [20], a valid physiological indicator in one environment might not be applicable elsewhere. The stronger relation of the OKN_{Freq} to the symptom questionnaires applied in D might not only be caused by the close temporal connection of assessment and measurement but also by inducing more oculomotor symptoms in general. Future studies should test this hypothesis with a focus on oculomotor symptoms.

The linear panel model found a time-dependent negative correlation between the OKN_{Freq} and the upcoming cybersickness rating. However, the results were only borderline significant and correspondingly the effect sizes were small (explaining 2% of the total variability). Equally, the negative correlation of the global OKN_{Freq} with the symptom questionnaire was only borderline significant. This effect in the same environment could be an indicator of discomfort with low external validity; with higher external validity the OKN could be applied as a diagnostic criterion for validating other cybersickness questionnaires. As different thresholds for valid and reliable data made the exclusion of data necessary, the small effect size might be attributable to conservative preprocessing. It is known that thresholds do directly impact the classification of eye events [21], thus it cannot be ruled out that different preprocessing rationales would lead to other conclusions. In case the reader likes to run an analysis with different thresholds on the same data set, the link to the repository is given in the supplementary materials section.

In order to compare the OKN parameters between subjects, we only included participants with a complete data set. However, this approach has missed the most interesting participants, those who had to terminate the experiment prematurely due to severe reports of cybersickness. Some researchers have utilised the maximum value [22, 23] to fill in missing data sets, which inappropriately aggravates the symptom severity.

In addition to excluding whole data sets, eye events could only be sampled validly as long as participants adhered to the task. During the VR exposure, behavioral adaptation e.g. voluntarily closing one's eyes (more blink events) to reduce the unpleasant effects of the D was a strategy reported by participants and also apparent in the gaze data [24]. With prolonged exposure, a greater amount of data had to be filtered out due to low confidence. As a result, the categorization of eye events has been biased especially for those who reported more cybersickness. Combining the findings of Kim, et al. [24] and our data, the negative correlation found in the eye events could also be attributed to less need for closing ones' eyes when less discomfort was experienced. Future studies could apply shorter VR exposures to increase the reliability of eye events.

By avoiding extensive VR exposures the likelihood of slippage known for all sorts of head-worn eye trackers [25] as well as the exclusion of participants and/or massive filtering of raw data would be reduced. Despite these limitations, the current paper offers valuable insights into transparent, efficient, and affordable open-source methods applicable to user-related research in VR.

5   Conclusion

While the applicability of any physiological indicator for predicting cybersickness in another environment might be challenging due to various reasons (e.g. environment dependent symptom facets, exclusion of participants, filtering data, etc.), the current study offers insights into affordable open-source methods for user-related VR research. Future studies should equally apply transparent and comprehensible rationales for exploring the relationship between eye movements and cybersickness.

Acknowledgements. We acknowledge A. Klingenfuss for collecting the experimental data.

Disclosure of Interests. The authors have no competing interests to declare that are relevant to the content of this article.

Supplementary Materials. The data analyzed in this study are publicly available (under Creative Commons License CC-By) and can be accessed here: http://dx.doi.org/10.25532/OPARA-245.

References

1. Aronson, E., Wilson, T.D., Brewer, M.B.: Experimentation in social psychology. In: The Handbook of Social Psychology, 4th edn., vol. 1–2, pp. 99–142. McGraw-Hill, New York (1998)
2. Caserman, P., Garcia-Agundez, A., Gámez Zerban, A., Göbel, S.: Cybersickness in current-generation virtual reality head-mounted displays: systematic review and outlook. Virtual Real. **25**, 1153–1170 (2021)
3. Rebenitsch, L., Owen, C.: Review on cybersickness in applications and visual displays. Virtual Real. **20**, 101–125 (2016)
4. LaViola, J.J., Jr.: A discussion of cybersickness in virtual environments. ACM SIGCHI Bull. **32**, 47–56 (2000)
5. Ebenholtz, S.M., Cohen, M.M., Linder, B.J.: The possible role of nystagmus in motion sickness: a hypothesis. Aviat. Space Environ. Med. **65**, 1032–1035 (1994)
6. Yates, B.J., Miller, A.D., Lucot, J.B.: Physiological basis and pharmacology of motion sickness: an update. Brain Res. Bull. **47**, 395–406 (1998)
7. Oman, C.M.: Are evolutionary hypotheses for motion sickness "just-so" stories? J. Vestib. Res. **22**, 117–127 (2012)
8. Nooij, S.A.E., Pretto, P., Oberfeld, D., Hecht, H., Bülthoff, H.H.: Vection is the main contributor to motion sickness induced by visual yaw rotation: implications for conflict and eye movement theories. PLoS ONE **12**, 1–19 (2017)
9. Guo, C.C., Chen, D.J., Wei, I.Y., So, R.H., Cheung, R.T.: Correlations between individual susceptibility to visually induced motion sickness and decaying time constant of after-nystagmus. Appl. Ergon. **63**, 1–8 (2017)
10. Pupil Labs: Pupil Tutorials (2022). https://github.com/pupil-labs/pupil-tutorials
11. Hoffman, D.M., Girshick, A.R., Akeley, K., Banks, M.S.: Vergence–accommodation conflicts hinder visual performance and cause visual fatigue. J. Vis. **8**, 33 (2008)
12. Pupil Labs: hmd-eyes Unity Package, 10 December 2020. https://github.com/pupil-labs/hmd-eyes/releases
13. Pupil Labs: 2. Pupil (Pupil Core Apps), 24 October 2022. https://github.com/pupil-labs/pupil
14. Kim, H.K., Park, J., Choi, Y., Choe, M.: Virtual reality sickness questionnaire (VRSQ): motion sickness measurement index in a virtual reality environment. Appl. Ergon. **69**, 66–73 (2018)
15. Bos, J., Mackinnon, S., Patterson, A.: Motion sickness symptoms in a ship motion simulator: effects of inside, outside and no view. Aviat. Space Environ. Med. **76**, 1111–1118 (2006)
16. Bach, M.: The Freiburg Visual Acuity Test-Variability unchanged by post-hoc re-analysis. Graefes Arch. Clin. Exp. Ophthalmol. **245**, 965–971 (2007)
17. Ophthalmic Instruments Pte Ltd.: Random Dot Stereo Acuity Test with Lea Symbols® (2021). https://www.ophthalmic.com.sg/product/random-dot-stereo-acuity-test-with-lea-symbols/
18. Brown, P., Spronck, P., Powell, W.: The simulator sickness questionnaire, and the erroneous zero baseline assumption. Front. Virtual Real. **3**, 118 (2022)
19. Holmqvist, K., Nyström, M., Andersson, R., Dewhurst, R., Jarodzka, H., Van de Weijer, J.: Eye Tracking: A Comprehensive Guide to Methods and Measures. Oxford University Press, Oxford (2011)
20. Josupeit, J.: Cybersickness as the virtual reality sickness questionnaire (VRSQ) measures it!? –An environment-specific revision of the VRSQ. Front. Virtual Real. **4** (2023)
21. Alhashim, A.G.: Eye movement classification algorithms: effect of settings on related metrics. In: Stephanidis, C., Kurosu, M., Degen, H., Reinerman-Jones, L. (eds.) HCII 2020, pp. 3–19. Springer, Cham (2020). https://doi.org/10.1007/978-3-030-60117-1_1
22. Jung, S., Li, R., McKee, R., Whitton, M.C., Lindeman, R.W.: Floor-vibration VR: mitigating cybersickness using whole-body tactile stimuli in highly realistic vehicle driving experiences. IEEE Trans. Visual Comput. Graphics **27**, 2669–2680 (2021)

23. Rebenitsch, L., Owen, C.: Individual variation in susceptibility to cybersickness. In: Proceedings of the 27th Annual ACM Symposium on User Interface Software and Technology, pp. 309–317 (2014)
24. Kim, Y.Y., Kim, H.J., Kim, E.N., Ko, H.D., Kim, H.T.: Characteristic changes in the physiological components of cybersickness. Psychophysiology **42**, 616–625 (2005)
25. Niehorster, D.C., Santini, T., Hessels, R.S., Hooge, I.T.C., Kasneci, E., Nyström, M.: The impact of slippage on the data quality of head-worn eye trackers. Behav. Res. Methods **52**, 1140–1160 (2020)

SongScape: A Song Dynasty-Style Architectural Scene Design System Based on CGA Rules and Virtual Reality

Ruyi Li and Chunrong Liu[(✉)]

School of Design, Shanghai Jiao Tong University, Shanghai, China
{lry_sjtu,cheeronliu}@sjtu.edu.cn

Abstract. The digital preservation and representation of ancient architecture hold significant importance, and the rapid and effective creation of stylized ancient buildings is a worthy research topic within this field. This paper, based on the ancient Chinese text "Yingzao Fashi," analyzes the external features of Song dynasty architecture, including both palace-style and mansion-style buildings. Utilizing the CGA (Computer Generated Architecture) grammar rules, we propose CGA rules capable of generating Song-style architecture and explore the design concepts and implementation strategies. Building on this foundation, we have developed a design system within a virtual reality environment that supports the adjustment of parameters for individual buildings and collaborative design among multiple users. This system facilitates the rapid creation of Song-style architecture and offers new practical examples for immersive collaborative design.

Keywords: Procedural content generation · Ancient architecture · Virtual reality

1 Introduction

Ancient architecture, as a carrier of history, holds profound significance in the transmission of cultural and spiritual heritage. Virtual reality technology and three-dimensional digital modeling enable us to preserve and present ancient architectural scenes in the virtual domain, which is crucial for the protection and study of cultural heritage. Yet, the challenge lies in how to rapidly and effectively produce stylized ancient buildings in the context of the expanding volume of the virtual world.

Against this backdrop, Procedural Content Generation (PCG) has emerged as one of the key methods to address this challenge [1]. By analyzing the internal structure and stylistic features of ancient architecture, we can use rules to automatically generate buildings with similarities and variations, offering innovative avenues for the digital preservation and design of ancient architecture. However, current research efforts have been primarily focused on the procedural generation

© The Author(s), under exclusive license to Springer Nature Switzerland AG 2024
C. Stephanidis et al. (Eds.): HCII 2024, CCIS 2116, pp. 67–74, 2024.
https://doi.org/10.1007/978-3-031-61950-2_8

of classical castle forms, with limited exploration into ancient Chinese architecture [6–8]. Moreover, there is a relative lack of research on the interaction with individual buildings after procedural generation.

This study focuses on Song dynasty architecture, proposing a system designed for Song architectural scenes using CGA grammar rules and virtual reality technology. The CGA (Computer Generated Architecture) shape grammar language is mainly suited for procedural architectural modeling, providing design flexibility [5]. Based on ancient Chinese texts, such as "Yingzao Fashi," we analyzed the external characteristics of the palace hall and the common hall, and proposed the design concept and implementation strategies for CGA rule files. On this basis, we implemented a design system in a virtual reality environment that supports the adjustment of parameters for individual buildings and collaborative design among multiple users. This system offers users an immersive interactive experience and explores cutting-edge collaborative design modes, thereby advancing the digital preservation and presentation of ancient architectural heritage.

2   Procedural Generation of Individual Song-Style Buildings Based on CGA

2.1   CGA Programming Language

The CGA (Computer Generated Architecture) language is used for procedural architectural modeling, involving operations like translation, splitting, extrusion, scaling, and roof construction. It utilizes parameters and functions for diverse modeling. CityEngine supports CGA rule files for designing and scripting, enabling efficient procedural architecture generation.

2.2   Characteristics of Song Dynasty Architecture

This study focuses on the architectural styles of palace and mansion buildings from the Song dynasty, conducting an analysis and extraction of the appearance characteristics of Song-style architecture. According to the ancient Chinese text "Yingzao Fashi," the wooden frame structure of the palace is formed by vertically overlapping multiple layered wooden frameworks [2–4]. A typical palace usually comprises three structural layers: the column frame layer, the puzuo (bracket sets) layer, and the roof layer (Fig. 1). The mansion structure is based on the palace structural system, differing only in specific dimensions and roof styles, thus exhibiting minimal differences in external structural features. Therefore, the characteristics of both are discussed together.

Column Frame Layer. This layer consists of internal and external columns of essentially the same height, predominantly utilizing cylindrical columns. In the double-eaved palace structures that incorporate auxiliary steps around the perimeter, an additional circle of columns around the palace supports the structure, forming the basic structure of a high-grade palace. In terms of facade

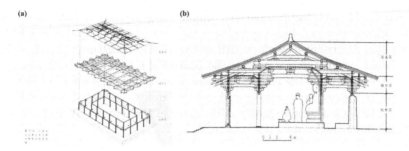

Fig. 1. Figure (a) is a layered diagram of the wooden framework of Song Dynasty architecture, divided into the column frame layer, the puzuo layer, and the roof layer. Figure (b) is a side view diagram of the wooden framework of the Great Hall of Foguang Temple on Mount Wutai in China.

structure, the number of frontal bays in palace-type buildings generally ranges from three to thirteen, while mansion-type buildings range from three to seven, indicating a certain difference in the scale of the two types of architecture.

Puzuo (Bracket Sets) Layer. As the most complex structural layer of the building, it exhibits a high degree of regularity both in the dougong (bracket sets) themselves and their planar arrangement. The categories of dougong primarily include column head puzuo, inter-column puzuo, and corner puzuo at the building's corners. A common form of inter-column puzuo involves two sets of brackets for the central room and one set of brackets on each side of the central room.

Roof Layer. Significant differences emerge between the palace and mansion at this layer. The palace often employs wudian (hip) and xieshan (saddle) roofs, with relatively high ridges; while the mansion typically uses xieshan (saddle) and xuanshan (suspension) roofs to differentiate architectural ranks and categories.

2.3 Design of CGA Rules for Song-Style Architecture

The design approach for CGA rules is based on the three layers analyzed in Sect. 2.2, serving as the foundation for overall hierarchical division, with iterative subdivision and detail enhancement applied at each layer.

Column Frame Layer. The central focus of the column frame layer's design is on doors and windows, which are symmetrically aligned along the central axis. In traditional Song dynasty palaces and mansions, the number of rooms varies from three to thirteen. The central room is termed "dangxinjian," while the rooms to its left and right are called "cijian," and the outermost rooms are known as "jinjian." The sizes of the dangxinjian and cijian can be identical.

Adhering to this architectural pattern, jinjian are generated on both sides of the facade, within specified boundaries, and the central space is allocated for the dangxinjian, determined by the width of the middle door (middleDoorWidth). To maintain symmetry and ensure the central alignment of the dangxinjian, cijian are produced between the jinjian and dangxinjian. The middleDoorWidth command is utilized to evenly distribute the area that cannot be subdivided further to the cijian. The dynamic adjustment of the main body's width of the building follows the formula outlined in Eq. (1):

$$middleWidth = 2 * sideDoorWidth + (roomNum - 2) * middleDoorWidth \quad (1)$$

In the equation, middleWidth represents the main width of the building, sideDoorWidth denotes the width of the jinjian, roomNum indicates the total number of rooms, and middleDoorWidth refers to the width of the dangxinjian and cijian (Fig. 2).

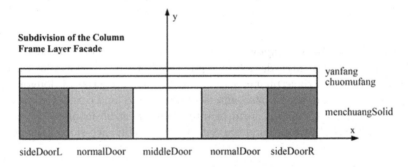

Fig. 2. Schematic diagram of the column frame layer elevation segmentation.

Upon completing the initial subdivision, it is necessary to iteratively refine the details of the doors and windows. The overall design is governed by rules set according to the specification that the dangxinjian and cijian feature four doors, while the jinjian have either two doors or windows. This part is primarily achieved through multiple recursive subdivisions, with the relevant areas utilizing the insert (i) command to place lattice door or mullioned window model resources (Fig. 3).

Puzuo Layer. Considering the level of detail and workload, the dougong (bracket sets) themselves are modeled geometrically, with their planar arrangement being regularly procedurally generated. The arrangement of dougong follows three principles: firstly, a single bracket set is placed on top of each cylindrical column head; secondly, one to two additional bracket sets are inserted between column heads; thirdly, corner bracket sets are positioned at the four corners of the building. To ensure that each column is topped with a bracket set

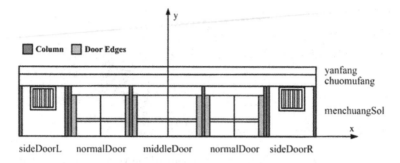

Fig. 3. Architectural facade detail iteration diagram.

and to dynamically adjust the insertion method for the intermediate bracket sets based on their number, the approach involves calculating the distance between the column head bracket sets and the intermediate bracket sets. The specific calculation method is given by Eq. (2):

$$X = middleDoorWidth/(bujianNum + 1) \qquad (2)$$

In the equation, X represents the distance between the column head puzuo and the intermediate puzuo, middleDoorWidth is the width of the dangxinjian, and bujianNum is the number of intermediate dougong. Upon completion of the calculation, the dougong areas corresponding to the dangxinjian and the cijian are segmented according to these parameters.

Considering the issue of the rotation angle of corner puzuo, it is necessary to formulate rules separately for the front two jinjian and the rear two jinjian. The method involves partitioning a portion of the area on either the left or right side to serve as the corner puzuo region. After segmentation, the rotate command is used to adjust the orientation of the corner puzuo model, ensuring its alignment with the Song dynasty architectural style (Fig. 4).

Roof Layer. Given the complexity and predominance of curved shapes in the roof decorations of Song dynasty architecture, it is not feasible to generate these elements through rules. Therefore, a geometric modeling approach is chosen for the creation of roof models, while tiles and bricks are inserted using procedural modeling.

This paper discusses the procedural design of the roof framework using a saddle roof as an example, which is divided into upper and lower eaves; the upper eave resembles a suspension roof, while the lower eave resembles a hip roof, with brick and tile models inserted onto each eave. The first part of the implementation involves using the offset command to divide the bottom surface of the lower eave into interior and edge parts. The interior utilizes the roofHip function to create a hip roof, inserting the lower eave model. The exterior employs a combination of insert (i), component splitting (comp), scaling, and rotation commands to insert a series of curved brick and tile sequences. This method allows for the

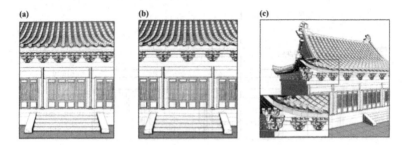

Fig. 4. Figures (a) and (b) illustrate the generated outcomes when the number of intermediate puzuo is set to 1 and 2, respectively, while figure c depicts the generation result for corner puzuo construction.

dynamic insertion of bricks and tiles according to the size of the house, providing more detail and precision than simply scaling the architectural length with a stretch command, thus enriching architectural details and enhancing modeling efficiency. The second part involves using the roofHip function on the bottom surface of the upper eave to generate a dual-sloped roof, inserting the upper eave model to achieve the creation of a saddle roof (Fig. 5).

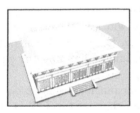
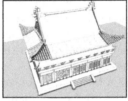

Fig. 5. Saddle roof procedural generation.

Generation Results of Song-Style Architecture. The final generation results of the Song-style palace and mansion using CGA rules are as illustrated in the Fig. 6.

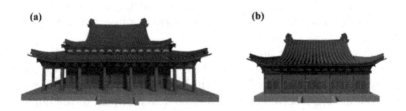

Fig. 6. Procedural modeling effects of Song-style architecture based on CGA rules.

3   Song-Style Architecture Scene Design System

This paper utilizes the Oculus Quest 2 virtual reality hardware, with the assistance of OculusVR, Vitruvio, and Prefab Tool plugins, to implement interactive functionalities. The system supports the adjustment of parameters for individual buildings as well as collaborative design among multiple users.

3.1   Adjustment of Parameters for Individual Buildings

The functionality for adjusting parameters of individual ancient buildings in VR interaction is based on the "raycasting metaphor." Rays emitted from the controller capture real-time intersections with the collision boxes of the generated architectural primitives. These architectural primitives are primarily generated using the Vitruvio plugin, which can import CGA rule files from CityEngine into Unreal Engine for generation and modification. Upon capture, the Vitruvio primitive component detected is stored in the blueprint as the architectural primitive variable to be adjusted, and the Generated Models component under this primitive is accessed.

After the primitive capture is completed, as shown in Fig. 7, a user panel generated at the controller displays adjustable architectural parameters, including the number of rooms, door and window styles, and roof types. When the user moves the slider or selects a roof type, the new parameters are instantly fed back to the captured Vitruvio component, changing the corresponding CGA rule data for regeneration. This allows users to immediately see the updated Song-style architecture. The implementation of this interactive functionality enables users to intuitively observe the generation effects and make improvements, thereby making the scene generation results more satisfactory to the designer's needs.

(a)   **(b)**

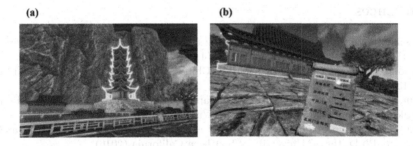

Fig. 7. Figures (a) and (b) demonstrate the operational outcomes of the Song-Style Architecture Scene Design System, wherein users can adjust parameters of individual buildings through a panel within the scene to design the layout.

3.2   Collaborative Design Among Multiple Users

The collaborative design within this system is facilitated by the session system in Unreal Engine. Through a local area network, multiple users can join the same session to design and adjust ancient scenes. When an architectural parameter is changed by any client, it should be reflected in real-time across all clients and modify the corresponding architectural primitives. This synchronization is achieved using the replication of properties in blueprints. When there are data changes on the server side, the modified architectural parameters and the indices of the changed architectural primitives are shared with the corresponding blueprints of all clients. This enables clients to access the architectural primitives within their scene under that index and regenerate the individual ancient building with new parameters. Consequently, this allows multiple users to communicate and immersively modify ancient architecture within the scene, achieving better design outcomes.

4   Conclusion

Based on the ancient Chinese text "Yingzao Fashi," this paper analyzes the external features of palace-style and mansion-style buildings. Taking into account the characteristics of their wooden frameworks, we designed CGA grammar rules for the column frame layer, the puzuo layer, and the roof layer, and discussed design concepts and implementation strategies. On this basis, we developed a design system in a virtual reality environment that supports the adjustment of parameters for individual buildings and collaborative design among multiple users. This system allows multiple users to connect to the same ancient architectural scene via a local area network and complete the design. The system preliminarily realizes the procedural generation of Song-style architecture and supports immersive collaborative design, offering new practical insights into the digital preservation of ancient architecture.

References

1. Freiknecht, J., Effelsberg, W.: A survey on the procedural generation of virtual worlds. Multimodal Technol. Interact. **1**(4), 27 (2017)
2. Guo, Q.: Yingzao fashi: twelfth-century Chinese building manual. Archit. Hist. **41**, 1–13 (1998)
3. Lin, W.C.: Chinese architecture and metaphor: Song culture in the "Yingzao Fashi" building manual by Jiren Feng. J. Song-Yuan Stud. **46**, 241–247 (2016)
4. Luo, D.: A grain of sand: Yingzao Fashi and the miniaturization of chinese architecture. Ph.D. thesis, University of Southern California (2016)
5. Müller, P., Wonka, P., Haegler, S., Ulmer, A., Van Gool, L.: Procedural modeling of buildings. In: ACM SIGGRAPH 2006 Papers, pp. 614–623 (2006)
6. Whiting, E., Ochsendorf, J., Durand, F.: Procedural modeling of structurally-sound masonry buildings. In: ACM SIGGRAPH Asia 2009 Papers, pp. 1–9 (2009)
7. Xinjuan, L., Jiasheng, W.: 3d modeling of the Miao residences based on CityEngine CGA. Bull. Surv. Mapp. (12), 112 (2017)
8. Yu, G., Yuan, L., Liang, W., Yong, L.: Research and implementation of CGA-based parametric fast modeling–taking ancient temples in the Yu-Mu mountain as an example. Bull. Surv. Mapp. (4), 112 (2017)

XR Empowers a New City Landmark in Qingdao: Hi Metaverse

Jing Liang[1]([✉]), Siqi Fan[1], and Fan Chen[2]

[1] College of Design and Innovation, Tongji University, Shanghai, China
12046@tongji.edu.cn
[2] College of Architecture and Urban Planning, Tongji University, Shanghai, China

Abstract. The concept of the metaverse, centered around XR (Extended Reality) technology, has explosively impacted the market. XR technology, playing an important role in digital planning in urban development, is expected to innovate models in urban smart governance. Against this backdrop, we have created the "Hi Metaverse" project in Qingdao, China, integrating actual maritime scenery with augmented reality. This project marks global firsts with a marine XR show, user co-created digital landmarks, and a massive metaverse media publicity. Through the "Hi Metaverse" application, users can experience a comprehensive, free XR encounter in real urban environments. It transcends the constraints of physical space and promotes maritime culture and knowledge. With the advent of the new era of spatial computing and the emergence of smaller devices, the continuous innovation of XR-based virtual and real content is anticipated, providing users with more immersive experiences and ushering in new modes of consumption, entertainment, and production.

Keywords: XR · Metaverse · Co-creation · Urban Planning

1 Introduction

In recent years, the concept of Metaverse centered on virtual experiences such as XR (Extended Reality) has continued to spark the market, and the continuous iteration of XR technology and equipment continues to optimize users' digital life experience. XR-based digital services are penetrating around all kinds of scenarios, deeply affecting every aspect of people's lives. In addition, the entire metaverse ecosystem is enriched by the development of industrial chain and technology, the gradual prosperity of content applications, and the accelerated entry of ecological players [1].

In the field of urban planning, XR technology has also sparked the rise of digital planning. By adding real-world geospatial data to Unity's 3D development platform, it will help to better operate and manage large-scale infrastructure and urban spaces in an immersive environment [2]. The virtuality, human participation, and reality that the metaverse possesses make it expected to play an important role in urban smart governance and break the urban smart governance dilemma, thus realizing the model innovation of urban smart construction and governance [3].

C. Stephanidis et al. (Eds.): HCII 2024, CCIS 2116, pp. 75–81, 2024.
https://doi.org/10.1007/978-3-031-61950-2_9

2 Design and Implement: Hi Metaverse

"Hi Metaverse" is a revolutionary XR project that combines actual seascapes and architectures with augmented reality. This project seamlessly encourages interactions between the real-world scenes of Qingdao West Coast and the virtual imagery constructed from digital content, providing a truly immersive experience.

It achieved three global firsts: The first marine XR Show, which performs on over 50,000 square meters of sea surface; the first user co-created digital landmark, which recreates future landmark buildings on a 1:1 scale using XR technology; and the first massive metaverse media publicity that overlays virtual elements and digital identifiers on real buildings, enabling commercial promotion.

"Hi Metaverse" is experienced through mediums like electronic or wearable devices (see Fig. 1). Users only need to download the "Hi Metaverse" application and follow the tutorial to go to the specified location. By scanning the real urban scene on-site from the optimal viewing angle indicated on the screen, users can enjoy a comprehensive free XR experience. The application is based on the principle of VPS (Visual Positioning System). It collects real-time environmental data through sensors such as cameras, utilizing computer vision technology for environment recognition and modeling. Through a positioning algorithm, it determines the user's accurate location and viewing angle in the real world. Subsequently, it precisely overlays virtual information in the user's field of view.

Fig. 1. The user experiences 'Hi Metaverse' through the mobile app.

It transcends the limitations of physical space, incorporating local historical stories from Qingdao and technological elements such as the Jiaolong submersible, popularizing local marine culture and knowledge to tourists and public (see Fig. 2).

Fig. 2. Inserting local historical stories, marine culture from Qingdao and technological elements to the "Hi Metaverse" marine XR Show.

"Hi Metaverse" dynamically generates and updates virtual elements. Once the user's position is determined, the system will retrieve relevant virtual information for that location, including 3D models, labels, virtual objects, and more. Real-time updates involve communication with AR cloud services, fetching the latest virtual information corresponding to the user's current location and perspective from the cloud. Virtual information can be adjusted and transformed in real-time based on different scenes or user interactions. For instance, at Q Bridge, the ambient elements displayed are varied based on users' age and gender: children may see candies, while adults might see flower petals or ginkgo leaves.

Furthermore, "Hi Metaverse" encourages users to participate and co-create. By allowing users to vote on their preferred design solutions on Q Bridge (see Fig. 3), users are able to participate in the creation of digital city landmarks, which in turn integrates them into the construction of the metaverse. In this platform, users are encouraged to interact with the platform, future prospects, and other users, bringing new ideas and content to the metaverse.

Fig. 3. Q Bridge: Envisioning future city landmarks through AR technology.

The "Hi Metaverse" system is designed and built based on a three-tier architecture in cloud computing (see Fig. 4). It is primarily divided into the IaaS layer (including infrastructure and network layers), PaaS layer (including the middle platform and central platform), and SaaS layer (including application and user layers). Data communication is established between the layers, with internal data exchange primarily handled through the platform layer.

Considering scenarios involving large-scale concurrent user access to the client app, and aiming to enhance the convenience, reliability, and security of the system for future use, maintenance, and upgrades, a B/S model based on web application architecture is proposed. Stable, efficient, and secure Linux cloud servers are employed as the service runtime environment with externally exposed interfaces. The storage system utilizes MySQL database, and Redis serves as a caching medium. The entire underlying business logic is developed in Java. The client-side is developed natively, integrating functionalities such as WeChat login, Apple login, and phone number login.

For the PC operating platform, VUE is used as the page framework for the management system. CentOS 7.9 is selected as the server operating system, and Nginx is configured as the proxy server.

3   Evaluation and Discussion

During the first week after the project was officially launched, the design team conducted user surveys (see Fig. 5), collecting real feedback and impressions from users of different age groups, and made daily optimizations to enhance the user experience based on the

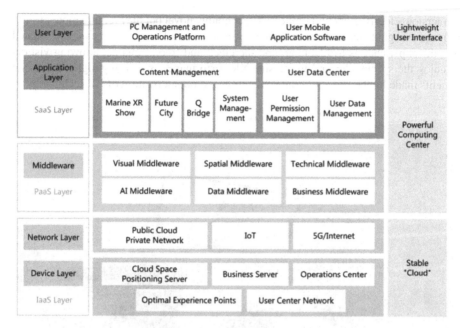

Fig. 4. Overall Design of the "Hi Metaverse" System.

gathered insights. The research used on-site interviews to tap into the opinions of local residents and tourists about their experience of the "Hi Metaverse".

Fig. 5. On-site user surveys.

Through the "Hi Metaverse" app, residents and tourists can experience the full content of the "Hi Metaverse" by performing real-time scanning and registration (see Fig. 6). In general, children are curious and interested in the virtual elements in "Hi Metaverse," hoping to see more interesting virtual content; young users appreciate its rich interactive experience and expect stronger 3D effects and AR glasses viewing functionality; middle-aged users acknowledge the effectiveness of AR applications and wish to enhance immersion; elderly users find immersive technology novel but may require more promotion and user guidance to enhance their usage experience. The scenic area manager stated that the experience is available around the clock and free of charge, allowing visitors to enjoy the spectacular and immersive XR performance, which highlights the social benefits made by the project in the application and popularization of XR technology.

Fig. 6. The interface of "Hi Metaverse" app.

As for the economic benefits, we also created a super-large metaverse publicity media, superimposing virtual elements and digital logos on the real buildings (see Fig. 7), attracting brands to enter, and promoting the transformation of the digital economy of

Fig. 7. Future city: Metaverse Mega Advertising Platform.

enterprises. For businesses and brands near Qingdao West Coast, XR technology provides a more convenient advertising channel. Businesses can cooperate with Hi Metaverse to integrate advertisements or promotional information into XR scenes, allowing tourists to naturally understand the relevant information of the businesses and brands in XR scenes [4]. This enhances the businesses' and brands' exposure, increases customer flow and sales, and also provides more information for tourists' choices.

4 Conclusion

Based on the regional characteristics of Qingdao, this project has strong characteristics of marine culture, and has a great reference for other coastal cultural regions in content creation. However, due to the strong regional cultural characteristics, this study lacks a more universal XR experience content creation method to promote to digital landmark construction projects around the world.

On June 5, 2023, Apple's Worldwide Developers Conference announced the Apple Vision Pro, along with the new operating system VisionOS. VisionOS breaks the limitations of traditional displays with a new 3D user interface that allows natural interaction with the user's eyes, gestures and voice. The advent of the Apple Vision Pro represents the beginning of a new era in spatial computing. Its popularity and slick performance could portend a future of smaller devices in which humans interact with virtual overlays on the real world. A wearable computer instead of a handheld computer [a mobile phone] could be the future [5]. Based on the support of hardware facilities, combined with the virtual and real content innovation based on XR technology such as "Hi Metaverse", it will bring more immersive experience to users and open a new consumption, entertainment and production model.

References

1. Pu, Q.L., Pang, Y.P., Peng, B., Hu, J.N., Zhang, Y.D.: Metaverse Series White Papers-The Future is Coming: Global XR Industry Insight. Deloitte, China (2021)
2. Hudson-Smith, A.: Incoming metaverses: digital mirrors for urban planning. Urban Plan. **7**, 343–354 (2022)
3. Peng, G.C., Wu, S.Y.: Metaverse: a new approach to exploring urban smart governance scenarios. Library Forum. **43**, 86–92 (2023)
4. Zhang, Y.N., Han, H.: The design strategy of AR-based travel experience in the post-pandemic era – an exploratory case study in China. In: Stephanidis, C., Antona, M., Ntoa, S., Salvendy, G. (eds.) HCI International 2023 Posters, vol. 1836, pp. 355–363. Springer, Cham (2023). https://doi.org/10.1007/978-3-031-36004-6_49
5. O'Callaghan, J.: Apple Vision Pro: what does it mean for scientists? Nature (2024). https://doi.org/10.1038/d41586-024-00387-z

ColorIt: An Augmented Reality Application for Object Recoloring

George Margetis⬤, Stavroula Ntoa⁽✉⁾ ⬤, Eirini Sykianaki,
Konstantinos C. Apostolakis⬤, Eleni Papadaki, Georgios Mathioudakis,
and Maria Bouhli

Institute of Computer Science, Foundation for Research and Technology-Hellas (FORTH),
70013 Heraklion, Crete, Greece
stant@ics.forth.gr

Abstract. Selecting the color of a consumer product during a preproduction phase can be a time-consuming and costly process, requiring the involvement of specialized professionals and multiple iterations. However, the integration of Augmented Reality technology offers an easy-to-use solution by streamlining decision-making processes for individuals and companies, effectively reducing the required resources in terms of effort and time. This poster introduces ColorIt, an AR mobile application designed to facilitate the virtual recoloring of objects, applied in the context of plastic objects. This innovative tool allows users to explore different shades, select preferred tones, and customize the color of plastic objects in real-time, using a diverse range of plastic colorants. The application enhances efficiency and accuracy in the selection of plastic object colors, offering the potential to revolutionize manufacturing, reduce costs, and increase customer satisfaction.

Keywords: Recoloring Objects · Augmented Reality · Mobile Application

1 Introduction

Plastics come in various forms and are present in almost every aspect of daily life [1]. They are used in clothing, food packaging, and public health products, among other things. To enhance their aesthetic appeal and make them more suitable for their intended use, pigments are incorporated into plastics to add colors [2]. A color masterbatch is a granular form of densely concentrated pigments or pigment blends, often supplemented with additives such as antioxidants, antistatic agents, and plasticizers [3].

The production process involves multiple stages, including ingredient dosing, melting, mixing, and cooling in the extruder, as well as cutting the material into uniform granules using a granulator [4]. However, fabricators need their color delivered on schedule, and therefore obtaining approval right away is crucial for production [5]. Any adjustments to color not only result in financial waste, but also hinder the ability to quickly respond to customer needs, potentially risking loss of business opportunities. For this

© The Author(s), under exclusive license to Springer Nature Switzerland AG 2024
C. Stephanidis et al. (Eds.): HCII 2024, CCIS 2116, pp. 82–91, 2024.
https://doi.org/10.1007/978-3-031-61950-2_10

reason, it is important to make prompt and informed decisions when choosing colors for plastics, ensuring both efficiency and reliability.

Previewing colors on plastic objects before production can streamline the process and allow for extensive testing of various hues before finalizing a selection. By utilizing Augmented Reality (AR) technology, previewing colors becomes not only a streamlined processes, facilitating the process of testing a wide range of hues before a final selection can be made, but also an enhanced one for stakeholders who are not experienced in specialized software.

In more detail, AR involves the integration of real-world and virtual elements, facilitating real-time user interaction [6]. In the context of the production of plastic objects, this technology could enable users to view real-world objects through a smart device and apply any desired color, thus capitalizing on the opportunities offered by AR to expedite the production cycle, offering enhanced efficiency and effectiveness.

This work presents a mobile application that uses AR technology to recolor plastic objects in real-time. The application enables users to choose from a variety of colors and preview them by pointing their smartphone camera at the object. This technology allows them to make informed decisions before purchasing and applying any color, thus reducing any waste of resources and materials by avoiding the production of objects that may ultimately be rejected for aesthetic or other reasons. In addition, the application provides various features, including the ability to recolor objects within photos retrieved from the user's gallery, review their activity history, and access detailed information about selected colors. The application was designed with the active participation of field experts, adopting a Human-Centered Design approach [7]. Furthermore, to ensure that the application abides by user requirements and by usability standards, evaluation of the application was iterative [8], with the active involvement of stakeholders as well as a heuristic evaluation conducted by User Experience (UX) experts.

The paper is structured as follows: Sect. 2 provides an overview of related works, Sect. 3 describes the system's functionality, Sect. 4 presents the results of the heuristic evaluation process, and Sect. 5 offers the conclusion and insights for future work.

2 Related Work

AR technology has a wide range of applications in various domains, including marketing, medicine, education, entertainment, and architecture [9, 10]. Several researchers, as described below, have explored the application of AR for recoloring objects across various contexts. However, none have specifically focused on real-time recoloring of plastic surfaces. Addressing this gap could create new opportunities for innovation and advancement across various industries, including color masterbatch manufacturing.

AR Museum [11] is a mobile app where users can interact with paintings using AR. By pointing their device's camera at a painting, users can view a virtual version overlaid on the real one. They can then personalize the artwork by adding colors to different areas. However, the user modifies the virtual version of the painting instead of directly altering its form as captured by the camera. Marino et al. [12] presented AR recoloring methods to improve visualization by adapting virtual content to real backgrounds, but once again, the recoloring was applied only to virtual objects. Moreover, Meka et al.

[13] presented a framework for live AR applications that enables dynamic features such as recoloring. Their framework allows users to interact with objects by simply touching them to select them and then using gestures such as swiping or tapping to change their color. However, to achieve real-time performance, their solution is computationally demanding and requires a state-of-the-art graphics card. Additionally, some studies [14–16] have introduced systems tailored for individuals with visual impairments, such as color blindness, utilizing AR to adapt colors in their visual experience. Nevertheless, these systems do not provide the functionality to selectively modify and replace specific colors with those preferred by the user. Recoloring applications are also valuable in the beauty industry, with recent efforts employing AI techniques for recoloring and area masking. For instance, Levinshtein et al. [17] demonstrated how a modified MobileNet CNN architecture can effectively segment hair in real-time, while Qin et al. have employed convolutional networks for skin and hair masking [18].

Overall, AR recoloring of real objects, persons, or images is a technique widely reported in the literature. The proposed approach offers an effective and efficient solution for recoloring plastic objects, addressing challenges such as the intricate shape of objects or glare effects due to light reflections on the object surface.

3 System Overview

ColorIt is an innovative application designed to enable users to easily modify the colors of plastic objects, using their smart mobile device, to find those that suit their preferences. It allows users to easily customize colors, save their preferred selections, and request information about each hue. The recoloring of objects can be achieved instantly through the use of AR technology or retrospectively through previously taken pictures. The application was implemented using the React Native framework[1], offering platform adaptability of the developed native mobile app, whereas the recoloring algorithm was implemented via a GLSL shader[2].

3.1 User Interface

Upon opening the ColorIt application, users are given the option to either use the camera to recolor an object immediately, which is the main feature of the application, or to explore all of its functionalities through the home page (see Fig. 1). On each page of the application, accessing the camera to recolor an object is made very easy through the main button in the menu. The menu remains constantly available, with the button for this functionality distinctively standing out from the rest of the options.

When activating the AR functionality, the device's camera is enabled, prompting users to select an object or surface in their environment for color modification with a simple tap (see (a) (b) (c) Fig. 2). To optimize results, they are advised placing the object against a clear background and ensuring ample natural light. After selecting an item, users

---

[1] https://reactnative.dev/.

[2] https://developer.mozilla.org/en-US/docs/Games/Techniques/3D_on_the_web/GLSL_S haders.

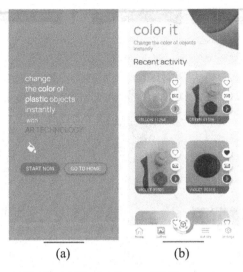

(a)   (b)

Fig. 1. (a) Starting Screen, (b) Home page.

can choose a color from the palette to recolor it, and they can adjust the color threshold (i.e., the extent to which the new color is applied to the selected object surface) until they achieve the desired result. In order to facilitate color selection, colors are grouped according to their shade, and there are also color filters based on attributes such as heat resistance, light fastness, polymer type, and production methods. Furthermore, there is a category featuring users' favorite colors for quick access. By selecting a color, users can view through the camera how the item would appear when the color is applied. They also have access to the color card, where they can view its attributes, request more information, or save it to their favorites. Subsequently, they can capture a picture, which they can save, share, or utilize to request more information from the selling company. Moreover, users have the option to take a photo through the application before selecting any color, and then use this photo for recoloring. Another option for recoloring is through the "Gallery" menu option, where users can select photos from their gallery, regardless of whether they were taken within the application or not.

Additionally, users can review their past activities within the application by accessing the "Activity" menu option. These activities are categorized into three tabs: "SAVED", "FAVORITES", and "REQUESTS" (see (a) (b) (c) Fig. 3). The "SAVED" tab includes all of the saved camera captures, along with information about the selected color. Options are available to save the color to favorites, share it, request information about it, and delete the activity entry. The "FAVORITES" tab displays the colors that the user has saved as their favorites, which can be filtered by shade. Users can also access information about each color or remove any colors they no longer prefer. Finally, the 'REQUESTS' tab contains all previous requests for additional information on specific colors. Users have the option to delete any request entries or examine more information about the selected color within a specific request.

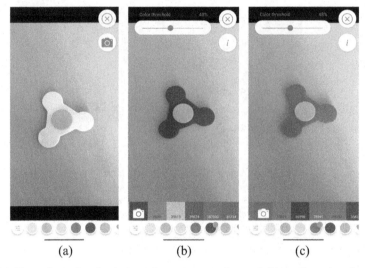

Fig. 2. (a) User selects the plastic item they want to color, and (b) applies one color, then (c) applies another color.

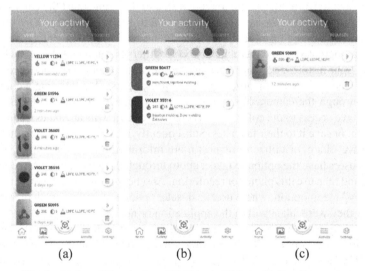

Fig. 3. (a) Saved Recolorings, (b) Favorite Colors, (c) Past Requests.

Regarding the request process, users have the option to generate an email to the corresponding company directly from the application to inquire about a specific color they tried and liked. The email includes, as an attached file, the capture taken by the application with the recolored plastic object and the code of the applied color. To generate the request, users also need to fill out a form that includes their full name, email address, affiliated company name (if applicable), and a brief explanation of their request (see Fig. 4). This ensures that all necessary information is included in the email. After submitting the form, users will be redirected to their preselected email client where they will find a pre-filled email. Additionally, they will be informed that the company manufacturing the color masterbatches will be in contact with them soon.

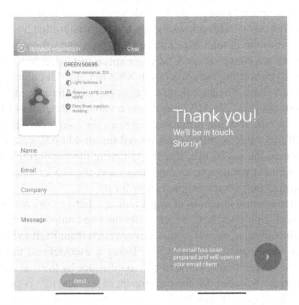

Fig. 4. The form for requesting additional color information.

The application currently supports two languages, English and Greek, and users can switch between them in the settings. Within the "Settings" menu option, users can also access crucial information, including the terms and conditions governing the application's usage, as well as answers to frequently asked questions regarding its functionalities.

3.2   Recoloring Algorithm

At the core of the application, a recoloring method was implemented, which determines, for each pixel in an input image: (a) whether the pixel should be recolored; and (b) the new color of the pixel, in case the pixel has been flagged for recoloring. Using several color space transformations and operations, the algorithm preserves the lighting and shading information, so as to retain, as much as possible the integrity of the original image. The recoloring operation is implemented using a GLSL shader, which allows the app to leverage GPU-based processing for real-time performance.

The algorithm accepts a source image as its main input, alongside the source (c_σ) and target (c_t) colors (e.g., the color samples when the user last tapped on the image on the screen, thereby indicating the color to be changed; and the color from the list of masterbatches, with which to replace the original). Both colors are fed into the algorithm, formatted as 3-dimnensional color vectors with red, green and blue components (normalized in the $[0 \ldots 1]$ range). In its output, the algorithm produces the final color to display on the screen.

The first step of the algorithm is to determine whether to actually apply the recoloring operation on the current pixel being rendered (p). This is done by first converting p and c_σ in CIELAB color space (which is device-independent, and approximates the way the human eye perceives color). This allows the algorithm to determine how similar the two colors appear to be to the human eye. The conversion is carried out in two stages: (i) first, the two colors are converted to XYZ color space (referring to a D65/2° standard illuminant); and (ii) converting the colors from XYZ to CIELAB color space. Using the two CIELAB color values, we then calculate the perceived difference in color, according to Delta E 94 formula (ΔE_{94}^*). ΔE_{94}^* represents a value in the scale of 0–100, where, the lower the value, the less the difference between the two colors is perceivable by the human eye. If this value is below a designated threshold ($\Delta E_{tolerance}$), p and c_σ are considered similar to the naked eye, thereby initiating the recoloring operation for p, as described in the next paragraph. In any other case, the shader skips the recoloring operation, and simply outputs the original color for p.

The second step (should the result of step 1 indicate that a color change is warranted) is to apply the recoloring operation, which shifts the hue component of p to match the target's c_t hue value. First, p, c_σ and c_t must be converted from RGB to HSV color space (resulting in new values p^{hsv}, c_σ^{hsv} and c_t^{hsv}). Using a user-defined threshold value t, which indicates the range of colors around c_σ^{hsv} to influence by the hue shifting function, the absolute distance d between the hue component of p^{hsv} and c_σ^{hsv} is calculated (taking into account the 360-degree representation of color hues). If d is found to be below t, then the new color p'^{hsv} is calculated from the components of c_t^{hsv} as follows:

$$
p'^{hsv} = \begin{cases} c_t^{hue} \\ c_t^{sat} + (p^{sat} - c_\sigma^{sat}) \\ c_t^{val} + (p^{val} - c_\sigma^{val}) \end{cases} \tag{1}
$$

This color is then converted back into RGB color space, so that it can be rendered by the GLSL fragment shader.

Some additional checks and optional operations are executed prior to the recoloring algorithm, if the color the user wants to change (c_σ) is perceived as "achromatic" (i.e., the a* and b* values in CIELAB color space are in a sufficiently small area around 0). If c_σ is achromatic, and its luminance indicates the achromatic color is closer to white than it is to black, then both p and c_σ are "changed" into another color (via a sepia filter), allowing the algorithm to apply the recolor, given the new yellow/brown appearance of the image. If the luminance value indicates the achromatic color is closer to black, an inversion operation is executed on both p and c_σ, prior to the application of the sepia filter. These operations account for the algorithm's (e.g., hue shifting) limitation in handling achromatic image data.

4   Evaluation

The research utilized the heuristic evaluation method [19] to assess the ColorIt application. Specifically, four evaluators consisting of two UX experts and two domain experts employed heuristics (i.e., established usability principles) [20] to evaluate the user interface through multiple iterations and identify any potential violations. In each interaction, the evaluators documented the findings they discovered and specified the corresponding violated principles. These findings were then consolidated into a single report, with each issue addressed only once. Afterward, the evaluators reviewed the consolidated list and assigned severity ratings to each finding. The final severity score for each problem was calculated by averaging the ratings provided by each evaluator.

The application has been evaluated iteratively, until all identified problems were resolved. Throughout the evaluation iterations, several issues were identified and resolved until the application was deemed usable. The key modifications made following the evaluation process are outlined below:

- A confirmation popup has been implemented, prompting users to confirm their intention to exit the application. This feature aims to prevent accidental exits caused by unintentional gestures.
- The photo captured by the user within the application failed to appear in the gallery until the user exited and then re-entered the application. This inconsistency could cause confusion, but the issue has been resolved.
- Experts agreed that in order to optimize the AR functionality, it is critical to streamline the process of capturing a picture after navigating through colors. Therefore, the selected color's visibility was prioritized by placing it at the forefront of the color palette. This ensures that the selected color is prominently displayed and the capture button is easily accessible, preventing it from being accidentally hidden beyond the edge of the screen.
- The issue of displaying incorrect language in certain application components that did not previously match the selected language has been successfully resolved.
- The color threshold has been updated from initially providing theree options (low, high, and medium) to a slider selector to improve the user's ability to precisely adjust the color of the selected object.
- Another improvement was the way the images in the gallery were displayed, depending on their orientation. In the early stages, all images were displayed horizontally, resulting in a lot of white space, which made it difficult to recolor the object.
- Several iterations were required to enhance the AR functionality for live recoloring. Initially, the application experienced frequent crashes or freezes when using the camera.
- Numerous iterations were also conducted to ensure the application's compatibility across all devices. Issues such as difficult-to-read text, due to wrapping or truncation, and low-quality graphics were also addressed.

5   Conclusions and Future Work

Given the time-consuming and costly nature of producing colored plastic, it is crucial to make the right decision on color before starting the process. ColorIt is a mobile application that allows users to explore various colors in real-time through their mobile camera and apply them to any plastic surface, using AR technology. Through the application, users can effortlessly visualize how each hue can color their desired object, empowering them to make informed decisions about the color they wish to proceed with for production. The application's user interface has undergone multiple evaluation iterations to ensure full functionality and optimal usability. Following, the application has been deployed in production and became available through mobile app stores.

Although ColorIt was initially developed for recoloring plastic objects, its potential extends beyond that to any surface, enabling users to visualize them in a variety of colors of their choice. For instance, it can be readily employed for changing the color of surfaces and objects for interior decoration purposes, similar to [21], or for eCommerce purposes to recolor apparel [22, 23], thus offering customers the option to select the color of their choice for a product without trying it out again. In this regard, future work will focus on applying the developed algorithm across different contexts and carry out a comparative performance analysis as well as a user-based evaluation to further enhance the described system.

Acknowledgments. The authors would like to thank Plastika Kritis S.A. for their collaboration and support.

References

1. Andrady, A.L., Neal, M.A.: Applications and societal benefits of plastics. Philos. Trans. R. Soc. B Biol. Sci. **364**, 1977–1984 (2009). https://doi.org/10.1098/rstb.2008.0304
2. Zhao, X., Wang, J., Yee Leung, K.M., Wu, F.: Color: an important but overlooked factor for plastic photoaging and microplastic formation. Environ. Sci. Technol. **56**, 9161–9163 (2022). https://doi.org/10.1021/acs.est.2c02402
3. Koz\lowska, M., Lipińska, M., Okraska, M., Pietrasik, J.: Polypropylene color master-batches containing layered double hydroxide modified with quinacridone and phthalocyanine pigments—rheological, thermal and application properties. Materials **16**, 6243 (2023)
4. Chorobinski, M., Skowronski, L., Bielinski, M.: Methodology for determining selected characteristics of polyethylene dyeing using CIELab system/Metodyka wyznaczania wybranych charakterystyk barwienia polietylenu z wykorzystaniem systemu CIELab. Polimery **64**, 690–697 (2019)
5. Harris, R.M.: Coloring Technology for Plastics. William Andrew, Norwich (1999)
6. Azuma, R.T.: A survey of augmented reality. Presence Teleoperators Virtual Environ. **6**, 355–385 (1997)
7. Margetis, G., Ntoa, S., Antona, M., Stephanidis, C.: Human-centered design of artificial intelligence. In: Salvendy, G., Karwowski, W. (eds.) Handbook of Human Factors and Ergonomics, pp. 1085–1106. Wiley, New York (2021)
8. Ntoa, S., Margetis, G., Antona, M., Stephanidis, C.: User experience evaluation in intelligent environments: a comprehensive framework. Technologies **9**, 41 (2021). https://doi.org/10.3390/technologies9020041
9. Billinghurst, M., Clark, A., Lee, G.: A survey of augmented reality. Found. Trends® Hum.–Comput. Interact. **8**, 73–272 (2015)
10. Gavgiotaki, D., Ntoa, S., Margetis, G., Apostolakis, K.C., Stephanidis, C.: Gesture-based interaction for AR systems: a short review. In: Proceedings of the 16th International Conference on PErvasive Technologies Related to Assistive Environments, pp. 284–292. Association for Computing Machinery, New York (2023)

11. Ryffel, M., et al.: AR museum: a mobile augmented reality application for interactive painting recoloring. In: Proceedings of the International Conference Interfaces and Human Computer Interaction 2017, pp. 54–60. IADIS Press, Lisbon (2017)
12. Marino, E., Bruno, F., Liarokapis, F.: Color harmonization, deharmonization and balancing in augmented reality. Appl. Sci. **11**, 3915 (2021)
13. Meka, A., Fox, G., Zollhöfer, M., Richardt, C., Theobalt, C.: Live user-guided intrinsic video for static scenes. IEEE Trans. Vis. Comput. Graph. **23**, 2447–2454 (2017)
14. Tanuwidjaja, E., et al.: Chroma: a wearable augmented-reality solution for color blindness. In: Proceedings of the 2014 ACM International Joint Conference on Pervasive and Ubiquitous Computing, Seattle Washington, pp. 799–810. ACM (2014)
15. Ananto, B.S., Sari, R.F., Harwahyu, R.: Color transformation for color blind compensation on augmented reality system. In: 2011 International Conference on User Science and Engineering (i-USEr), pp. 129–134. IEEE (2011)
16. Valakou, A., Margetis, G., Ntoa, S., Stephanidis, C.: A framework for accessibility in XR environments. In: Stephanidis, C., Antona, M., Ntoa, S., Salvendy, G. (eds.) HCI International 2023 – Late Breaking Posters, vol. 1958, pp. 252–263. Springer, Cham (2024). https://doi.org/10.1007/978-3-031-49215-0_31
17. Levinshtein, A., Chang, C., Phung, E., Kezele, I., Guo, W., Aarabi, P.: Real-time deep hair matting on mobile devices. In: 2018 15th Conference on Computer and Robot Vision (CRV), pp. 1–7. IEEE (2018)
18. Qin, S., Kim, S., Manduchi, R.: Automatic skin and hair masking using fully convolutional networks. In: 2017 IEEE International Conference on Multimedia and Expo (ICME), Hong Kong, Hong Kong, pp. 103–108. IEEE (2017)
19. Nielsen, J.: Usability Engineering. Morgan Kaufmann, San Francisco (1994)
20. Nielsen, J.: Enhancing the explanatory power of usability heuristics. In: Proceedings of the SIGCHI Conference on Human Factors in Computing Systems Celebrating Interdependence - CHI 1994, pp. 152–158. ACM Press, Boston (1994)
21. Tong, H., Wan, Q., Kaszowska, A., Panetta, K., Taylor, H.A., Agaian, S.: ARFurniture: augmented reality interior decoration style colorization. Electron. Imaging **31**, 175-1–175-9 (2019). https://doi.org/10.2352/ISSN.2470-1173.2019.2.ERVR-175
22. Margetis, G., Ntoa, S., Stephanidis, C.: Smart omni-channel consumer engagement in malls. In: Stephanidis, C. (ed.) HCII 2019. CCIS, vol. 1034, pp. 89–96. Springer, Cham (2019). https://doi.org/10.1007/978-3-030-23525-3_12
23. Birliraki, C., Margetis, G., Patsiouras, N., Drossis, G., Stephanidis, C.: Enhancing the customers' experience using an augmented reality mirror. In: Stephanidis, C. (ed.) HCI 2016. CCIS, vol. 618, pp. 479–484. Springer, Cham (2016). https://doi.org/10.1007/978-3-319-40542-1_77

A Comparative Study on Methods to Interact with Close-Distance Objects in Mixed Reality Environment: Direct Method vs. Raycasting Method

Sang Jun Park⬭, Min Joo Kim⬭, Yu Gyeong Son⬭, Donggun Park⬭, and Yushin Lee(✉) ⬭

Pukyong National University, 45, Yongso-Ro, Nam-Gu, Busan, Republic of Korea
{dgpark,ysl}@pknu.ac.kr

Abstract. Mixed Reality (MR) technology allows users to interact with virtual objects generated in the real world intuitively. The raycasting method, which uses hand gestures, is a useful way to interact with virtual objects located at a distance in a controller-free environment. However, considering a real-world situation where various obstacles may block the user's view, it is necessary to study how to interact with close objects. This study aimed to compare the usability of the direct and raycasting methods for interacting with close virtual objects. In the experiment, participants were instructed to manipulate the buttons that were randomly generated at nine specified locations (3 by 3 array) with a distance of 0.5 meters. They were asked to perform the task using both methods and then evaluate the usability and preference of each method. Additionally, task completion time and error frequency were measured to quantitatively compare task performances of them. The results showed that the participants preferred the raycasting method, even though the errors occurred more frequently. It was also found that there was a difference between the two methods in the variation of task performance and preference by button location. This result may be due to the fact that there are some differences between the two methods in terms of interaction characteristics and required body movements. The results of this study are expected to contribute to design more user-friendly user interfaces in MR environments.

Keywords: Mixed reality · Hand direct method · Hand raycasting method · Usability · Preference

1 Introduction

In mixed reality (MR), users can interact with virtual objects placed in the real physical world, and intuitively explore three-dimensional (3D) virtual information. The goal of MR environment is to effectively perform tasks through seamless integration between the real world and augmented virtual content. However, when using an MR application with the placement of various objects in front of a user, visual occlusion due to the overlap between the virtual and real objects may confuse the user's visual perception [1]. In addition, this can potentially cause secondary problems such as eye fatigue and motion sickness hindering the accurate execution of object manipulation tasks. [2–6]. Due to this nature, interaction with objects within an MR environment occurs with objects close to the user.

In 3D environments like MR, accurately selecting and manipulating objects are fundamental interactions, particularly crucial for user immersion [7]. Therefore, several input technologies have been proposed to aid intuitive interaction with virtual objects. Free Hand is an input system tracking the movement of a hand and fingers without additional trackers or controllers. This method enables natural and intuitive interaction through hand and finger movements [8].

Free Hand can be classified into hand direct interaction and hand raycasting interaction based on the interaction metaphor. The hand direct interaction method (direct method) is essentially an extension of the real-world object manipulation method to a 3D virtual environment [9, 10]. This enables more natural and intuitive interaction because it directly maps the user's hand movements to the virtual hand movements [11]. Thus, it was favored by many users in early virtual reality research [12, 13]. The hand raycasting interaction method (raycasting method) utilizes raycasting metaphors for object selection. The direction of the light rays coming out of the virtual hand is determined by the direction of the user's hand. By tracing a ray to the target object and performing a pinch gesture with an index finger and thumb, it provides metaphorical object manipulation similar to a mouse click in desktop environments. The raycasting interaction is commonly used in virtual environments and is known for its high performance and user preference when performing selection tasks due to the simplicity of the interaction procedure [14]. Unlike the direct method, it allows the manipulation of objects beyond the reach of the user's hand and requires less body movement [14]. Therefore, direct and raycasting methods can differ in usability due to differences in mapping mechanisms when the user's movement is reflected in MR environments within physically constrained real-world space.

This study aims to compare the usability of the direct and raycasting methods when manipulating a virtual controller of button type. In addition, since the physical arrangement of the virtual controller can affect the manipulation performance, the placement of buttons at the nine locations by 3 rows and 3 columns in a virtual grid was considered to identify the pattern of usability.

2 Method

2.1 Participants

Twenty Korean students (11 male, 9 female) between the ages of 21 and 27 (M = 23.4, SD = 1.64) participated in the experiment. All participants were free from mental or physical disabilities. All participants gave consent for the experiment protocol approved by the Pukyong National University Institutional Review Board (IRB NO. 1041386-202403-HR-27-02).

2.2 Experimental Setting

The test environment was displayed by Meta Quest Pro (resolution: 1800×1920 QD-LCD 90 Hz per eye; viewing angles: up to 120°). It is equipped with five internal and external cameras each and with the implementation of color-mixed reality [15]. The Unity 2021.3.16.f1 program was used to develop the test environment. The screen User Interface (UI) was displayed at a distance of 50 cm from the user, which is the minimum comfortable viewing distance for objects. The overall UI size was set to 57.74 $\times$ 36.40 cm, considering the comfortable rotation range of -30° ~ 30° horizontally and -20° ~ 20° vertically [16]. The overall UI (Fig. 1 (a)) was divided evenly into 9 areas (from A to I) by a gray grid with a transparent background. A button was located in the center of an area, with a size of 9×9 cm (Fig. 1 (b)). Visual feedback was provided by lowering the chromaticity during pointing (Fig. 1(c)).

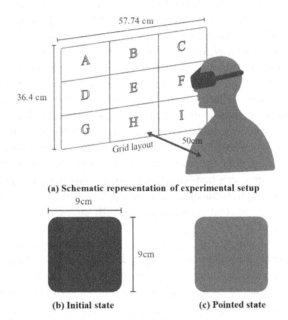

(a) Schematic representation of experimental setup

(b) Initial state   **(c) Pointed state**

Fig. 1. Experimental setup. (a) virtual layout grid, (b) button in initial state (c) button in pointed state

2.3 Experimental Design

The experiment was conducted to find out the effects of two interaction methods and the patterns by location while manipulating a virtual button. This experiment was designed as a within-subject study based on performing the direct and raycasting methods. The sequence of performing the task between the interaction methods was randomly designed for each participant. The direct method is a method of selecting a virtual object with an index finger for operation (Fig. 2 (a)). On the other hand, the raycasting method is defined as pointing a target object through a ray and performing a selection task through a pinch gesture without a physical controller (Fig. 2 (b)). The dependent variables included both objective and subjective measures for usability. Objective measures included the task completion time and the number of errors to assess manipulation performance. The task completion time was defined as the time from the presentation of the stimulus to pressing a correct button, and the number of errors was defined as the number of times the participant selected the surrounding background or another area instead of the target button. The subjective measures comprised subjective preference and the System Usability Scale (SUS) [17]. Subjective preference was assessed on a 100-point scale for the preference across nine locations, while the SUS which is a standardized instrument blending ten positively and negatively worded items evaluated perceived usability on a 5-point scale.

(a) Direct method   (b) Raycasting method

Fig. 2. Illustration of the two interaction methods. (a) Direct method, (b) Raycasting method

2.4 Experimental Procedure and Task

After participants were explained about the experimental procedure, they had time to adapt to the button operation. Then, the main experiment for selecting buttons randomly generated at 9 areas (3 × 3 arrangements) was conducted (Fig. 3).

At the beginning of each trial of selection, participants stood straight with their right arm at the side and were allowed to use only their right hand throughout the experiment in order to control the experimental condition. During the trial, they were asked to perform the selection task as quickly as possible. Once the selection trial of a button was completed, the button was deactivated and disappeared. Then, a new button appeared at a random location after a maintenance time of 3 seconds. The task trials were presented 3 times at every 9 locations in resulting a total of 27 trials for each interaction method. After the task was completed for one interaction method, participants responded to subjective questionnaires and had a break at least for 2 minutes and more when requested. The entire experiment lasted for 30 minutes on average.

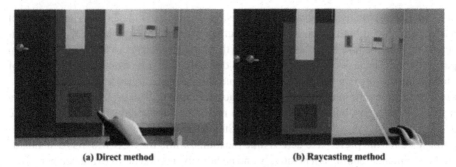

(a) Direct method   (b) Raycasting method

Fig. 3. Experimental scene views of participants. (a) Direct method, (b) Raycasting method

2.5 Data Analysis

IBM SPSS Statistics 29 was used for data analysis. Paired t-test was conducted to analyze the effect of the manipulation method on objective and subjective measures. In addition, descriptive statistics on objective and subjective measures for each location were also examined. The statistical significance level of all tests was determined based on $\alpha = 0.05$.

3 Results

3.1 Task Performance

Task Completion Time. The results showed that there was no significant difference

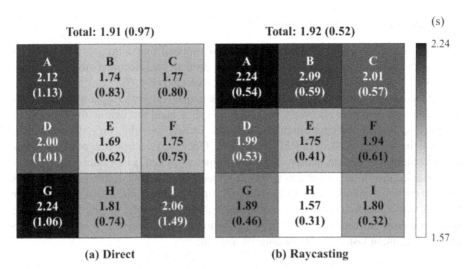

(a) Direct   (b) Raycasting

Fig. 4. Mean and standard deviation of task completion time at each location. (a) Direct method, (b) Raycasting method (Note. Darker color means higher value.)

between two methods in task completion time. However, the difference in task completion time by location was observed between the methods (Fig. 4). The task completion time was lowest on the center and higher on the left side and the bottom right corner for the direct method (Fig. 4(a)). However, it was lowest on the bottom center area and higher on the top side for the raycasting method (Fig. 4(b)).

Error Frequency. It was found that error frequency was significantly lower in the direct method ($t(8) = -4.530$, $p < 0.001$). Comparing the error frequency by location for the two methods, the error frequency was higher on the top side for the raycasting method (Fig. 5(b)), while there was no clear trend for the direct method (Fig. 5(a)).

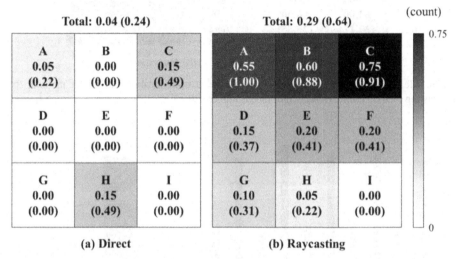

(a) Direct   (b) Raycasting

Fig. 5. Mean and standard deviation of error frequency at each location. (a) Direct method, (b) Raycasting method (Note. Darker color means higher value.)

3.2 Subjective Evaluation

Preference. The result indicated that participants significantly more prefer to use raycasting method rather than the direct method. ($t(8) = 4.088$, $p < 0.01$). The additional analysis on the preference by location showed that the preference is highest on the center and lower on the left side for both methods (Fig. 6).

System Usability Scale (SUS). SUS total score was slightly higher for raycasting method but it was not statistically significant (Fig. 7).

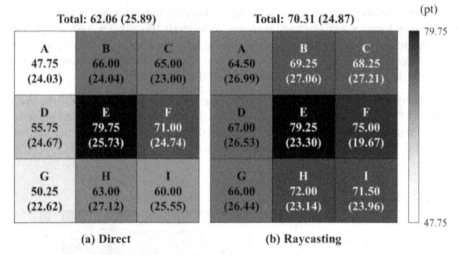

Total: 62.06 (25.89)   Total: 70.31 (24.87)   (pt)

(a) Direct   (b) Raycasting

Fig. 6. Mean and standard deviation of preference at each location. (a) Direct method, (b) Raycasting method (Note. Darker color means higher value.)

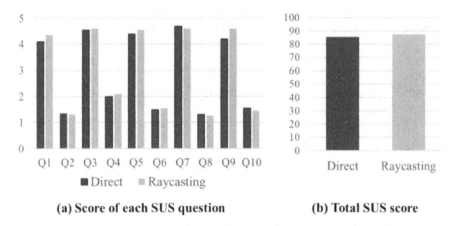

(a) Score of each SUS question   (b) Total SUS score

Fig. 7. The results of SUS evaluation. (a) Score of each question, (b) Total score

4   Discussion

As a result, there are no significant differences in mean task completion time between the two methods. However, error frequency was significantly higher in the raycasting method. The raycasting method requires more precise control of hand movement because it has lower control-response ratio [18]. This suggests that interaction with a relatively small object using the raycasting method may introduces error more frequently.

Despite inferior task performance, the raycasting method was more preferred. The cause of this result can be inferred from the presence of tactile feedback. In direct method, users only can notice the result of their action by visual cue. It does not provide tactile cues as to whether or not a button has been pressed and how much it has been pressed, so it may not be preferred despite being a more intuitive method. However, raycasting method, including pinch gesture, gives tactile feedback [19]. Moreover, there is no need to consider the depth of the object [20]. There was no significant difference in perceived usability between the two methods, but it can be concluded that raycasting method was superior in subjective evaluation.

The results also showed the differences of variation in task performances and preferences by location between the methods. In case of direct method, the task completion time and preference were lower on the left side. This result can be explained by the characteristics in posture to perform the task. The direct method requires the arm movement to point the target [21]. In the experiment, the participants were asked to use only right hand, so they had to adduct their shoulder excessively to control the object on the left side. Kee and Karwowski [22] found that people felt more comfortable flexing the shoulder than adducting the shoulder. Therefore, the left side, which requires a more uncomfortable posture, is not recommended for locating the interaction elements when using the direct method. Moreover, the participants had to move their arm more to tap the button on the left side because the horizontal length of the UI grid was longer. In the experiment, it was observed that the participants flexed their wrist to control the button on the top side and rotated their shoulder in a medial direction to control the button on the left side. The study of Kee and Karwowski also found that wrist flexion was more sensitive to comfort decrement than medial shoulder rotation [22]. Although the results of the preference ratings were not consistent, it can be concluded that placing the button on the top is not recommended.

5   Conclusions

The aim of this study was to investigate the effect of interaction method on task performances, perceived usability, and preference when manipulating static control element at close range in an MR environment. In the experiment, participants were asked to select a button which is presented randomly on the nine different locations using direct and raycasting method. The results showed that the direct method had an advantage in performing the task but the raycasting method was more preferred. It was also found that task performances varied differently depending on the location of the button in each method. In the direct method, it was observed that the errors were rare in all locations. However, both task completion time and error frequency were higher on the top side for the raycasting method. This study did not consider any other type of controller. In addition, the number of participants is relatively small. However, it is expected that this study could contribute to the design of a user-friendly user interface in the MR environment.

Acknowledgements. This research was supported by the MSIT(Ministry of Science and ICT), Korea, under the ICAN(ICT Challenge and Advanced Network of HRD) support program supervised by the IITP(Institute for Information & Communications Technology Planning & Evaluation) (IITP-2023-RS-2023-00259806).

Declaration. All the co-first authors equally contributed.

References

1. Shah, M.M., Arshad, H., Sulaiman, R.: Occlusion in augmented reality. In: 2012 8th International Conference on Information Science and Digital Content Technology (ICIDT2012), Jeju, Korea (South), pp. 372–378 (2012)
2. Zhu, J., et al.: Handling occlusions in video-based augmented reality using depth infor-mation. Comput. Anim. Virtual Worlds **21**, 509–521 (2009)
3. Tian, Y., et al.: Real-time occlusion handling in augmented reality based on an object tracking approach. Sensors **2010**, 2885–2900 (2010)
4. Wang, Y. et al.: Key technique of assembly system in an augmented reality environment. In: Second International Conference on Computer Modeling and Simulation, 2010, pp. 133–137 (2010)
5. Feng, W.D., Guan, Y.X., Gao, F., Chen, Y.: Realization of multilayer occlusion between real and virtual scenes in AR. In: Proceedings of the 10th International Conference on Computer Supported Cooperative Work in Design (2006)
6. Fuhrmann, A. et al.: Occlusion in collaborative augmented environments. In: Computers Graphics (1998)
7. Stanney, K.: Realizing the full potential of virtual reality: human factors issues that could stand in the way. In: Proceedings Virtual Reality Annual International Symposium 1995, pp. 28–34. IEEE (1995). https://doi.org/10.1109/VRAIS.1995.512476
8. Cabric, F., Dubois, E., Serrano, M.: A predictive performance model for immersive interactions in mixed reality. In: 2021 IEEE International Symposium on Mixed and Augmented Reality (ISMAR), Bari, Italy, pp. 202–210 (2021). https://doi.org/10.1109/ISMAR5 2148.2021.00035
9. Poupyrev, I., Weghorst, S., Billinghurst, M., Ichikawa, T.: A study of techniques for selecting and positioning objects in immersive VEs: effects of distance, size, and visual feedback. In: Proceedings of ACM CHI, Vol. 98 (1998)
10. Lemmerman, D.K., LaViola Jr, J.J.: Effects of interaction-display offset on user performance in surround screen virtual environments. In: Proceedings - IEEE Virtual Reality, pp. 303–304 (2007).
11. Mine, M.R., Brooks, Jr., F.P., Sequin, C.H.: Moving objects in space: exploiting proprioception. In: Virtual Environment Interaction. In: Proceedings of ACM SIGGRAPH 1997, pp. 19–26 (1997). https://doi.org/10.1145/258734.258747
12. Argelaguet, F., Andújar, C.: A survey of 3D object selection techniques for virtual en-vironments. Comput. Graph. **37**, 121–136 (2013)
13. Vanacken, L., Grossman, T., Coninx, K.: Exploring the effects of environment density and target visibility on object selection in 3D virtual environments. In: 2007 IEEE Symposium on 3D User Interfaces, IEEE (2007)
14. Grossman, T., Balakrishnan, R.: The design and evaluation of selection techniques for 3D volumetric displays. In: Proceedings of the 19th Annual ACM Symposium on User Interface Software and Technology - UIST 2006, p. 3. ACM Press, New York, New York, USA (2006)
15. Azuma, R.T.: A survey of augmented reality. Presence Teleoper. Virtual Environ. **6**(4), 355–385 (1997)
16. Vodilka, A., et al.: Designing a workplace in virtual and mixed reality using the meta quest VR headset. In: Ivanov, V., Trojanowska, J., Pavlenko, I., Rauch, E., Pitel, J. (eds.) Advances in Design, Simulation and Manufacturing VI DSMIE 2023. LNME, pp. 71–80. Springer, Cham (2023). https://doi.org/10.1007/978-3-031-32767-4_7

17. Chu, A.: VR design: transitioning from a 2D to a 3D design paradigm. In: Samsung Developer Conference, vol. 19 (2014)
18. Brooke, J.: SUS: A "quick and dirty" usability. Usabil. Eval. Indus. **189**(3), 189–194 (1996)
19. Ro, H., et al.: A dynamic depth-variable ray-casting interface for object manipulation in AR environments. In: 2017 IEEE International Conference on Systems, Man, and Cybernetics (SMC), Banff, AB, Canada, pp. 2873–2878 (2017). https://doi.org/10.1109/SMC.2017.812 3063.
20. Kim, W., Xiong, S.: Pseudo-haptics and self-haptics for freehand mid-air text entry in VR. Appl. Ergon. **104**, 103819 (2022)
21. Lu, Y., Yu, C., Shi, Y.: Investigating bubble mechanism for ray-casting to improve 3D target acquisition in virtual reality. In: 2020 IEEE Conference on Virtual Reality and 3D User Interfaces (VR), pp. 35–43 (2020)
22. Bellarbi, A., Benbelkacem, S., Belghit, H., Otmane, S., Zenati, N.: Design and evaluation of a low-cost 3D interaction technique for wearable and handled AR devices. In: 4th International Conference on Image Processing Theory Tools and Applications (IPTA), pp. 1–5, October 2014
23. Kee, D., Karwowski, W.: The boundaries for joint angles of isocomfort for sitting and standing males based on perceived comfort of static joint postures. Ergonomics **44**(6), 614–648 (2001)

Spatial Computing Through an HCI Lens - UX Evaluation Based on Situatedness

Katja Pott[(✉)][iD] and Doris Agotai[iD]

University of Applied Sciences and Arts Northwestern Switzerland FHNW, Institute of Interactive Technologies IIT, Windisch, Switzerland
`katja.pott@fhnw.ch`

Abstract. The field of spatial computing is attracting increasing attention. Despite this, aspects related to user experience and evaluation methods are not yet established. The current state of the art in UX and UX evaluation needs to be extended to include aspects that are usually not considered when interacting with mobile or desktop applications.

In spatial computing, devices are aware of 3-dimensional physical space and enable human actions with spatial meaning. However, it is important that applications consider not only the user's environment from a spatial perspective, but also other relevant contextual aspects such as the emotions of a place, the surrounding community, and the broader goals of the activity. This approach provides a new perspective and is complementary to the current state of the art.

This paper presents three examples of applications in spatial computing and demonstrates the potential aspects to be considered in the context of the experience and how the interaction could be evaluated, using an open-ended interpretive methodology. It explores methods and aspects relevant to spatial computing, highlighting opportunities and tools for evaluating the user experience. This encourages a more comprehensive approach and allows to analyse a situation holistically. The results indicate that while methods and considerations exist, there is currently no coherent methodology that integrates all relevant aspects. This finding may provide the basis for a new perspective on spatial computing and highlights the great potential of this technology to provide exceptional user experiences.

Keywords: Spatial Computing · Augmented Reality · UX Evaluation · 3D Interaction · Perception

1 Introduction

Individuals move within their environment and engage in activities, however not independently. Each action is intertwined with a situation, encompassing numerous components and social interactions. All of these components can be

C. Stephanidis et al. (Eds.): HCII 2024, CCIS 2116, pp. 102–113, 2024.
https://doi.org/10.1007/978-3-031-61950-2_12

viewed as *context* for a given action [9]. Thus, we recognise context not solely from a viewpoint of spatial organisation and its corresponding objects, but also in consideration of the social dynamics present within the space and within human activities [9]. Context is situational, thus it is essential to consider what is relevant in each circumstance [8]. Humans create the situation and make sense of their surroundings through their actions and social interactions [8].

Spatial Computing applications augment physical space with digital content. The devices are aware of the 3-dimensional space and allow human actions with spatial meaning [10]. This technology offers new user experiences (UX), where the context and situation in which the interaction occurs are fundamental factors shaping experience and perception in contrast to traditional interactions with mobile or desktop devices. However, these interactions also create uncertainties regarding the evaluation of the applications. Aspects that were not very important in the past need to be taken into account, highlighting the need to enrich the current state-of-the-art in UX and UX evaluation ([1,7,45,51]). It remains unclear which elements should be analysed to holistically evaluate the user experience in spatial computing. A more comprehensive analysis is required as it is embedded in the environment and includes spatial aspects which does not apply compared to traditional technologies. Additionally, it becomes visible that spatial computing is susceptible to various external influences that cannot be controlled, but must still be taken into account during development.

This paper presents three suitable example applications for spatial computing, demonstrating potential aspects to consider in the context of the experience and how to evaluate the interaction, using an open-ended interpretive methodology. Literature from augmented reality, information visualisation, human-computer interaction, spatial computing, and other related fields is used to identify the aspects for consideration. The results demonstrate that there are existing instruments for the holistic evaluation of spatial computing applications. However, these tools are not yet well established and extensive research is necessary to identify the potential aspects to be considered in the context and to determine how they should be evaluated. The aim of this paper is to highlight the great potential of this technology and to contribute to the body of knowledge on how to provide outstanding user experiences with spatial computing.

2   Subject of Investigation: Example Applications

As the field of spatial computing is extensive, three promising example applications are being chosen for in-depth analysis and which aspects may have an influence on the user experience. The aspects presented are currently not widely considered in applications, but are highly relevant to spatial computing. The three applications will be the subject of an investigation in order to identify considerations in the user experience and potential instruments for the evaluation of the introduced aspects.

Spatial computing includes various technologies, which can be categorized as: (1) Mobile Augmented Reality, the use of mobile devices to augment the physical space with digital content that can be viewed through the devices. (2) Head-Mounted Displays, headsets which give the possibility to interact with the physical space and the digital content embedded within. (3) Spatial Augmented Reality, projection of digital content onto physical objects, taking into account their shape and allowing to interact with the projection.

For each application area, an appropriate subject of investigation is selected for analysis, with consideration of what potential aspects might have an impact on the experience and how the evaluation might be facilitated. For mobile AR, the subject is a collaborative analysis of a simulation of plants in an online shop; for head-mounted displays, a procedural task for mixing radioactive substances with a 3D model; and finally for spatial augmented reality, an interactive installation combined with physical books in the context of museums.

2.1   Subject 1: Mobile Augmented Reality

(a) Simulation of plants in physical room with Mobile AR

(b) Collaboration with expert through Mobile AR

Fig. 1. Mobile AR Application of feey

Mobile Augmented Reality can be a useful way to visualise products in the physical space and help users make decisions through simulation [30]. Elements can be analysed based on aspects such as size, appearance, and integration into the real world. The online shop *feey* provides such an example for buying plants as illustrated in Fig. 1.

Feey's AR application is used in consultation with an expert to find the right plant for the user, serving as a decision support system [30]. It is a web application which allows to have a video call with the expert and at the same time show the environment of the user, providing information through simulation of the plant in the space and expertise by the remote consultant [29,37]. In collaboration, the expert and the user can discuss the room settings as well as the user's needs with regard to the plants. By sharing the environment, the user can provide the expert with relevant contextual information in order to gain a richer experience of the place and thus enable informed recommendations [22]. They can also select different plants and position them in the room to simulate their appearance and discuss their suitability. By highlighting objects in the augmented environment, visual references are being created, which can simplify communication by using deictic references, allowing expressions such as "this one" [20, 38]. Through the simulation, the user is able to gain meaning and analyse the plant based on contextual data, leading to a higher level of decision comfort and a reduction in cognitive load [21, 29, 32]. However, manipulating digital objects in multiple degrees of freedom to simulate different spatial positions can make interaction uncomfortable and complex [15]. Ergonomics must also be taken into account, as prolonged holding of a smartphone or tablet in an upright position can lead to pain and fatigue [3, 41].

Possible Evaluation Methods and Findings

A method for evaluating the effectiveness of a decision support system (DSS) is presented by Häubl et al. [19]. Their approach evaluates *amount of search for product information* (the number of products for which detailed information is obtained), *consideration set size* (the number of products the user considers for purchase), *consideration set quality* (the proportion of products in the consideration set that are suitable for given attributes), and *decision quality* (whether the final product selected is the best product given the desired attributes of a product and the degree of confidence in a purchase decision) for a DSS.

The impact of augmented reality (AR) simulation and visual reference cues on communication and collaboration can be evaluated using the Social Presence Questionnaire (SoPQ) [18]. The SoPQ measures attention and social presence, with subscales for co-presence, attention allocation, and perceived message understanding. It assesses whether attention is more focused on the partner in collaborative settings or on other items, such as the AR simulation. It can also provide information on whether communication was easy to facilitate, even with the use of deictic references, using the principle of *least effort for collaboration*.

The *Handheld Augmented Reality Usability Scale* (HARUS) evaluates the manipulability and comprehensibility of digital objects for mobile AR [41]. Manipulability evaluates the ease of manipulating the application during use and identifies ergonomic problems, while Comprehensibility evaluates the ease of understanding the content presented in AR and considers perceptual problems. The *Rapid Upper Limb Assessment* (RULA) provides further information on ergonomics [31]. It assesses the user's upper body posture based on the position of the upper and lower arm, wrist, neck, trunk and leg. The result indicates whether the posture is acceptable for the application or requires further investigation, suggesting possible changes either soon or immediately.

Lastly, the *Intrinsic Motivation Inventory* (IMI) could be useful to analyse the perceived usefulness and competence after using the application [40]. This could deliver insights as how useful the application is seen overall for the use case of purchasing a plant and if the feelings of competence for making a purchase decision could be increased.

2.2 Subject 2: Head-Mounted Displays

Head-mounted displays (HMD) are suitable for scenarios where both hands are required to perform actions, without restricting the dexterity of the user which can be useful for guiding users through sensitive procedural tasks [2]. Such an application represents Arigo, a non-overlayed AR guidance using a 3D model in radiopharmacy (Fig. 2) [43]. This project aims to substitute paper instructions for the creation of radioactive mixtures with AR via a Microsoft Hololens by showing step-by-step instructions on a 3D-model.

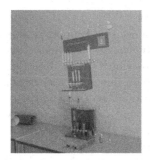 

(a) Non-Overlayed AR User Guidance with 3D-Model [43]   (b) Creating a mixture with the step-by-step guidance through Microsoft Hololens

Fig. 2. Head-Mounted Display Application of Arigo

As the field of view is limited of the HMD, the user needs support in orientation and navigation in the scene [49] [33]. However, the awareness of the surrounding should not be diminished as reduced situational awareness, known as information tunneling, can lead to a higher risk of accidents and distraction [33]. It is therefore important to blend the digital content with the real environment to reduce the dominant perception of the digital content [52]. A higher level of blending could also lead to a higher sense of presence, which is defined as *being consciously engaged in the augmented world* [42]. To achieve this state, the spatial connection of the digital content should also be considered in order to anchor the elements appropriately in the real environment [33] and not to disturb the spatial mental model of the users [50]. There are different possibilities of spatial connections, which are also crucial as spatial references from objects are used for providing natural language guidance [39], such as "to the left" or "on top," [50]. The attention of a user can also be guided through visual cues [44]. Visual cues can also disrupt presence if they are not properly integrated. It is important to consider how they are integrated, either as part of the scene or outside of immersion, and whether they are communicated explicitly or implicitly [44].

Possible Evaluation Methods and Findings

To evaluate whether the visual cues are effective for orientation and navigation, the spatial mental model may be assessed using the technique of drawing in combination with a verbal report [12], [24]. This allows the user to draw the spatial references they for orientation and to verbalise the relationship between the different objects to assess if the spatial link of information objects are appropriate. If the application aligns with the spatial mental model of the users, the interaction is less cognitively demanding [17], which could be assessed with the questionnaire by Leppink et al. [27]. It measures the intrinsic load (task complexity & prior knowledge of the user), the extraneous load (unsuitable instructional features) and the germane load (beneficial instructional features). The distinction in the cognitive load could also indicate whether the temporal aspects of the step-by-step instructions are being used in an appropriate way.

Whether the visual cues reduce situational awareness by drawing too much attention could be assessed with the *Augmented Reality Immersion* (ARI) questionnaire [14]. It is a potentially useful tool that covers a number of aspects and can provide useful cues for situational awareness, by including usability and attention. Further insights could be gained through an analysis of the semiotics of space [28] to assess the perception of a visual cue (sign) and its interpretation, followed by an action of the user. Combined with spatial mental model analysis, it provides more detail if the visual cues are linked correctly, which influences interpretation and the resulting action.

2.3 Subject 3: Spatial Augmented Reality Based on Projection Mapping

Exhibitions often pursue hedonic qualities in technology which promotes discussions about the content in society, in ways other presentation forms couldn't [6]. Spatial Augmented Reality (SAR) can promote those qualities as it breaks out of the traditional screen and shows information in a different form which can promote visual storytelling [35]. Such an installation are the interactive books from i-art [4]. They use projectors and sensors placed on the ceiling to show information on a physical book and allow for interaction with the digital content as in Fig. 3.

The books are usually placed in museums to provide an interactive experience that is novel to many visitors, which may increase attention of the installation by its novelty [23]. The physical integration opens up new possibilities and allows multi-user scenarios with different interaction possibilities compared to traditional screens. It has the ability to involve multiple people to varying degrees as it is not only visible to active users but also to bystanders or observers [34,46], which creates an opportunity for social learning [53]. The experience is created by the relationship between the installation, the space in which it is placed, the architectural design and layout of the space, and the other people in the space [13]. This creates a complex model of influence that needs to be taken into account in public space installations for successful social interaction [13].

(a) Physical books overlayed with digital content allowing for interaction [4]

(b) Interactive books with several users, either active or bystanders

Fig. 3. Spatial Augmented Reality Application of i-Art

The books are placed on special stands allowing for tactile interaction by tracking the user's touch gestures on the pages [5]. The projector is installed in the ceiling and projects digital content onto the physical books, facilitating object recognition without markers as recognition is based on shape and depth [48]. It further allows haptic interaction to explore new content by turning the page of the book [5] which is a familiar way of interaction and does not require much explanation. This in turn is supportive to maintain the user engaged as the difficulty of interaction is not too high [23]. To increase the probability of extended interaction the immersion should be high [23], which can also be beneficial for spatial and social presence to support creating empathy [25]. It is shown that a higher level of spatial presence can be achieved with SAR, which influences attitudes and possible changes in behaviour [25].

Possible Evaluation Methods and Findings

As SAR installations are placed in the environment, the space, community and interaction require further consideration. SAR also allows for social interactions and learning to take place through the installations, provided that the space allows for these interactions [13]. This can be evaluated through contextual enquiries to analyse the installation in a public space and whether social learning and encounters are possible and how they are formed [13,53]. Unlike other AR technologies, SAR not only allows interaction as an active user, but passive bystanders can also be considered users in SAR [53]. They can observe active users and learn one in the next phase which increases attention, thus also the probability for interaction [23]. Once the user's attention is captured, it can be maintained through high levels of engagement and immersion which can be assessed with the *Augmented Reality Immersion* (ARI) questionnaire [14] as it takes into account the user's engagement, involvement and immersion in AR.

The interaction modalities can also differ from traditional technologies, as users can interact not only with touch gestures, but also with haptic interaction. In order to evaluate the usefulness and the usability of the interaction method, the first subscale of the questionnaire *Modular Evaluation of key Components of User Experience* (meCUE) can be used [47].

SAR is a versatile technology that breaks out of the traditional screen and can be used in a variety of contexts to convey information that is not possible with other technologies [6]. For this reason, it can also be particularly useful for evoking feelings of empathy, which can be stronger with greater social and spatial presence [25]. To evaluate sympathy and empathy induced through media the *Ad Response Sympathy* (ARS) and *Ad Response Empathy* (ARE) questionnaire [11] can be used and adapted as in [16]. To avoid disrupting the immersion provided by SAR, the object detection needs to be facilitated accordingly. Either with appropriate markers that blend into the physical space, or without markers, which presents other difficulties in detection. The *User Experience Questionnaire* (UEQ) is one way of assessing how object detection and projection mapping are perceived, as it assesses efficiency, perspicuity and dependability [26].

3   Discussion

We associate different norms and values with spaces, depending on the context. Not only does the space influence how we perceive a place, but the community inhabiting the space and their interaction with it shapes our experience, and our interaction with AR shapes their experience of the space. Relevant aspects for spatial computing have different characteristics depending on the technology, context and scenario. This requires an in-depth analysis of the context and its aspects that break down to the definition of situatedness: space, place, activity, community and time. *Space* encompasses the physical environment and its digital content, *Place* the meaning of a space, *Community* refers to individuals in relation to a particular place, *Activity* to the relationship between a person and the goals and *Time* to the relationship of data collection or temporal relevance.

The analysis shows that in order to realise its full potential, spatial computing needs a multidisciplinary approach, as is common in HCI. This is because there are many aspects from different fields of research that influence the experience of spatial computing. It also shows that in order to evaluate the novel interaction, it is necessary to make use of evaluation tools from other fields as well, whether all tools are applicable is however questionable. In the current state of the art there are still a lot of open questions about the user experience and how to evaluate it. This also reflects the fact that the field is less mature than virtual reality or traditional web/mobile development.

4   Conclusion and Future Work

This paper analyses how the user experience in spatial computing could be evaluated, based on three different example applications. It highlights a number of different aspects that need to be considered, but when placed in a broader context, it is apparent that these aspects can be grouped into five issues: space, place, activity, community and time, which are the categories of *situatedness*. It states that the human mind is influenced by its natural, social and cultural environment [9]. According to this theory, the actions of individuals should be interpreted in relation to their specific environmental and contextual factors [9].

To provide exceptional experiences, it is important to consider the various relevant aspects of a situation. However, it can be challenging to identify these aspects and appropriate evaluation methods. Consequently, the development teams look at current applications and common evaluation methods, thus they end up using traditional and simple methods [36]. However, it is evident that methods and considerations do exist, but they are not yet well-established and there is currently no coherent methodology that integrates all relevant aspects. This raises the question of how these considerations and methods can be established in the field to enhance spatial computing experiences.

Further research may develop a comprehensive model of influence in spatial computing which can be used to assist in the creation of applications. It should identify potential scenario-relevant issues that might otherwise be overlooked, and provide guidance on how to assess them by recommending appropriate tools.

References

1. Alexandrovsky, D., et al.: Evaluating user experiences in mixed reality. In: Extended Abstracts of the 2021 CHI Conference on Human Factors in Computing Systems, pp. 1–5 (2021)
2. Aromaa, S., Väätänen, A., Aaltonen, I., Goriachev, V., Helin, K., Karjalainen, J.: Awareness of the real-world environment when using augmented reality head-mounted display. Appl. Ergon. **88**, 103145 (2020)
3. Aromaa, S., Väätänen, A., Kaasinen, E., Uimonen, M., Siltanen, S.: Human factors and ergonomics evaluation of a tablet based augmented reality system in maintenance work. In: Proceedings of the 22nd International Academic Mindtrek Conference, pp. 118–125 (2018)
4. i art: The magic of interactive books. https://iart.ch/en/next/interaktive-buecher
5. Besançon, L., Ynnerman, A., Keefe, D.F., Yu, L., Isenberg, T.: The state of the art of spatial interfaces for 3d visualization. Comput. Graph. Forum **40**(1), 293–326 (2021)
6. Boletsis, C.: The Gaia system: a tabletop projection mapping system for raising environmental awareness in islands and coastal areas. In: Proceedings of the 15th International Conference on PErvasive Technologies Related to Assistive Environments, pp. 50–54 (2022)
7. Börsting, I., Heikamp, M., Hesenius, M., Koop, W., Gruhn, V.: Software engineering for augmented reality-a research agenda. Proc. ACM Human-Comput. Interact. **6**(EICS), 1–34 (2022)
8. Bressa, N., Korsgaard, H., Tabard, A., Houben, S., Vermeulen, J.: What's the situation with situated visualization? A survey and perspectives on situatedness. IEEE Trans. Visual Comput. Graphics **28**(1), 107–117 (2021)
9. Costello, M.: Situatedness, pp. 1757–1762. Springer New York, New York, NY (2014)
10. Delmerico, J., et al.: Spatial computing and intuitive interaction: bringing mixed reality and robotics together. IEEE Robot. Autom. Mag. **29**(1), 45–57 (2022)
11. Escalas, J.E., Stern, B.B.: Sympathy and empathy: emotional responses to advertising dramas. J. Consum. Res. **29**(4), 566–578 (2003)

12. Fiore, S.M., Schooler, J.W.: How did you get here from there? verbal overshadowing of spatial mental models. Appl. Cogn. Psychol. **16**(8), 897–910 (2002)
13. Fischer, P.T., Hornecker, E.: Urban HCI: spatial aspects in the design of shared encounters for media facades. In: Proceedings of the SIGCHI Conference on Human Factors in Computing Systems, pp. 307–316 (2012)
14. Georgiou, Y., Kyza, E.A.: The development and validation of the ARI questionnaire: an instrument for measuring immersion in location-based augmented reality settings. Int. J. Hum Comput Stud. **98**, 24–37 (2017)
15. Grandi, J.G., Debarba, H.G., Nedel, L., Maciel, A.: Design and evaluation of a handheld-based 3d user interface for collaborative object manipulation. In: Proceedings of the 2017 CHI Conference on Human Factors in Computing Systems, pp. 5881–5891 (2017)
16. Guarese, R., Pretty, E., Fayek, H., Zambetta, F., van Schyndel, R.: Evoking empathy with visually impaired people through an augmented reality embodiment experience. In: 2023 IEEE Conference Virtual Reality and 3D User Interfaces (VR), pp. 184–193 (2023)
17. Hanisch, K.A., Kramer, A.F., Hulin, C.L., Schumacher, R.: Novice-expert differences in the cognitive representation of system features: mental models and verbalizable knowledge. Proc. Human Factors Soc. Ann. Meet. **32**(4), 219–223 (1988)
18. Harms, C., Biocca, F.: Internal consistency and reliability of the networked minds measure of social presence. In: Seventh Annual International Workshop: Presence 2004 (2004)
19. Häubl, G., Trifts, V.: Consumer decision making in online shopping environments: the effects of interactive decision aids. Mark. Sci. **19**(1), 4–21 (2000)
20. Heer, J., Agrawala, M.: Design considerations for collaborative visual analytics. In: 2007 IEEE Symposium on Visual Analytics Science and Technology, pp. 171–178 (2007)
21. Heller, J., Chylinski, M., de Ruyter, K., Mahr, D., Keeling, D.I.: Let me imagine that for you: transforming the retail frontline through augmenting customer mental imagery ability. J. Retail. **95**(2), 94–114 (2019)
22. Hilken, T., Keeling, D.I., de Ruyter, K., Mahr, D., Chylinski, M.: Seeing eye to eye: social augmented reality and shared decision making in the marketplace. J. Acad. Mark. Sci. **48**, 143–164 (2020)
23. Hong, S., Jo, Y., Kang, Y., Lee, H.K.: Interactive experiential model: Insights from shadowing students' exhibitory footprints. J. Mus. Educ. **48**(2), 92–108 (2023)
24. Jonassen, D., Cho, Y.H.: Externalizing mental models with mindtools. In: Understanding Models for Learning and Instruction, pp. 145–159 (2008)
25. Jung, S.: The message effect of augmented health messages on body. In: Virtual, Augmented and Mixed Reality: Applications in Health, Cultural Heritage, and Industry: 10th International Conference, VAMR 2018, Held as Part of HCI International 2018, Las Vegas, NV, USA, July 15-20, 2018, Proceedings, Part II, pp. 86–93 (2018)
26. Laugwitz, B., Held, T., Schrepp, M.: Construction and evaluation of a user experience questionnaire. In: HCI and Usability for Education and Work: 4th Symposium of the Workgroup Human-Computer Interaction and Usability Engineering of the Austrian Computer Society, USAB 2008, Graz, Austria, November 20-21, 2008. Proceedings, pp. 63–76 (2008)
27. Leppink, J., Paas, F., Van der Vleuten, C.P., Van Gog, T., Van Merriënboer, J.J.: Development of an instrument for measuring different types of cognitive load. Behav. Res. Methods **45**, 1058–1072 (2013)

28. Määttänen, P.: Semiotics of space: Peirce and lefebvre (2007)
29. Marques, B., Santos, B.S., Araújo, T., Martins, N.C., Alves, J.B., Dias, P.: Situated visualization in the decision process through augmented reality. In: 2019 23rd International Conference Information Visualisation (IV), pp. 13–18 (2019)
30. Martins, N.C., Marques, B., Alves, J., Araújo, T., Dias, P., Santos, B.S.: Augmented reality situated visualization in decision-making. Multimed. Tools App. **81**(11), 14749–14772 (2022)
31. McAtamney, L., Corlett, E.N.: Rula: a survey method for the investigation of work-related upper limb disorders. Appl. Ergon. **24**(2), 91–99 (1993)
32. Moncur, B., Galvez Trigo, M.J., Mortara, L.: Augmented reality to reduce cognitive load in operational decision-making. In: International Conference on Human-Computer Interaction, pp. 328–346 (2023)
33. Müller, T.: Challenges in representing information with augmented reality to support manual procedural tasks. AIMS Electron. Elect. Eng. **3**(1), 71–97 (2019)
34. Nofal, E., Stevens, R., Coomans, T., Moere, A.V.: Communicating the spatiotemporal transformation of architectural heritage via an in-situ projection mapping installation. Digital App. Archaeol. Cult. Herit. **11**, e00083 (2018)
35. Pezzullo, P.C.: Between crisis and care: projection mapping as creative climate advocacy. J. Environ. Med. **1**(1), 59–77 (2020)
36. Picardi, A.: User-centred evaluation methods for augmented and mixed reality. A working framework to inform and choose the best user evaluation methods based on multiple structured field surveys (2020)
37. Regenbrecht, H., Zwanenburg, S., Langlotz, T.: Pervasive augmented reality-technology and ethics. IEEE Pervas. Comput. **21**(3), 84–91 (2022)
38. Reski, N., Alissandrakis, A., Kerren, A.: User preferences of spatio-temporal referencing approaches for immersive 3d radar charts. arXiv preprint arXiv:2303.07899 (2023)
39. Román, A., Flumini, A., Lizano, P., Escobar, M., Santiago, J.: Reading direction causes spatial biases in mental model construction in language understanding. Sci. Rep. **5**(1), 18248 (2015)
40. Ryan, R.M., Mims, V., Koestner, R.: Relation of reward contingency and interpersonal context to intrinsic motivation: a review and test using cognitive evaluation theory. J. Pers. Soc. Psychol. **45**(4), 736 (1983)
41. Santos, M.E.C., Taketomi, T., Sandor, C., Polvi, J., Yamamoto, G., Kato, H.: A usability scale for handheld augmented reality. In: Proceedings of the 20th ACM Symposium on Virtual Reality Software and Technology, pp. 167–176 (2014)
42. Schubert, T., Friedmann, F., Regenbrecht, H.: The experience of presence: Factor analytic insights. Presence: Teleoper. Virtual Environ. **10**(3), 266–281 (2001)
43. Simmen, Y., Eggler, T., Legath, A., Agotai, D., Cords, H.: Non-overlayed guidance in augmented reality: User study in radio-pharmacy. In: Zaynidinov, H., Singh, M., Tiwary, U.S., Singh, D. (eds.) Intelligent Human Computer Interaction. IHCI 2022. LNCS, vol. 13741, pp. 516–526. Springer, Cham (2022). https://doi.org/10.1007/978-3-031-27199-1_52
44. Speicher, M., Rosenberg, C., Degraen, D., Daiber, F., Krúger, A.: Exploring visual guidance in 360-degree videos. In: Proceedings of the 2019 ACM International Conference on Interactive Experiences for TV and Online Video, pp. 1–12 (2019). https://doi.org/10.1145/3317697.3323350
45. Stefanidi, H., Leonidis, A., Korozi, M., Papagiannakis, G.: The Argus designer: Supporting experts while conducting user studies of AR/MR applications. In: 2022 IEEE International Symposium on Mixed and Augmented Reality Adjunct (ISMAR-Adjunct), pp. 885–890. IEEE (2022)

46. Stephanidis, C., et al.: Seven HCI grand challenges. Int. J. Human-Comput. Interact. **35**(14), 1229–1269 (2019)
47. Thüring, M., Mahlke, S.: Usability, aesthetics and emotions in human-technology interaction. Int. J. Psychol. **42**(4), 253–264 (2007)
48. Tone, D., Iwai, D., Hiura, S., Sato, K.: FibAR: embedding optical fibers in 3d printed objects for active markers in dynamic projection mapping. IEEE Trans. Visual Comput. Graphics **26**(5), 2030–2040 (2020)
49. Tran, T.T.M., Brown, S., Weidlich, O., Billinghurst, M., Parker, C.: Wearable augmented reality: research trends and future directions from three major venues, pp. 1–12 (2023). https://doi.org/10.1109/TVCG.2023.3320231, https://ieeexplore.ieee.org/document/10269051/
50. Tversky, B.: Cognitive maps, cognitive collages, and spatial mental models. In: Frank, A.U., Campari, I. (eds.) COSIT 1993. LNCS, vol. 716, pp. 14–24. Springer, Heidelberg (1993). https://doi.org/10.1007/3-540-57207-4_2
51. Vi, S., da Silva, T.S., Maurer, F.: User experience guidelines for designing HMD extended reality applications. In: Lamas, D., Loizides, F., Nacke, L., Petrie, H., Winckler, M., Zaphiris, P. (eds.) INTERACT 2019. LNCS, vol. 11749, pp. 319–341. Springer, Cham (2019). https://doi.org/10.1007/978-3-030-29390-1_18
52. Wickens, C.D., Alexander, A.L.: Attentional tunneling and task management in synthetic vision displays. Int. J. Aviat. Psychol. **19**(2), 182–199 (2009)
53. Wouters, N., et al.: Uncovering the honeypot effect: how audiences engage with public interactive systems. In: Proceedings of the 2016 ACM Conference on Designing Interactive Systems, pp. 5–16 (2016)

Exploring the Impact of Virtual Reality on Viewer Experience: A Cognitive and Emotional Response Analysis

Soo-Min Seo[✉] and Ju Young Lim

The Graduate School of Metaverse, Sogang University, Seoul, South Korea
metaversimone@gmail.com

Abstract. The film industry has a history of embracing innovative technologies like 3D and 4D to enhance audience engagement (Slater & Sanchez-Vives, 2016). Today, with the rise of the metaverse, Virtual Reality (VR) is revolutionizing the film experience. This paper focuses on VR movies, which utilize head-mounted devices like VR headsets to immerse users in virtual environments, transcending traditional cinematic boundaries. By integrating embodiment theory, it explores how VR movies offer a unique blend of narrative absorption and interactivity, revolutionizing storytelling and audience engagement. This study aims to understand how VR technology is transforming the film industry and shaping the future of cinematic experiences.

Keywords: Metaverse · Virtual Reality · Virtual reality films · Virtual reality movies · HMD movies · Metaverse Films

1 Introduction

Virtual Reality (VR) films represent a groundbreaking shift in cinematic experiences, drawing on cognitive response and embodiment theories to immerse viewers in unparalleled ways. Cognitive response theory suggests that viewers actively construct meaning from content, intensified in VR films due to their immersive nature. Embodiment theory emphasizes the sense of physical presence and agency within the virtual environment. This paper explores how these theories manifest in VR movies, analyzing features like field of view and social interaction, which deepen viewer engagement. By unraveling these complexities, we aim to understand how VR films redefine cinematic experience, offering a more profound and emotionally resonant engagement with audiences, thereby revolutionizing storytelling in the film industry.

1.1 Immersive Storytelling by Technology

Technological advancements in film, from basic cameras to immersive 4D experiences, have revolutionized storytelling by expanding the ways stories are told and experienced. The film industry's continual embrace of new technologies demonstrates its dedication

C. Stephanidis et al. (Eds.): HCII 2024, CCIS 2116, pp. 114–118, 2024.
https://doi.org/10.1007/978-3-031-61950-2_13

to delivering sophisticated and engaging cinematic experiences globally. These advancements push the boundaries of visual and sensory stimulation, captivating audiences and fostering deeper emotional connections with the narrative.

Latest Technological Advancements in Movies.   The journey of cinematic evolution is marked by the adoption of groundbreaking technologies that have redefined the art of storytelling. In this era, two technologies stand out for their transformative impact: Virtual Reality (VR) and Artificial Intelligence (AI).

Virtual Reality (VR).   The advent of VR technology has ushered in a new paradigm in the movie-watching experience. By leveraging headsets and interactive interfaces, VR immerses viewers within a virtual world, transcending traditional passive viewing. This technology allows audiences to become active participants in the narrative, providing an opportunity to explore and interact with the story's elements in a fully immersive manner. VR's ability to create a sense of presence and agency takes cinematic storytelling into uncharted territories, offering a uniquely personal and engaging experience.

The Interplay of Movies and Technology.   The evolution of movies is deeply intertwined with technological advancements. From the invention of the camera to the immersive capabilities of VR and the creative prowess of AI, these innovations have continuously transformed the way stories are told and experienced. The film industry's commitment to leveraging cutting-edge technology is pivotal in its growth and evolution. It enables filmmakers to not only captivate audiences with compelling narratives but also to explore new horizons of immersive and interactive storytelling. As technology continues to evolve, so too will the cinematic experiences, promising a future where movies are not just watched but lived.

Method.   This study conducts a comprehensive analysis of the unique elements of VR movies, with a focus on their impact on audience engagement and immersion. The research centers on VR films available on platforms like Steam VR Films, Meta Original Films, Google Original VR Films, and accessible VR films on YouTube. Through a methodical content analysis of 30 VR films, this study aims to provide insights that could inform the development of future VR films and enhance the viewer experience.

2 Sample Selection and Characteristics

Our analysis sampled 30 VR films based on their availability and popularity across various platforms. These films were selected for their diverse representation of the current VR film landscape and their accessibility to a broad audience. A significant observation is the genre distribution within these films. Most of the VR films in our sample fall into the animation or horror/thriller categories. This trend is not coincidental but reflects specific attributes of VR filmmaking:

Animation in VR: The prevalence of animated films in VR can be attributed to the relative ease of creating virtual worlds and characters in animation compared to live-action. Animation in VR allows for more control over the environment and a smoother integration of interactive elements, making it a popular choice for VR filmmakers.

Horror/Thriller Genres: The horror and thriller genres have found a natural fit in VR due to the medium's immersive nature. These genres effectively leverage VR's capabilities to create intense, engaging experiences. The immersive aspect of VR heightens the suspense and emotional impact of horror and thriller narratives, making them particularly compelling for VR audiences.

The length of the films in our sample varied considerably, ranging from brief experiences of 1 min to more extended narratives of up to 20 min. This variation in length reflects the filmmakers' intentions and the narrative requirements of each story. It also indicates the evolving nature of VR filmmaking, where the duration is adapted to suit the immersive qualities of the medium rather than conforming to traditional film lengths.

The selection of VR films for this analysis provides a window into the current state of VR cinema. By examining these films, we gain valuable insights into how specific genres and narrative lengths align with the unique capabilities of VR. This analysis not only sheds light on current trends but also offers guidance for future VR film projects, emphasizing the importance of genre selection and narrative duration in enhancing the immersive experience for viewers.

Table 1. List of the VR films available.

	Subject	FOV	Bodily movement	Direct Eye contact	Direct Calling	Body part visuability	Out Of Field characters
1	We live here	360	10	0	0	1	0
2	THE INVISIBLE MAN	360	10	1	1	0	1
3	INVASIONE	360	10	1	1	1	1
4	Avatar 2	360	10	1	1	1	1
5	Tom and Jerry Are Friends	360	10	1	0	1	1
6	THE MISSING FIVE	180	0	1	0	1	1
7	Glace à l'eau	180	0	1	0	0	1
8	But my Grandad Still Sees Gentian	180	0	0	0	0	0
9	Out of the Cave Part 2	180	0	0	0	0	0
10	Henry	360	3	1	0	0	0
11	Moss	180	0	1	1	0	0
12	Dunkerque - 360°	360	7	0	0	0	1
13	The Martian Trailer	180	0	0	1	1	1
14	IT: FLOAT	360	3	0	1	0	1
15	The Hunger Games	360	3	0	1	0	1
16	Vader Immortal: A Star Wars VR Series	180	0	1	1	1	0
17	Father is gone	360	7	1	0	0	1
18	The monkey wrench gang	360	7	1	0	1	1
19	Oh DeBu	360	3	1	0	0	1
20	The seven story building	360	3	1	1	0	1
21	Pearl	360	7	0	0	1	1
22	Back to the Moon	360	10	1	0	0	1
23	Buggy Night	360	10	0	0	0	1
24	Son of Jaguar	360	10	1	0	0	1
25	Rain or Shine	360	10	1	0	0	1
26	Dear Angelica	360	7	0	0	0	1
27	Always	360	10	0	1	0	1
28	Blade Runner 2049: Memory Lab	180	0	1	1	1	0
29	I PHILIP	360	3	1	1	0	1
30	Wolves In the Walls	360	10	1	1	1	1

3   Related Works

Recent advancements in immersive film formats, including Augmented Reality (AR), Virtual Reality (VR), and Extended Reality (XR), challenge traditional cinematic concepts like Point Of View (POV). While POV, film speed, and camera angles remain relevant, VR films introduce new dimensions critical for immersion, moving beyond traditional techniques (Kang, 2020). Unlike conventional movies and games, VR films demand a first-person perspective to immerse viewers fully (Chen et al., 2020). This study expands on these elements, focusing on the Field of View (FOV), direct eye contact with characters, interaction with the viewer, visible body parts of the viewer's avatar, and the significance of out-of-view characters or events.

In traditional cinema, the audience is presented with a flat, front-facing 180-degree FOV. VR films, however, provide a spherical 360-degree FOV, requiring viewers to turn their heads or bodies for full engagement, particularly in genres like horror where unpredictability enhances immersion. The story unfolds mainly in the front view, but VR films use the entire 360-degree space, compelling physical interaction and differentiation from traditional media.

Interaction with out-of-view characters introduces a dynamic element to character interaction. Viewers are aware of characters out of view, heightening presence and realism. Out-of-view characters engage the audience's attention and encourage physical movement, fostering stronger emotional responses compared to virtual objects or environments. This study explores how VR movies utilize out-of-view characters to enhance audience engagement.

Breaking the fourth wall in VR involves direct eye contact and addressing the audience directly, creating profound connection and immersion. When characters make eye contact or speak to the viewer, it engulfs them into the narrative, dissolving traditional boundaries and fostering a sense of presence and telepresence. This technique transforms storytelling and audience engagement in VR films, offering a more intimate and engaging experience than traditional formats.

Direct interaction in VR films, such as direct eye contact and calling out to the audience, enhances intimacy and involvement. This dynamic element alters the viewer's role from passive observer to active participant, elevating the VR film experience. Breaking down conventional barriers, VR films offer a more immersive, intimate, and interactive narrative experience, redefining storytelling in cinema.

Embodiment in VR films enhances immersion by depicting the viewer's body within the virtual environment, creating a profound sense of presence. Seeing their virtual limbs respond to movements blurs the line between physical reality and the film world, making the experience more visceral and impactful. This heightened embodiment provides a deeper connection between the audience and characters, offering a unique means of experiencing narrative and setting a new standard for immersive cinema.

This study explores the portrayal of characters in VR films who directly address the audience, enhancing engagement with fiction. It discusses the implications of direct address within film theory and investigates the concept of trans-diegetic music and its impact on narrative functions. By examining these elements, the study aims to understand how VR films redefine storytelling and audience engagement, paving the way for new possibilities in cinematic experiences.

Acknowledgement. This research was supported by the MSIT (Ministry of Science and ICT), Korea, under the graduate school of Metaverse Convergence support program (IITP_2023-RS-2022- 00156318) Supervised by the ITTP (Insitute for Information & Communication Technology Planning and Evaluation).

References

1. Chen, H.-L., Lin, T.-J., Wu, H.-C.: An immersive storytelling approach for virtual reality movies: a case study of 3D audio design. J. Inf. Display **21**(3), 115–122 (2020)
2. Cuddon, J.A.: A Dictionary of Literary Terms and Literary Theory. John Wiley & Sons, New York (2012)
3. Hochberg, J., & Brooks, J. (2016). Movies in the age of media convergence. ABC-CLIO
4. Kang, S.H.: Effects of virtual reality experience in movie theaters on the decision-making process of moviegoers. J. Hosp. Leis. Sport Tour. Educ. **27**, 100242 (2020)
5. Liu, J., Yang, F.: A study on the evolution of virtual reality film art. J. Phys: Conf. Ser. **1777**(1), 012052 (2021)
6. Llorens, A., Borrego, A., Llorente, S.: A critical review of immersive virtual reality technologies: applications in storytelling. Int. J. Interact. Multimed. Artif. Intell. **5**(7), 18–24 (2019)
7. Makransky, G., Lilleholt, L., Aaby, A.: Development and validation of the multimodal presence scale for virtual reality environments: a confirmatory factor analysis and item response theory approach. Comput. Hum. Behav. **64**, 682–691 (2016)
8. Makransky, G., Lilleholt, L., Aaby, A.: Development and validation of the VR-Cope: a virtual reality - cognitive behavioral therapy for coping with social anxiety. Br. J. Psychiat. Open **2**(6), 318–325 (2016)
9. Makransky, G., Lilleholt, L., Aaby, A.: The effect of using virtual reality head-mounted displays in class on science teaching and learning. J. Educ. Psychol. **108**(3), 369–374 (2016)
10. McAllister, G., Bregman, J., Garry, M., Gholson, B.: Reliable content analysis without human coders. J. Broadcast. Electron. Media **37**(2), 195–202 (1993)
11. McAllister, H.A., West, S.G., Bootzin, R.R.: The reliability and validity of content analyses of ratings data: a meta-analysis. J. Appl. Psychol. **78**(4), 587–603 (1993)
12. Pimentel, J.S., Vinkers, C.H.: Virtual characters and emotions: effects of the identity of the avatar and the emotional content of the environment on affective responses in virtual reality. J. Affect. Disord. **282**, 258–267 (2021)
13. Schoeller, F., Hunziker, S., Gut, U., Landau, A., Mast, F.W., Bente, G.: Social presence in virtual reality: towards understanding differentiation in empathy and social influence. Front. Robot. AI **7**, 40 (2020)
14. Slater, M., Sanchez-Vives, M.V.: Enhancing our lives with immersive virtual reality. Front. Robot. AI **3**(74), 1–6 (2016)
15. Warhol, A.: Break a Leg, Darlings': Feminist theatre and its effects on the audience. Perform. Arts J.**1**(1), 45–50 (1975)

Research on Interactive Design of AR Books

Juanjuan Shi$^{(\boxtimes)}$, KaiXiang Wang$^{(\boxtimes)}$, and Jie Hao

Beijing Institute of Fashion Technology, Beijing 100029, China
sjjzgy@126.com, wkx05@163.com

Abstract. AR technology has been widely used in AR books, bringing readers an unprecedented reading experience by embedding virtual elements into the real environment. In the design of AR books, interactive design is a crucial factor. Based on the analysis of the interactive design principle of AR books, this paper carries out the application research on the interactive design of AR books "Lost Time". In the process of design and research practice, "empathy" is constantly used to simulate the user's experience and feelings, and the interactive design of this series of books is mainly studied from the aspects of emotion, narrative, and functionality. The interactive design of AR books is proposed from the perspective of emotion, narrative, and functionality, so that users can naturally interact with AR books functionally, provide users with pleasant communication methods close to human and physical world, and make the interactive experience between users and AR books natural and efficient.

Keywords: Augmented reality · Interactivity · AR books

1 Introduction

In recent years, augmented reality technology has developed rapidly and widely used in many industries, such as education, military, industry, medical treatment, and publishing. Although the reading experience of traditional paper books is one-way, static, flat, and linear, it has the characteristics of slow reading, deep reading, and high user recognition. AR (Augmented reality) technology skillfully integrates virtual information after simulation with the real world, and the two kinds of information complement each other to realize the "enhancement" of the real world. It has three characteristics: virtual-real combination, real-time interaction, and three-dimensional registration [1]. The combination of augmented reality technology and paper books can not only retain the habit of slow reading and deep reading but also allow users to enjoy the beautiful text and the pleasing narrative and presentation mode of paper books, also allow users to experience the dynamic sense, fun, immersion, and interactive experience brought by augmented reality technology. Effectively change the flat, one-way, and static reading experience of paper books, realize the real interaction between users and books, perceive the interest, and enhance the exploration of book knowledge and the extension of book content. At present, in the field of publishing, many books such as popular science books, children's books, medical, physics and other professional books have been combined with augmented reality technology to enhance the interactive reading experience of users. AR books are composed of virtual and real space, and users need to face the dual information of real books and virtual space. How to effectively design the interaction of AR books and let users interact with AR books naturally is a crucial factor in AR books design and is also the focus of this paper.

2   The Interactivity of AR Books

Augmented reality books are based on traditional paper books, taking the current book pages or the reader's reading environment as the real environment, superimposing, and displaying the produced virtual digital objects (images, videos, audio, three-dimensional models, three-dimensional animations, etc.). They can interact in real-time, to enhance the reader's perception and understanding of the reading content. [2] Interaction design is "human-centered", focusing on connecting the digital virtual world with the human objective world. With the development of VR and AR technology, AR interaction design needs to let users naturally and efficiently integrate into the AR environment, and natural and efficient interaction is the goal and development trend of AR interaction design.

Fig. 1. AR interactive picture book "Science Runs Out Series Dinosaurs Run Out"

Interactive design of AR books refers to from the perspective of users, based on research and analysis of target users, determine the specific needs of target users, clarify the psychological and behavioral characteristics of users when interacting with AR books, take books as the carrier, based on user psychology and cognitive theory, and use AR technology to study the ways of interaction between users and AR books. Let users immerse in it, so that the interactive experience of books is stronger, knowledge memory is more profound, more intuitive, and easier to understand, and provide users with a natural and pleasant interactive reading experience. As shown in Fig. 1, the AR interactive popular science book "Science Comes Out Series Dinosaurs Come Out" written by Claire Smith in the UK studies the psychological and cognitive characteristics of children users. Children have strong curiosity and pay attention to visual impact and perceptual interactive experience. Because of this, the 3D reality AR interactive book is developed. Children use the mobile phone camera to interact with the book, jump on the paper book and appear a virtual dinosaur, which can be interactively controlled by touching the finger. The dinosaur leaves the book step by step and steps on the floor tile of the objective world, and the floor tile cracks along with the footsteps of the dinosaur in the mobile phone lens, realizing the interaction effect of the virtual and real combination. It gives users a magical and shocking reading experience, improves users 'interest in reading dinosaur related knowledge, and lets children users learn happily in a natural interactive experience, to grasp the relevant science knowledge better.

3 Interactive Design Principle of AR Books

3.1 The Importance of Interactive Design

In the design of AR books, interactive design is a crucial factor. Interactive design can provide a platform to interact with readers, so that readers can be more deeply involved in the book's content, and it provides readers with a richer reading experience.

Interactive design is important in AR books because it captures the reader's attention and increases their interest. In traditional book reading, readers are usually passive receivers of information. Through interactive design, readers can actively participate in the book's content, interact with the book by operating the book interface, touching, rotating, or clicking AR elements, etc., thus making the book more attractive and participatory. Interactive design can make the book's content easier to understand and digest and give readers with a richer and more personalized reading experience.

3.2 The Basic Principles of Interactive Design for AR Books

The interactive design of AR books is the product of the combination of augmented reality technology and book reading, aiming to provide a richer and more diversified reading experience. When designing interactive AR books, some basic principles need to be followed.

First, the interactive design of AR books should pay attention to user experience. User experience is a core goal of design, and designers need to consider users' needs and expectations, as well as how they interact with AR books. Designers should simplify the interface operations as much as possible, provide an intuitive, easy-to-understand user interface, and focus on the seamless connection of book content and interaction.

Secondly, the interactive design of AR books should make full use of the characteristics of augmented reality technology. Augmented reality technology can provide a more direct, immersive experience and designers can combine virtual content with physical books through AR technology to create a richer and more diverse way to read. For example, dynamic effects and interactive elements can be added to the book content through AR technology, enabling readers to interact with the book content in real time.

In addition, the interactive design of AR books should complement the book content. Designers need to have a deep understanding of the theme and content of the book and integrate interactive elements with the book's content to make it more organically integrated into the reading experience. Designers can design corresponding AR inter-action functions according to different book contents, such as displaying dioramas in books through AR technology, interacting with readers, or providing virtual experiences related to book themes.

Finally, the interactive design of AR books should continue to innovate and improve. As technology evolves, new AR interaction methods and features continue to emerge. Designers should pay close attention to the latest technological developments and con-stantly explore and apply new interaction design principles and techniques to enhance the reading experience and attractiveness of AR books.

4 Research on Interactive Design Application of AR Books "Lost Time"

Based on the above interactive design principles of AR books, research on the application of interactive design of AR books "Lost Time" is carried out. In design and research practice, "empathy" is constantly used to simulate users' experiences and feelings, and users can naturally interact with AR books functionally from the perspective of emotion and narrative.

4.1 The Design Concept of "Lost Time"

"Lost Time" is a series of idiom picture books based on AR technology for children, including three-story picture books and the AR interaction design of an APP. The overall design is shown in Fig. 2. After investigation and user demand analysis, the story content of the picture book is positioned in the type of adventure, taking the zodiac as the entry point to accompany the protagonist Xiaoyu's adventure and bring users into the idiom learning. The Land of Time is thrown into chaos because Xiaoyu wastes time. Which has lost important hour hands, minute hands and second hands, and it is necessary to help the residents of the land of Time to recover these hands, so that the land of time can return to normal, to achieve the purpose of cultivating children's sense of time. Using a storyline that moves from real life to a fantasy world and back again to give users a sense of immersion, Xiaoyu experiences adventures in three different scenarios, each of which encounters different characters of the four zodiac signs. The three AR picture books under the main story line are cleverly combined with the learning content of 35 idioms such as "ear life", "suddenly enlightened" and "at a loss". The idiom content of the first book is mainly toward emotional expression, the idiom content of the second book is the description of seasons and scenery, and the third is the idiom content of interpersonal communication. By embedding idioms into the story content of picture books, the author pays attention to the educational significance of the whole storyline and skillfully combines it with idiom learning. Many hidden education parts are added to the design of picture books so that children can constantly discover "little accidents" in reading, increase their reading interest, increase user stickiness, open a variety of interac-tive ways, achieve the purpose of cultivating children's physical and mental intelligence, and easily master and use idioms in the process of reading interesting stories. Combined with AR technology, AR interactive animation of idiom allusion analysis is introduced when idioms have allusion analysis, AR interactive dynamic game picture is introduced when the paper static picture is difficult to explain the connotation of idioms, and AR interactive three-dimensional game characters are introduced in character design, which integrates story picture books, situational education, idiom learning and AR interaction. The interactive experience between paper culture and virtual world can be realized, so that children can feel tangible and perceptible cognitive embodiment, experience the connotation of idiom culture in an interesting way, and stimulate children's interest in independent learning [3].

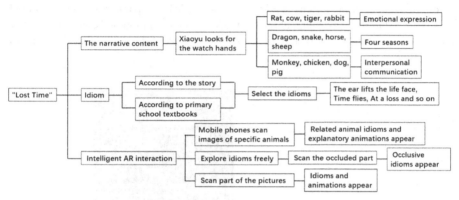

Fig. 2. The overall design of "Lost Time"

4.2   The AR Interactive Design of "Lost Time"

Interactive Design of AR Books Based on Emotion. Emotional design is a design method that takes the poten-tial emotional needs as the main design principle in the design process [4]. Human beings have the richest emotions, for book users, the correct AR interaction is not only the physical level of interaction, but also the emotional resonance and commu-nication at the ideological level. Integrate user emotions and experiences into AR book interaction design to create a more interesting and inspiring reading experience. The "Lost Time" series of books adopt bright and bright colors, and the character modeling reflects the modern sense and fashion sense, and the overall design of the scene adopts the fantasy style, unique composition, and magical color matching, which can accurately convey the meaning of the imagination and creativity while showing the imagination and creativity, and visually stimulate the emotional reso-nance of users.

A good storyline and theme are crucial elements in AR books' interaction design. According to the story plot and the theme of time, AR elements of corresponding idioms are formulated to increase readers' deep emotional resonance and make them feel a more profound and vivid reading experience. The main character of the picture book is Xiaoyu, a child with extreme "procrastination" who always likes to put things off until later. Once by chance, she enters a wonderful world, the "Land of Time", and finds it desolate and lifeless. After hearing the guardian mouse of the "Land of Time" say that the clock of life, which guards the balance of the "Land of Time", has been lost. As a result, the "Land of Time" which was originally full of vitality appeared in chaos and became so desolate. So Xiaoyu followed the mouse on the road to find the lost hour hand. In the process of searching, Xiaoyu experienced many interesting adventures, met many lovely friends, and gradually realized that the loss of the clock of life in the "Land of Time" guarded by the zodiac is inextricably linked to his serious "procrastination", and understood the importance of cherishing time. As shown in Fig. 3, Xiaoyu unexpectedly came to the "Land of Time" because of the delay, and everything around her made her feel strange and afraid. Combined with AR technology, the picture moves to an interactive display of the digital content of the idiom "at a loss", showing Xiaoyu's panic and confused mood toward the unfamiliar environment so that readers can have emotional connection while understanding the meaning of the idiom, and be conveyed the theme that they should cherish time.

Fig. 3. Scene design

Interactive Design of AR Books Based on Narrative.   The information added by AR technology can't be included in the central axis of the story or can't strengthen the theme of expression, and the information will be a mutual loss or overflow, and the result can only destroy the integrity of the work and affect the effect of reading. [5] Narration-based AR book interaction design requires comprehensive use of various technologies and methods to integrate the information added through AR technology with the central axis or theme of the story.

Designers should use a variety of elements and technologies to present diverse and information-dense content to users. AR books involve different interaction methods such as vision, sound, and touch, so integrating diverse AR elements can provide a richer, real, and sensory shock reading experience, and the connection between readers and virtual content can be enhanced by adding 3D models. The 3D model combined with the paper narrative content gives full play to the multidimensional characteristics and dynamic advantages of AR three-dimensional space narrative, and better explains and explains the characteristics of objects based on the original text narrative, to realize the complementary benefits of AR three-dimensional space narrative and paper narrative.

[6] As shown in Fig. 4, to reflect the "rich in learning" of the ox, the zodiac ox image is designed to wear a doctoral cap and glasses, reflecting the image of the scholar, making the image of Dr. Ox more vivid, guiding readers to find the "hidden content" quickly, and combining AR technology with the three-dimensional image of Dr. Ox, vividly explaining the meaning of "rich in learning and five cars" to the user, and metaphorically representing the theme of cherishing time. The use of 3D characters, video, audio, and other diversified and comfortable AR elements overlay to bring users a richer reading experience, further improve the readability of books, and enhance the immersive experience.

Fig. 4. "Learning rich five cars" zodiac ox

Interactive Design of AR Books Based on Functionality.   In the interactive design of functional AR books, we must determine the interaction scene and choose the appropriate functional interaction mode and display means according to the scene's characteristics. This series of picture books mainly focuses on experiencing the function of "finding idioms" according to the theme scene and designing corresponding interactive ways. The interactive design of "finding idioms" in the text part. A special graph is designed to cover up the idioms in the text content of the picture book. Users can first guess the corresponding idioms by understanding the story scene (annotate the beginning of the picture book, indicating the hidden AR idiom interaction in the masked part). Further, after scanning the corresponding graphics with mobile phones, idioms and related explanations of the idioms will appear in the masked text part. The interactive design of "finding idioms" in the hidden content. In the picture book, some idioms of related animals are arranged for the zodiac characters and corresponding digital interaction is designed, at the same time the mobile phone is set as a magnifying glass, and children can use the mobile phone to find out which animals have idioms hidden on the screen, as shown in Fig. 5. This process of "finding idioms" provides readers with a rich, novel, and functional experience with practical value, completely breaks the limitations of traditional paper books, and creates a new reading experience with surreal nature for users. Through the combination of digital information and the real world, readers can expand their horizons.

Fig. 5. AR interaction design for hidden idioms of animal characters

5 Conclusion

AR books are the product of integrating traditional books and AR technology. Their advantage is that they can integrate virtual information and real scenes to provide a more vivid reading experience. The purpose of this paper is to explore the interactive design of AR books to meet the individual needs of users and improve the reading experience of users. Based on the analysis of the interactive design principle of AR books, the application research of the interactive design of AR books "Lost Time" is carried out. In the process of design and research practice, "empathy" is constantly used to simulate the user's experience and feelings, and the interactive design of this series of books is mainly studied from the aspects of emotion, narrative, and functionality. The interactive design of AR books based on emotion needs to integrate the user's emotions and experience into the interactive design of AR books to create a more interesting and inspiring reading experience. The interactive design of AR books based on narrative requires the comprehensive use of various technologies and methods to integrate the information added through AR technology with the central axis or theme of the story. In the interactive design of AR books based on functionality, the interaction scene must be determined, and the appropriate functional interaction and display means must be selected according to the scene's characteristics. The interactive design of AR books needs to pay attention to user experience, make full use of the attributes of augmented reality technology, complement each other with the book content, and continue to innovate and improve. This research allows users to interact with AR books naturally and functionally from the emotional and narrative aspects, provides users with pleasant communication methods close to human beings and the physical world, makes the interactive experience between users and AR books natural and efficient, and makes users feel the benefits brought by interaction in the reading experience.

Acknowledgments. This study was funded by the project "Practice Teaching and Innovation of Redesigning Traditional Culture under New Media Environment" (Project No: JG-2215).

References

1. Azuma, R.T.: A survey of augmented reality. Presence Teleoper. Virtual Environ. **6**(4), 355–385 (1997)
2. Hui, W., Jincheng, L.: Application research of augmented reality technology in the field of book publishing. China Publ. **38**(17), 38–40 (2015)
3. Yikai, Z.: Application and optimization of AR books in the era of digital publishing. Publ. Wide Angle **09**, 58–60 (2021)
4. Ni, Y.: School of Industrial Design and Engineering, Delft University of Technology. Design Methods and Strategies: The Delft Design Guide. Huazhong University of Science and Technology Press, Wuhan, 1 August 2014
5. Min, S.: Situational interaction: the core of AR children's book design. China Publ. **04**, 47–51 (2019)
6. Yanxiang, Z., Weiwei, Z.: Research on narrative design of augmented reality publications. Sci. Technol. **06**, 134–139 (2018)

Research on Human-Computer Re-Interaction in AR Books

KaiXiang Wang, Juanjuan Shi$^{(\boxtimes)}$, and Chunpeng Wang

Beijing Institute of Fashion Technology, Beijing 100029, China
sjjzgy@126.com

Abstract. With the advancement of technology, the application of Augmented Reality (AR) technology in the field of books is becoming increasingly widespread. The common application of this technology involves presenting different virtual elements by combining them with the real environment. Aimed at enhancing the fun and richness of the reading experience, this paper explores the enrichment of human-computer interaction design through the recognition of reader actions using a camera after the presentation of virtual elements. For action recognition, the color differences in the image are compared, noise and irrelevant information are removed, and the color coding of the effective information area is converted into a binary graphic form, displayed as "bright" (assigned "1") in the constructed matrix; while the ineffective area is displayed as "dark" (assigned "0"). When actions change, the areas of "1" and "0" in the matrix also adjust accordingly, thus achieving real-time recognition of dynamic actions. Based on this process, human-computer interaction design captures reader actions through the camera and triggers responses related to the invoked virtual elements. This not only provides readers with a more immersive reading experience but also enhances the richness of the displayed virtual reality content. Additionally, it offers new perspectives for interactive book design. The focus of this paper is on exploring the potential application of action recognition technology in interactive design methods within AR books.

Keywords: Human-Computer Re-Interaction · Skin color detection · Building a Matrix

1 Introduction

With the maturity and widespread adoption of Augmented Reality (AR) technology, its application in the field of book reading has gradually become a research hotspot. In comparison to the singular, static, and linear reading approach of traditional books, AR technology introduces a dynamic, interactive, and non-linear reading experience. This transformation not only challenges traditional reading methods but also offers a new perspective for real-time, interactive content display, showcasing tremendous developmental potential. On the design level, the theory of "Developmentally Situated Design" proposed by scholars [1] provides guidance and suggestions for various aspects of reading behavior, including body, recognition, emotion, and social aspects. Building upon this foundation, AR books exhibit several notable characteristics over time.

© The Author(s), under exclusive license to Springer Nature Switzerland AG 2024
C. Stephanidis et al. (Eds.): HCII 2024, CCIS 2116, pp. 128–136, 2024.
https://doi.org/10.1007/978-3-031-61950-2_15

Firstly, they can provide specific content that aligns with particular times and locations, allowing readers to access information matching their environment at any given moment. Secondly, AR books can guide reading interests and behavioral motivations, sparking readers' curiosity for exploration. Lastly, they emphasize the experiential enjoyment and diversity of reading, providing readers with an immersive reading experience. Currently, the design of AR books is mainly focused on the development of dynamically displayed content. However, the design of interactive methods remains in its early stages, primarily involving the presentation of virtual content combined with the real scene through scanning. After presenting virtual content, how to further achieve multiple interactions with AR books, thereby increasing the dimensions of reading in the post-presentation phase, remains a subject requiring in-depth exploration.

Therefore, this paper will primarily explore how to engage in multiple interactions with the virtual content of AR, aiming to further enhance the dimensions of reading. Through a thorough analysis of the current application status and development trends of AR technology in the field of book reading, the intention is to provide valuable references and insights for future research and practice.

2 Interaction and Presentation Modes of AR Books

In traditional book reading, paper serves as the primary medium of information, offering readers a static, two-dimensional reading experience. However, with the development of Augmented Reality (AR) technology, the interaction methods of books are undergoing profound changes. By integrating AR technology with traditional books, people can overlay and present pre-made virtual content in a real environment, providing readers with a more intuitive and multidimensional reading experience. The interaction design of AR books typically builds upon the content of traditional paper-based books. It involves scanning specific objects through a camera, thereby displaying various virtual elements such as images, audio, animations, and videos in the real environment. These diverse forms of content not only enhance the intuitiveness of book content but also offer readers a richer reading experience. Claire Spillane's work "Dinosaurs Run Out" (as shown in Fig. 1) serves as a typical example. In this book, readers can scan specific content to see corresponding virtual dinosaur animations on the screen. Simultaneously, these virtual elements are combined with the actual hand scenes captured by the camera, presenting readers with an augmented reality scene that merges the virtual and the real. This design makes the book content more vivid and three-dimensional, further boosting readers' interest and engagement. Through this approach, AR books provide readers with an entirely new reading experience, making book content more diverse and enjoyable. In the future, as technology continues to advance, AR books can further expand their interaction methods and content forms, delivering an even more immersive reading pleasure to readers.

Fig. 1. Dinosaurs Run Out

Currently, this interactive format often involves a process of "presenting after a one-time scan," and in terms of post-presentation re-interaction design, it typically only employs screen tapping. For example, as shown in Fig. 1, after scanning and presenting virtual content, the re-interaction involves guiding the dinosaur's movement through simple screen taps. While this approach produces decent results, it still appears somewhat monotonous in terms of interaction. A more enriched interactive experience can be achieved by utilizing the front camera, in addition to scanning and capturing real scenes with the main camera, to recognize reader's gesture actions. Combining the recognized gesture actions with virtual content is sure to generate a more diverse interactive experience. For instance, if the front camera captures and recognizes a "waving" motion (as shown in Fig. 2), it could make the virtual object turn in the direction of the reader's movement. Similarly, if the front camera captures a "hand with five extended fingers" gesture (as shown in Fig. 3), it could halt the movement of the virtual object towards the reader. Another example is when the front camera captures a "pointing with a single finger" gesture (as shown in Fig. 4), causing the virtual object to move in the direction pointed by the finger, and so forth. This represents a process of re-recognizing reader gestures through the front camera, where the recognized results can trigger a secondary response to the invoked virtual elements.

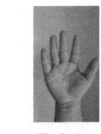

Fig. 2. Wave   **Fig. 3.** Stop   **Fig. 4.** Finger pointing

Understanding gestures for machine devices is challenging [2]. The key to achieving such relatively complex re-interaction processes lies in addressing the recognition issue of actions captured by the camera.

3 Gesture Recognition and Methods

In the AR interaction process, after scanning the book and presenting the corresponding visuals, it is imperative to further recognize gesture actions through the front camera of the terminal device. This is a crucial requirement for achieving a more enriched interactive experience with AR books. The gestures to be recognized can be broadly categorized into two types: finger gesture recognition and entire hand gesture recognition. Finger gesture recognition can be employed to control the forward or backward, left or right movement of virtual elements, or even the swaying motion of these elements. On the other hand, recognizing the overall hand gesture can be utilized to control fundamental movements such as rolling or pitching of virtual elements. Of course, gesture recognition can extend to control various aspects of virtual elements, including image elements, sound elements, 3D model elements, control of displaying spatial depth, and much more. It can even transform the presentation of the book into a gamified format or engage in more complex interactive processes. The design of these controlled elements needs to commence at the inception of creating virtual elements, integrating the entire process of gesture recognition with the creation of virtual display elements to achieve the desired outcome.

4 Skin Color Recognition and Binary Image Conversion

Gesture recognition can leverage human skin color [3] as a reference, comparing the captured image based on skin color. To achieve this, the image needs to be converted from the RGB mode to the YC_bC_r encoding mode [4]. This approach separates the luminance information from the chrominance information in a color image, thereby enhancing the efficiency and effectiveness of image processing. The encoding conversion formula is as follows:

$$Y = 0.299R + 0.587G + 0.114B \tag{1}$$

$$C_b = -0.169R - 0.331G + 0.5B + 128 \tag{2}$$

$$C_r = 0.5R - 0.419G - 0.081B + 128 \tag{3}$$

Among these, Y represents brightness, C_b represents chrominance blue-difference component, C_r represents chrominance red-interpolation component, while R, G, and B denote the red, green, and blue color components, respectively. Taking the skin color of the yellow race as an example, based on experimental statistics, the C_r component is approximately between 140 and 175, and the C_b component is roughly between 100 and

120. The image color content is then compared with the specified ranges, and according to Formula 4, the threshold is set according to the skin color range:

$$dst(x,y) = \begin{cases} 255(100 \leq Cb \leq 120, \quad 140 \leq Cr \leq 175) \\ 0 \text{ (non-skin color)} \end{cases} \tag{4}$$

In the above equation, dst constructs a target array, where x and y represent the indices of specific elements in the array. After the computer reads the image, the pixel values in the image are compared with the skin color range according to the formula. Pixels that meet the skin color conditions are set to 255 (white), and pixels that do not meet the conditions are set to 0 (black), thus generating a binary image corresponding to the original gesture. This achieves the goal of recognizing and extracting actions corresponding to the respective skin color parts, as shown in Figs. 5, 6, 7.

Fig. 5. Waving Binary Image   **Fig. 6.** Stop Binary Image   **Fig. 7.** Finger Binary Image

Hand Gesture Storage and Detection.

For gesture recognition, the identification of actions can be accomplished by constructing relevant matrices based on the size of the binary image. Following a specific scanning sequence to traverse each pixel in the binary image, the color matching of the image is used to eliminate noise and irrelevant information. Pixels with a value of 255, representing "bright" areas in the image, are assigned a value of "1" in the matrix, while ineffective areas are assigned a value of "0." When there is a change in hand gestures, the recognition of relevant information areas also changes simultaneously. Therefore, the values "1" and "0" in the matrix are constantly changing, completing the process of dynamic gesture recognition. The matrices corresponding to the binary images from the previous section are depicted in Figs. 8, 9, and 10. This completes the basic recognition of gestures, and it can also recognize actions involving limbs, facial expressions, etc., thereby achieving more sophisticated interactive designs.

5 Re-Interaction After Gesture Recognition

Building upon the foundation of gesture recognition discussed earlier, the common one-time virtual reality interaction processes in AR books can be further enriched. This enhancement aims to improve knowledge exploration and content expansion [5]. The solitary content presentation process may appear somewhat limited in terms of interactivity. By leveraging both the front and rear cameras of smart terminal devices and

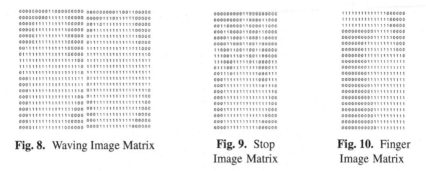

Fig. 8. Waving Image Matrix   **Fig. 9.** Stop Image Matrix   **Fig. 10.** Finger Image Matrix

incorporating the actions they capture into a second interaction, the initially mechanical content playback transforms into a purposeful and controlled presentation, resulting in a much more engaging experience.

5.1 Re-Interaction Based on the Motion of Virtual Elements

In the display of virtual elements in AR books, the movement of characters is a commonly used expressive form, such as walking, running, jumping, sitting, etc. When user actions are integrated, it enhances the controllability of characters, thereby elevating the richness and enjoyment of interaction. For example, when recognizing hand gestures through the front camera, if identified as a "waving" motion, the character turns to move in the direction facing the user, simultaneously controlling the perspective relationship of the receding background. When the gesture changes to "stop," the character halts in the current position. If the gesture shifts to a "finger-pointing" direction, the character turns in the direction of the finger and moves accordingly.

In this process, character control can be achieved through two commonly used methods. Firstly, creating videos for different movement modes, and during program invocation, loading different videos based on different gesture actions. The playback position of the video is then controlled according to the needs of action continuity. Secondly, treating the character as a separate control object for loading, adjusting its position, angle, magnification, and all other attributes through the program. The control flow is illustrated in Fig. 11.

5.2 Re-Interaction Based on Facial Expressions

User's facial expressions can also be utilized for redesigning the interaction between virtual elements in AR books. By capturing facial expressions, the behavior of virtual characters can be controlled, achieving synchronous or asynchronous interactive effects. Building on the skin color detection discussed earlier, the analysis of facial features such as lips and eyes involves monitoring color changes to accurately identify distinct facial expressions. The program can preset several common expression types, swiftly invoking corresponding virtual elements once recognition is complete. For example, when the user expresses a "smile," the virtual character will display a joyful expression (as shown

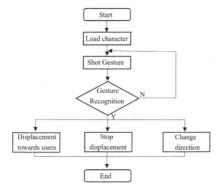

Fig. 11. "Action Control" Flowchart

in Fig. 12); when the user exhibits a "cry," the virtual character will portray an exaggerated weeping appearance. However, the requirements for facial interaction should be customized and refined based on the specific content of the AR book, recognizing that virtual expressions may not always align with real expressions. For instance, upon recognizing a "smile," the virtual character might present a celebratory "cheering" or "jumping" state; detecting a "rolling eyes" expression could prompt the virtual character to showcase a thoughtful "pondering" state; identifying a "cry" expression might lead the virtual character to adopt a comforting posture. The technical core lies in the precise recognition of collected facial expressions, enabling subsequent re-interaction design. This approach adds more fun and interactivity to AR books.

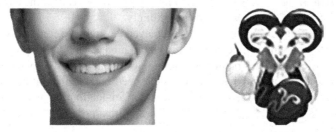

Fig. 12. Correspondence of facial expressions

5.3 User-Subjective Intervention Interaction Redesign Based on Color Recognition

When the user's body interacts with the virtual character, this interaction becomes a process of subjective intervention. Visual subjective intervention can provide users with a more immersive experience, significantly enhancing their sense of involvement. To achieve this subjective intervention in interaction design, the specific elements in the virtual content of AR books need to undergo a process of color recognition and comparison with elements captured by the camera. For instance, when the user's body part (using the hand as an example) enters the camera's capture range and aligns with the virtual character, determining the spatial relationship between the two becomes a crucial factor in deciding whether further interaction is possible.

For the virtual character, the coordinate position can determine its contour edges. However, the user's "hand" appearing within the camera range is not a pre-designed virtual element, making it impossible to directly obtain its coordinate position. Nevertheless, utilizing skin color recognition methods, once the color of the "hand" is identified, it becomes feasible to calculate the color's position information within the camera frame. Comparing this position with the virtual character's position can unlock additional interactive possibilities. When the two positions coincide (as shown in Fig. 13), the virtual character can be moved in the opposite direction to the hand. If the positions gradually move apart, within a certain distance threshold, the virtual character can be shifted towards the direction of the user's hand, once beyond this distance threshold, the virtual character ceases interaction with the user's hand and resumes its predetermined display. To further enhance interaction complexity and user experience, combining skin color recognition with motion detection technology allows the design of various interactive processes between the user and the virtual character, such as petting, repelling, pressing, and fighting. These interactive processes provide users with a richer experience, significantly boosting engagement and satisfaction in the augmented reality environment.

Fig. 13. Subjective intervention interaction

6 Conclusion

In summary, against the backdrop of rapid advances in computer technology, the application of AR technology in the field of books has brought about a revolutionary transformation in traditional reading. The field of books is undergoing a shift from traditional paper-based reading to digital reading, and augmented reality technology injects new vitality into this transformation. With the technical support of computer graphics, AR's content-based interactive design holds tremendous potential in enriching the ways books are read. Through the human-computer interaction process, it activates relevant visual elements of virtual reality, contributing to improved readability, interest, and comprehensibility of books. This not only enhances the reader's reading experience but also establishes a more intuitive and natural connection between the book's content and the reader, offering new directions and perspectives for the future development of books.

References

1. Bekker, M.M., Antle, A.: Developmentally situated design(DSD): making theoretical knowledge accessible to designers of children's technology. In: Proceedings of the 2011 Annual Conference on Human Factors in Computing Systems (2011)
2. Ying, C., Yong-biao, H., Jin, X.: Human-computer interaction gesture recognition model based on artificial intelligence. Comput. Simul. **38**(3), 360–364 (2021)
3. Wenbing, F.A.N., Lianjie, Z.H.U.: A gesture detection and recognition method based on skin color feature extraction. Mod. Electron. Technol. **40**(18), 85 (2017)
4. Microchip, G.: gm6010 /gm6015 Programming Guide. Genesis Microchip Company, California, US, 85p. (2002)
5. Juan-juan, S.H.I., Qian, N.I.E., Kai-xiang, W.A.N.G.: Interactive design of fashion idioms based on AR technology. Educ. Teach. Forum. **42**, 88–89 (2018)

A Comparative Analysis of Spectator Placement Methods in Virtual Reality Environments

Oliver Wang[1,2], Simon Smaczny[1], Gabriel Unmüßig[1],
and Florian van de Camp[1(✉)]

[1] Fraunhofer Institute of Optronics, System Technologies, and Image Exploitation
(IOSB), Karlsruhe, Germany
{simon.smaczny,gabriel.unmuessig,florian.vandecamp}@iosb.fraunhofer.de
[2] Berlin University of Applied Sciences and Technology (BHT), Berlin, Germany
s86824@bht-berlin.de

Abstract. Virtual reality (VR) is becoming increasingly popular, necessitating the development of methods to enhance the viewing experience in VR presentations. This paper compares three different spectator placement methods designed to optimize immersion and engagement in VR environments. The first method, Formations, uses predefined patterns such as circles or lines for positioning spectators. The second, Dynamic Positioning, involves automatic teleportation around a designated point with adjustments for visibility and spacing. The third method, Personal Perspective, allows spectators to share the navigator's exact position and view. These methods were assessed based on immersion, comfort, and overall experience through a combination of subjective questionnaires and objective tracking data analysis. The paper discusses the advantages and limitations of each method, providing valuable insights for VR content creators, designers, and developers to improve VR presentations. The results aim to guide the selection of the most effective spectator placement strategies, leading to more captivating and memorable VR experiences.

Keywords: Virtual reality · collaboration

1 Introduction

This paper presents a comparison of three different methods for placing spectators in a virtual reality (VR) environment to optimize their positioning for an immersive and captivating presentation. With the growing popularity of VR technology, it is crucial to explore techniques that enhance the viewing experience for individuals observing VR content (Fig. 1).

2 Related Work

Navigation methods in VR are crucial for allowing users to move freely and intuitively in virtual environments. There are several navigation approaches,

C. Stephanidis et al. (Eds.): HCII 2024, CCIS 2116, pp. 137–146, 2024.
https://doi.org/10.1007/978-3-031-61950-2_16

Fig. 1. Sample positioning of users using the formations method.

including controller-based movement, on-the-spot walking (Room-Scale Tracking and Locomotion), and teleportation. Controller-based movement offers precise control using controllers, similar to video games, but often leads to motion sickness [1]. Room-Scale Tracking uses special cameras and sensors to capture the user's physical movement in space. Treadmills or controller movements can simulate walking, aiming to replicate real walking and minimize motion sickness. However, this method has drawbacks such as space requirements for equipment like treadmills and limited freedom of movement. While Locomotion systems can create the illusion of movement, they are still confined to the user's limited physical space and cannot provide the sensation of complete freedom and actual physical movement. Moreover, walking in place is the slowest method of movement [2].

In contrast, teleportation is often seen as a better navigation method in Virtual Reality, especially in terms of reducing motion sickness. It allows users to cover large distances instantly, making it highly efficient, and it does not require additional space. However, teleportation can lead to a phenomenon called Spatial Desynchronization [6], where the user's VR positions no longer match their real-world positions. This issue is only relevant in scenarios where multiple users are present in the same physical space.

Previous research on this topic exists but focused on less complex environments and did not concentrate on the specific use case of content presentation in VR. Weißker et al. [9] explored the properties and challenges of group navigation in VR and its previous implementations in the literature. They differentiated between Single Workspace and Multiple Workspaces scenarios: in a Single Workspace, all participants are in the same physical space, while in Multiple

Workspaces, participants can be distributed across different locations as long as an internet connection is available. Users were accordingly classified as Collocated or Distributed Users. Weißker et al. referred to Tuckman's model [8] and categorized the group navigation process into four phases: Forming, Norming, Performing, and Adjourning. The main issue for Collocated Users is Spatial Desynchronization, where the user's spatial perception does not match their actual position in the virtual environment, leading to confusion and collision risks with other participants. One solution suggested by Weißker et al. is to treat Collocated Users as a single entity and navigate them together through virtual space. For Distributed Users, the problem of Spatial Desynchronization does not exist. However, past experiences showed that virtual avatars could evoke negative feelings when too close to a person. It was found to be challenging to stay together or find each other in a large virtual space when users navigated individually. It would be beneficial to assign control over group navigation to the person with the most knowledge and expertise in a field. Additionally, navigation should be understandable to all group members, avoid obstacles, and position everyone to clearly view displayed objects [5,7]. The conclusion was that group navigation in Multi-User VR is still at the beginning of research and four broad areas are relevant for future research:

Scalability: Previous research mainly focused on small groups. A study with more participants, from three to seven simulated users, revealed that the biggest challenges in group navigation are avoiding obstacles and optimizing visibility while maintaining sufficient distance between participants. For larger groups, these tasks become more difficult, and a possible solution could be to divide large groups into smaller subgroups, displaying only avatars from these subgroups and allowing switching between them to not limit social interaction.

Diversity: Future studies on group navigation should consider more diversity among subjects, examining participants with different levels of experience and prior knowledge. It is also important to study the diversity of hardware, as users may use different VR headsets in real cases, leading to varying results.

Social Factors: It is important to further investigate social factors during the group navigation process. Especially for Distributed Users, it would be interesting to determine which aspects contribute to social cohesion and a sense of belonging. Focusing on these effects in the future could help create a better collective understanding of the virtual environment or improve the analysis of information in virtual space.

Alternatives to Group Navigation: Which have been discussed due to some users' dissatisfaction with losing control when navigation is directed by a single person. There is potential for improvement, such as allowing participants to object to or block group navigation moves if they feel uncomfortable. Research has shown that sometimes splitting the group can lead to better task outcomes. Therefore, it's important to investigate how users can navigate individually and later regroup.

In a study by Berger and Wolf [1], the World-in-Miniature (WiM) principle was examined as an alternative to other VR locomotion methods. WiM presents a miniature version of the virtual environment, allowing users to interact with it to change perspective and position. This is important in VR, where spatial orientation can be more challenging. The study compared WiM with two conventional navigation methods: continuous motion using controller joysticks and teleportation using a line and target marker. WiM was activated on the user's right palm, with a marker for changing position within the miniature representation. WiM caused the least motion sickness, outperformed other methods in speed and efficiency for distances over 45m, and provided the best spatial orientation.

Chheang et al. [3] analyzed group navigation specifically for WiM, focusing on usability, efficiency, and the experience of both the navigator and the group. A user study with 20 participants was conducted in a virtual space based on a real medical training environment. In WiM, the navigator could rotate and scale a miniature version of the environment and choose from four group formations: circle, semicircle, grid, and line. The avatars were automatically positioned to face the center after teleportation, so users could immediately see all other participants and the intended view.

Obstacle avoidance was addressed by marking preview avatars with a Mesh Collider in red if they collided with objects or walls, blocking teleportation. Participants received haptic feedback when selecting a group formation and could view a miniature map on a virtual tablet to understand group navigation better. The WiM navigation method was compared to a conventional teleportation function that also allowed group formation placement but without the WiM view. Results indicated that WiM is advantageous for complex environments and long distances, while the alternative teleportation method was positively received for navigating immediate surroundings.

3   Methods

3.1   Formations

Positioning with Formations involves the selection of predefined formations, such as circles, semicircles, or lines, by the navigator. Using a laser pointer, a preview of the formation is displayed at the endpoint of the pointer. Participants are then teleported and positioned according to the chosen formation. This method is based on a previously published implementation.

3.2   Dynamic Positioning

Dynamic Positioning allows the navigator to designate a point in the 3D environment. Participants are automatically teleported within a limited radius around this point. To ensure a clear line of sight and maintain sufficient distance from other participants, automatic positioning adjustments are made.

3.3 Personal Perspective

In the Personal Perspective method [4], the navigator enters a 3D mode and aligns themselves with a specific point of interest. The position and viewing direction are saved and transmitted to all participants, who are subsequently teleported to the same position with the same viewing direction. Avatars are hidden to prevent clipping issues.

4 Evaluation

To enable a comparison between the three placement methods, we will conduct a user study (n = 9).

To evaluate the effectiveness of these methods, several factors will be considered, including time to complete the assignment, correctness, immersion level, user comfort and overall user experience. A combination of qualitative and quantitative metrics will be employed, such as questionnaires and tracking data analysis. The findings from this study will contribute to a more in-depth understanding of the strengths and limitations of each method, helping VR content creators, designers, and developers make informed decisions regarding spectator placement techniques. By identifying the best approach, VR experiences can be enhanced, leading to more engaging and memorable presentations (Fig. 2).

Fig. 2. Possible view on the target building during trial. Blue and red markings are visible. (Color figure online)

The user study consists of three sets of assignments, each representing a different method that were mentioned in the previous chapter. A training set is run before the real cases start to let the users familiarize with the VR environment and the controls. Before the teleportation happens, the participant will be prompted to agree to it in order to reduce the feeling of loss of control. If they decline, teleportation will not happen. After agreeing, a fade in/out transition is played during teleportation to minimize the risk of motion sickness. Afterwards, the user is placed into the trial environment.

The task will be to count coloured markers on a target building as accurately as possible. Each side of the building will have markers in a different colour respectively. This means participants will have to give back the correct number of markings **and** their colours, which will provide insight on how well they were able to spot markers depending on their positions. A task counts as completed when the participants themselves confirm that they are done and could not find any more markings. Additionally, the constellation and number of markers will be different for each set to avoid bias by memorization. Dummy avatars will be placed in the environment along with the user to represent a group of participants. The user is able to switch their position with a dummy to obtain its view. A total of 5 positions and dummy avatars are available during Formation and Dynamic testing, while the Personal Perspective method will only have one view and no avatars. For the Formation method, the group is configured in a **semicircle** position around the trial object while the Personal Perspective method will have static coordinates, ensuring that each trial and participant will not have deviating conditions. The Formation and Personal Perspective positions were placed in a way that a clear view without obstacles was given to mimic the behaviour of a navigator placing the group optimally.

Only in the Dynamic method the positions of the users and dummy avatars will be different each time since they will be dynamically generated. After each set, the participants will answer a few questions regarding visibility of the markings and usefulness of the available positions to find them. When completing all sets, they will be asked to rank all three methods based on their personal preference and also give their reason.

5   Results

The participants were people aged from 21 to 55 (5 male and 4 female) and with mixed fields of professions that range from logical/analytical to creative thinking such as IT administrator, software architect, interface design or firefighter operations manager. Of the 9 participants examined, 5 had beginner to intermediate level of VR experience ($5 <$ on a scale up to 10) while 4 were considered advanced users or experts ($5 >$ on a scale up to 10). The results indicate that the Formation method seemed to be best suited for this case and had the highest rating score of 95.1% markings found (see Fig. 3). It is followed by the Dynamic method and then Personal Perspective (Blue bars). However, it must be considered that for the Personal Perspective, only one view is given and thus a considerable number

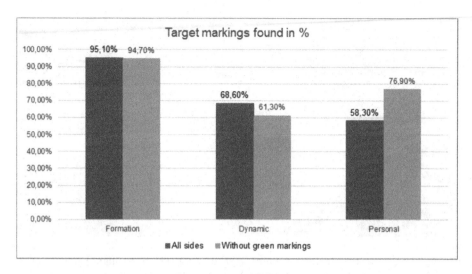

Fig. 3. The rate of target markings found represented in percentage. Blue shows the rating with all markings included, and orange shows the rating without counting green markings that were hidden from Personal Perspective. (Color figure online)

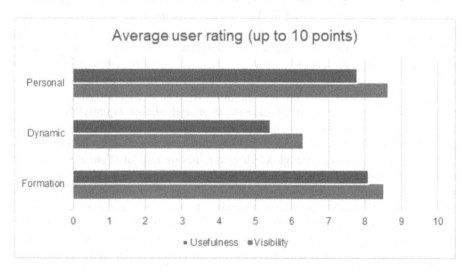

Fig. 4. Average user rating for visibility of markings in the different methods. Up to 10 points could be given.

of markings is always hidden. In the study, these hidden markings happened to be coloured green. If we disregard these green markings from the calculation, we get another score which puts the Dynamic method at last place. The Formation method remains the best (Orange bars). On average, participants needed 63.2 s to complete the Formation-based task, 67.2 s for the Dynamic method and

Fig. 5. Bad perspective during a dynamic method trial. The participant is too far away from the target and the view is obstructed by obstacles and an avatar.

26.8 s in Personal Perspective. They required slightly more time to complete the Dynamic assignment compared to the Formation method. The considerable discrepancy between Personal Perspective and the other two methods is due to the fact that participants only had one view available, and thus were only able to count the immediately visible markings. Questionnaires regarding the visibility and usefulness seem to support the notion that the Dynamic method performed worse than the others. One interesting thing to note is that although Personal Perspective had a lower rate of success, it scored almost equally to the Formation method regarding user opinion on visibility and usefulness (see Fig. 4). Every participant agreed that more perspectives are beneficial to finding markings, compared to a singular view. However, about half of them also said the Personal Perspective was still 'quite helpful' and 'felt good' as it showed many markings at once and had no obstacles in its view. The Dynamic method was most critiqued for having positions of varying distances to the target building, as they made it confusing and harder to find markings. It was also mentioned that some obstacles happened to be in the way, including dummy avatars (see Fig. 5). These results also align with the user-based ranking of the different methods (see Fig. 6).

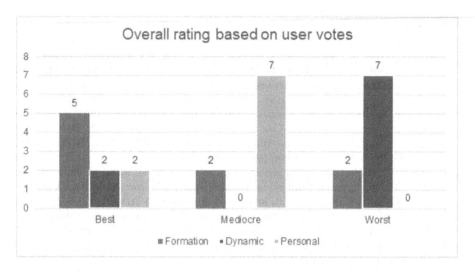

Fig. 6. Overall ranking of the three methods based on user votes.

6   Conclusion and Future Work

Considering the collected data, we can conclude that static positions placed by a navigator seem to outperform a dynamically generated approach in both efficiency of viewing-based tasks and overall user experience. During the study, we were able to observe that often than not, the Dynamic method placed participants too far away or too close to the target building. In some cases, it was still possible for the view to be obstructed by objects and dummy avatars, meaning the algorithm needs to be more precise and detailed regarding placement calculation. The obstruction by objects and other participants (dummy avatars) is not only perceived to be annoying by the user but also negatively affects the efficiency of tasks, as expected. Data from Personal Perspective suggests that a high quality singular view with no obstacles is also viable but will be outperformed by more perspectives if not obstructed. This could be improved by allowing the navigator to place multiple Personal Perspectives, for instance.

It should be mentioned that this study only depicted a limited use case in a contained experiment. It is important to conduct further research and to test with more participants, environments, and use cases. The potential for improvement and optimization on any of the three showcased methods is still vastly unreached. The results of the study should give an estimation on what aspects of spectator placement should be thought about when implementing such a system. It reveals problems and also highlights some information about what users perceive as essential for a good user experience. For future research, one could also think about utilizing AI technology to enhance decision-making about placement or create a system that places spectators automatically. All in all, it is clear that further research into these topics should be conducted.

References

1. Berger, L., Wolf, K.: Wim: Fast locomotion in virtual reality with spatial orientation gain & without motion sickness. In: Abdennadher, S., Alt, F. (eds.) Proceedings of the 17th International Conference on Mobile and Ubiquitous Multimedia, pp. 19–24. ACM, New York, NY, USA (2018). https://doi.org/10.1145/3282894.3282932
2. Bozgeyikli, E., Raij, A., Katkoori, S., Dubey, R.V.: Point & teleport locomotion technique for virtual reality. In: Cox, A., et al. (eds.) Proceedings of the 2016 Annual Symposium on Computer-Human Interaction in Play, pp. 205–216. ACM, New York, NY, USA (2016). https://doi.org/10.1145/2967934.2968105
3. Chheang, V., et al.: Wim-based group navigation for collaborative virtual reality. In: 2022 IEEE International Conference on Artificial Intelligence and Virtual Reality (AIVR), pp. 82–92. IEEE (2022). https://doi.org/10.1109/AIVR56993.2022.00018
4. Hoppe, A.H., van de Camp, F., Stiefelhagen, R.: Personal perspective: using modified world views to overcome real-life limitations in virtual reality. In: 2018 IEEE Conference on Virtual Reality and 3D User Interfaces (VR), pp. 577–578 (2018). https://doi.org/10.1109/VR.2018.8446311
5. Katz, I.R. (ed.): Human Factors in Computing Systems: CHI 1995 Conference Companion - Mosaic of Creativity. ACM Press and Addison-Wesley, New York, NY and Reading, Mass (1995)
6. Lacoche, J., Pallamin, N., Boggini, T., Royan, J.: Collaborators awareness for user cohabitation in co-located collaborative virtual environments. In: Fjeld, M., et al. (eds.) Proceedings of the 23rd ACM Symposium on Virtual Reality Software and Technology, pp. 1–9. ACM, New York, NY, USA (2017). https://doi.org/10.1145/3139131.3139142
7. Pausch, R., Burnette, T., Brockway, D., Weiblen, M.E.: Navigation and locomotion in virtual worlds via flight into hand-held miniatures. In: Proceedings of the 22nd Annual Conference on Computer Graphics and Interactive Techniques (SIGGRAPH 1995), pp. 399–400. ACM Press, New York, NY (1995). https://doi.org/10.1145/218380.218495
8. Tuckman, B.W.: Developmental sequence in small groups. Psychol. Bull. **63**(6), 384–399 (1965). https://doi.org/10.1037/h0022100
9. Weißker, T.: Group Navigation in Multi-User Virtual Reality. Ph.D. thesis, Bauhaus-Universität Weimar (2021). https://www.tim-weissker.de/preprints/2021-dissertation-group-navigation.pdf

Exploring the Relationship Between the Interactive Range of Objects and the Performance of Freehand Grasping Interaction in Glasses-Free 3D Scenes

Hongrun Wang[1], Wenjun Hou[1,2,3(✉)], Yucheng Cao[1], and Benzhi Yang[4]

[1] School of Digital Media and Design Arts, Beijing University of Posts and Telecommunications, No.10 Xitucheng Road, Beijing 100876, China
hwj1505@bupt.edu.cn

[2] Beijing Key Laboratory of Network System and Network Culture, No.10 Xitucheng Road, Beijing 100876, China

[3] Key Laboratory of Interactive Technology and Experience System, Ministry of Culture and Tourism, No.10 Xitucheng Road, Beijing 100876, China

[4] China Mobile Research Institute, Beijing, China

Abstract. Target selection is one of the most essential and common tasks in 3D interaction. Grasping interaction is an innate ability of human beings. As the most basic form of target selection interaction, it is widely used in target selection tasks. Previous work has explored the impact of various feedback factors on the interaction efficiency of grasping target selection. However, research has yet to focus on the impact of the interactive range of objects on target selection efficiency. This study takes the interactive range of objects as the research goal, builds an experimental platform based on a glasses-free 3D display, and evaluates the impact of the interactive range of objects on grasping performance and task load under different interactive object layouts. The results show that the interactive range of objects significantly impacts the performance and accuracy of grasping interaction. Reducing the interactive range can improve accuracy and increase the time spent on the task. Increasing the interactive range can shorten the time spent on the task. However, it will also reduce the accuracy. We also observe that the interactive range does not significantly impact the task load. This study initially reveals the relationship between the interactive range of objects and target selection task performance and experience. It provides suggestions for the design of three-dimensional interactive applications.

Keywords: Glasses-free 3D · Freehand Interaction · Grasping Interaction · Interactive Range

1 Introduction

Glasses-free 3D technology is regarded as the next-generation display technology [1]. It can naturally display three-dimensional objects, allowing users to

C. Stephanidis et al. (Eds.): HCII 2024, CCIS 2116, pp. 147–158, 2024.
https://doi.org/10.1007/978-3-031-61950-2_17

obtain an immersive three-dimensional experience without wearing any display devices [2]. Therefore, creating an environment with high immersion has interested researchers. Interacting naturally and realistically with virtual objects in a virtual environment is the key to improving immersion.

Interacting with virtual objects can be divided into two stages: virtual target selection (considered one of the most basic interactions in the 3D environment [3]) and virtual object manipulation. Because hands are our most powerful tools for interacting with the world around us [4], freehand interaction is considered a natural way of target selection [5]. Freehand interaction collects the user's natural gestures and maps them into the virtual scene to complete the interaction process. In addition to eliminating the need for input devices, it also has the advantage of being more natural and convenient for humans [6]. In order to improve the experience and efficiency of freehand target grasping interaction in a 3D interactive environment, the usability and performance of various combinations of factors that affect grasping task performance need to be weighed and compared [7]. Current research on grasping performance's effects mainly focuses on interactive feedback and human grasping behavior.

Many researchers have studied the influencing factors of interactive performance, and the results show that color feedback on virtual hands and interactive objects can improve user performance when performing virtual interactive grasping tasks [8]. The impact of interactive feedback on grasping performance has been widely studied. However, more work needs to be done on the factors that influence interactive performance from the perspective of human behavior. Interaction using the distance between thumbs and fingertips is the most common way to interact with virtual objects in virtual environments that lack execution feedback [9]. Al-Kalbani's research show that the distance between the thumb and index finger decreases when the hand moves to the virtual interaction target [10]. This phenomenon will cause the user to trigger the grasping interaction in advance in scenarios where the distance between the thumb and index finger is used as an interaction intention judgment. Therefore, different interactive ranges of the same object may affect the interaction experience and performance. This phenomenon is visually similar to the interactive feedback method in which fingers can penetrate objects [11] in grasping interactions, so it is often regarded as a type of visual feedback for research. More research is needed on the impact of this phenomenon on interaction performance from a human behavioral perspective.

This study regards the interactive range as a potential factor affecting grasping interaction efficiency from the perspective of human grasping behavior. It experimentally evaluates the impact of the interactive range on grasping performance and task load under different spatial layouts of interactive objects. We focus on the interactive range parameters corresponding to the best interaction performance to ensure the conclusions can provide a reference for building glasses-free 3D interactive applications. This study mainly makes contributions in the following aspects: 1. Proposes the interactive range as a parameter that may affect the performance of grasping interaction. 2. Explores the impact of the interactive range on the performance of virtual grasping interaction. 3. Make suggestions for the interaction design of glasses-free 3D applications.

2   Related Work

2.1   Freehand Grasping Interaction in the 3D Environment

In the virtual 3D interactive environment, freehand interaction refers to collecting the position and skeletal information of the user's hand through computer vision or data gloves. It constructs a virtual hand model of the user and displays it in three dimensions, providing a visual reference for the user to operate the target object directly. Cui et al. believe that gesture interaction aligns more with the user's psychological model of 3D interaction [12] and allows users to manipulate virtual objects like natural objects [13]. However, human experience with gesture interactions on natural objects cannot be directly applied to grasping virtual objects. Ganias et al. believes that existing finger-tracking methods have the shortcoming of lack of tactile feedback, resulting in users being unable to clearly express their intentions for a particular virtual operation [14]. Therefore, freehand grasping interaction in a 3D environment is regarded as a technical challenge [15], and many researchers have explored the grasping performance. Geiger et al. verified that color feedback on the virtual hand or object can improve the user's performance during grasping interaction [8]. Through user experiments, Blaga et al. verified that translucent hands significantly improved interaction performance [9,12]. The research mainly focuses on the impact of factors such as feedback during interaction on interaction performance and experience.

2.2   Grasping Interaction Behavior Research

There are few studies on the influencing factors of grasping performance from the perspective of human behavior, and many factors derived from human grasping interaction behavior that may affect grasping interaction performance have yet to be studied. Some studies have compared the differences between grasping interactions in natural and virtual scenes and believe that when interacting with natural objects, the shape evolution of the hand gradually conforms to the object's outline [16] while interacting with virtual objects lacks sensory feedback. Users often interact using the distance between thumbs and fingertips [9]. Therefore, using the distance between the index finger and thumb for grasping operations is more suitable for grasping interaction of virtual objects. This technology is also a common method of grasping virtual objects. Al-Kalbani et al. studied the changes in gestures in the transition stage from making a grasping gesture to grasping an object. The results showed that when interacting with virtual objects, the distance between the thumb and index finger will change when the hand moves to the interaction target. It becomes smaller and is unaffected by task categories and interactive object attributes [10]. This phenomenon is easily confused with whether the finger can penetrate the object in the visual feedback of the grasp interaction. For example, Blaga et al. studied the impact of the positional relationship between virtual hands and objects on the performance of freehand interaction from the perspective of interactive feedback. They believed that virtual hands penetrating interactive objects could provide better performance [9,11]. However, few studies explore the impact of this phenomenon on interactive performance from the perspective of human grasping behavior, which is the direction of our research.

3 Experiment Design

3.1 Device Setup

This experiment uses the Unity3D engine to build the experimental scene. It uses the Leap Motion gesture sensor running in desktop mode as the input device to collect the position information of the hand nodes in space as well as the direction and position information of the hand. The display device used in the experiment is the Sony ELF-SR2 glasses-free 3D 3D display. The screen size is 27 in., and the resolution is 3840*2160. It can sense the pupil position and render spatial images for both eyes in real-time, allowing users to see three-dimensional images using only the naked eye.

3.2 Experiment Content

This experiment takes the interactive range of virtual objects as the main research object. It explores the impact of the interactive range on grasping interaction performance under different interactive object layouts.

Fig. 1. Three layouts

We conducted tests on three virtual object layouts: vertical layout, horizontal layout, and dispersed layout. In the vertical layout, 12 cubes are placed in a matrix of 3 rows and four columns. Each cube's length, width, and height are 14cm, the distance between adjacent cubes is 2cm, the entire matrix is perpendicular to the ground, and the distance between the plane of the cube and the camera is 64cm. In the horizontal layout, the number, size, and spacing of the 12 cubes are the same as in the vertical layout. The entire matrix is parallel to the ground. The first row is 32cm away from the camera, the second is 48cm away from the camera, and the third is 64cm away from the camera. In the distributed layout, cubes of the same size as the above two layouts are randomly distributed

Fig. 2. Three interactive ranges

within the Leap Motion gesture interaction range and adjusted appropriately to avoid mutual occlusion. The three layouts are shown in Fig. 1.

The interactive range of virtual objects refers to the range within which the target object can successfully achieve the grasping operation when the grasping operation occurs. In this experiment, three interactive ranges of different sizes were set, represented by bounding boxes of 80%, 100%, and 120% of the cube volume(see Fig. 2). When grasping occurs within the bounding box, an interaction is triggered.

4   User Study

4.1   Participants

We recruited 15 participants, including six women and nine men. Participants ranged from 22 to 25 years old, with a mean age of 23.47 ($SD = 0.834$). Participants were all graduate students majoring in art, design, and computer science. Six participants had experience using VR, and 9 had no experience using VR. Only one participant used a glasses-free 3D display screen, and the rest had no experience using it.

4.2   Measure

Interaction Performance. Measure the time required for each task based on the performance of this group of experiments. After the broadcast is completed, the task start time is recorded as t_{start} until the user successfully grabs any object, the task end time is recorded as t_{end}, and the time difference is $time = t_{end} - t_{start}$, which is the time it takes the user to complete the task.

Interaction Accuracy. Record the number of virtual squares selected by participants that differ from the voice broadcast as the number of errors. The error rate is the ratio of the number of errors to the total number of tasks.

Interaction Task Load. This experiment uses the NASA-LTX Task Load Index Questionnaire [17] to evaluate task load. The task load index questionnaire includes a comprehensive task load and sub-items such as mental, physical, and performance loads.

Semi-structured Interviews. We conducted semi-structured interviews after the task to better understand the user interaction experience under different parameters. Questions included, "Can you feel the difference in interaction experience caused by the interactive range?" "Which interactive range do you like best and why?" "Which interactive range do you think is more accurate and why?" "Which interactive range do you think is faster and why?" We used semi-structured interviews to understand participants' operational processes and explain possible outcomes.

4.3   Tasks and Experiment Procedure

Fig. 3. A participant is in the process of grasping interaction

The participant's task is to select the target object according to the voice command. There are three layouts * 3 interactive ranges * 2 types with or without feedback = 18 repeated measurement experiments. The system randomly selects eight letters in each experiment and broadcasts them in sequence. The participant grasps the cubes marked with the corresponding letters until eight corresponding random objects are selected. The number of errors in the eight grasps is recorded to calculate the error rate, and the average time is recorded to reflect the grasping performance. In order to avoid inaccurate identification caused by pronunciation problems, the experiment removed letters such as B, D, G, and J. Before the experiment, Leap Motion and the Sony ELF-SR2 spatial reality display were adjusted to ensure that participants' gesture movements could be recognized and scene information displayed correctly. A simple demonstration program provides participants with detailed instructions for gesture-grasping interaction and display usage. After completing each interactivity range experiment, participants completed questionnaires to assess the perceived task load. After completing all tasks, participants will be invited for a semi-structured interview, which takes approximately 55 min. The process of participants' grasping interaction is shown in Fig. 3.

5   Result

5.1   Task Completion Time

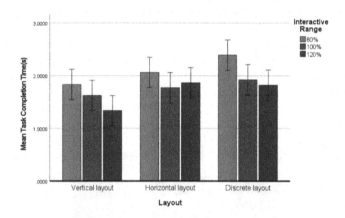

Fig. 4. Task Completion Time

ANOVA analysis of variance was performed on the interactive range in different layouts. The results showed that different interactive ranges in a vertical layout and dispersed layout significantly impact task completion time. In the vertical layout, the interactive range significantly impacts the interaction completion time $(F(2,87) = 4.078, p = 0.020, \eta_p^2 = 1.883)$. The 120% volume interactive range consumes the least time (M = 1.335, SD = 0.407). In the discrete layout, the interactive range significantly impacts the interaction completion time $(F(2,87) = 3.347, p = 0.039, \eta_p^2 = 2.756)$. Among them, 120% of the volume surrounding the interactive range consumes the least time $(M = 1.823, SD = 0.547)$. In the above two layouts, the interaction in the 120% volume interactive range is completed faster, and the 80% volume interactive range is completed slower. The task completion time of tasks with different interactive ranges is shown in Fig. 4. In the horizontal layout, the impact of the interactive range on the interaction completion time is insignificant $(F(2,87) = 1.022, p = 0.346, \eta_p^2 = 0.660)$. The interaction completion time of 120% of the volume interactive range is not the shortest.

5.2   Error

ANOVA analysis was performed on different layouts' interactive ranges. The results showed that in the three vertical, horizontal, and dispersed layouts, the interactive range significantly impacted the error rate ($F(2,87) = 3.249, p = 0.042, \eta_p^2 = 0.102; F(2,87) = 5.728, p = 0.005, \eta_p^2 = 0.251; F(2,87) = 3.145, p = 0.048, \eta_p^2 = 0.135$). The 80% volume interactive range has the lowest error rate ($M = 0.150, SD = 0.152; M = 0.117, SD = 0.199; M = 0.163, SD = 0.177$). The task error rate of tasks with different interactive ranges is shown in Fig. 5. The opposite trend to the time consumption is reflected in the three layouts. The error rate of the interactive range of the smaller volume is reduced, and the interactive range of the larger volume is higher.

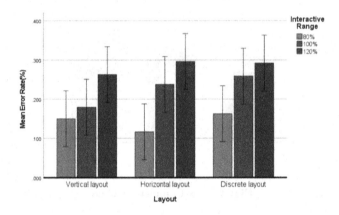

Fig. 5. Error

5.3   Task Load

Perform an analysis of variance on the interaction range in different layouts. The results show that the interactive range has no significant effect on task load in vertical, horizontal, and distributed layouts ($F(2,87) = 2.330, p = 0.103, \eta_p^2 = 564.668; F(2,87) = 0.730, p = 0.485, \eta_p^2 = 255.604; F(2,87) = 0.215, p = 0.807, \eta_p^2 = 72.330$). From the average task loads of different interaction ranges in all layouts, it can be found that the interaction range of 120% volume interaction range has the highest total task load score, and all sub-item loads are the highest except for the time requirement sub-item as shown in Fig. 6.

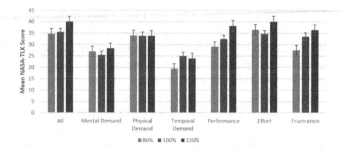

Fig. 6. Mean NASA-TLX Score

6   Discussion

We comparatively analyzed the impact of interactive range on grasping task performance and user experience under different object layout scenes.

In terms of task completion time, compared with the interactive range of the same size as the visual volume, the interactive range with a smaller volume consumes more time, and the interactive range with a larger volume consumes less time. The reasons for this phenomenon are as follows: (1) In a scene with a larger interactive range, participants can move their hands within the interactive range of the object in a shorter time to complete the grasp, thus reducing task consumption. (2) During the movement, the participants' hands are prone to accidentally touching objects with larger interactive ranges passing by, causing the task to end early and resulting in a shorter overall task completion time. It is worth noting that in the horizontal layout, the interactive range does not significantly impact the task completion time, and the larger interactive range does not reduce the task completion time. This phenomenon may be because users need to perform horizontal movements that are relatively difficult in three-dimensional interactions in horizontal layouts. In a horizontal layout, a more extensive interactive range will make participants worry about accidental touches and pay more attention to their actions during the interaction, causing the task time to increase instead of decrease. This explanation is also consistent with the results of the participant interviews.

Compared with the interactive range of the same size as the visual volume, the error rate of interactive tasks is lower in the interactive range scenario of smaller volume, and the error rate is higher in the interactive range scenario of larger volume. This is because when the interaction range is small, the user needs to be closer to the object to grab it so that the correct object can be grasped more accurately. The more extensive interactive range can easily lead to false touches, increasing errors.

In terms of task load, changes in the interactive range did not significantly impact the task load. It is worth noting that the more extensive interactive range only has the highest average value among the other loads regarding time requirements is not the highest. This phenomenon is because a larger interactive range will reduce the time consumed by the task, making the user feel that the time requirement is lower. At the same time, users must operate more carefully to avoid accidental touches, resulting in more effort on the user's part, which will bring concerns about performance and frustration to participants.

To sum up, when designing interactive applications related to virtual object grabbing, it is necessary to consider the impact of the interactive range of objects on interactive performance. In general, it follows the rule that a smaller interactive range can improve the accuracy but also increase the time spent on the task, and a more extensive interactive range can reduce the time spent on the task but reduce the accuracy. Changes in the interactive range have no impact on task load. The designer needs to weigh the interactive range based on the attributes of the interactive application. Consider appropriately reducing the interactive range for applications with high interaction accuracy. Consider appropriately increasing the interactive range for applications with higher interaction time requirements.

7   Conclusion

In this work, we proposed the interactive range as a potential factor affecting the efficiency of grasping interaction from the perspective of human grasping behavior. We evaluated the effect of the interactive range on grasping performance under different interactive object spatial layouts. In general, the interactive range significantly impacts grasping interaction performance and accuracy. The impact of changes in the interactive range in different layouts is roughly the same and has no significant impact on task load. Therefore, we recommend that designers consider the impact of interactive range on task interaction efficiency and accuracy during the design process of 3D interactive applications. Designers should choose an appropriate interactive range based on the importance of interaction efficiency or accuracy in actual tasks without worrying about the impact of changes in interactive range on task load.

8   Future Work

In this study, we preliminarily verified the impact of interactive range on grasping interaction efficiency. However, due to the limitation of experimental time, the number of interactive range divisions in the experiment is limited, and the granularity of the interactive range changes could be more precise. Therefore, it is impossible to precisely determine the trend of grasping efficiency as the interactive range changes. In subsequent work, we will refine the granularity of changes in the interactive range and more accurately study the impact of the interactive range on interaction efficiency. It also focuses on studying the optimal threshold for changes in the interactive range to provide more precise guidance and suggestions for interaction design.

References

1. Hua, J., Qiao, W., Chen, L.: Recent advances in planar optics-based glasses-free 3d displays. Front. Nanotechnol. **4**, 829011 (2022)
2. Dodgson, N.A.: Autostereoscopic 3d displays. Computer **38**(8), 31–36 (2005)
3. El-Shimy, D., Marentakis, G., Cooperstock, J.R.: Tech-note: multimodal feedback in 3d target acquisition. In: 2009 IEEE Symposium on 3D User Interfaces, pp. 95–98. IEEE (2009)
4. Adhikarla, V.K., Woźniak, P., Barsi, A., Singhal, D., Kovács, P.T., Balogh, T.: Freehand interaction with large-scale 3d map data. In: 2014 3DTV-Conference: The True Vision-Capture, Transmission and Display of 3D Video (3DTV-CON), pp. 1–4. IEEE (2014)
5. Yu, D., Liang, H.N., Lu, F., Nanjappan, V., Papangelis, K., Wang, W., et al.: Target selection in head-mounted display virtual reality environments. J. Univers. Comput. Sci. **24**(9), 1217–1243 (2018)
6. Santos, B.S., Cardoso, J., Ferreira, B.Q., Ferreira, C., Dias, P.: Developing 3d free-hand gesture-based interaction methods for virtual walkthroughs: using an iterative approach. In: Handbook of Research on Human-Computer Interfaces, Developments, and Applications, pp. 52–72. IGI Global (2016)
7. Bowman, D.A., Hodges, L.F.: An evaluation of techniques for grabbing and manipulating remote objects in immersive virtual environments. In: Proceedings of the 1997 Symposium on Interactive 3D Graphics, pp. 35–ff (1997)
8. Geiger, A., Bewersdorf, I., Brandenburg, E., Stark, R.: Visual feedback for grasping in virtual reality environments for an interface to instruct digital human models. In: Ahram, T., Falcão, C. (eds.)Advances in Usability and User Experience: Proceedings of the AHFE 2017 International Conference on Usability and User Experience, 17-21 July 2017, The Westin Bonaventure Hotel, Los Angeles, California, USA, pp. 228–239. Springer, Cham (2018). https://doi.org/10.1007/978-3-319-60492-3_22
9. Blaga, A.D., Frutos-Pascual, M., Creed, C., Williams, I.: A grasp on reality: understanding grasping patterns for object interaction in real and virtual environments. In: 2021 IEEE International Symposium on Mixed and Augmented Reality Adjunct (ISMAR-adjunct), pp. 391–396. IEEE (2021)
10. Al-Kalbani, M., Frutos-Pascual, M., Williams, I.: Freehand grasping in mixed reality: analysing variation during transition phase of interaction. In: Proceedings of the 19th ACM International Conference on Multimodal Interaction, pp. 110–114 (2017)
11. Adkins, A., Lin, L., Normoyle, A., Canales, R., Ye, Y., Jörg, S.: Evaluating grasping visualizations and control modes in a VR game. ACM Trans. Appl. Percept. (TAP) **18**(4), 1–14 (2021)
12. Cui, J., Sourin, A.: Mid-air interaction with optical tracking for 3d modeling. Comput. Graph. **74**, 1–11 (2018)
13. Al-Kalbani, M., Williams, I., Frutos-Pascual, M.: Analysis of medium wrap freehand virtual object grasping in exocentric mixed reality. In: 2016 IEEE International Symposium on Mixed and Augmented Reality (ISMAR), pp. 84–93. IEEE (2016)
14. Ganias, G., Lougiakis, C., Katifori, A., Roussou, M., Ioannidis, Y., et al.: Comparing different grasping visualizations for object manipulation in VR using controllers. IEEE Trans. Visual Comput. Graph. **29**(5), 2369–2378 (2023)

15. Borst, C.W., Indugula, A.P.: Realistic virtual grasping. In: IEEE Proceedings. VR 2005. Virtual Reality, 2005, pp. 91–98. IEEE (2005)
16. Santello, M., Flanders, M., Soechting, J.F.: Postural hand synergies for tool use. J. Neurosci. **18**(23), 10105–10115 (1998)
17. Hart, S.G., Staveland, L.E.: Development of NASA-TLX (task load index): results of empirical and theoretical research. Adv. Psychol. **52**, 139–183 (1988)

Virtual Reality: A Window into the Future of Journalism

Weilong Wu[✉] and Liyang Ling

School of Film Television and Communication, Xiamen University of Technology, Xiamen, China

wu_academic@163.com

Abstract. This article explores the application of virtual reality technology in news reporting, aiming to reveal the great potential and potential advantages of virtual reality technology in the field of news reporting. First, the inconveniences and limitations of current news reporting are analyzed, including the limitations of limited immersive experiences, the inability to participate in reporting remotely, the limitations of information delivery, the limitations of audience engagement, the lack of depth of reporting, and the traditional constraints of the news narrative, which highlight the inadequacies of traditional reporting methods in terms of information delivery and audience engagement.

Secondly this article explains how virtual reality technology will fill these gaps. By analyzing the specific use of virtual reality technology in journalism, the enhancement of the immersive experience brought by virtual reality is highlighted, allowing the audience to perceive the actual situation of the report more deeply. Then also detailed in the panoramic experience and interactive enhancement of 360-degree video, panoramic photos and other technical means, which expand the three-dimensionality of the news coverage, so that the audience can freely explore and actively participate in the scene.

Finally, the results of the study show that the application of virtual reality technology in news reporting can provide a more realistic and comprehensive reporting experience, and at the same time break through the geographical limitations, so that viewers do not need to travel thousands of miles, they can participate in the whole report, which increases the degree of audience participation. This innovative narrative not only empowers viewers with a richer perceptual experience, but also helps to improve their cognitive level of news events, bringing about a technological and narrative revolution in the field of news reporting.

The significance of this research is to promote technological innovation in the field of news reporting to enhance audience understanding and engagement with the news, as well as to provide media outlets and content creators with an innovative narrative approach that promises to change the paradigm of traditional news reporting, ushering in a more vivid and engaging narrative future.

Keyword: News Reporting · Virtual Reality Technology · Media Technology · Immersive Experience

C. Stephanidis et al. (Eds.): HCII 2024, CCIS 2116, pp. 159–168, 2024.
https://doi.org/10.1007/978-3-031-61950-2_18

1 Introduction

With the continuous development of modern science and technology, the field of news reporting is undergoing profound changes. The traditional approach to news reporting is gradually revealing several limitations, including restricted immersive experiences, limited audience participation, and insufficient depth of coverage. These challenges impede the effective dissemination of news. Against this backdrop, this study aims to explore the application of virtual reality technology in news reporting, with the objective of unveiling its potential advantages and significant possibilities.

Reflecting on the traditional approach to news reporting, one can observe numerous limitations, particularly in terms of depth of coverage and audience interaction. Viewers often face constraints in understanding reporting due to limited immersive experiences and remote participation. Additionally, the conventional model of news narratives restricts the depth of reporting. These challenges compel us to seek innovative solutions as a means to advance journalism.

The development of virtual reality technology opens up new possibilities for news reporting. This study delves into the specific application of virtual reality in journalism, elucidating how it addresses the limitations of traditional news reporting methods. Technological tools like 360-degree videos and panoramic photos enhance the immersive and interactive aspects of news reporting, allowing viewers to gain a profound understanding of the reported content.

Overall, the application of virtual reality technology marks a revolution in the field of news reporting. This technology not only delivers a more realistic and comprehensive reporting experience but also transcends geographical limitations, enhancing the audience's sense of participation. This innovative approach opens up new possibilities for news creators and foreshadows a more vivid future in news reporting.

2 Limitations of Current News Coverage

2.1 Limitations of Traditional News Reporting

Traditional news reports primarily employ text and static images to convey information to the audience [1]. However, this approach restricts the audience's ability to deeply immerse themselves. Simultaneously, the absence of real-time interaction and multimedia elements in traditional news reports hinders viewers from becoming thoroughly engaged in the content. This limitation affects their perception of event authenticity and may lead to inaccurate evaluations of the news' objective accuracy.

2.2 Limitations of Remote Participation and Journalism

Traditional news coverage faces challenges in engaging viewers remotely during real-time events, potentially resulting in coverage that appears limited, one-sided, and lacking in comprehensiveness. Simultaneously, the absence of remote participation can also diminish viewers' depth of understanding regarding complex events.

2.3 Limitations of Passive Audience Reception and Interaction

Viewers are merely passive as information receivers in traditional news reports [2]. This long-standing pattern of one-way interaction weakens the effectiveness of traditional news reporting and may impact the value of traditional media applications [3]. For example, paper newspapers have developed online versions as part of the digital transformation, but some online news platforms conduct editorial reviews of comments to ensure compliance with community guidelines and regulations. This results in delayed display of comment board content, hindering real-time interaction between viewers and news content. The online versions of some paper newspapers offer only limited interactive features. Comments are the only means of interaction, while other more real-time forms of interaction, such as instant polls, real-time surveys or real-time quizzes are not online on the site.

2.4 Challenges in an Interactive Environment

Some online news platforms do not adequately integrate social media, limiting viewers' ability to interact in a more real-time manner through social media platforms [4]. This makes journalism less interactive. And some online news platforms allow anonymous comments, which can lead to abusive and low-quality comments, making it more difficult for editors to filter and maintain an interactive environment of high quality.

3 Specific Applications of VR Technology

3.1 Enhance Audience Immersion

Relative to traditional news reporting, VR news has the quality of significantly enhancing audience immersion. Through the virtual reality headset, the audience seems to travel to the actual scene of the report, and perceives the real space and depth of the reporting environment in an all-round, 360-degree way, so that they can understand the spatial layout and background of the event in a more comprehensive way. Audiences are able to interact in real time with the characters and environment of the story, experiencing the news story with the subject of the event. This interactivity allows the audience to be less of a passive bystander and more directly involved in the news situation. Immersive experiences make it easier for audiences to build emotional resonance, and this first-hand experience triggers a stronger emotional response that can deepen their understanding of and attention to news events. The immediacy of VR news allows viewers to access up-to-the-minute stories quickly, no longer having to wait for the sorting and editing process of traditional media, resulting in a swifter, more immediate immersive experience. This unique sensation is unmatched by any other form of news.

3.2 Use of Panoramic Photos

The application of panoramic photographs has attracted widespread attention in the field of news reporting [5]. The technology creates a 360-degree visual integration experience between the viewer and the news event by providing an immersive viewing experience, thus deepening the perception of the authenticity of the report. Panoramic photographs excel in restoring the scenes of reported events, and through a high degree of restoration, viewers are able to understand the background of the news story in a more comprehensive and in-depth manner. Its interactive feature provides viewers with the opportunity to adjust their perspective independently, enabling them to dig deeper into the details and environment of the reported event, further enhancing their sense of participation in the report. In addition, panoramic photos offer the possibility of expanding the geographical coverage of the report, allowing viewers to experience the news scene remotely. In terms of narrative, through the skillful integration of information points, text description and other elements, panoramic photos bring more innovative and vivid narrative means for news reporting, presenting a more layered form of reporting.

3.3 The Important Role of 360-Degree Video

360-degree video with VR technology plays a key role in the field of news reporting. Its immersive experience provides viewers with a 360-degree all-around visual perception, making viewers feel as if they were in the scene of the report, deeply participating and strengthening the perception of the authenticity of the event. Selective viewing from a panoramic perspective allows viewers to independently explore multiple perspectives of a reported event, helping to present a more comprehensive and objective report and reduce the limitations of information. The application of this technology breaks through the traditional limitations of news narratives, giving viewers the initiative in news reporting and stimulating in-depth thinking and participation. The 360-degree video of VR technology provides a rich expression of interactivity and immersion for news reporting, deepens the form of reporting, and enhances the audience's deep involvement in the news.

3.4 Applied to News Reporting in Complex Environments

When virtual reality technology is used in news reporting, it is often applied to cover complex and dangerous environments [6]. For example, fires and accident scenes. By wearing VR equipment, viewers can look around the place of the incident in 360 degrees in virtual reality and feel the real scene of smoke and fire. This way of reporting not only allows the audience to more intuitively understand the extent of the disaster, but also makes the news report more emotional resonance, stimulating the audience's concern for the people in the disaster area. The CCTV network VR immersion news in the "heard" flood "and move, dikes built" orange Great Wall "special report on aerial photography, 360-degree video and the integration of VR video panels, full of highly advanced VR technology in the field of news reporting significant value [7].The use of panoramic pictures plays a vivid and intuitive descriptive role in the aerial photography of the Yonglexu board in Xinzhou Township, which profoundly presents the severity of the flood disaster through the high degree of reproducibility of the images. This not only enhances the information density of the report, but also gives viewers a more intuitive understanding of the actual situation of the affected areas. The Emergency Rescue of Armed Police Officers and Soldiers section was presented in the form of a 360-degree video, an interactive visual experience that not only reinforced the immersion of the report, but also provided an interactive media environment with a strong sense of audience participation. The audience felt as if they were there, and felt the heroic struggle of the officers and soldiers in the emergency rescue mission. The dike construction and rescue section utilizes VR video form to vividly present the process of rescue work carried out by officers and soldiers in the rain. Through the technical means of virtual reality, the report successfully introduced the audience to the perspective of the officers and soldiers, making them understand more intuitively the various complex situations in the rescue process. This kind of situation reproduction adds a lot of color to the report, showing the unique expressive power of VR technology in news reporting.

3.5 VR Immersion News on CCTV

CCTV's VR immersive news brings viewers into the heart of news events through 360-degree video and panoramic photo technology, providing a more comprehensive and in-depth reporting experience. This immersive reporting method not only enhances the news dissemination effect, but also brings a richer sensory experience to the audience, provides a deep interactive experience, injects a brand new era into the field of news reporting, and at the same time promotes the innovation of news reporting methods.

4 Possible Challenges of VR Technology in Live Interviews

4.1 Network Quality and Stability

In live interviews, the presentation of virtual reality images requires real-time transmission of the content of the screen, so as to ensure that the audience can participate in a timely manner, which puts high demands on the quality and stability of the network, and if the quality of the network fails to meet the requirements, it may lead to problems such as transmission delays and delays in the quality of the picture [8].

4.2 Equipment Costs and Deficiencies

Interviewers and viewers are required to wear appropriate virtual reality equipment, the current market, no matter which type of virtual reality equipment, the price is not expensive, for news organizations and viewers are a lot of money, and nowadays the technology is not perfect enough, the mainstream equipment of virtual reality equipment is still dominated by the VR helmet, but are generally present in the weight of the large, short duration, low permeability, wear too long will lead to Dizziness and other problems.

4.3 Insufficient Skilled Personnel

The lack of virtual reality talent in news organizations and the lack of maturity of the technology.

4.4 Level of Technology Affects Immersion

Creating a real-feeling virtual environment requires strong technical support in order to match the virtual environment with the real environment, and the insufficient level of technology will also affect the user's immersion and reduce the user experience. In the process of real-life interviews, the interview site often has many uncontrollable factors, such as unchangeable lighting, noise in the background, etc., which creates difficulties in the practical application of virtual reality technology, and requires continuous improvement of technology to adapt to different environments.

4.5 Threshold of Use and Cumbersome Steps

At present, the steps of using virtual reality equipment are still cumbersome and set a certain threshold for the audience, which requires the technology sector to simplify the steps of using the equipment as a way to improve the universality of virtual reality equipment [9].

5   VR Technology Future Directions

The key to the future development of virtual reality technology is still continuous technological innovation, including higher resolution, lower latency, and lighter devices, as a way to enhance the user experience. Developing interactive virtual reality news applications allows viewers to participate in reporting in their own way, e.g., viewers can select specific events they are interested in and interact with elements in the virtual scene to enhance the user's personalized experience [10]. On the other hand, future research should also focus on the sustainable development and popularization of virtual reality technology [11]. The cost of the technology, the acceptance of the audience, and the application experience of news practitioners are all aspects that need to be studied in depth. Research in this area can help expand the practical application of virtual reality technology in the field of journalism and promote its wider and more effective integration into media business.

6   Experiment Investigation

6.1 Experimental Method

In order to explore the feasibility of applying virtual reality technology in news reporting, this study used a questionnaire survey to gain insight into this viewpoint. A total of 500 questionnaires were distributed to the audience and the survey data were statistically analyzed to understand the audience's knowledge of virtual reality technology, their views on the application of virtual reality technology in news reporting, and the limitations of using virtual reality technology.

6.2 Experimental Subjects

The respondents of the questionnaire were mainly journalists, such as reporters, editors, photographers and other professionals, technicians with extensive experience in the field of virtual reality technology, and general audience covering all age groups, professions and geographic locations.

6.3 Experimental Content

Analysis of the Audience Situation. As can be seen from Table 1, most of the industry insiders have a high level of understanding of the application of virtual reality technology in news reporting, while the general audience has a low level of understanding of virtual reality technology, so it seems that there is a need to publicize and promote the virtual reality technology, so that the general audience also has a certain understanding of virtual reality technology.

Table 1. Level of knowledge of VR technology

Level of understanding	Journalists(%)	Technicians(%)	General audience(%)
Profound Understanding	28.15	42.54	6.32
Thorough Understanding	20.17	38.32	12.67
Moderate Understanding	35.42	15.59	22.27
Limited Understanding	12.23	2.33	30.69
No Understanding	4.03	1.22	28.05
Total	100.0	100.0	100.0

From Table 2, we can learn that most news practitioners have a supportive attitude towards the application of virtual reality technology in news reporting, with a relatively high percentage of strong support and stronger support. Among technologists, supportive attitudes toward virtual reality technology are relatively balanced, including strong support, stronger support, and neutrality. Among the general audience, views on virtual reality technology are relatively scattered, including a variety of attitudes such as neutral, less supportive, and not supportive at all. Overall, supportive attitudes are dominant in response to the use of virtual reality technology in news reporting, especially among news practitioners with relatively high levels of support.

Table 2. Perspectives on the use of virtual reality technology in journalism

Opinion	Journalists(%)	Technicians(%)	General audience(%)
Strongly Supportive	45.25	34.56	24.46
Strongly Favorable	40.82	35.46	26.73
Neutral	13.46	25.67	32.56
Somewhat Opposed	0.34	2.35	12.69
Completely Unsupportive	0.13	1.96	3.56
Total	100.0	100.0	100.0

From Table 3, it can be learned that the cost of equipment, network quality, and comfort of use are the common core concerns of the interviewees of virtual reality technology in news reporting. Technologists focused more on technical challenges, while news professionals and general audience were more concerned with the actual experience of using it. Security issues raised high concerns among the general audience, while journalists and technologists were relatively less concerned.

Table 3. Limitations in the use of VR technology

Limitations	Journalists(%)	Technicians(%)	General audience(%)
Network quality	24.56	22.43	12.36
Equipment cost	25.65	20.39	13.56
Technical proficiency	12.35	23.09	19.80
Security Concerns	19.64	13.53	28.34
Comfort of use	16.46	15.11	25.69
Other	1.34	5.45	0.25
Total	100.0	100.0	100.0

Result. The results of the questionnaire survey can be learned that, in terms of immersive experience, most of the industry insiders said that virtual reality technology really enhances the audience's immersive experience of news reporting, while the general audience's views are more diverse, part of the audience believes that it really improves the audience's sense of participation, while the other part believes that there are many limitations in the use of virtual reality technology, for example, the cost of acquiring virtual reality equipment limits some of the audience's participation [12]. Audience's participation; there is a certain threshold for getting started with virtual reality equipment, which becomes an obstacle to participation for some audience members; some audience members are still skeptical about the comfort and safety of virtual reality equipment, and feel that there are still more considerations about whether the prolonged use of virtual reality equipment will have an impact on health and whether virtual reality equipment is able to guarantee the user's privacy and information security; at present, the network requirements of most virtual reality equipment are relatively high, and some audience members believe that virtual reality technology has many limitations. At present, the network requirements of most of the virtual reality devices are relatively high, which poses a limitation to the areas where the network conditions are not good enough.

Overall most of the respondents are looking forward to the future development of virtual reality technology in the field of news reporting, the industry focuses mainly on the hope that the technology can be widely used in the practice of reporting, especially in complex and dangerous environments, which can greatly reduce the investment in manpower, and the audience cares about the point to focus on improving the universality of virtual reality equipment, lowering the threshold of learning virtual reality technology, so that households can enjoy the news immersion brought by virtual reality technology without any hindrance.

7 Discussion and Analysis

This study emphasizes the potential impact of virtual reality technology in news reporting [13]. Through the case study, it can be found that virtual reality technology can significantly enhance viewers' understanding and engagement with the news. Immersive experiences, panoramic photos, 360-degree videos and other technological means create a more realistic and in-depth reporting experience for viewers, enabling them to perceive the context of the reported events in a more comprehensive and detailed way. The impact lies not only in the innovation of the technology itself, but also in the fundamental change in the paradigm of news dissemination, which has transformed the audience from passive receivers of information to active participants [14].

Acknowledgments. This work was funded by Social Science Foundation of Fujian Province, China (Funding Number: FJ2022C071). And funded by Xiamen Education Scientific Planning Project: Application of VR in art design courses in the post-epidemic era Innovative Teaching Reform Study (Funding Number:22002). And funded by High-level Talent Research Project of Xiamen University of Technology (Funding Number: YSK22018R).

References

1. Hanbo, D.: Exploring the practice of journalism aesthetics in media convergence–Taking the winning works of the 32nd China news award as an example. J. Res. Guide **22**, 99–101 (2023)
2. Vladimir, S., Yanmei, W.: Research on the innovation of Chinese calligraphy's foreign communication practice: an example of interactive video empathy design. Beijing Cult. Creativity **S2**, 67–76 (2023)
3. Xue, C.: The integration development of traditional media and new media under "Internet+" mode. News Commun. **12**, 52–54 (2023)
4. Liu, J.: Analysis of synergistic effect between traditional newspaper and new media. J. Res. Guide **05**, 92–95 (2024)
5. Yingxue, W.: Research on innovative communication of immersive major theme reporting of CCTV (Master's thesis, Communication University of China) (2023)

6. Lee, R.: An analysis of the public opinion guiding function of immersive news–Taking Xinhua News Agency as an example. Picking Writing Editorial **12**, 52–54 (2023)

7. Pang, H.-N., Luo, J.-J., Huang, H.-J.: Exploration and inspiration of "VR+News" in the context of media deep integration–Taking CCTV.com's "VR immersion news" as an example. News Front **20**, 112–114 (2021)

8. Yao, J.D.: Volumetric photography to build an innovative model of MR intelligent art teaching. Sino-Arab Sci. Technol. Forum (in English and Chinese) **12**, 123–127 (2023)

9. Xiao, T., Xiu, J.T.: Research on the innovation path of network ideological and political education in colleges and universities under 5G+VR technology. J. Chongqing Electric Power Higher Specialized School **03**, 61–64 (2022)

10. Liu, F.: The re-branding of paper media in the new media environment. J. Cradle **03**, 144–146 (2024)

11. Yuan, X., Lv, X., Feng, D., Wang, Z.: Research on the development of virtual reality industry based on technology-driven and service innovation. China Eng. Sci. (2024)

12. Zhang, C.: Virtual reality system development and application in teaching new energy vehicles. Autom. Pract. Technol. **04**, 139–142 (2024). https://doi.org/10.16638/j.cnki.1671-7988.2024.004.028

13. Zhang, Z., Pu, X., Bian, X., Ma, T., Liu, F.: VR interactive virtual power generation equipment modeling and simulation. Orient. Electr. Rev. (01), 1–6+10 (2024). https://doi.org/10.13661/j.cnki.issn1001-9006.2024.01.008

14. Tao, Q.-Y., Li, Y.: Exploring the innovative teaching path of news camera and video editing experiment. J. Res. Guide **04**, 109–111 (2024)

Does the Metaverse Conflict with Social Goods? Challenges at the Intersection of the Metaverse and SDGs

Arisa Yasuda(✉)

School of Computing, Australian National University, Canberra, Australia
arisa.yasuda@anu.edu.au

Abstract. Information technologies have impacted society and thus the social good in various fashions. The metaverse is one of the notable technologies today enabling an immersive virtual meta-world. The metaverse is a technological novelty and at the same time a social novelty with diverse implications for the way we live. In this paper we analyze the societal impacts of the metaverse from the perspective of Sustainable Development Goals (SDGs). We thereby shed light on how the metaverse impacts the social good and based upon that we finally consider ethical design principles for the metaverse to support the SDGs.

Keywords: Metaverse · SDGs · Social goods

1 Introduction

From 2016 we are in the Web 3.0 era [1], when various technologies such as blockchain, big data, mobile, and VR/AR have been introduced and are active in various fields. One of the notable technologies today is the metaverse, i.e., an immersive virtual meta-world. The metaverse today is more than just a technology. It is also being recognized as a platform for the next generation of social connections and networking [2,3]. It is also used as a way to solve social issues and contribute to the social good [4–6].

In this paper we adopt the concept of Sustainable Development Goals (SDGs) to evaluate the metaverse's impact on social good. SDGs are a set of 17 goals and 169 targets by the United Nations General Assembly [7], aimed at addressing the most pressing global challenges and promoting sustainable development. The metaverse has the potential to both support and hinder progress toward the SDGs. This paper sheds light not only on the opportunities of the metaverse to positively contribute to the SDGs but also on the challenges of the metaverse negatively impacting the SDGs. We also briefly discuss ethical design principles to address the challenges that arise at the intersection of the metaverse and the SDGs.

© The Author(s), under exclusive license to Springer Nature Switzerland AG 2024
C. Stephanidis et al. (Eds.): HCII 2024, CCIS 2116, pp. 169–179, 2024.
https://doi.org/10.1007/978-3-031-61950-2_19

2   Metaverse's Impact on SDGs: Positive Contributions

The advantages and disadvantages of the metaverse are outlined in the figure below, along with possible scenarios. First, we evaluate the contributions in a nutshell. For detailed information, please refer to the Table 1.

First, the metaverse contributes to social issues through the creation of space. It can create an unlimited number of virtual spaces tailored to our needs. For example, the metaverse allows users to immerse themselves in the situation, which encourages a deeper examination of the topic, making it suitable for educational purposes. In addition, it allows customized education and training. The metaverse serves as a means of connecting and matching purposes, including fundraising, recruitment, and trade. Furthermore, it can also serve as a communication platform for different social networks, providing real-time communication options.

Secondly, the metaverse is well-suited for managerial purposes; for instance, organizations may implement remote work arrangements. Furthermore, it is suitable for recording and monitoring purposes. For example, blockchain technology in the metaverse can be important in securing transactions and the trustworthy flow of financial transactions by being used as a virtual ledger.

Third, the metaverse can create a virtual economy referred to as the "metaverse economic zone", where various economic activities may take place. Consequently, new demands and opportunities may emerge from the metaverse.

Fourth, the metaverse can be utilized for simulation purposes, providing a way to minimize risks and conserve resources in the physical world while exploring different scenarios and ideas for optimal outcomes. In addition, its vivid and realistic visualization with XR technologies and 3D modeling contributes to more realistic experiments and simulations.

Finally, the metaverse has the potential to promote human rights, foster a more inclusive environment, and facilitate respectful interactions between users from different backgrounds. It transcends physical boundaries and provides access to virtual spaces for anyone with the necessary infrastructure.

3   Metaverse Versus SDGs: Identifying Conflicts

In this section we detail how the metaverse conflicts with the SDGs.

3.1   Metaverse Causes Gap

The metaverse can cause and widen disparities. One reason is that there are high hurdles to accessing the metaverse. We require not only minimal infrastructure to access the Internet but also expensive VR goggles and other gadgets to make themselves an immersive environment. For instance, the popular VR Google, Meta Quest 3.0 starts at US$499.99 [8] and PlayStation VR2 at US$549.99 [9]). This would be a heavy burden for those with financial hardship. Once the initial hurdles are overcome, we can enter a positive cycle of platform opportunities,

Table 1. Metaverse's Impact on SDGs

No.	Expected Contributions	Challenges
1 NO POVERTY	– Visualize poverty with XR and immerse people in the reality of poverty for educational purposes. – Raise funds to eliminate poverty. – Introduce a tax system tailored to each country's circumstances (i.e. preferential treatment for developing countries). – Implement blockchain technology to secure and record transactions to prevent exploitation.	– The shift of certain activities to the metaverse can lead to job losses and reduced income for some individuals who maintain the traditional way in the real world.
2 ZERO HUNGER	– Visualize hunger with XR and immerse people in the reality of hunger for educational purposes. – Raise funds to support agriculture development. – Manage market by collecting stock data, analyzing it, and forecasting supply and demand.	– A small group of influential entities control or manipulate food trading within the metaverse, it may heighten the susceptibility of the food supply chain, potentially compromising food security.
3 GOOD HEALTH AND WELL-BEING	– Educate people about good health and well-being. – Raise funds to support well-being. – Use the metaverse as a tele-hospital place. – Facilitate collaboration among researchers and promote medical development. – Enable healthcare professionals to simulate surgery in a virtual environment to improve their skills.	– Share sales information regarding illegal drugs, alcohol, and tobacco in the metaverse. – Excessive metaverse use can result in symptoms resembling a "Cyber-Syndrome", which affects physical and mental well-being. – Virtual medical consultations could lead to decreased diagnostic accuracy and missed diseases. – Failure to manage e-waste containing hazardous substances can lead to health hazards.
4 QUALITY EDUCATION	– Train teachers to increase experienced teachers. – Improve accessibility with XR, ensuring inclusion for children and people with disabilities. – Enable personalized educational programs. – Raise funds to support education in developing countries (i.e. higher educational training).	– Individuals without access are unable to reach high-quality educational content within the metaverse. – Reduces face-to-face interaction and collaboration, compromising education quality.
5 GENDER EQUALITY	– Train women in the metaverse to improve their skills. – Create remote work opportunities especially for women to help balance work and family life. – Allow users to customize their appearance, including gender, race, and other characteristics.	– Sexual harassment in the metaverse can feel more realistic and uncomfortable due to the physical interaction between users. – There is a need to ensure equal access to asset ownership, access to financial services, and inheritance regardless of gender.

(continued)

Table 1. (*continued*)

No.	Expected Contributions	Challenges
6 CLEAN WATER AND SANITATION	– Visualize wastewater and sanitation methods with XR for educational purposes. – Simulate freshwater production, efficient water use, wastewater treatment, recycling, and reuse technologies in the metaverse.	– Large amounts of water are used to cool data centers and equipment in the metaverse, resulting in increased digital wastewater.
7 AFFORDABLE AND CLEAN ENERGY	– Educate people about affordable and clean energy. – Conduct simulations on renewable energy, energy efficiency, and environmentally friendly technologies.	– The metaverse that operates the infrastructure lacks renewable energy and energy conservation technologies.
8 DECENT WORK AND ECONOMIC GROWTH	– Conduct virtual job fairs to post job opportunities. – Monitor the working progress and performance. – Establish virtual trading platforms to create new trading opportunities and facilitate business. – Monitor and record the work to avoid overwork.	– All activities in the metaverse are recorded and monitored, which can cause employees to feel watched, leading to stress and anxiety.
9 INDUSTRY, INNOVATION AND INFRASTRUCTURE	– Train people to boost information and communication technology skills. – Increase economic opportunities such as new types of jobs by expanding the metaverse economy.	– Issues related to intellectual property may arise, posing the risk of rampant theft of knowledge and ideas.
10 REDUCED INEQUALITIES	– Utilize blockchain technology for a secure virtual ledger to prevent exploitation or manipulation. – Raise funds to reduce inequalities. – Establish a virtual remittance platform that allows efficient income transfers with reduced fees. – Transcend physical limitations to reach people with access difficulty in real life.	– The cost of accessing the metaverse causes inequality between the individuals who can access or not.
11 SUSTAINABLE CITIES AND COMMUNITIES	– Provide a virtual construction platform. – Analyze tragedy impacts like natural disasters. – Simulate the population of migrants in urban areas and its impact (i.e. logistics, environment, economy).	– Privacy and security concerns can impact community trust and safety. – Virtual currency value fluctuations can lead to credit losses for the economy. – Disconnection from the real world and isolation within communities.

(*continued*)

Table 1. (*continued*)

No.	Expected Contributions	Challenges
12	– Educate people about consumption and production. – Implement a system to allocate and report consumption and production. – Implement customized tax reforms prioritizing preferential treatment for developing nations. – Utilize blockchain technology for secure transactions to prevent falsehood.	– More e-waste such as VR goggles will be generated in the future, requiring proper waste management.
13	– Visualize climate change and how it affects the ecosystem with XR for education purposes. – Raise funds to support climate change mitigation. – Conduct a simulation for climate change. – Monitor the contributions of entities to address climate change.	– The metaverse utilizes advanced graphics and processing power, causing carbon dioxide emissions through activities such as streaming and transactions, which finally affect global warming.
14	– Visualize oceans and ecosystems for education purposes. – Raise funds to support the ocean environment. – Simulate suffocating oceans and ocean acidification. – Monitor illegal activities like illegal fishing.	– Information sharing within the metaverse allows illegal fishing activities to spread in the real world.
15	– Visualize the land situation like deforestation for education purposes. – Raise funds for sustainable forest management. – Simulate biodiversity, ecosystem, deforestation, and food chain disruption. – Monitor wildlife poaching and illegal wildlife trading.	– Information sharing within the metaverse allows illegal deforestation to spread in the real world.
16	– Facilitate international collaboration. – Simulate natural disasters like earthquakes, terrorism scenarios, and pandemic preparedness. – Establish a trusted flow of financial transactions through blockchain technology to prevent fraud and malfeasance, and improve economic reliability. – Improve the metaverse's security by adding mechanisms to monitor violent activity.	– Privacy breaches and fraudulent activities have arisen in the metaverse. – Violent behavior, bullying, discrimination, and harassment occur in the metaverse. – Fluctuating virtual currency values can cause economic credit losses and social security issues. – There is a need for appropriate governing bodies and develop judicial procedures.
17	– Connect people and encourage partnerships.	– There is a need to establish a legal framework that can be universally applied across countries.

access resources including educational content, acquire the necessary skills, leverage those skills in the metaverse market, and finally make money. Conversely, those who do not are left behind (No.10). The metaverse can provide people with high-quality, customized educational content, however, it becomes meaningless for those who do not have access to it. Inequality of initial access may even increase other equalities such as educational inequality (No.4). Another reason is that some people may be adversely affected by the transition of some activities to metaverse activities. For example, if certain jobs transition to the metaverse or technologies and know-how are shared within the metaverse, those who have maintained the traditional way in the real world may experience temporary loss of jobs and income, possibly leading to poverty (No.1).

3.2   Concentration of Power

Metaverse causes a power concentration. It is because most of our information such as sight, hearing, speech, body movement, and possibly even the content of thought could in principle be acquired in the fully developed metaverse, which may accelerate the hyper-supervised society so-called surveillance capitalism [10]. In addition, the metaverse is addictive and immersive [11], users then tend to spend a significant amount of time there, which increases the overall amount of information gathered. The metaverse thus reinforces the problem of surveillance in terms of both the variety and quantity of information collected. As a result, the major technology companies and platforms that control the metaverse will have significant power. These platformers will control many things as governance and there is a risk of manipulating information and user behavior caused by them. Thus, the metaverse economy could allow some individuals and companies to dominate the market and build competitive advantages over the other participants, which sometimes poses additional risks. For example, if food traded in the metaverse is controlled or manipulated by a few key players, it can heighten the susceptibility of the food supply chain, potentially compromising food security (No.2). Another problem is people's growing anxiety about surveillance capitalism. People may feel uneasy about having their actions monitored. For example, working in a metaverse provides employees with flexibility and the freedom to choose when and where they work, but at the same time, it instills a sense of being watched, as all activities are recorded and monitored. This can lead to stress and anxiety (No.8). Besides, privacy and security concerns regarding the handling of personal information and digital assets within the metaverse may be raised against the platformer, which could affect the trust and safety of the community (No.11).

3.3   Crimes in the Metaverse

New types of criminal activities and amplification of existing crime may emerge in the metaverse. The first reason is simply the places where people can commit a crime will increase, there are new opportunities for people to cause the crime in the metaverse. In fact, concerns about privacy breaches and fraudulent activities such as hacking incidents, unauthorized sale of stolen data to external entities, and its misuse for fraud have arisen [12](No. 16). It is true that the same type of crime occurred on the previous web, however as we get new types of information, hackers can make use of them. In fact, voices are increasingly being stolen and used for fraud purposes [13]. Since the metaverse is a treasure trove of data from which sensitive personal information can be obtained, it is necessary to consider the possibility that it will be used for criminal purposes in the future [14]. The second reason is that the boundary between the real and virtual is blurred, and users could bring existing problems into the metaverse. Issues such as violent behavior, bullying, discrimination, and harassment have appeared in the metaverse (No. 16). Some of these issues are more serious than in the traditional web. Sexual harassment, in particular, individuals may encounter more realistic experiences in the metaverse, as users can physically interact with each other. This tactile dimension makes the impact on the victim feel more tangible and makes the discomfort (No. 5). The third reason is about abusing the metaverse as a place of communication. While the metaverse serves as a platform for information sharing, it can also be used for sharing criminal information. For example, sharing sales information regarding the distribution of illegal drugs, alcohol, and tobacco in the metaverse can present both legal and health risks (No. 3). In addition, if information about illegal fishing and deforestation could be shared in the metaverse, it would cause negative real-world ecological impacts (No. 14 and No. 15).

3.4   Lack of Governance

The metaverse currently does not have adequate governance. Its governance, including economic governance, political governance, social governance, and so on is dependent on specific platforms. However, users come from diverse backgrounds, and there is a need to establish a legal framework that can be universally applied across countries (No.17). Regarding social governance, there is still a lack of fair rules regarding gender within the metaverse, and regulations must be implemented to eradicate sexist practices in the real world. For example, there is a need to ensure equal access to asset ownership, access to financial services, and inheritance regardless of gender (No.5). In terms of economic and political governance, there are no uniform rules for doing business in the metaverse, including the protection of intellectual property rights. This may increase the risk of rampant theft of knowledge and ideas (No.9). Furthermore, the metaverse has its own economy, an example of which is virtual currency. However, these virtual currencies give value to things that do not physically exist, and because of their fluctuations in value, the lack of stability can lead to a loss of confidence in the market as a whole and finally affect social safety (No.11 and No.16). Finally, we do not have appropriate governing bodies and develop judicial procedures and penalties for misconduct in the metaverse (No.16).

3.5   Metaverse Addiction

Due to the immersive feature of the metaverse, it could blur the distinction between the real world and the virtual world. This causes a variety of problems, including health issues. For example, excessive metaverse use could cause what is known as "Cyber-Syndrome", which has a negative impact physically, socially, and mentally [14]. Examples include physical issues such as sleep disorders, social issues such as isolation, and mental issues such as delusional disorders (No.3). As the metaverse becomes more prevalent, there is a danger that people will become overly enthusiastic about it and eventually alienate themselves from the real community, feeling isolated, and the existing sense of community unity will fade away (No.11).

3.6   Transition from the Real to the Virtual

The cases of transitioning traditional real-world activities to the metaverse have been increasing. However, this transition brings difficulties. For example, medical consultations have moved significantly online since the COVID-19 pandemic [15]. In the future, some medical consultations will be conducted in the metaverse. Making a diagnosis without physically performing laboratory tests and examinations on a patient offers convenience, however, we have to consider that it also carries the potential for decreased diagnostic accuracy and missed diseases (No.3). Increased transience to the metaverse may reduce direct face-to-face encounters and interactions and influence negatively. Decreased direct interaction and cooperation, for instance, may limit opportunities for learning and knowledge sharing, which may negatively impact the quality of education (No.4).

3.7   Environmental Problems

The rapid growth and widespread adoption of the metaverse may cause various environmental problems.

This trend accelerated the demand for the data center which is a facility or building where servers are securely stored. According to [16], data centers in 2022 account for 1%–1.5% of global electricity consumption. These days, many new data centers were constructed, in 2023, data center construction in major markets will be the largest ever [17]. Each data center indeed requires many high-performance servers to process large amounts of data at high speed, which accelerates power consumption and heat generation, resulting in high temperatures inside the data centers. For high temperatures, these data centers require significant cooling facilities. Data centers use large amounts of water for cooling, which results in increased digital wastewater (No.6).

Carbon neutrality, which is one of the global action plans to deal with rising global greenhouse gas concentrations and temperatures, is a vital perspective to consider environmental problems. It is necessary to not only reduce CO_2 emissions but also to remove CO_2 from the atmosphere to achieve net-zero carbon or negative carbon emissions through various social, economic, environmental, and technological measures [18]. The metaverse can indeed play a role in reducing the amount of emission of transportation, manufacturing, and energy generation [19]. For example, the metaverse curbs emissions through activities such as holding virtual meetings instead of in-person meetings. For example, according to a recent study, shifting physical meetings to virtual meetings can reduce carbon emissions by as much as 94% [20]. At the same time, however, the metaverse utilizes advanced graphics and processing power, causing carbon dioxide emissions through activities such as streaming and transactions, which potentially affect global warming (No.13) [21]. Thus, there is a trade-off between the amount of CO_2 emitted by the metaverse and the amount of CO_2 that can be reduced by using the metaverse.

While it is possible to reduce the amount of carbon dioxide emission, it is impossible to eliminate it. One of the solutions to reduce carbon dioxide emissions from the metaverse is the introduction of renewable energy, and we can cover energy consumption with renewable energy. Thus, investing the sustainable energy solutions and effective energy management is important. Clean solutions to energy and water consumption are required because currently there is a lack of renewable energy and energy conservation technologies installed in the infrastructure operating metaverse (No.7).

Finally, E-waste/WEEE (Waste Electrical and Electronic Equipment) has increased so far and poses a serious challenge in disposal and recycling for both developed and developing countries [22]. The more widespread the metaverse becomes, the more e-waste such as VR goggles will be generated in the future, requiring proper waste management (No.12). Failure to manage them could lead to health problems due to the hazardous substances they contain (No.3). There are problems not only in hardware waste problems but also in software. For example, data accumulation in the metaverse leads to increased costs associated with increased data storage and the presence of unnecessary data can degrade overall system preferences.

4 Ethical Design Principles

Based on the aforementioned social issues, we propose ethical principles in terms of environmental, economic, social, legal, and governance aspects. For environmental problems, the core principle concerns should involve enhancing energy efficiency, alongside integrating renewable energy sources to offset any excess energy consumption. In the economy, we suggest several guidelines to ensure the proper operation of the metaverse economy. These include guidelines for the proper handling of data in business activities, guidelines to prevent excessive concentration of power, and guidelines to promote employment and a good working environment. From a social perspective, education needs to take advantage of the technology and virtual collaboration used in the metaverse, as well as a better understanding of literacy in the use of the metaverse. Some problems like criminal activities in the metaverse can be solved by technology and legislation. It is also important to take steps to lower the barriers to metaverse use so that the gap between rich and poor does not widen. In the area of law, we examine the basic principles that guide the formulation of regulations in the metaverse. For example, it is imperative to avoid implementing discriminatory laws that reflect real-world inequalities. Legal considerations are approached through the lens of various industries. With regard to economic facets, the prioritization of intellectual property rights emerges as an immediate necessity. Finally, the establishment of an appropriate governance structure is an urgent issue in the operation of the metaverse. for the governance structure, equal distribution of power and transparency are essential. It is also essential to take proactive measures and coordinate with the appropriate agencies to prepare for unforeseen events.

5   Conclusion

We have so far discussed metaverse contribution to the social good, while referring to the ethical issues that would arise in the metaverse and may lead to potential threats to the SDGs. This study brings attention to the significance of the metaverse in contributing to the achievements of SDGs. We have finally referred to ethical design principles for the sustainable metaverse, the proposals provide guidelines to ensure that the development of the metaverse is socially sound. The detailed solution for each SDGs and how to implement the ethical design principles realistically through the coordination of various stakeholders and relevant policies would need to be explored further and thus be our future work.

References

1. Nova, S.: Web 3.0: The Third Generation Web is Coming (2011). http://lifeboat.com/ex/web.3.0
2. Park, S.M., Kim, Y.G.: A metaverse: taxonomy, components, applications, and open challenges. IEEE Access **10**, 4209–4251 (2022)
3. Hwang, G.J., Chien, S.Y.: Definition, roles, and potential research issues of the metaverse in education: an artificial intelligence perspective. Comput. Educ. Artifi. Intell. **3**, 100082 (2022)
4. Duan, H., Li, J., Fan, S., Lin, Z., Wu, X., Cai, W.: Metaverse for social good: a university campus prototype. In Proceedings of the 29th ACM international conference on multimedia, pp. 153-161 (2021)
5. BUANA, I. M. W.: Metaverse: threat or opportunity for our social world? In understanding Metaverse on sociological context. J. Metaverse **3**(1), 28-33 (2023)
6. De Giovanni, P.: Sustainability of the metaverse: a transition to industry 5.0. Sustainability **15**(7), 6079 (2023)
7. Nations U: Transforming our world: The 2030 agenda for sustainable development. New York: United Nations, Department of Economic and Social Affairs.(2015)
8. Meta.: Meet Meta Quest 3, Our Mixed Reality Headset Starting at $499.99.(2023). https://about.fb.com/news/2023/09/meet-meta-quest-3-mixed-reality-headset/
9. Shop PS VR2. https://direct.playstation.com/en-us/playstation-vr2

10. Zuboff, S.: The age of surveillance capitalism. In Social Theory Re-Wired, pp. 203-213. Routledge (2023)
11. Mystakidis, S.: Metaverse. Encyclopedia.: 2(1):486-497 (2022). https://doi.org/10.3390/encyclopedia2010031
12. Wu, J., Lin, K., Lin, D., Zheng, Z., Huang, H., Zheng, Z.: Financial crimes in web3-empowered metaverse: taxonomy, countermeasures, and opportunities. IEEE Open J. Computer Soc. **4**, 37–49 (2023)
13. Verma, P.: They thought loved ones were calling for help. It was an AI scam. The Washington Post (March 5 2023). https://www.washingtonpost.com/technology/2023/03/05/ai-voice-scam/
14. Yasuda, A.: Human-computer interaction in the emerging metaverse: social implications and design principles for the sustainable metaverse. In: International Conference on Human-Computer Interaction (pp. 492-504). Cham: Springer Nature Switzerland (2023). https://doi.org/10.1007/978-3-031-48057-7_31
15. Hong, J.Y., He, J., Lam, B., Gupta, R., Gan, W.S.: Spatial audio for soundscape design: recording and reproduction. Appl. Sci. **7**(6), 627 (2017)
16. Data Centres and Data Transmission Networks. https://www.iea.org/energy-system/buildings/data-centres-and-data-transmission-networks
17. North America Data Center Trends H1 2023 (6 September 2023). https://www.cbre.com/insights/reports/north-america-data-center-trends-h1-2023
18. Chen, L., et al.: Strategies to achieve a carbon neutral society: a review. Environ. Chem. Lett. **20**(4), 2277–2310 (2022)
19. Allam, Z., Sharifi, A., Bibri, S.E., Jones, D.S., Krogstie, J.: The metaverse as a virtual form of smart cities: Opportunities and challenges for environmental, economic, and social sustainability in urban futures. Smart Cities **5**(3), 771–801 (2022)
20. Tao, Y., Steckel, D., Klemeš, J.J., You, F.: Trend towards virtual and hybrid conferences may be an effective climate change mitigation strategy. Nat. Commun. **12**(1), 7324 (2021)
21. Liu, F., Pei, Q., Chen, S., Yuan, Y., Wang, L., Muhlhauser, M.: When the Metaverse Meets Carbon Neutrality: Ongoing Efforts and Directions. arXiv preprint arXiv:2301.10235 (2023)
22. Needhidasan, S., Samuel, M., Chidambaram, R.: Electronic waste-an emerging threat to the environment of urban India. J. Environ. Health Sci. Eng. **12**, 1–9 (2014)

Interacting with Cultural Heritage, Art and Creativity

Exploring Relationships Between Personality and Creativity

Daniel Badro, Olayele Adelakun$^{(\boxtimes)}$, and Xiaowen Fang$^{(\boxtimes)}$

DePaul University, Chicago, IL 60604, USA
dbadro@depaul.edu, XFang@cdm.depaul.edu

Abstract. Extensive research has been conducted on personality and creativity. Scholars have been able to identify various factors that influence personality and creativity. For examples, scholars allude to the fact that those that are creative exhibit various levels of openness to new experiences and extroversion. However, the relationship between personality and creativity has yet to be established in a coherent framework. In this research in progress paper, the authors propose establishing a new framework to encompass the relationships between personality and creativity.

Keywords: Relationships · Personality · Creativity

1 Introduction

Creativity in nature is a unique human trait. Scholars argue that it is creativity that allows for the visualization, imagination, and reconstruction of certain events regardless of past, present, or future. While the literature is ambiguous on the definition of creativity, Guilford [11] defines creativity in terms of two criteria: novelty and adaptability. The creative person must be novel in their approach as well as adaptable to various situations. It is important to note that other scholars have identified other criteria that coincides with the definition of creativity. For example, Madjar et al. [9] argue that creativity refers to the production of new and useful ideas by an individual or group of individuals working together. Past research conducted does not provide a clear overview on which specific personality traits can contribute to creativity. For example, Feist [9] alludes to the fact that creative individuals are high in autonomy, more ambitious, hostile, dominant, impulsive, confident, extraverted, and open to new experiences. McCrae et al. [21] indicate that creative individuals are those that are open to new experiences. Leith [15] concludes that those that exhibit high extroversion and low neuroticism proved to be more creative in comparison to others.

Scholars in the field have been unable to coherently list the personality traits that contribute to creativity. In addition, past research focused on the use of subjective data collected in an artificial environment. This data collection process was also administered during a short period of time. For example, Heinen et al. [12] conducted two experiments. These experiments were conducted over a short duration of time and the results indicate that the offering of guidance on how to be more creative resulted in creative responses that were more semantically distant in comparison to uncreative responses. These experiments focus on the use of subjective data collected in an artificial environment within a short period of time.

The purpose of this research is twofold. First, the researchers will try and explore the different relationships between personality traits and different creativities. First, the researchers will attempt to explore the relationship between various personality traits and different creativities. Second, the researchers will explore different types of creativity. This paper is organized to present the readers with a literature review. Within this literature review, the subsections of creativity, personality and creativity, and other factors that influence personality and creativity are discussed. The subsequent sections consist of the research framework, the research methodology, and the conclusion as well as the next steps.

2   Literature Review

2.1   Creativity

Creativity has previously been defined as a process that results in a novel work that is accepted as tenable or useful or satisfying to a group at some point in time [30]. However, there are additional definitions of creativity. Simpson [29] defines creativity as the intuition which one manifests by their power to break away from the usual thought routine and into an altogether different pattern of thought. Wertheimer [33] proposes that creative thinking is the successful transposition of a member from one configuration to another. Drevdahl [6] maintains that the primary method of creative thought is the deducing of correlates, the transplanting of an old relation, and in consequence, the generation of a new correlate. Ribot [27] attributes creativity to the motor activities produced by appetites, tendencies, and desires as well as the possibilities of spontaneous revival of images that become grouped in new combinations. Klavir et al. [14] define creativity as a product or behavior that satisfies criteria of originality and appropriateness. Tyler [32] argues that creativity is best defined as the recognition of possibilities. MacKinnon [18] considers creativity as an attribute of personality or a particular kind of response style.

The differences in these definitions lie wherein each scholar offers different characteristics of what comprise creativity. While the definitions mentioned in this subsection have been used in previous literature, the most common definition used revolves around creativity being defined as an idea that is novel and adaptable. It is these definitions that have enabled a productive discussion as to what creativity is. It is important to note that there is not an all-purpose definition of creativity. The definition of creativity has the potential to be one that is subjective depending on the context in which it is used. In addition to the definitions provided, scholars have also alluded to frameworks to further describe creativity. Lin [16] alludes to the notion that creative pedagogy is dependent on teaching for creativity, creative learning, and creative teaching (Fig. 1).

Nijstad et al. [24] conclude that creative ideas are dependent on attention controlled, outside factors, and flexible/persistence pathways. These pathways have a subset of different factors (Fig. 2).

Fig. 1. Lin's framework.

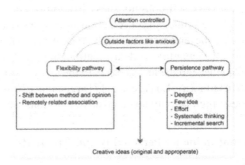

Fig. 2. Nijstad's framework

Jain et al. [13] conclude that employee creativity is comprised of characteristics of individuals as well as characteristics of organizations (Fig. 3).

Fig. 3. Jain's framework.

While the frameworks included do provide some context around creativity and what comprises creativity, the frameworks do not coherently illustrate the personality factors that comprise of creativity.

2.2 Personality and Creativity

It is understood that personality and creativity intertwine one another. Mumford et al. [23] argue that creativity is a syndrome that requires multiple resources within a person. Mayer [20] defines personality as the system of psychological attributes that describe how one feels, thinks, interacts with the social world, and regulates behavior. Goldberg [10] classifies the Big Five as a dominant model for describing broad personality traits. The Big Five lists openness to experience, neuroticism, conscientious, agreeableness, and extraversion as the five factors that influence personality and creativity. Zhao et al. [36] define openness to experience as a personality dimension that characterizes someone who is intellectually curious and tends to seek new experiences and explore novel ideas. Widiger et al. [35] describe neuroticism as the trait disposition to experience negative affect, including anger, anxiety, self-consciousness, irritability, emotional instability, and depression. Roberts et al. [28] allude to conscientiousness as the relatively stable pattern of individual differences in the tendencies to follow socially prescribed norms for impulse control, to be goal-directed, planful, to delay gratification, and to follow norms and rules. Ellis et al. [8] state that agreeableness refers to the tendency to concur with others, especially others high in authority. Lucas et al. [17] argue that extraversion encompasses sociability, assertiveness, high activity level, positive emotions, and impulsivity.

2.3 Other Factors that Influence Personality and Creativity

Scholars in the creativity research area have conducted research on the various factors that influence creativity. Mittone et al. [22] list risk preferences, past performances, and the consequences of failing to innovate as factors that influence creativity. Chen et al. [5] allude to the fact that there are certain domains of work that improve creativity. Du et al. [7] conclude that positivity can affect creativity. Scholars have found consensus as it pertains to the importance of innovation as an influencing factor. Oldham et al. [25] argue that skill variety, challenges, task identity, task significance, task feedback, and autonomy predict innovation at work. Caldwell et al. [4] allude to support for risk taking, tolerance of mistakes, teamwork, and speed of action as factors that influence innovation. Burpitt et al. [3] mention that leader empowering behavior is a factor that influences innovation. Ramirez et al. [26] conclude that mutual trust, open exchange, regular contact, democracy, attendance, and team management influence innovation.

3 Research Framework

The researchers will build upon the framework proposed by Amabile [1]. Thomson et al. [31] describe Amabile's framework as a framework that included three dominant components: domain-relevant skills, creativity-relevant skills, and task motivations. Within each component, specific factors are needed and they are dependent on other factors to be realized. For example, within the domain-relevant skills, individuals must have knowledge, technical skills, and special talents within the domain and these variables are contingent on innate cognitive, motor, and perceptual abilities in the combination with formal and informal education. Creativity-relevant skills include appropriative cognitive styles (divergent thinking, remembering accurately, perceiving novelty), implicit or explicit knowledge regarding idea generation, and effective work styles. These skill sets are dependent on past training and experience in generating new ideas coupled with personality traits that support creative exploration. Within task motivation, individuals must perceive that they are initiating the motivation to undertake the task and that the task is worth pursuing. Task motivation is dependent on intrinsic motivation, extrinsic constraints and rewards, and an ability to minimize the constraints. West et al. [34] argue that Amabile's framework is one that provides a link between the work environment, individual and team creativity, and organizational innovation. This framework is one that is suitable for our research as it clearly depicts the most important and influential personality factors as it pertains to creativity. However, the framework is not too clear as it pertains to relationships between the specific personality trait and creativity. The researchers will need to do additional research to determine the exact relationship between each specific personality trait and creativity (Fig. 4).

Fig. 4. Amabile's framework

4 Research Methodology

To further investigate the relationships between Personality Traits and Creativity, an observational study has been designed in a university in the Midwest region of the United States. The study will be conducted in an innovation lab within the university. In this innovation lab, students form teams of 6 to 10 members and work on various innovative projects with real industry clients for six months or longer. When a project team is formed, all members will be asked to respond to a 50-item NEO-IP Inventory of Personality [2]. This inventory is based on the Big-Five Personality Model and assesses the five personality traits: intellect, conscientiousness, extraversion, agreeableness, and emotional stability. At the completion level of a project, each team member will be asked to evaluate the creativity of all other peers on the team by answering the two following questions. First, what is the most creative talent of this member in comparison to other team members? Second, could you provide concrete examples of his/her creative talents demonstrated in this project? The creativity assessment reports will be integrated with the personality measure in order to examine the relationships between personality traits and creativity. This content analysis of various creativity assessment reports will also help explore the different types of creativity.

5   Conclusions and Next Steps

This paper poses an observational study to investigate how personality traits are related to creativity and to further explore different types of creativity. Due to the fact that the data will be collected in a natural environment rather than an artificial one, the results will provide a unique perspective and new insights on individual creativity.

References

1. Amabile, T.M.: The social psychology of creativity: a componential conceptualization. J. Pers. Soc. Psychol. **45**(2), 357–376 (1983)
2. Ashton, M.C., Lee, K.: A theoretical basis for the major dimensions of personality. Eur. J. Pers. **15**, 327–353 (2001)
3. Burpitt, W.J., Bigoness, W.J.: Leadership and innovation among teams: the impact of empowerment. Small Group Res. **28**(3), 414–423 (1997)
4. Caldwell, D.F., O'Reilly, C.A.: The determinants of team-based innovation in organizations. the role of social influence. Small Group Res. **34**(4). 497–517 (2003)
5. Chen, C., Himsel, A., Kasof, J., Greenberger, E., Dmitrieva, J.: Boundless creativity: evidence for the domain generality of individual differences in creativity. J. Creative Behav. **40**(3), 179–199 (2006)
6. Drevdahl, J.E., Cattrell, R.B.: Personality and creativity in artists and writers. J. Clin. Psychol. 14, 107–111 (1958)
7. Du, J., Ma, E., Cabrera, V., Mei, J.: Keep your mood up: a multilevel investigation of hospitality employees positive affect and individual creativity. J. Hosp. Tour. Manag. **48**, 451–459 (2021)
8. Ellis, L., Hoskin, A.W., Ratnasingam, M.: Personality and Behavioral Factors. Handbook of Social Status Correlates, pp. 75–118. Academic Press, (2018)
9. Feist, G.J.: A meta-analysis of personality in scientific and artistic creativity. Pers. Soc. Psychol. Rev. **2**(4), 290–309 (1998)
10. Goldberg, L.R.: The structure of phenotypic personality traits. Am. Psychol. **48**, 26–34 (1993)
11. Wreen, M.: Creativity. Philosophia **43**(3), 891–913 (2015). https://doi.org/10.1007/s11406-015-9607-5
12. Heinen, D.J.P., Johnson, D.R.: Semantic distance: an automated measure of creativity that is novel and appropriate. Psychol. Aesthet. Creat. Arts **12**(2), 144–156 (2018)
13. Jain, R.K., Jain, C.: Employee creativity: a conceptual framework. Manag. Labor Stud. **41**, 294–313 (2016)
14. Klavir, R., Gorodetsky, K.: Features of creativity as expressed in the construction of new analogical problems by intellectually gifted students. Creat. Educ. **2**, 167–173 (2011)
15. Leith, G.: The relationships between intelligence, personality, and creativity under two conditions of stress. J. Educ. Psychol. **42**(3), 240–247 (1972)
16. Lin, Y.S.: Fostering Creativity through education – a conceptual framework of creative pedagogy. Creat. Educ. **2**, 149–155 (2011)
17. Lucas, R.E., Diener, E.: Extraversion. International Encyclopedia of the Social & Behavioral Sciences, pp. 5202- 5205 (2001)
18. MacKinnon, D.W.: The nature and nurture of creative talent. Am. Psychol. **17**(7), 484–495 (1962)
19. Madjar, N., Oldhman, G.R., Pratt, M.G.: There's no place like home? The contributions of work and nonwork creativity support to employees' creative performance. Acad. Manag. J. **45**(4), 757–767 (2002)

20. Mayer, J.D.: A tale of two visions: can a new view of personality help integrate psychology. Am. Psychol. **80**, 294–307 (2005)
21. McCrae, R., Costa, P.J.: Validity of five factor model of personality across instruments and observers. J. Pers. Soc. Psychol. **52**, 81–90 (1987)
22. Mittone, L., Morreale, A., Vu, T.: What drives innovative behavior? an experimental analysis on risk attitudes, creativity, and performance. J. Behav. Exper. Econ. **98** (2022)
23. Mumford, M.D., Gustafson, S.B.: Creativity syndrome: integration, application, and innovation. Psychol. Bull. **103**, 24–43 (1988)
24. Nijstad, B.A., Carsten, K.W., Rietzschel, E.F., Baas, M.: The dual pathway to creativity model: Creative ideation as a function of flexibility and persistence. Eur. Rev. Soc. Psychol. **21**, 34–77 (2010)
25. Oldham, G.R., Cummings, A.: Employee creativity: personal and contextual factors at work. Acad. Manag. J. **39**(3), 607–634 (1996)
26. Ramirez, B.H., Berger, R., Brodbeck, C.F.: Does an adequate team climate for learning predict team effectiveness and innovation potential? a psychometric validation of the team climate questionnaire for learning in an organizational context. Proc.– Soc. Behav. Sci. **114**, 543–550 (2014)
27. Ribot, T. Essay on Creative Imagination. Open Court Publishing (1906)
28. Roberts, B.W., Jackson, J.J., Fayard, J.V., Edmonds, G.: Handbook of individual differences in social behavior, pp. 369–381. The Guilford Press (2009)
29. Simpson, R.M.: Creative imagination. Am. J. Psychol. **33**, 234–243 (1922)
30. Taylor, C.W.: Widening Horizons in Creativity. John Wiley and Sons Inc. (1964)
31. Thomson, P., Jaque, S.V.: Understanding creativity in the performing arts. Creativity and the Performing Artist, Explorations in Creativity Research, pp. 3–16 (2017)
32. Tyler, L.: Individuality: Human Possibilities and Personal Choice in the Psychological Development of Men and Women. Jossey-Bass (1978)
33. Wertheimer, M.: Productive Thinking. Harper (1959)
34. West, M.A., Sacramento, C.A.: Creativity and innovation: the role of team organizational climate. Handbook Organizat. Creat. **359**, 385 (2012)
35. Widiger, T.A., Leary, M.R., Hoyle, R.H.: Handbook of individual differences in social behavior, 129–146. The Guilford Press (2009)
36. Zhao, H., Seibert, S.E.: The big five personality dimensions and entrepreneurial status: a meta-analytics review. J. Appl. Psychol. **91**(2), 259–271 (2006)

Study on the Vivification Pathway of Lingnan Cantonese Opera in the Virtual Reality Interaction: A Case Study of Cantonese Opera "Di Nv Hua (The Emperor's Daughter)"

Lijian Chen, Xinru Zhang, and Yuanfang Zhao[(✉)] [iD]

College of Art and Design, Shenzhen University, Shenzhen 518060, People's Republic of China
zhaoyuanfang@szu.edu.cn

Abstract. With the rapid development of information technologies such as big data, the Internet of Things, virtual/augmented/mixed reality, a new technological revolution centered around three-dimensional virtual reconstruction and virtual heritage restoration exhibitions has emerged. As a vital component of the intangible cultural heritage represented by Cantonese opera in Guangdong Province, Cantonese opera costumes hold a significant position in local Chinese opera costumes and represent a crucial feature of Lingnan culture. However, Cantonese opera and its costume culture are facing a dual challenge of talent gap and insufficient value transformation, leading to the risk of no one inheriting this rich cultural tradition. This study takes the Cantonese opera "Di Nv Hua" as a case study, exploring the construction elements of characters, costume culture, and scenes through three dimensions: three-dimensional virtual reconstruction, design practice, and innovative promotion. Employing technical methods such as CLO 3D virtual costume production, Cinema 4D (C4D), Unreal Engine 5 (UE5) modeling, and Touch Designer (TD) interactive design, the study creates virtual Cantonese opera digital characters, showcases virtual Cantonese opera costumes, and simulates interactive scenes. Combined with related digital cultural and creative product design, NFT digital collections, and cultural and creative events, this "real + virtual" dual communication approach promotes dynamic heritage. It aims to attract more young individuals to understand and experience the charm of traditional Cantonese opera and its costume culture, contributing to the inheritance of this intangible cultural project with Lingnan cultural characteristics.

Keywords: Vivification Pathway · Cantonese Opera · Case Study · Virtual Reality Interaction · Virtual Clothing

1 Introduction

Cantonese opera, a gem among Chinese traditional dramas originating from southern China, bears profound cultural heritage. The costumes in Cantonese opera, constituting a vital component, encapsulate distinct regional characteristics and embody elements of China's rich traditional culture. Despite this cultural richness, Cantonese opera and its costume heritage face a dual challenge of insufficient succession and dwindling cultural relevance. The pressing issue is how to protect existing Cantonese opera and costume culture and engage the younger generation in its preservation. The Chinese government actively promotes the digitization of intangible cultural heritage, outlining a path for utilizing technology to revitalize cultural heritage digitally.

The article takes the real-time space interaction as its core. The CLO 3D completes three-dimensional virtual reconstruction such as the character, clothing, C4D headdress, and UE5 Cantonese theater of the Cantonese opera "DI NV HUA". The innovative practice module is based on the digital collection mode under the BigVerse NFT China Blockchain and the two paths of the 3D printed and creative IP built by C4D. The main line of the Guanshanyue Art Museum and the Douyin Short Video Platform launched an innovative promotion module as the main line. It is committed to inheriting and protecting traditional culture in the virtual environment, injecting new vitality into Lingnan Cantonese opera, alleviating Lingnan The problem of the fault and value of the Cantonese opera culture.

2 Virtual-Real Space Interaction and Dynamic Inheritance of Cantonese Opera

In a broad sense, virtual and real-space interaction refers to the bidirectional interaction between physical space and digital space. This is achieved through the collaborative use of technologies such as the Internet of Things (IoT), Augmented Reality (AR), Virtual Reality (VR), human-computer interaction, and sensors, facilitating the fusion, control, and feedback between virtual and real spaces 11. However, the scope of this study on virtual and real space interaction utilizes sensors (Leap Motion), enabling gesture-driven interactions in the real environment to achieve an interactive visual experience in the virtual environment. This technology allows users to interact with the real world in the virtual environment, creating a more immersive and realistic experience. Digital technology plays a crucial role in the dynamic inheritance of Cantonese opera. By combining virtual and real space interaction technology with Cantonese opera's dynamic inheritance, it achieves the virtualization and immersion of real space, providing new pathways to address the challenges faced in the inheritance, innovation, and promotion of Cantonese opera's intangible cultural heritage.

2.1 Dual Dilemma of Cantonese Opera Intangible Cultural Heritage Inheritance

Talent Gap. In the rapidly changing society of today, one of the primary challenges faced by Cantonese opera heritage is the phenomenon of talent fragmentation. Traditional skills require extensive professional training and practice to master. However, in the fast-paced modern lifestyle, the younger generation tends to prefer more contemporary and lucrative professions, showing reluctance to invest substantial time in learning and inheriting the artistic skills of Cantonese opera. This trend has led to a gradual decline in traditional skills, making the talent shortage a primary obstacle to the inheritance of Cantonese opera. According to empirical studies, the percentage of young people disliking Cantonese opera culture has reached 87%, and the overall public affection for Cantonese opera culture tends to be skewed towards an older demographic. The phenomenon of talent fragmentation has become one of the core issues threatening the inheritance of Cantonese opera.

Lack of Value Transformation. Cantonese opera faces significant challenges in value transformation. In modern society, audiences seek diversified forms of entertainment, and although traditional Cantonese opera performances are rich in cultural content, they may appear too old-fashioned and outdated for contemporary viewers. Analyzing survey data, it is evident that Cantonese opera actors face challenges with low professional income and weak value transformation, becoming a major factor hindering the development of Cantonese opera and its costume culture. Consequently, to survive, a majority of Cantonese opera actors are compelled to opt for professions that offer higher and quicker returns (see Fig. 1).

Through a detailed analysis of survey data, it is observed that current users predominantly acquire knowledge about Cantonese opera and its costume culture through online channels such as the internet and television. This indicates a shift in the way users access cultural information from traditional physical venues to digital platforms with the development of technology. Online media, particularly the internet, has become the primary medium for information dissemination, offering users a more convenient and extensive means of understanding Cantonese opera culture (see Fig. 1).

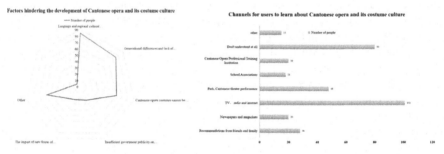

Fig. 1. Visualization of questionnaire survey data

2.2 Innovative Application of Virtual-Real Space Interaction in Cantonese Opera

The fundamental concept of virtual-real space interaction involves the integration of virtual and real environments, allowing users to perceive, comprehend, and interact within this merged environment. The goal of this interaction method is to create a space that is more realistic and experiential compared to traditional virtual environments, enabling users to engage in more natural and intuitive operations.

The scope of this study on interactive methods extends beyond virtual reality (VR) and encompasses sensor technologies and computer technologies. In the context of Cantonese opera heritage, leveraging virtual-real space interaction technology enables the creation of three-dimensional virtual Cantonese opera elements, including characters, costumes, headpieces, and scenes, using computer technology. Utilizing Leap Motion technology allows users to perform mid-air gestures in the real environment, steering virtual visuals and creating a more intuitive interactive experience, allowing users to appreciate the artistic charm of Cantonese opera in the virtual environment. At the technological level, enriches the means of heritage for Cantonese opera and provides users with a more immersive and engaging experience in terms of human-computer interaction [2].

3 Research Path of "Dynamic Inheritance" Using "Di Nv Hua" as an Example

This study focuses on Cantonese opera "Di Nv Hua" and selects the prototype foundation of two acts, "Di Nv Hua-Ying Feng" and "Di Nv Hua-Xiang Yao." It completes the digital models of the core characters, namely the positive female role Chang Ping, the secondary female role Zhou Ruiran, the martial male role Zhou Shixian, and the martial male role Zhou Zhong. The research is divided into three modules: three-dimensional virtual reconstruction, design practices, and innovative promotion.

3.1 Three-Dimensional Virtual Reconstruction Module

Cantonese Opera Costume and Virtual Digital Character Model Construction Based on CLO 3D. The core of this phase involves utilizing CLO 3D technology to conduct three-dimensional virtual modeling of costumes from the Cantonese opera "Di Nv Hua." This includes restoring the details of Cantonese opera costumes, such as fabric texture and pattern details. Additionally, it involves creating virtual character models with relatively lifelike movements to inject more vivid performance qualities. If we designate the role's costume as C, then Chang Ping's costume is C1; Zhou Ruiran's costume is C2; Zhou Shixian's costume is C3; and Zhou Zhong's costume is C4 (see Fig. 2).

Based on the analyzed information of characters and costume elements, a human body model is created in CLO 3D, providing the human body with basic hair models, skin textures, and physical attributes. Analyzing the characteristics of the characters, integrating with Photoshop software to draw character makeup. Utilizing CLO 3D models to modify digital character makeup and actions, drawing panels in the 2D interface, and dynamically adjusting the relationships between panels in the 3D interface. Applying matching colors and embroidery patterns to costume characters, conducting real-time fabric simulation for the trial-wearing effect. Throughout this process, continuously adjusting fabric physical properties and optimizing panel fitting issues to achieve the best results in virtual simulation.

Modeling Headpieces with Cinema 4D as the Core. After the completion of character roles and virtual costume creation, headpiece models are produced using modeling techniques centered around Cinema 4D (C4D) to enhance the fidelity of the characters. The virtual character models created in CLO 3D are exported in FBX format and imported

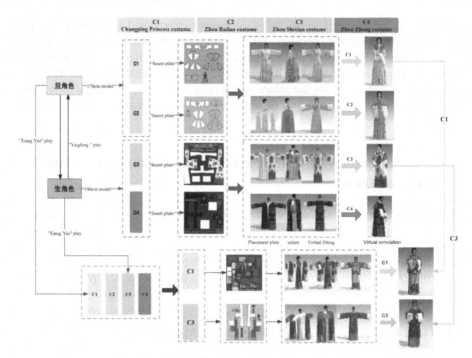

Fig. 2. CLO 3D virtual clothing production process

into C4D. Analyzing the headpiece features based on images saved from film and television, along with traditional elements of Cantonese opera culture, detailed sculpting is performed using C4D's sculpting tools (see Fig. 3). Appropriate material textures and texture maps are applied to ensure harmony between the textures and overall costume and stage design.

Scene Construction and Digital Character Debugging for "Di Nv Hua" Using UE5 and Motion Capture Devices

① *UE5 Construction of Cantonese Opera "Di Nv Hua" Scene.* In accordance with the plot and scene requirements of "Di Nv Hua", design the overall layout and structure of the scenes, determining the placement of the stage, background, and props, taking into consideration the visual effects and audience experience. For the "Ying Feng" act, the scene is set at Zhou Zhong's residence, with the main storyline involving Zhou Shixian meeting Princess Changping. Accordingly, it is necessary to arrange the placement of items in the indoor scene. The "Xiang Yao" act is an outdoor scene, requiring a focus on arranging outdoor plants, bridges, and the relationship between characters, along with adjustments to the rendering effects of nighttime lighting.

② *Motion Capture and Digital Character Debugging.* Before conducting motion capture tests, it is necessary to prepare devices such as sensors and cameras and calibrate the equipment to ensure synchronization between the sensors, obtaining accurate three-dimensional motion data. Subsequently, Cantonese opera actors are equipped with motion capture devices to perform Cantonese opera movements. The capture includes

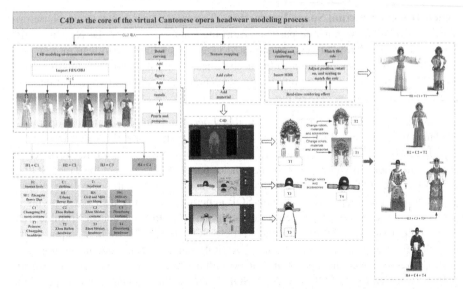

Fig. 3. C4D as the core of the virtual Cantonese opera headwear modeling proces

hand movements and the recording of facial expressions. In the motion capture area, a radar sensing range is established to allow the system to accurately track the position and posture of the motion capture performer, ensuring the fit and comfort of the equipment without affecting the actor's normal performance (see Fig. 4).

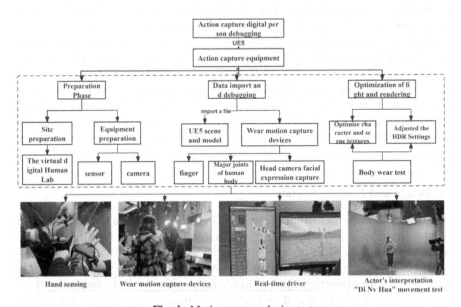

Fig. 4. Motion capture device test

Touch Designer Virtual Space Interaction. The virtual space interaction phase primarily utilizes TD to generate particles from the Cantonese opera "Di Nv Hua" OBJ Models, PNG rendering effects, or animated videos. Combined with leap motion gestures, the screen is manipulated to break the one-way information transmission issue during the exhibition, enhance interaction between users and the artwork, and increase interest in cantonese opera (See Fig. 5).

Taking the virtual space interaction with a video clip from the Cantonese opera "Di Nv Hua: Fragrant and Bewitching" as an example, first, import the video into Touch Designer. You can use the Movie File In TOP by dragging it into the network editor, selecting the desired video file in the parameter panel. Next, connect the Trace SOP to the Movie File In TOP, adjusting parameters such as Threshold to control the contour generation of the image. The Sprinkle SOP generates randomly distributed points or geometry on the image, often used for creating particle effects. Connect Sprinkle SOP to the output of Trace SOP and input Particle SOP to Sprinkle SOP's output. If the particle effect appears too flat, the Extrude SOP can stretch the geometry along the normal direction, creating a geometric shape with thickness. Therefore, add the Extrude SOP between Sprinkle SOP and Trace SOP to adjust the thickness and shape of the geometry, then combine TD rendering components such as Geometry COMP, Camera COMP, Light COMP, Constant CHOP, and Render TOP for rendering.

To further enhance interaction, MouseIn CHOP and Leap Motion devices can be integrated into TD. The MouseIn CHOP is a type of CHOP used for capturing mouse inputs, generating channels containing mouse position information for interactive design within a project. The MouseIn CHOP can be combined with Metaball SOP and Force SOP, where Force SOP simulates external forces affecting particle systems, such as gravity and wind. Observing the Metaball effect in real-time preview mode, parameters can be adjusted to achieve dynamic mouse interaction effects.

The Leap Motion device captures the user's hand movements through an infrared camera, utilizing infrared light to create a three-dimensional hand model. It can recognize key points on the hand, finger positions, gestures, and other information. To use Leap Motion effectively, there needs to be sufficient space in front of the device for accurate hand motion capture. By inputting Leap Motion CHOP into TD, it retrieves user hand information from the Leap Motion device, converting this data into channel information for real-time data processing and visualization in TD, thereby achieving real-time interactive effects.

3.2 Design and Practice Module

NFT Digital Collectibles Model Under BIGVERSE Blockchain. The blockchain digital collectibles in the design and practice module primarily utilize BIGVERSE as the main medium. The NFT digital collectibles model on the BIGVERSE official website involves collaboration with the platform for sales. Its blockchain technology ensures the uniqueness and traceability of digital collectibles, providing a reliable foundation for the protection and dissemination of digital art. This contributes to increasing the visibility and market influence of Cantonese opera culture. BIGVERSE utilizes Non-Fungible Token (NFT) technology to transform digital works of Cantonese opera into unique

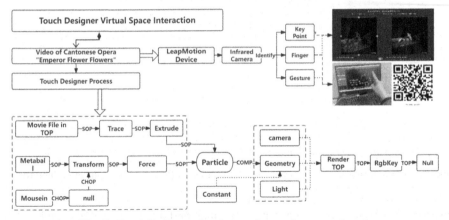

Fig. 5. Touch Designer virtual space interaction research path

digital artworks. This not only offers creators new means of digital copyright protection but also enhances the unique value of Cantonese opera digital cultural and creative products.

3D Printing of "Di Nv Hua" Character Cultural and Creative IP Products. Leveraging C4D technology, the modeling of cultural and creative IP products for the characters of "Di Nv Hua", including the lead heroine, supporting heroines, martial arts character, and warrior character, is completed. Collaborating with future factories for product creation, this module aims to implement the practical application of 3D printing.

3.3 Innovation and Promotion Module

Douyin (TikTok) Virtual Headgear Special Effects Promotion Model. Utilizing C4D-produced virtual headgear models, export them to supported file formats such as FBX. Import these models into the "Xiangsu" platform to create special effects. Export the special effects files to upload them to Douyin's creator tools for a final preview and publication of the special effects. Set parameters for the use conditions of the headgear effects to enhance the user experience. After passing the review, users can search for keywords like "Cantonese opera headgear effects" on the Douyin platform to experience Cantonese opera virtual headgear effects. Within 30 days of launch, the exposure of Princess Changping's virtual Cantonese opera headgear effect reached 95,000, and Zhou Ruilan's virtual Cantonese opera headgear effect reached 92,000 (see Fig. 6).

China Guanshanyue Art Museum Offline Exhibition Experience. In 2023, the project's works were exhibited offline at the China Guanshanyue Art Museum. The initial version 1.0 of the exhibition mode used VR technology to immerse users in the virtual Cantonese opera "Di Nv Hua" performance video. Currently, through continuous iterations and updates, the optimized version 2.0 of the virtual Cantonese opera digital characters played the role of guides, providing the audience with a more novel interactive

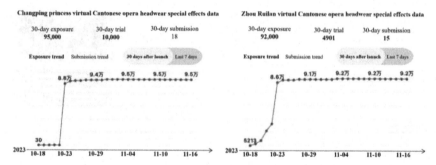

Fig. 6. Data of virtual Cantonese opera headwear effect of Princess Changping and Zhou Ruilan

experience, enriching the exhibition's dissemination format. Through the guidance of virtual Cantonese opera characters, the audience can interactively explore the character settings and costume culture of the otherwise mundane "Di Nv Hua" performance, presenting a more creative and enjoyable side to the entire exhibition.

The virtual-real space interaction mode transforms the originally unidirectional exhibition space and exhibit content output experience into a bidirectional interaction. Visitors, through participating in interactive activities in the interaction area, can more deeply and immersively experience the charm of the Cantonese opera performance. This mode transforms visitors from passive observers into integral parts of the entire production, fostering a closer interaction with Cantonese opera as a traditional Chinese theatrical form (see Fig. 7). It enhances the user's sense of participation and interactive experience, making the entire exhibition more engaging and educational.

Fig. 7. Virtual Cantonese Opera online exhibition effect picture

4   Conclusion

Through in-depth empirical research and practical exploration, this study draws the following conclusions: within the context of virtual space interaction, the dynamic inheritance path based on three-dimensional virtual reconstruction, design practices, and innovative promotion demonstrates significant potential applications in the inheritance of Cantonese opera in the Lingnan region. In the process of application and promotion, the constructed virtual Cantonese opera digital characters, virtual Cantonese opera costumes and virtual headgear special effects experiences, as well as the interaction between real and virtual spaces, have enhanced users' profound understanding of Cantonese opera culture, laying a solid foundation for the realization of "digital + Cantonese opera" dynamic inheritance.

Practical results indicate that through the mode of virtual and real space interaction, the inheritance of Cantonese opera in the Lingnan region has not only found new channels of dissemination but has also revitalized under the catalysis of modern technology. Users, through virtual experiences, not only participate but also deepen their understanding of traditional culture. However, to further promote the application of this inheritance path, continuous improvement and optimization of technological means and user experiences are still necessary. In future research, the author will continue to delve into innovative applications of virtual and real space interaction in the protection and utilization of cultural heritage, contributing more beneficial experiences and practical outcomes to the inheritance and development of intangible cultural heritage.

Acknowledgements. The authors acknowledge the funding support by the "High-Level Achievement Cultivation Project" of Shenzhen University's Phase III Construction of High-Level Universities (Project No: 24GSPCG18).

References

1. Li, L., Hu, Y.: Connotation, architecture, and promotion path of digital twin campus. Digital Educ. **9**(6), 22–29 (2023)
2. Xu, J., Xi, T.: Research on interactive digital art based on multi-modal sensory theory. Indust. Design **3**, 97–99 (2018)
3. Wen, B., Xiao, Y.: Research on the spread of cantonese opera on douyin short video platform in the new media era. New Media Res. **7**(23), 48–50 (2021)
4. Wang, T.: Application of Digital Interaction Technology in the Promotion of Cantonese Opera Culture. Beijing University of Technology (2017)
5. Fu, X., Su, R.: Logical evolution, space interaction, and sensory thinking of the logic of symbiotic communication. Youth Journalist **22**, 9–13 (2023)
6. Chen, S., Zhang, Q.: Di Nv Hua. Hong Kong and Taiwan Original Edition, Hong Kong Commercial Press, Reader (2020)

"Landscape-Drama": Innovative Applications of Digital Projection Art in the Renewal of Chinese Old City Communities

Xingyu Chen[1,2], Xiang Liu[2], and Hongtao Zhou[1(✉)]

[1] College of Design and Innovation, Tongji University, Shanghai 200092, China
hongtaozhoustudio@qq.com
[2] Sichuan Fine Arts Institute, Chongqing 401331, China

Abstract. Amidst the backdrop of China's urban renewal entering a new phase, digital projection art has garnered significant attention as an effective, communicative, interactive, and experiential art form with the potential to inject innovation and sustainability into the renovation of old urban communities. However, current research on domestic digital projection predominantly revolves around technical aspects, resulting in relatively uniformity in content and visual representation. Therefore, against this backdrop, this study innovatively introduces theatrical arts into the projection mapping of old urban community building facades to achieve deep interaction between dramatic content and community environments. Using the example of the digital projection artwork "The Magic Flute" at the Chongqing International Light and Shadow Art Festival in the Huangjueping community, the study primarily analyzes spatial forms, visual characteristics, digital interactions, and related interviews. This research contends that "The Magic Flute" transcends the realm of digital technology by establishing a unique binary structure of "landscape-drama" that deeply integrates landscape forms with dramatic content in the community, enriching the cultural content and narrative structure of digital projection works in old urban areas. Additionally, it proposes experimental methods led by theatrical arts, creates more delicate immersive experiences in community theaters, and uncovers the media art creation process closely aligned with the reality of old urban areas, thereby offering valuable insights to support the sustainable revitalization of old urban communities in China.

Keywords: Old Urban Communities · Digital Projection Art · The Magic Flute · Landscape-Drama

1 Introduction

In the current context, the Chinese government is actively seeking more flexible and adaptable approaches to promote the revitalization of old urban communities. Digital projection art, utilizing augmented reality technology to create dynamic immersive audio-visual performances, has garnered significant attention due to its effectiveness, communicability, interactivity, and experiential nature. It is poised to inject innovation and sustainability into the revitalization of old urban communities, aligning with the contemporary demands of urban renewal. However, with the widespread adoption of digital projection techniques in urban spaces, it has become apparent that the discourse in this field tends to be predominantly focused on the technological aspects, leading to a proliferation of similar artistic expressions across various cities. Whether it's standalone 3D Mapping projections on individual building facades or large-scale light art festivals, the artistic expressions on urban facades appear strikingly similar, regardless of the scale of the works. Therefore, in future applications of digital projection art, it is crucial to delve deeper into the content and essence of digital image artworks, fostering deeper connections and collaborations between the essence of digital projection art and the everyday life of old urban communities. This endeavor will contribute to the exploration of the depth and quality of digital projection art content, diversify residents' experiences, and establish genuine symbiotic relationships between old urban communities and digital imaging media.

2 Literature Review

With the continuous development and innovation of digital technology, the forms of expression of digital projection art in the revitalization of old cities are also constantly enriched and expanded. From static digital images to dynamic interactive experiences, from singular projection forms to the complex integration of multimedia presentations, the rapid iteration of digital technology has provided artists with a broader and more diverse creative space and richer means of expression. "New media" has become a ubiquitous element in shaping contemporary urban public spaces (Chen 2020), including the application of technologies such as holographic projection and stereoscopic projection, as well as the integration with augmented reality (AR) and virtual reality (VR) technologies. Moreover, the widespread use of increasingly complex intelligent algorithms, digital life, synthetic models, software editing, and multimedia integration tools has led to the evolution of a new creative direction in digital projection, centered around the essence of "technological culture."

The diverse technological interventions undoubtedly lead to a richer variety of forms and experiences in digital projection works in today's old city communities. Residents and audiences often have more opportunities and ways to perceive, experience, and participate in the digital projection art created, enhancing their daily lives. Therefore, exploring how digital projection art can leverage interactive technology and virtual reality to achieve audience perception and experience has become a major focus of research. Rush (2002) argues that the development of new urban digital media supports the widespread transformation of "technological forms of life," where the meaning of social life gradually becomes a matter of technical systems. Consequently, driven by this trend, the creative development of digital projection art will increasingly focus on innovative technological approaches, seeking to diversify exploration in digital projection creation to further enrich people's sensory experiences in digital interpretation.

Therefore, the significant technological exploration leads to the influence and control over digital projection works, encompassing the embedded social significance within the projection works, the involvement of public participation, and the expression of regional cultural inheritance and innovation. However, in this process, they are all subjected to a restrained and restricted state, where the prevalence of certain (technological) applications becomes commonplace, while the development of other applications gradually becomes isolated, resulting in the existing communities becoming generalized into what is termed as media cities (McQuire 2008). Even if the artistic concepts behind the creation of works differ, they often appear to share significant similarities in form. Consequently, digital projection art deployed in various urban communities and on a larger urban scale exhibits homogenized formal characteristics, with considerable similarities observed in production methods, visual techniques, presentation methods, and sound effect selection, thus losing the genuine connection between community public spaces and digital projection works.

Mumford (1967) argues that technology has always been life-centered since its inception. Throughout human evolution, technology has merely served as an auxiliary tool for human development, rather than being the primary force or intrinsic driver of human progress. Instead, there has been a greater emphasis on the creation of human culture and the enrichment of spiritual life (Sun 2019). Similarly, Mitcham (1999) shares this perspective, asserting that technology is generally oriented towards life development rather than being centered around work or power. Zielinski (2006) suggests that all analyses of technological media are inherently interdisciplinary and diverse. Therefore, in the context of old urban communities, considering the complex relational elements and cultural spaces, how to achieve high-quality creation of the intrinsic content of digital projection remains a challenging question. What genuine breakthroughs can be made in enriching the spiritual connotations expressed through innovative forms of artwork, thus breaking free from the limitations imposed by technology? How can we truly establish a deep integration between old urban communities and visual media, thereby fostering genuine public engagement through digital projection works to promote the symbiotic development of both?

3 Method

The proposed methodology of this study involves a shift from technological focus to a focus on the creative spirit, with a particular emphasis on in-depth discussions surrounding the essence of digital projection creation within old urban communities. Through this, the aim is to explore new possibilities for the development of this field beyond technological constraints, thereby expanding the expressive forms and connotations of digital projection art. Building upon this foundation, the research will focus on the construction strategies and design logic inherent in the content of digital projection artworks within old urban communities, aiming to investigate more diverse, varied, and profound modes of expression. It is hoped that through these efforts, a new form of digital projection art can be reshaped within old urban communities, thereby redefining its relationship with the environment, culture, technology, and audience.

3.1 Site Selection

Taking the intervention of the Chongqing International Light and Shadow Art Festival into the Huangjueping Old Town Community as an opportunity, we will focus on the architectural digital projection section of the Light and Shadow Art Festival for research, and select the main exhibition building for digital projection, the facade area of the 5-story 501 Warehouse located in the core area of the community, as the target area (Fig. 1). This building once played an important role as a local defense logistics warehouse from the 1960s to the 1990s, but was later abandoned. With an area exceeding 5,000 m², it was once the spiritual landmark of the old community, surrounded by residential areas witnessing the lives and work of local residents, representing the spiritual essence of the Huangjueping community.

Fig. 1. On-site Image of Warehouse 501 in Huangjueping Community, Chongqing, China

3.2 Drama Case Selection

This study aims to analyze and research the intervention of drama art in the digital projection creation on the facades of old urban community buildings. The digital projection artwork "The Magic Flute" showcased at the Chongqing International Light and Shadow Art Festival is chosen as the primary subject of investigation (Fig. 2). The original drama "The Magic Flute" is a classic by Mozart, renowned worldwide, with the story revolving around the prince and princess. It begins with the prince embarking on an adventurous journey to rescue the princess, leading to their encounter, the emergence and resolution of misunderstandings, the prince undergoing arduous trials, and ultimately succeeding in the rescue mission. The point of attraction in this research lies in the emphasis on the metaphorical similarity between the original drama's storyline and the process of old city renewal. Through the protagonist's arduous struggle for pursuing the ideals of light and eternal love, it metaphorically reflects the era-changing pains experienced during the renewal iterations of Chinese old cities, which similarly require steadfast courage to adhere to the right direction and confront challenges.

3.3 Analysis of the Creative Language Used in "The Magic Flute"

The research entails analyzing comprehensive documentation of the entire creative process behind "The Magic Flute," obtained from the creative team. This includes conducting interviews with team members to explore their creative language. The objective is to dissect and organize the most pivotal visual elements of the work, culminating in a comprehensive synthesis and summary of the visual data.

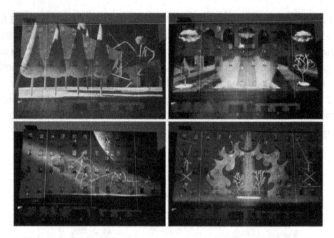

Fig. 2. Images of the live performance of "The Magic Flute"

Spatial Form Construction. The work consists of sixteen scenes interconnected to form the entire plot, with the performance content progressing layer by layer according to the storyline (Fig. 3). The core of spatial form construction lies in the utilization of abstract symbols and symbolic techniques to deeply integrate the landscape forms of the old community with relevant content from the drama, thereby achieving spatial scene handling and "actor and character" shaping. Specifically, the creators observed and documented the old community's architecture, streets, and cultural landscapes, acquiring rich visual materials including unique colors and forms found in the local environment. Simultaneously, elements such as characters, plotlines, and spatial symbols from the drama narrative were extracted. These two aspects—the images in the community landscape and the related content characters in the drama—were synthesized and unified through a minimalist abstract symbolic language, creating new character features that encompass both the old city environment and the story characters, without excessive embellishment. In essence, all spatial elements are involved in every part of the performance (Schechner 2001). Additionally, with the expressive power of minimalist stage lighting, an organic connection and interpretation between the community and the drama, landscape and characters, light and shadow, and plotlines were achieved.

Surface Visual Shaping. In the research process, the surface visual language of the creation was interpreted. The creative team conducted extensive on-site image shooting, totaling over 600 images, aimed at capturing various surface conditions in the Huangjueping community environment, including natural traces, industrial remnants, and life imprints (Fig. 4). These photographs covered various surface features at different locations within the community, encompassing natural traces such as tree textures, vegetation growth status, as well as material textures presented by residential wall remnants, and features like wear, rust, weathering, and life imprints such as graffiti on buildings and traces on streets. These surface visual features are integral components of the community environment. The image captures not only provided important references and valuable material resources for the scene creation of digital images but also aided

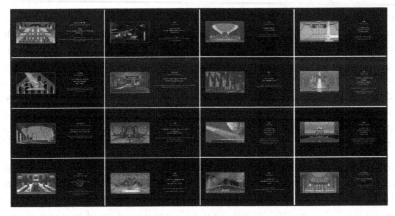

Fig. 3. Content Overview of "The Magic Flute"

artists in better understanding the development changes and cultural connotations of the community. Through the collection and analysis of these image textures, the creative team utilized it as textures for the environmental space, set materials, and costumes for various characters in the "Magic Flute" production, ultimately constructing the surface visual features of all scenes.

Fig. 4. Textures of the Environment in Huangjueping Community, Chongqing, China

Digital Modeling and Interaction. The entire production process of the artwork "The Magic Flute" relies entirely on digital modeling, primarily utilizing software such as CAD, 3D Max, Unity, Premiere, and TouchDesigner to create three-dimensional models of scenery, spaces, props, and characters for projection imagery. Initially, during the early stages of creation, CAD serves as a valuable tool for assisting design, enabling precise correspondence with architectural facades. Designers translate each scene's narrative content into accurately drawn scenarios, with the precise contour shapes of scenes providing a foundation for subsequent scene modeling (Fig. 5). During the modeling phase, 3D Max predominates, aiming to ensure accurate alignment with the predetermined positions in CAD. The relationship between spatial structures and individual models must be unified under the same camera perspective, resulting in disparities between model space and image space alignment. Subsequently, Unity and Premiere are utilized to produce lighting effects and rendering. By simulating the texture and light characteristics of real light sources, lighting design is completed around scene narrative, ensuring alignment with spatial morphology, plot performance, and visual effects. Additionally, artists conduct refined spatial modeling and local adjustments based on contour sketches and the features of the 501 warehouse wall, along with dynamic effects settings, to ensure compatibility with spatial morphology, plot performance, and visual effects in practical applications.

Ascott (2012) noted that the most distinctive feature of new media art is its connectivity and interactivity. The interactive use of TouchDesigner for image content creation establishes strong interactive relationships between partial graphics and architectural profiles. Particularly, the random variation and transformation of graphics at architectural window locations achieve unpredictable random effects, facilitating the dynamic integration of theatrical atmosphere with physical architecture, while also integrating with commonly used techniques in modern mapping projection art. Moreover, creators considered the audience's experiential participation and information reading during the digital exhibition process. Audiences can use their mobile devices to scan QR codes appearing during the broadcast to access relevant background information about the artwork, deepening their understanding of the plot and scenes and enhancing their engagement and immersion. This approach aims to satisfy the diverse experiential needs of users by combining online and offline experiences. However, due to the limited exhibition period, this aspect was not implemented in practice, and only feedback from related content audiences was obtained through interviews.

Interview. The study conducted interviews with 15 on-site spectators and 5 new media artists during the exhibition period (January 5–10,2023). For the general audience, questions focused on their comprehension of the artwork, viewing experiences, and the assistance provided by technology in understanding the artwork. As for the artists, inquiries were centered around their understanding of the artwork, artistic expression, and proficiency in technical utilization.

4   Result and Discussion

4.1   The Value of Drama Intervention

Expression of Drama. The expression of drama is one of the fundamental characteristics manifested in the creation of the digital projection artwork "The Magic Flute." The work highlights dramatic elements through performance, narrative, staging, characterization, and emotional intensity. Performance permeates the main design line, conveying character emotions and storylines; narrative coherence communicates content through a complete storyline; staging utilizes space, sets, props, lighting, and sound to create scene atmospheres; Characterization strategies manifest in the portrayal of actors with diverse personality traits;emotional intensity creates an emotional atmosphere in the interpretation; interactivity reflects interactive experiences of plot interaction and audience participation. The multifaceted display of these dramatic elements will bring new creative

Fig. 5. The Scene Design and Narrative Content of "The Magic Flute "

methods to digital projection art, breaking away from the previous unidimensional model dominated by "technology" in digital projection art.

Drama as Public Art. In the digital projection activities of light and shadow art in the Huangjueping old community, the creators transferred the classical drama "The Magic Flute" from traditional theaters to the public space of the old community, achieving an organic integration of regional community and theatrical performance. The connection between artistic works and localities is not necessarily a direct relationship; the creative team aims to popularize and publicize high art theatrical arts, akin to the modern art "coming off the shelf," stepping out of art galleries and museums and entering open public spaces to form public art. Through various artistic languages and forms, it portrays the daily lives and socio-cultural realities of the public while developing close interactive relationships with public life (Li, 2016), akin to the projection screening of ordinary movies in everyday public spaces. Therefore, this digital projection creation aligns closely with the nature of public art, evolving into a post-theatrical concept, and should be considered as an occurrence of a certain event (Lehmann, 2016).

4.2 The Organization and Composition of "Landscape-Drama"

Through the study of the author's creative approach, it is found that the design elements of "The Magic Flute" exhibit many unique compositional and organizational methods. These forms depart from traditional representational techniques and adopt a mode of expression similar to that of John Hejduk's "structuralism," even featuring a surrealistic imaginative style. This innovative design expression aims to ingeniously blend the characteristic features of the old community environment with the original elements of "The Magic Flute" drama, presenting a visual spectacle (Fig. 6). The flexibility in the design of each element's aesthetics and the peculiar language of expression in the artwork allow these design elements to manifest open-ended changes and developments, along with unpredictable characteristics. Moreover, these design elements also integrate various unrelated forms and structures in the surroundings, intending to establish new associative relationships. This association is not merely a matter of placing various elements together but, through the meticulous design layout and clever arrangement of forms, constructs a novel dual-layered connotative structure of "landscape-theater," organizing all content and elements together through rich and unique formal relationships. This innovative mode of expression opens up new paths for the development of digital projection art, providing audiences with a fresh artistic experience.

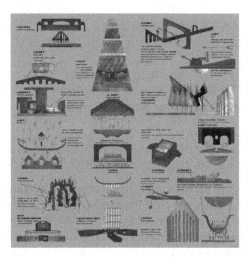

Fig. 6. Creative Organization and Composition of Elements in "The Magic Flute "

4.3   Shift in Technology

The core of "The Magic Flute" prioritizes dramatization and conceptual expression, yet the emphasis on creative content does not imply a negation of appropriate technological application. The more complex the concepts, the greater the need for diverse expressions at various creative levels to match them. Accordingly, achieving various aspects of "The Magic Flute" necessitated the utilization of a wider array of technological means for support. Correspondingly, behind the utilization of multiple technologies, creators established a systematic and procedural relationship with technological application to control and coordinate the overall effect of the work. This approach serves to guide the integration of the work's essence with the use of technology, fostering a mutually beneficial interaction between artistic content and technological implementation, rather than relying solely on flashy displays driven by technology. Thus, technology should be considered an integral component within the essence of digital projection art.

4.4 Interview Feedback

The Interviewed Audience. On the day of the exhibition, 15 audience members were selected for questioning. Given that "The Magic Flute" is an experimental contemporary digital art piece with interdisciplinary nature, it is not surprising to encounter comprehension barriers among the general public. Among the 15 interviewees, 9 respondents expressed support for using the online QR code-assisted reading function. They believed that this approach could facilitate a smoother understanding of the artwork throughout the entire exhibition process. Furthermore, individuals could choose to scan specific segments of the exhibition content that interested them, thereby making the presentation of the artwork more flexible and spontaneous, and diversifying the experience. Five individuals, particularly those aged 60 and above, were unable to use smart devices to scan QR codes. One person felt that the function was not particularly useful, preferring the continuity of the purely on-site experience. Regarding the overall impression of the artwork, 13 out of the 15 interviewees found it satisfactory, while 2 considered it average. Generally, the public's reception of the visual content of the artwork is positive, the online assistance system for comprehension is also deemed necessary to be integrated into future exhibitions.

The Interviewed Artists. The 5 new media artists interviewed unanimously regarded the experimental nature of the work as high, which contributes significantly to artistic exploration. They found that the artistic expression in the work is notably sophisticated, exhibiting an independent performance style distinct from typical digital projection works. Regarding the use of technology, 4 artists believed that the existing minimalist and low-tech creative approach suits the current content, while 1 artist suggested that technological advancements could enhance the diversity of expression and interpretation in the work. Overall, the artistic style and technical application in this production represent a challenging yet innovative attempt in artistic expression, demonstrating an appropriate choice in technology application.

5 Conclusion

The innovation of this study lies in proposing an experimental approach to digital projection creation in old urban communities led by drama cross-boundary exploration. Through the case analysis of "The Magic Flute" in Chongqing Light and Shadow Art Festival digital projection work, it establishes a unique binary structure of mutually supportive "landscape-drama" as the foundation. It breaks the traditional visual experience creation mode of digital projection art, where technology often takes precedence, by incorporating more aspects of community environment, drama, life, culture, and temporal memory into the creative framework, providing a more diverse creative perspective. This creative model enriches the narrative structure of digital projection works, explores the richer emotional aspects beyond technology in digital projection, creates a more subtle immersive experience in community theaters, and explores more closely the creative thinking closely tied to the daily reality of old cities. It integrates community daily life, technological interaction, and dramatic clues, providing a more mixed and diverse development direction for digital projection art. Through such diverse explorations in the field of digital projection art, it has provided robust support for the sustainable revitalization of China's old urban areas.

References

Chen, Y.Y.: New media art in public spaces. Tongji University Press, Shanghai (2020)

Lash, S.: Critique of information. Sage Publication, London (2002)

McQuire, S.: The Media City: Media, Architecture and Urban Space. Sage Publication, London (2008)

Mumford, L.: Technics and Human Development. A Harvest HBJ Book (1967)

Sun, H.: Commentson the relationship between "human" and technology-thinking based on the view of moundfo's humanistic technology. Sci. Econ. Soc. (01), 6–11 (2019)

Mitcham, C.: Introduction to the Philosophy of Technology. Tianjin Science and Technology Press, Tianjing (1999)

Zielinski, S.: Achaologie Der Medien. The Commercial Press, Shanghai (2006)

Schechner, R.: Environmental Theatre. China Theatre Press, Beijing (2001)

Ascott, R.: The Future is Now: Art, Technology, and Consciousness. Gold Wall Press, Beijing (2012)

Li, L.: The development and evolution of public art and its conceptual analysis. Art Res. (02),107–110 (2016)

Lehmann, H.T.: Postdramatic Theatre. Peking University Press, Beijing (2016)

The Interaction Between Architectural Heritage and the Public: Augmented Reality in Preservation Interpretation

Daoxin Chen[✉]

Graduate School of Architecture, Planning and Preservation, Columbia University,
New York City, NY 10027, USA
dc3590@columbia.edu

Abstract. This paper investigates the role of augment reality (AR) in enhancing heritage interpretation through digital technologies, specifically focusing on AR for engaging the public with historical buildings. It examines AR design processes, the integration of digital information and physical heritage, and AR's potential to deepen public understanding of cultural heritage. Drawing on ICOMOS principles and the PrEDiC framework, the study proposes a framework that merges heritage interpretation with AR technology. This framework guides the analysis of AR applications in heritage sites and leads to new design guidelines for AR in cultural heritage, ensuring alignment with interpretation needs. The application of these guidelines will be demonstrated through an AR project for Columbia University's Low Memorial Library. The paper aims to advance the use of AR in heritage interpretation, offering insights for both AR developers and heritage professionals.

Keywords: Augmented Reality · Architectural Heritage · Interpretation · User Experience

1 Introduction

Preservation interpretation, as defined by the International Council on Monuments and Sites (ICOMOS), "refers to the full range of potential activities intended to heighten public awareness and enhance understanding of cultural heritage sites" [1]. In recent years, digital methods have been introduced and applied to enhance the efficacy of heritage interpretation, among which digital tools, including Augmented Reality (AR), play a prominent role. AR stands as a promising avenue for enriching public engagement with historical buildings, offering immersive experiences. In this context, the design of AR experiences emerges as pivotal, serving as intermediaries that facilitate connections between cultural heritage practitioners and the broader public. AR designers must incorporate thoughtful recreation of heritage information, orchestrate immersive heritage experiences, and strategically utilize AR technology to realize these visions effectively.

This paper aims to explore the role of AR experience design in historic preservation and its contributions to heritage interpretation. Focusing on the design of AR products for

C. Stephanidis et al. (Eds.): HCII 2024, CCIS 2116, pp. 211–219, 2024.
https://doi.org/10.1007/978-3-031-61950-2_23

architectural heritage, it seeks to unravel current design processes, examine the symbiotic relationship between digital elements and physical heritage in AR interpretation, and elucidate how AR can aid the general public in understanding the heritage of historical buildings.

To address these inquiries, this paper draws upon established interpretation principles, including ICOMOS Interpretation and Presentation Principles [1] and the PrEDiC conceptual framework for digital heritage interpretation [2], and knowledge of AR application in cultural heritage. By amalgamating preservation interpretation principles with AR technical expertise, a design framework will be delineated. Subsequently, this framework will be applied to analyze case studies of AR utilization for on-site heritage interpretation, leading to the proposal of new design guidelines for AR designers. These guidelines aim to align AR product design more closely with the requisites of heritage interpretation, ensuring enhanced public engagement and a deeper appreciation for historical heritage.

2   The Dimensions of Heritage Preservation

In 2008, ICOMOS outlined seven principles for interpreting cultural heritage sites to enhance public appreciation and understanding, focusing on accessibility, context, authenticity, sustainability, inclusiveness, and ongoing research and evaluation [1]. Despite extensive discussions on heritage interpretation, there were no specific principles for digital heritage interpretation. Recognizing this gap, Hafizur Rahaman developed the PrEDiC framework for digital heritage interpretation, emphasizing presentation, cultural learning, and interactive engagement in a dialogic environment [2]. Rahaman's framework underscores the importance of a multi-faceted, user-oriented approach that fosters participant involvement and dialogue, aiming for a comprehensive interpretation of digital heritage [2].

The ICOMOS heritage interpretation principles and the PrEDiC framework both emphasize the importance of diverse content, user involvement, and creating personal connections between users and heritage. However, they diverge in their focus areas and approaches: ICOMOS primarily addresses broad cultural heritage interpretation with an emphasis on authentic, on-site experiences, while PrEDiC specifically targets digital heritage from an end-user perspective, covering various forms of digital interpretation. This paper explores the integration of both frameworks to enhance on-site heritage interpretation through digital tools.

The framework for evaluating digital heritage interpretation integrates principles from both ICOMOS and PrEDiC, focusing on five key aspects: effective presentation, authenticity, active participation, accessibility and inclusiveness, and cultural learning.

Effective Presentation: this aspect assesses how heritage values are represented comprehensively and innovatively, evaluating the diversity of heritage values presented and the novelty of the presentation methods.

Authenticity: crucial for both tangible and intangible value of architectural heritage, authenticity involves ensuring accurate and meaningful representations of heritage. It also focuses on whether AR experiences enhance or detract from the heritage's authenticity.

Active Participation: highlighting embodiment interaction and meaningful collaboration, this aspect examines if AR experiences facilitate user engagement and whether user feedback influences the AR experience's design and improvement.

Accessibility and Inclusiveness: this aspect assesses whether the AR experience accommodates people with diverse demographic and cultural backgrounds, and provides various modes or options to meet different user needs and preferences.

Cultural Learning: this aspect concerns whether the AR experience enables users to connect meaningfully with the heritage, promoting reflection, communication, and shared experiences that encourage further exploration.

3   The Dimensions of AR Experience

Bekele (2018) underscores AR technology's role in cultural heritage preservation, highlighting its use for three-dimensional reconstructions, enriching educational experiences, and boosting tourism at historical sites [3]. Hammady (2019) outlines the functionalities of AR in museums, such as visual communication, guidance, and interaction, which this paper further explores alongside the techniques supporting these functions [4]. AR is defined by three key features: combining real and virtual environments, real-time interaction, and 3D registration, supported by computer displays, tracking systems, and interaction interfaces [5]. This paper proposes three dimensions for analyzing AR in cultural heritage: information, interaction, and navigation, focusing on AR designers' considerations.

Information examines how heritage data is presented in AR, looking at the content's organization, and the modalities of virtual delivery to users.

Interaction explores user engagement with virtual heritage, including the range of interactive activities and types of input methods for user interaction.

Navigation assesses how AR aids users' spatial and contextual orientation within heritage sites, focusing on navigation tasks, guidance indicators, and user movement patterns within the virtual space.

These dimensions aim to provide a structured approach for investigating the design of AR products in cultural heritage, emphasizing the importance of information delivery, interactive engagement, and navigational support in enhancing the user experience.

4   The Proposed Framework

This chart is developed by combining the dimensions of digital heritage interpretation and the dimensions of AR experience design, which will be used to describe the design of AR experience for heritage and evaluate the function of AR for heritage interpretation (Table 1).

5   Case Studies

5.1   Mogao Caves AR Experience

The AR experience at Mogao Caves, a joint project by the Dunhuang Academy, Migu Animation, and Rokid AR, showcases five historically significant caves using archival data, animations, and interactive design via Rokid AR glasses linked to a mobile phone

Table. 1. The proposed framework

Dimensions	Information	Interaction	Navigation
Effective Presentation	How well does the information provided by AR enrich the content of the presentation?	How well does the interaction provided by AR enrich the content of the presentation?	How well does the navigation make it easy to follow the presentation?
Authenticity	How well does the information presented in AR respect the authenticity of heritage?	How well does the interaction methods respect authenticity of heritage?	How well does the navigation system respect authenticity of heritage?
Active Participation	How well does the information collection in AR encourage active participation?	How well does the interaction between users and digital heritage encourage active participation?	How well does the navigation system encourage active participation?
Inclusiveness and Accessibility	How well do the languages used in information presentation consider inclusiveness and accessibility?	How well do the interaction methods consider inclusiveness and accessibility?	How well does the navigation system consider inclusiveness and accessibility?
Cultural Learning	How well does the information supported by AR contribute to culture learning?	How well does the interaction supported by AR contribute to culture learning?	How well does the navigation supported by AR contribute to culture learning?

for content storage. Before starting, visitors are briefed on system usage by staff, and to protect the caves, groups are limited to 10 people.

AR Experience Design. The AR experience at Mogao Caves focuses on the narratives and symbolism of the cave paintings, highlighting stories and meanings related to the Buddha, religious narratives, and Chinese deities. Using strategic lighting, dynamic images, animations, and sound, the experience emphasizes specific characters and scenes. Notably, absent Buddhist statues are outlined with golden lines instead of 3D models. The unique contours of the cave are accentuated with golden lines, drawing focus to its architectural peculiarities. In addition to the visual aspects, audio significantly enhances the experience. For instance, a wall painting within the cave portrays an ancient gathering with musicians and dancers. The AR experience brings this scene to life by playing sounds of the musical instruments, offering visitors a unique auditory glimpse into the past.

Interaction is straightforward: visitors start animations by pressing a button on their phone and looking towards the Buddha statue. Additionally, the experience supports voice commands, which means that users can activate the experience by saying the number of the desired cave. The interaction primarily involves system control, with no direct engagement with the digital representations.

Navigation is guided by a deer avatar, which appears when the animation starts, directing users where to look. Incorrect movements prompt arrows to guide users back on track, ensuring a focused and immersive exploration (Fig. 1).

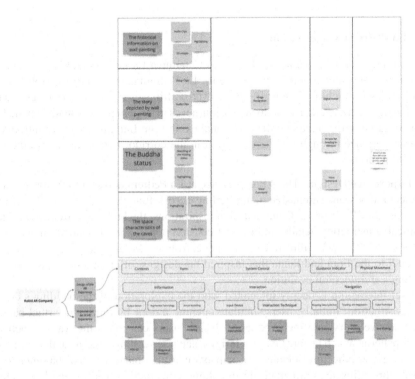

Fig. 1. The AR experience design of Mogao Cave

Evaluation in Interpretation Aspects. The AR experience at Mogao Caves focuses on the religious narratives and symbolism of the cave paintings, offering insights into the artistic significance while omitting broader historical context of Mogao Caves. The presentation employs animations, targeted lighting, and audio to highlight key elements and stories, with specific techniques enhancing learning, such as enlarging hard-to-see details for closer inspection. Despite its focus, the experience misses the opportunity to provide a comprehensive understanding of the caves' multifaceted significance.

Authenticity is preserved by limiting visitor numbers and drawing from archival research for content, ensuring an authentic representation of the heritage.

Active participation is limited, with users mainly engaging in a passive manner by watching animations and following the virtual tour guide. Interaction with virtual objects is minimal, and user feedback post-experience is not solicited.

Accessibility is addressed by offering the experience with simple terminology and multiple activation options (image recognition, screen taps, voice commands), accommodating diverse users.

Cultural learning is facilitated through detailed presentations and personal narratives, allowing users to closely observe the details on the paintings and obtain better understanding. However, the experience is individual-centric, limiting shared exploration or discussion.

5.2 La Pedrera Magic Vision

Xavi's Lab, in collaboration with Fundació Catalunya La Pedrera and Laie – Culture Experience, developed an AR experience for La Pedrera using Microsoft HoloLens 2, which took six months to develop [6]. It involved crafting a storyline, creating 3D visuals, and integrating these elements into an AR journey. The experience is situated on the first floor of La Pedrera, preceding the traditional exhibition. Initially, users are introduced to the experience through a training session in the corridor before moving to the first exhibition room.

AR Experience Design. The AR experience at La Pedrera delves into Antoni Gaudí's architectural vision, emphasizing storytelling across four themed rooms: the origins and context of La Pedrera, Gaudí's design inspirations, the building's architectural and technical construction details, and its post-construction history. Historical images, animations, and 3D models illustrate the narrative, from the Milan family's commissioning of Gaudí to the flora and fauna that inspired his designs, offering a deep dive into the building's architectural evolution.

User interaction is deeply integrated with the exploration of the building's design and construction. Initially, users simulate opening a door by turning a virtual handle, an immersive entry into the experience. Inside, users can touch the walls to activate flower patterns which inspire Gaudí's designs, and trace ceiling patterns with their hands to highlight architectural details. Participants can also hand a virtual hammer to an avatar, illustrating the craftsmanship in column construction, and manipulate a chain to delve into the building's construction techniques. These interactions, facilitated by direct hand movements, leverage sensor-based interfaces and hand-tracking technology for an interactive engagement with Gaudí's architectural marvel.

Navigation through the exhibition is facilitated by digital avatars—a feather in the first room and a hoopoe bird in subsequent rooms—guiding exploration and interaction. This markerless, camera-based tracking system ensures a seamless and intuitive journey through Gaudí's architectural masterpiece, enriching the educational and immersive experience of La Pedrera (Fig. 2).

Evaluation from Interpretation Aspects. For effective presentation, this AR experience offers an immersive exploration of Gaudí's architectural philosophy, combining historical context, design inspirations, and construction details. It employs historical images, animations, and 3D models to convey the rich narrative and intricate details of La Pedrera's architecture. The experience provides a multifaceted view of La Pedrera, integrating background information, societal context, and architectural insights. This

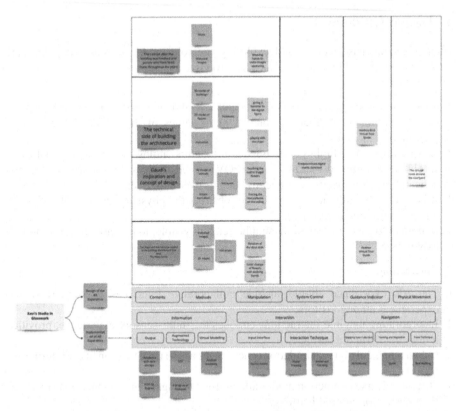

Fig. 2. The AR experience design of La Pedrera Magic Vision

comprehensive approach enriches the educational aspect and deepens appreciation for the architectural masterpiece.

For authenticity, utilizing historic images and archives, the AR design reproduces architectural features, ensuring an authentic representation of Gaudí's designs, despite potential color adjustments when it reproduces some flower patterns.

For active participation, users engage directly with digital elements, such as manipulating virtual objects and interacting with architectural features, fostering a hands-on experience that encourages personal insight and a deeper connection to the content. However, the lack of a clear feedback mechanism between users and the AR company hampers improvements to the experience.

For accessibility, information is available in eight languages, broadening accessibility. Yet, the experience's reliance on a single mode of interaction may limit accessibility for users with disabilities. The flying avatar for navigation is frustrating for those finding the virtual guide is hard to follow.

For cultural learning, hands-on activities highlight Gaudí's design details, supporting deep architectural appreciation. However, the focus on personal exploration over shared discovery and the sometimes challenging navigation system can diminish the educational potential of the experience.

6 Design Guidelines

After analyzing case studies and exploring the role of AR in supporting heritage interpretation, the following guidelines are proposed:

Information:

1. To enhance the appreciation of heritage, AR should incorporate diverse aspects of information while focusing on the main values of the heritage using varied presentation methods.
2. Artistic effects can highlight architectural features, aiding awareness without over-whelming the limited Field of View (FOV) of AR devices; this approach suggests concentrating on specific architectural details over large scenes.
3. It is crucial that digital overlays do not obstruct the physical heritage, allowing for direct observation of heritage.
4. Important digital information should remain visible long enough for thorough exploration.

Interaction:

1. The AR experience should include collaborative interfaces to support shared experiences among visitors.
2. Incorporating tangible interactions enriches the multi-sensory experience, provided it does not harm the heritage.
3. Enhancing hands-on manipulations encourages active participation in the interpretive process.
4. Offering diverse interaction modes allows users to engage in a manner that suits their preferences for cultural learning.
5. Users should have significant control over the system, enabling them to choose the aspects of the AR experience that interest them most.

Navigation:

1. In room-scaled AR experiences, navigation should prioritize the sequence and relevance of heritage information.
2. For larger, building-scaled experiences, careful consideration of the physical path and focus is essential.
3. Digital avatars used for storytelling should maintain a natural distance to foster engagement and empathy.
4. The size and movement speed of virtual guides must be tailored to fit the FOV and keep pace with users, preventing loss or confusion.
5. In expansive or complex heritage sites, combining various guidance indicators can aid in orientation, helping visitors navigate efficiently.

7 Conclusion and the Next Step

This paper is an attempt to establish the correlation between AR technology and preservation requirements, proposing ideas to ensure that AR applications meet the criteria for effective heritage interpretation. The next step involves putting forward design proposal of Low Memorial Library in Columbia University according to the guidelines, implementing the design proposal and conducting user testing to collect feedback.

Acknowledgments. Thanks for the guidance of my advisor, Halley Ramos, and the resources provided by GSAPP, Columbia University. I really appreciate the helps of Xavi Tribo and Clara Titos from Xavi's Lab, Glassworks, who provide information about the case study of Casa Mila - La Pedrera. Also, thanks for the support from my boyfriend, Zihao Zhang.

Disclosure of Interests. The authors have no competing interests to declare that are relevant to the content of this article.

References

1. International Council on Monuments and Sites, The ICOMOS Charter for the Interpretation and Presentation of Cultural Heritage Sites (4 October 2008)
2. Rahaman, H.: Digital heritage interpretation: a conceptual framework. Digital Creativity **29**(2), 208–234 (2018)
3. Bekele, M.K., et. al.: A survey of augmented, virtual, and mixed reality for cultural heritage. J. Comput. Cult. Herit. **11**(2), 1–36 (2018)
4. Hammady, R.: A framework for constructing and evaluating the role of MR as a holographic virtual guide in museums. Virt. Real. **25**, 895–918 (2020)
5. Schemalstieg, D., Hollerer, T.: Augmented Reality: Principles and Practice, 1st edn. Addison-Wesley Professional, Boston (2016)
6. Fundació Catalunya La Pedrera presents its first Mixed Reality tour in Spain. https://news.microsoft.com/es-es/2022/06/29/fundacio-catalunya-la-pedrera-presents-its-first-mixed-reality-tour-in-spain/, (Accessed 22 Mar 2024)

Han Opera Interactive Exhibition and App Design Based on the Theory of Cultural Three Factors

Xinyi Huang⊕ and Jie Xu(⊠)⊕

China University of Geosciences, Wuhan, No. 388, Lumo Road, Hongshan District, Wuhan, Hubei, China
xujie@cug.edu.cn

Abstract. As a colourful part of Chinese local opera, Han opera has made great contributions to the inheritance of Chinese traditional culture. However, with the social change and cultural transformation, Han Opera is facing difficulties in its inheritance and development. Many young people pay little attention to Han Opera and know less about its cultural content and spiritual connotation. In order to promote Han Opera as a precious cultural heritage and explore its deep cultural connotations, this study designs a series of interactive exhibition diagrams of Han Opera and its corresponding APP experience service based on the theory of three factors of culture, which condenses Han Opera's symbols, characteristics, and cultural contents into three levels according to the material, social organisation, and spiritual life. The APP contains interactive contents such as AR theatre model, culture, listening and watching theatre, etc. Users can explore the contents of interest in the exhibition in depth through the interactive service process of APP. It provides a novel way to enrich young people's understanding and immersive experience of Chinese opera.

Keywords: Han Opera Art · Cultural Three Factors · Digital Experience · Information Visualization

1 Introduction

Han Opera, one of the most influential operatic genres in the Hubei region of China, originated in the mid-Qing Dynasty within the boundaries of Hubei Province. It has had an impact on the development of other operatic genres such as Xiang Opera, Sichuan Opera, Gan Opera, Guangxi Opera, and Yunnan Opera. During the Jiaqing and Daoguang periods of the Qing Dynasty, Han tunes spread to Beijing, where they were incorporated into performances by Hui Opera troupes and gradually evolved into Peking Opera. In 1912, Yang Duo, a historian of Han Opera, in his work "Collected Discussions on Han Opera", first named the popular "Chu Tune" from Hankou, Hubei as "Han Opera" [1] and it was recognized by his peers.

Although Han Opera once flourished, since the 1960s, many plays and traditional techniques have faced the risk of being lost, and the overall situation and prospects of Han Opera are not optimistic. The diversity of products has made it impossible for theatrical arts to be the sole choice [2]. The contemporary younger generation has a special preference for learning methods and prioritizes modes of obtaining cultural heritage information, tending to learn and acquire cultural heritage content in an engaging manner.

However, the dissemination of traditional operas, characterized by "oral transmission" and "live stage performances" is limited by time and space. This traditional mode of theater is incompatible with the diverse market demands of the present, leading to a shrinking audience willing to enter theaters to "watch operas." Young people prefer to obtain information through digital platforms, social media, and online videos, which sharply contrasts with the traditional mode of theater dissemination. Han Opera, as an important genre of traditional Chinese opera, has a vast knowledge system and rich content, making it a daunting task to understand and learn about it. From the historical origins of Han Opera, performance techniques, music and dance, to theatrical performances, all require a considerable amount of time and effort to study.

In response to the new situations and problems facing the survival, protection, inheritance, and development of Han Opera, innovative methods of protection and development are urgently needed, especially those suitable for the cultural characteristics and progressive approaches of the times. In this article, we will explore the following questions:

1. How to categorize the knowledge content of Han Opera to facilitate user understanding?
2. How to make the process of appreciating opera interactive and enjoyable, thus more readily accepted by young people?

To address the above research questions, this paper selects Han Opera art exhibitions as the research object. Based on the theory of cultural three factors[3], the symbols, characteristics, and cultural content of Han Opera art are divided into three levels: material, social organization, and spiritual life, and presented through the production of Han Opera information visualization charts [4]. At the same time, combined with digital virtual reality technology and mobile applications [5, 6], a new experiential and immersive operatic exhibition is created. Through this form of exhibition, cultural traditions are transformed from passive consumer culture to active participant culture, injecting new vitality into the inheritance and development of Han Opera art.

2 Related Work

Digital technology is considered appealing to young visitors, and museums are increasingly adopting interactive digital media to complement their exhibits. This includes multimedia access in the 1990s, multitouch displays around 2010, and more recent developments such as smartphone/ tablet applications, VR, and AR.

Ren et al. [7] collected data on Arhat costumes from the collection of the Metropolitan Museum of Art in the United States, establishing a database and conducting examinations and analyses. They utilized three-dimensional modeling techniques to create "digital twin models" of Arhat costumes, facilitating the broad dissemination and creative transformation of overseas opera relics. Data on the intangible cultural heritage of the Li ethnic group in the Hainan Museum has been recorded through methods such as 3D scanning, photography, 3D modeling, and animation [8]. Interactive software is then used to access corresponding digital representations of cultural content (virtual scenes, objects, characters, sounds, etc.), which are superimposed onto existing museum arti-facts. Surround sound and projection of 3D images allow audiences to experience oceanic civilization and better explore ancestors' efforts to conquer the sea. The Street Museum app [9] was developed by the London Museum in 2009. Through this app, people can stroll through the city and use AR technology to admire urban landscapes depicted in engravings, oil paintings, and ancient photographs. Kitamura [10] researched a new tech-nology for digital exhibitions of Japanese classical texts and paintings. She developed two AR-based features: displaying Japanese characters corresponding to parts of images captured by the camera, and providing interesting website links related to Shukuba. The interactive exhibition at the National Palace Museum in Taiwan effectively integrates 4G technology into artistic creation, embodying the interdisciplinary, multicultural, diverse, and interactive characteristics of new media art [11]. Visitors can experience exhibitions and new technologies in combination, which blend virtual and real-time spaces, engaging all senses of the audience.

These initiatives often only scratch the surface of cultural heritage, combining new technologies with content or app design. This article aims to design an information visualization for effective classification of knowledge about Chinese opera based on the three-factor theory of culture. Through information visualization, the profound knowl-edge of Han Opera can be vividly presented in forms such as graphics, charts, and anima-tions, making it easier for users to understand and absorb. The combination of exhibitions and applications not only enhances the readability of knowledge but also increases user participation and interactivity. Through exhibitions, audiences can immerse themselves in the cultural charm of Han Opera in aspects such as its historical evolution, perfor-mance forms, and costumes and props, while through applications, they can further delve into and experience Han Opera knowledge, achieving interactive dissemination of knowledge.

3 Exhibitions Design

3.1 Visual and Scene Design

Malinowski (1884–1942) was a British social anthropologist and one of the founders of the functional school of culture. In his masterpiece "On Culture", he put forward the famous doctrine of "three factors of culture", which reveals the structure of culture from the bottom to the surface, that is to say, culture is composed of three factors: the material substratum, social organization and spiritual culture (language).

This study adopts Malinowski's theory of cultural structure from the perspective of cultural studies to categorize the symbols, characteristics, and cultural content of Han Opera into three levels: material, social organization, and mental life. The material level includes cosmetics, costumes, props (weapons), and musical instruments used in Han Opera performances, which fulfill the entertainment and functional aspects of theatrical arts. The social organization level encompasses the development of different schools within Han Opera, such as Fu River, Xiang River, Han River, and Jing River schools, as well as various renowned troupes. The mental life level refers to the philosophy, thoughts, and social concepts nurtured throughout the long-term development of Han Opera, which largely convey sentiments of loyalty, courage, honesty, dedication, and patriotism. This article divides Han Opera into three levels according to Malinowski's cultural three-factor theory and creates visualizations of this information, as shown in Fig. 1.

Fig. 1. Visual Infographics

3.2 Application Development

The information architecture of the Han Opera Art-HanSheng App is structured into three main parts. The first part encompasses two modules: "Exploration" and "Experience". The second part introduces the "Interaction" module, while the third part incorporates a "Memory" module at a spiritual level. As illustrated in Fig. 2, these three tiers of information architecture are integrated into the application's design to enrich users' cultural experiences, as elaborated in Fig. 3.

During the experiential phase of the first part, emphasis is placed on leveraging users' existing cognition and social experiences to unearth their points of interest in Han Opera through prior engagements. Users can actively explore Han Opera knowledge, browse graphics, and watch videos to gain a deeper understanding of its content. Subsequently, based on users' preferences, the system can precisely deliver content, helping users in furthering their understanding of cultural heritage [12].

In the second part, users primarily acquire long-term memory cognition through interactive experiences with cultural heritage products. Throughout this process, users accumulate additional knowledge through reflection and practice to facilitate better memory retention [13]. Augmented Reality (AR) serves as a pivotal experiential tool for cultural heritage learning. AR intervention guides users through a more natural and efficient learning process, incorporating narrative teaching, integrated offline experiences, and human-computer interaction, all aimed at helping users construct personalized behavioral memories [14].

In the third part, users delve into the spiritual dimension of cultural heritage through the "Memory" module, fostering cultural identification and emotional resonance, thereby further enhancing the user experience.

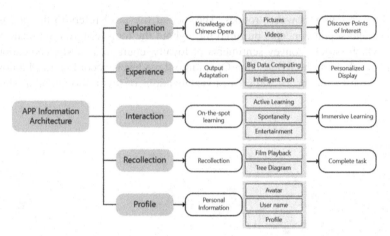

Fig. 2. APP Information Architecture

Fig. 3. Chinese opera software real-time learning interactive interface design

3.3 User Experience

The significance of exhibition design in cultural heritage cannot be overstated. Exhibitions emphasize interaction with visitors, transforming passive "viewing" behaviors into active participation. Visitors can explore and discover more about cultural heritage through exhibitions, thus sparking their interest [15, 16]. The Han Opera exhibition brings precious cultural artifacts to life using multimedia, showcasing the splendid culture of China in a tangible form while fostering interaction with visitors. The exhibition hall revolves around the associative effects of "material", "social organization", and "spiritual life", presenting the "cultural structure" of Han Opera through alternating spatial layouts. From the "material" aspects such as cosmetics, costumes, props (weapons), and musical instruments used in Han Opera performances, to the "social organization" aspects involving major social classes and factions, and further to the "spiritual life" aspects encompassing philosophical and social perspectives, visitors can explore the "cultural structure" of Han Opera within the space, sequentially experiencing the historical heritage of Han Opera culture.

The exhibition is divided into two spatial levels, as shown in Fig. 4. Visitors first encounter the material display of Han Opera on the ground floor, including cosmetics, costumes, props, and musical instruments used in Han Opera performances. Upon entering from the entrance, visitors are immediately intrigued by the Han Opera exhibition. The first thing that catches the eye is the circular array of exhibits, as indicated by the yellow dashed circle in the figure. On the right side is the first screen of the exhibition space, where visitors can scan and use their smartphones to explore the cultural connotations of Han Opera through images and videos. Based on visitors' browsing preferences, the system accurately guides them towards interactive directions for further engagement. As visitors reach the blue marked area in the middle of the circular path, they can scan different display platforms for interaction (the content on the platforms is visualized Han Opera knowledge charts segmented according to the three cultural factors). Here,

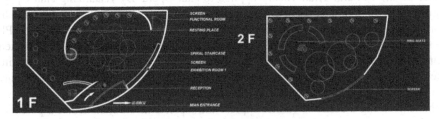

Fig. 4. Exhibition Venue Design

Fig. 5. The Effect of Augmented Reality Technology in Chinese Opera Exhibition

3D models and scene animations are used to showcase cultural heritage in augmented reality. Visitors not only learn face-to-face with virtual characters but also freely choose the content that interests them. By layering knowledge, the vast cultural system of Han Opera is presented in a more accessible and understandable way to visitors. Moving up to the second level, the content mainly focuses on "recollection". With its long history and rich content, Han Opera has experienced stages of development and decline, from inception, growth, peak, to decline. We have categorized and visualized this part of the content and set up a circular exhibition, hoping that visitors can further deepen their interest in Han Opera culture through observation on the second floor, as shown in Fig. 5.

4   Conclusion and Future Work

We developed an interactive exhibition and accompanying mobile application (APP) based on the Cultural Triad Theory applied to Han Opera. By visualizing Han Opera information through a series of charts and diagrams placed within the exhibition hall, participants can immerse themselves in the exhibition and use the accompanying APP to scan areas of interest within the visualized data. Based on user feedback collected during the actual exhibition, the majority of young attendees expressed satisfaction with the exhibition's effects, finding the experience both enjoyable and enlightening. Many actively engaged with the content and gained knowledge about Han Opera arts, with some expressing a desire to further explore the topic. This study indicates a potential increase in young people's interest in understanding Han Opera culture. Future efforts will focus on addressing any issues identified during the testing phase and validating the impact of this exhibition format on the public's perception of Han Opera culture.

References

1. Chen, Z.Y.: A hundred years of research on han opera: history, current situation, and reflection. Hubei Univ. (Philos. Soc. Sci.) **37**(06), 17–22 (2010)
2. Lu, A.: Impact and collision in an era of great changes: problems and challenges facing contemporary chinese opera. Northwest Normal Univ. (Soc. Sci. Edn.) **58**(05), 134–144 (2021)
3. Lin, Y.F.: Economic development and chinese culture. J. Peking Univ. Philos. Soc. Sci. Edn. **3**, 45–46 (2003)
4. He, X.M.: Research on the translation and regeneration of cultural resources for design carriers. Packaging Eng. **39**(20), 15–21 (2018)
5. Xu, L.: Traditional culture app design based on the concept of cultural transcreation. Hunan Packaging **36**(5), 34–37 (2021)
6. Zhang, X.: A study of digital display media for intangible cultural heritage. Packaging Eng. **36**(10), 20–23 (2015)
7. Ren, J.Y., Sun, Y., Shu X.: Digital twin of overseas opera relics: case study of arhat costumes in the collection of the metropolitan museum of art. In: 2022 IEEE 21st International Conference on Ubiquitous Computing and Communications (IUCC/CIT/DSCI/SmartCNS), pp. 350–356. IEEE Press, Chongqing, China (2022)

8. Wang, Y., Deng, Y.: Zhang, K., Lang, Y.: The Intangible cultural heritage show mode based on ar technology in museums - take the li nationality non-material cultural heritage as an example. In: 2018 IEEE 3rd International Conference on Image. Vision and Computing (ICIVC), pp. 936–940. IEEE Press, Chongqing, China (2018)
9. Source. http://www.clevelandart.org/gallery-one/artlens, (Accessed 7 April 2024)
10. Kitamura, K.: Common software for digital exhibition of japanese cultural heritage in literature. In: The International Conference on Culture and Computing 2013 proceedings, poster presentation PS1–05, pp. 137–138. National Institute of Japanese Literature, Tachikawa-city Tokyo, Japan (2013)
11. Liu, D.Y., Cheong, Y.J.: Historical cultural art heritage come alive: interactive design in Taiwan palace museum as a case study. In: 2016 22nd International Conference on Virtual System & Multimedia (VSMM), pp. 1–8. IEEE Press, Kuala Lumpur, Malaysia (2016)
12. Tan, G.X., He, Q.M.: Current research status, realistic dilemmas, and development path of digital communication of chinese intangible cultural heritage. Theoret. Monthly **9**, 87–94 (2021)
13. Wang, M., Peng, T., Ji, Y.: AR interactive design of cultural heritage based on experiential learning theory. Packaging Eng. **42**(04), 97–102 (2021)
14. Sun, J.X.: Research on the Cross-Cultural Communication Strategy of Traditional Chinese Opera. New China Press. Xinhua Publishing House, Beijing (2021)
15. Loannidis, P., Løvlie, A.S.: Exploring affordances through design-after-design: the re-purposing of an exhibition artefact by museum visitors. In Proceedings of the 14th Conference on Creativity and Cognition (C& C 20 22). , pp. 125134. Association for Computing Machinery, New York (2022)
16. Li, Y., Tennent, P., Cobb, S.: Appropriate control methods for mobile virtual exhibitions. In: VR Technologies in Cultural Heritage, pp. 165–183. CCIS. Springer, Cham (2019). https://doi.org/10.1007/978-3-030-05819-7_13

Realization of Kimono Fashion by Fusing Digital Art and Digital Textile Printing

Minori Jonoo, Miwa Rokudo, Harumi Kawamura, Naoko Tosa,
and Ryohei Nakatsu[⊠]

Kyoto University, Yoshida-Honmachi, Sakyo, Kyoto 606-8501, Japan
{jonoo.minori.84x,rokudo.miwa.72c,
kawamura.harumi.48z}@st.kyoto-u.ac.jp,
tosa.naoko.5c@kyoto-u.ac.jp, nakatsu.ryohei@gmail.com

Abstract. We have been working to create new art fashion by fusing digital art and digital textile printing. As a new attempt of this activity, we produced a Kimono, a traditional Japanese garment, using the same method. The challenge was creating a Kimono with an extended hem, called "Ohikizuri," used for weddings and other ceremonial occasions. The Kimono was designed using the "Sound of Ikebana," the digital art created by Naoko Tosa, one of the authors. In the production process, we learned and obtained much knowledge and advice from the chairman of a traditional Kimono company in Kyoto. We learned the know-how of Kimono pattern making and design placement through repeated prototyping of the Kimono using paper and polyester. We were finally able to create a Kimono using silk fabric, which was shown at the runway of the New York Fashion Week in September 2023 and was highly evaluated.

Keywords: Digital Textile Printing · Digital Art · Kimono Fashion · New York Fashion Week

1 Introduction

For a long time in the fashion world, clothes have been produced by analog methods: manual designing, textile printing on fabric, and sewing. In contrast, digital textile printing technology has recently been introduced to the fashion world [1]. Digital textile printing digitizes the textile printing process and is compatible with high-mix, low-volume production methods. Furthermore, since it is compatible with the art world based on one-of-a-kind items, the combination of art and digital textile printing can realize art fashion, in which one-of-a-kind art is developed into fashion. This will open new possibilities for fashion, and art, which used to be something to be appreciated, will become worn as fashion.

We started the challenge of creating art fashion within our laboratory environment. The fashion samples we have developed were shown to the public through exhibitions and accompanying fashion shows, demonstrating the new possibilities of fashion [2].

C. Stephanidis et al. (Eds.): HCII 2024, CCIS 2116, pp. 228–236, 2024.
https://doi.org/10.1007/978-3-031-61950-2_25

The next step is to produce Kimonos through a fusion of art and digital textile printing. Kimono is a traditional Japanese fashion; almost everything from designing to sewing has been done by hand. This is the reason why Kimono is recognized as highly artistic. Therefore, it is a great challenge to incorporate digital art into the Kimono production process by using digital textile printing technology to print designs on fabric. The research themes targeted in this paper is the following.

1. To see if digital textile printing technology can be applied to producing Kimono, a traditional Japanese fashion item.
2. To see if digital art-based design suits Kimono design.

2   Digital Art "Sound of Ikebana"

One of the authors, Naoko Tosa, found that by giving sound vibrations to fluids such as color paints and shooting the phenomenon with a high-speed camera, the jumping-up fluid makes beautiful forms. Using this environment, Tosa confirmed that various fluid shapes can be generated by changing the shape of the sound, the frequency of the sound, the type of fluid, and the viscosity of the fluid [3]. Tosa further edited the resulting video to match the colors of the Japanese seasons and created a digital artwork called "Sound of Ikebana" [4]. Figure 1 shows a scene from the work.

Fig. 1. A scene from " Sound of Ikebana"

The Sound of Ikebana is video art created by filming physical phenomena with a high-speed camera and is characterized by its organic and abstract shapes. Also, many overseas art professionals have pointed out that "Tosa's digital art, which expresses the beauty hidden in physical phenomena in an abstract form, contains a unique Japanese consciousness and sensibility." Therefore, the artwork is suitable for Kimono and other Japanese fashion designs.

Fig. 2. Inkjet printer for sublimation transfer (left) and thermal transfer device (right)

3 Fashion Production Using Digital Textile Printing Technology

An inkjet printer for sublimation transfer and a thermal transfer equipment (Fig. 2) were installed in the Tosa Laboratory, Kyoto University. In addition, sewing machines and other equipment were installed to create an environment where the entire fashion-making process, from design to sewing, is possible.

4 Kimono Production Using Digital Textile Printing Technology

4.1 Acquisition of Basic Knowledge

We decided to create a luxurious-looking Kimono called "Ohikizuri. The Ohikizuri is a style of Kimono born in the Edo period (1603–1868), characterized by a longer hem. We purchased a special Ohikizuri, a Kimono worn by a Maiko-girl in Gion. Figure 3 shows the scene when our student is wearing the "Ohikizuri." Then, we asked Mr. Suzuki,who runs a Kimono production company in Kyoto, to share his knowledge of Kimono with us.

4.2 Production of Prototype 1

We decided to create a prototype of the Kimono based on the knowledge provided by Mr. Suzuki. The Kimono pattern has a simple shape, a horizontal rectangle divided by rectangles (Fig. 4).

Fig. 3. A student wearing the Ohikizuri.

We asked Mr. Suzuki to unravel the Ohikizuri shown in Fig. 3 into multiple parts and then produced a Katagami (paper pattern) for each section. The first step was to use the paper pattern to prototype the Kimono. Figure 5 shows the design placed on the paper pattern and printed using a printer. The resulting prototype 1 is shown in Fig. 6.

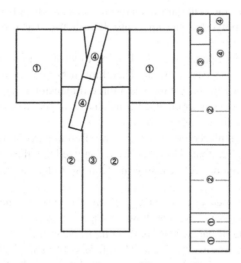

Fig. 4. Correspondence between Kimono and paper pattern.

Mr. Suzuki checked the finished prototype and confirmed that each part of the Kimono was made correctly and assembled correctly to form the Kimono.

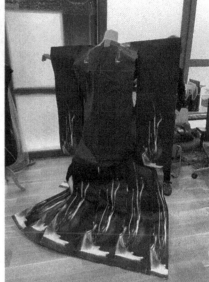

Fig. 5. Cutting out the necessary parts.   **Fig. 6.** Finished Kimono protype 1.

4.3   Creation of Prototype 2 and 3

Based on the knowledge obtained from Mr. Suzuki, the Sound of Ikebana design was rearranged. In addition, the material was changed from paper to polyester. The production of the Kimono using polyester was done entirely in-house. The resulting prototype 2 is shown in Fig. 7.

Prototype 1, made of paper, was challenging to wear and see. However, prototype 2, made of polyester, was easy to wear. Therefore, it became possible for us to study in detail the appearance of the Kimono as a three-dimensional object when worn by a person, as well as the design arrangement, such as the appearance of the Kimono when the person walks or performs other actions.

For prototype 2, we placed designs cut from different parts of the Sound of Ikebana to suit each part of the Kimono. However, we recognized that the different designs used in each part of the Kimono were causing the Kimono to lose a sense of unity from an overall perspective.

Therefore, we decided to place designs from the exact moment of the Sound of Ikebana. The resulting Prototype 3 is shown in Fig. 7.

Prototype 1, made of paper, was challenging to wear and see. However, prototype 2, made of polyester, was easy to wear. Therefore, it became possible for us to study in detail the appearance of the Kimono as a three-dimensional object when worn by a person, as well as the design arrangement, such as the appearance of the Kimono when the person walks or performs other actions.

For prototype 2, we placed designs cut from different parts of the Sound of Ikebana to suit each part of the Kimono. However, we recognized that the different designs used

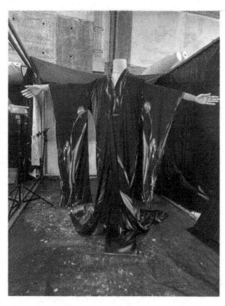

Fig. 7. The resulting protype 3.

in each part of the Kimono were causing the Kimono to lose a sense of unity from an overall perspective.

Therefore, we decided to place designs from the exact moment of the Sound of Ikebana. The resulting Prototype 3 is shown in Fig. 7.

4.4 Final Kimono Production

We decided to produce the final Kimono fashion based on prototype 3. For the final Kimono production, we decided to ask a specialized company to produce it, considering our plan to use it for fashion shows.

The Kimono fabric was purchased from Itoko, a company in Kyoto specializing in silk fabrics for Kimono. The printing of the design on the fabric was subcontracted to a digital textile printing company with equipment capable of printing on silk. The printed fabric is shown in Fig. 8.

The printed fabric was then sewn at Mr. Suzuki's company. Figure 9 shows the finished Kimono worn by a Japanese dancer in our project.

4.5 Fashion Show

The developed Kimono fashion was shown on the runway of the New York Fashion Week in the fall of 2023 and was featured in prominent fashion magazines such as Vogue (Fig. 10).

Fig. 8. Silk fabric on which the design wax printed

Fig. 9. A Japanese dancer wearing a Kimono.

Fig. 10. The Kimono featured by the Vogue (https://www.vogue.it/moda/branded/global-fashion-collective-edizione-estate-2024)

5   Conclusion

We have been researching the creation of art fashion, which combines digital textile printing technology and digital art to develop art into fashion. In this paper, we have extended this activity and challenged to create a traditional Japanese Kimono by combining digital textile printing technology and digital art.

For the digital textile dyeing technology, an environment enabling in-house fashion production in the laboratory was established based on joint research with Seiko Epson. As for digital art, we used the "Sound of Ikebana," which features abstract and organic shapes based on a technique created by Naoko Tosa, one of the authors of this project, of using a high-speed camera to photograph liquids scattered by sound vibrations.

Starting with no knowledge of Kimonos, there was some uncertainty about how far the combination of digital textile printing and digital art would go in traditional Kimono making. However, with the help of many companies and people who have been involved in Kimono making in Kyoto for many years, including Seiko Epson, with whom we have been conducting joint research, Mr. Suzuki and his company, and Itoko, a company specializing in silk fabric, we were able to create a prototype using called "Ohikizuri," which is considered difficult to make even among Kimono. We were able to open new possibilities in the world of traditional Kimono.

The finished Kimono was shown on the runway at New York Fashion Week in September 2023, one of the four primary fashion weeks in the world. Therefore, we can conclude that the two research themes presented in the Introduction were successfully met.

References

1. Susan Carden, "Digital Textile Printing," Bloomsbury Academic (2015)
2. Shibatani, M.: Latest advances in inkjet technology for industry applications. J. Printing Sci. Technol. **48**(4), 12–16 (2011)
3. Amo, Y., et al.: Development of Art Fashion by Integrating Art and Digital Textile Printing. In: EAI ArtsIT 2022 (Nov 2022)
4. Pang, Y., Zhao, L., Nakatsu, R., Tosa, N.: A study on variable control of sound vibration form (SVF) for media art creation. In: 2015 Conference on Culture and Computing. IEEE Press (2015)
5. Tosa, N., Pang, Y., Yang, Q., Nakatsu, R.: Pursuit and expression of Japanese beauty using technology. Arts journal, MDPI **8**(1), 38 (2019). https://doi.org/10.3390/arts8010038

The Relationship Between Sound of VR Concert and Motion Activity of Audience

Aki Kishimoto$^{(\boxtimes)}$ and Yasuhiro Oikawa

Waseda University, 3-4-1, Ohkubo, Shinjuku, Tokyo, Japan
aki_ksmt@suou.waseda.jp, yoikawa@waseda.jp

Abstract. In studies on the spectators of events, there have been several attempts at analyzing the excitement of spectators. In this work, we focus on the music performance using VR technology (VR concert) and propose the kinect-based motion recording system to analyze the relationship between the sound of VR concert and the motion activity of the audience in VR concert. For the motion recording system, we used a head mounted display (HMD), motion capture equipment and two host computers to show a music performance video to the audience by Unity and to record motion data of the audience by MATLAB®. Moreover, we used the equation to calculate the motion activity of the audience from the mean of whole joint's inter-frame coordinate translation in recorded motion data. To evaluate the motion recording system, we conducted experiments of watching a music performance video including background sound and recording motion data on examinees including 3 different conditions: Resting state (C1), watching a music performance video (C2) and watching a music performance video with sound of studio version (C3). The result shows that the mean of motion activity in C3 is larger than one in C2 and that there is few difference in the standard deviation of motion activity in each condition; which found that the background sound does not always increase the audience's motion.

Keywords: Virtual Reality · Kinect-Based Motion · Music Performance

1 Introduction

We have come to reach virtual reality (VR) content within recent years, and music performance using VR technology (VR concert) have spread throughout the world. In studies about VR concert, many systems, such as the VR-based remote live music support system [1] and the system using virtual instruments and virtual stage [2], were developed. On the other hand, there could be room for improvement in evaluation of user experience, especially the excitement of users. Unlike Likert scale [1] or interview [2], the quantitative way of evaluation should be found to omit bias from examiner and examinee.

To evaluate the excitement quantitatively, there are many studies about several approach to visualizing the excitement of spectators. For examples, Abe

C. Stephanidis et al. (Eds.): HCII 2024, CCIS 2116, pp. 237–244, 2024.
https://doi.org/10.1007/978-3-031-61950-2_26

et al. analyzed the excitement of spectators in a sports event by two-stream convolutional neural network (CNN) with object-based face and upper body detection [3]. Moreover, the biosignal-based approaches to quantify the excitement of spectators were taken, such as haptic feedback in remote-sports watching [4] and skin conductance response in video experience [5]. However, these approaches have yet to be improved because object-based detection would fail to find the slight motion of body parts [3] and installation of measuring devices to human directly [4,5] would not be suitable for a large number of people.

In this work, we focus on kinect-based motion data of the audience in VR concert, and propose that the relationship between the sound of VR concert and the movement of audience's motion (motion activity) in VR concert can be analyzed by kinect-based motion data. Conversion of the motion data to the motion activity could quantify the audience's motion and would not need to install to audience's head or body, and the motion activity could lead to analyzing the excitement of audience. Furthermore, we conducted evaluation experiments to examine whether the motion activity is changed by the sound of VR concert.

2   Proposed System

To record the motion data of the audience, we built the system using a head mounted display (HMD), motion capture equipment and two host computers as shown in Fig. 1.

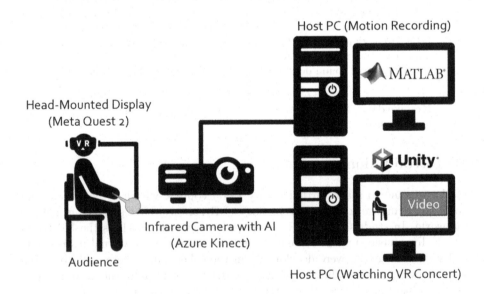

Fig. 1. Overview of the proposed system.

In this system, a host computer and the HMD are used to show a music performance video to the audience, and another host computer and motion capture equipment are used to record motion data of the audience. We introduced two host computers for distribution of load by video viewing in VR and motion recording. The HMD which we introduced is Meta Quest 2, and the motion capture equipment which we introduced is Azure Kinect DK, the infrared camera with AI.

2.1   VR Concert Viewer

In the host computer to show a music performance video, we developed the VR concert viewing system in VR space by Unity. There is a large screen to show the video in VR space, and the video starts on the screen when the Unity's scene is played. Moreover, we installed Oculus Integration, the plug-in to make the HMD available in Unity, and the HMD is connected to a host computer by Quest Link and to reflect the Unity's scene.

2.2   Motion Recording

We used the motion capture equipment and MATLAB®to capture and record the kinect-based moiton data of audience in another host computer. In MATLAB®, we referred to the program with the motion capture equipment in library developed by Terven [6]. The library includes the kinect-based body tracking program with the motion capture equipment and MATLAB®, but there is no motion recording program in the library. Therefore, we made motion recording available in MATLAB®by added motion recording program: Exporting the each coordinate joint saved in the body tracking program.

2.3   Analysis of Motion Activity

For analyzing motion activity of the audience, we referred to the equation of the video viewer's motion activity in Hanjalic's study [7]. The equation is used for analysis of viewer's block-based motion in video, and we redefined the equation for kinect-based motion as shown in Eqs. (1) and (2).

$$m(k) = \frac{100}{J|\boldsymbol{v}_{max}|}\left(\sum_{i=1}^{J}|\boldsymbol{v}_i(k)|\right)\%, \qquad (1)$$

$$m(k) = \frac{1}{J}\left(\sum_{i=1}^{J}|\boldsymbol{v}_i(k)|\right), \qquad (2)$$

where $m(k)$ is the score of motion activity between kth to $k+1$th frames, $|\boldsymbol{v}_i(k)|$ is each joint's coordinate parallel moving distance and J is the number of joints; we assumed J as 32 because the motion capture equipment is able to capture 32 joints [8].

These equations show that the motion activity is evaluated by the mean of whole joint's inter-frame coordinate parallel shifting from recorded motion data. In Eq. (1), the motion activity is expressed in ratio of the average of the parallel shifting motion's distance $|\boldsymbol{v}_i(k)|$ to the distance of the most parallel shifting motion $|\boldsymbol{v}_{max}|$ [7]. On the other hand, we provide Eq. (2), which does not include $|\boldsymbol{v}_{max}|$ as the distance of the most parallel shifting motion, to analyze when the divisor in the right-hand side of equation is constant in every frame.

3   Evaluation Experiment

For evaluation of the proposed system, we conducted evaluation experiments for 4 university students to examine whether the motion activity of audience is different from the sound of a music performance video in the system; the background sound, such as the audience's clapping and cheer, would increase the motion activity.

3.1   Procedure

We had an examinee sit on a chair with wearing an HMD, controllers and earphones as shown in Fig. 2, and the experiments was proceeded on 3 different conditions: Resting state (C1), watching a music performance video (C2) and watching a music performance video with sound of studio version (C3). The music in video which we used was "Virtual Insanity" by Jamiroquai [9].

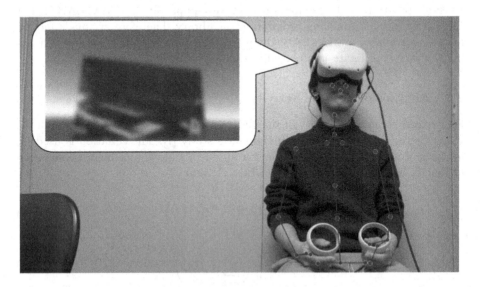

Fig. 2. Evaluation experiment.

In C1, we had the examinee stay at rest without the music performance video, and we instructed the examinee to move the examinee's body in rhythm if the examinee wants to do in both C2 and C3. The music performance video used in both C2 and C3 is same, but the sound of videos are different; the sound of C3's video is replaced by the studio version of the music to examine the difference by the background sound of the videos. At the same time, we recorded the examinee's motion by the system in each condition in the constant time, and evaluated the motion activities in MATLAB®.

3.2   Result

Figure 3 shows the time series graphs of the motion activity in each condition by Eqs. (1) and (2) and sound waveform of music performance videos in C2-3, and Table 1 shows the mean and standard deviation of the motion activity in each condition.

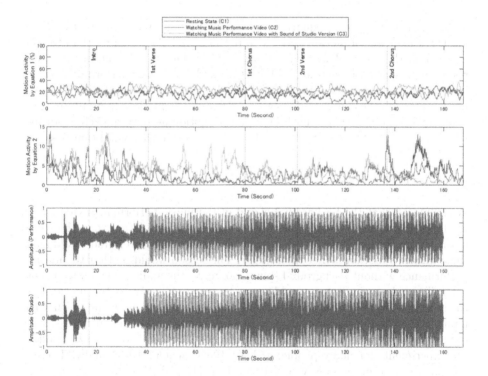

Fig. 3. The time series graphs (upper: motion activity of examinees' mean by Eqs. (1) and (2) in each condition, lower: sound waveform of music performance video in C2 and C3).

In means and standard deviations of the motion activity in each condition, as shown in Table 1, there is few difference between Eqs. (1) and (2), and it could be said that the motion activity is almost same regardless of whether the divisor

Table 1. Mean and standard deviation of the motion activity in each condition.

	Resting State (C1)	Watching Music Performance Video (C2)	Watching Music Performance Video with Sound of Studio Version (C3)
Mean (Eq. (1))	15.3	21.0	23.4
Standard Deviation (Eq. (1))	16.1	15.1	14.2
Mean (Eq. (2))	2.1	2.9	3.8
Standard Deviation (Eq. (2))	5.1	4.4	5.0

in the right-hand side of equation is constant or not. According to Fig. 3 and Table 1, the means of motion activity in both C2 and C3 are larger than the one in C1, and the mean of motion activity in C3 is larger than one in C2. These results represent that the sound of both C2's and C3's music performance videos increase the audience's motion and that the background sound of the video does not increase, on the contrary, decreases the audience's motion. In addition, there is few difference in the standard deviation of motion activity in each condition; which shows that the variation of audience's motion in each condition is same.

4   Discussion and Future Work

We supposed that the background sound of the music performance video, such as clapping and cheer, could make the audience's motion larger than the sound of the studio version, but it could be said that the background sound would make the audience's motion rather than larger. The reason would be that the musical performance without background sound can make the audience listen to it more carefully, and the audience would come to move its body to the music more easily in this situation. Furthermore, another assumed reason would be that the number of examinees is not enough to examine the relationship between the sound of videos and the motion of examinees. Therefore, we have to conduct the experiments for many people, at least 10–20 people. Additionally, There is few difference of motion activity between Eqs. (1) and (2) because the motions of all joints were used in both equation. To analyze the motion activity more clearly, we would need to choose the motion data of the joints related to moving in rhythm.

The weight of the HMD which we used could affect the motion activity because the examinees would not move their body because many people would not be accustomed to move their body with the HMD. The motion activity would be different if the examinees wear GOOVIS Pro (200g) [10] which is lighter than Meta Quest 2 (503g) [11]. In addition, there would be room for the research of the sound of music performance video. It could be thought that not only replacement of the video's sound but the sound of studio version with background sound should be examined to compare the motion activity's difference between live music and studio music; the difference between including background sound and excluding it should be also compared.

5   Conclusion

We proposed that the kinect-based motion of audience could be the important factor in the relationship between the sound of a VR concert and the audience's movement, and we built the system of recording motion with viewing a music performance video to quantify the audience's movement as motion activity and to measure without putting on audience directly. Moreover, we assumed that the music performance video's background sound could increase the audience's motion activity. However, the evaluation experiments showed that the video's background sound decrease the motion activity probably due to difficulty of listening and lack of examinees.

In the future, we will conduct the experiments for a large number of people to examine precisely the effect of the video's background sound, and investigate whether the weight of a HMD and other type of the video whose sound is fixed can affect the motion activity. In analysis of motion activity, we focus exclusively on the joints which is more noticeable during moving in rhythm.

References

1. Kaneko, T., et al.: Supporting the sense of unity between remote audiences in VR-based remote live music support system KSA2. In: 2018 IEEE International Conference on Artificial Intelligence and Virtual Reality (AIVR), pp. 124–127. Institute of Electrical and Electronics Engineers, New York (2018). https://doi.org/10.1109/AIVR.2018.00025
2. Pfafff, S., Lervik, O., Spoerri, R., Berra, E., Jahrmann, M., Neukom, M.: Games in concert: collaborative music making in virtual reality. In: SIGGRAPH Asia 2018 Virtual Augmented Reality, pp. 1–2. Association for Computing Machinery, New York (2018). https://doi.org/10.1145/3275495.3275509
3. Abe, K., Nakamura, C., Otsubo, Y., Koike, T., Yokoya, N.: Spectator excitement detection in small-scale sports events. In: Proceedings of the 2nd International Workshop on Multimedia Content Analysis in Sports (MMSports '19), pp. 100–107. Association for Computing Machinery, New York (2019). https://doi.org/10.1145/3347318.3355521
4. Peng, S.: Excitement projector: augmenting excitement-perception and arousal through bio-signal-based haptic feedback in remote-sport watching. In: Extended Abstracts of the 2022 CHI Conference on Human Factors in Computing Systems (CHI EA '22), pp. 1–6. Association for Computing Machinery, New York (2022). https://doi.org/10.1145/3491101.3519619
5. Shirokura, T., Munekata, N., Ono, T.: E3-player: emotional excitement enhancing video player using skin conductance response. In: Proceedings of the Companion Publication of the 2013 International Conference on Intelligent User Interfaces

Companion (IUI '13 Companion), pp. 47–48. Association for Computing Machinery, New York (2013). https://doi.org/10.1145/2451176.2451192

6. jrterven/KinZ-Matlab, https://github.com/jrterven/KinZ-Matlab. Accessed 09 Mar 2024

7. Hanjalic, A.: Multimodal approach to measuring excitement in video. In: 2003 International Conference on Multimedia and Expo. ICME '03. Proceedings (Cat. No.03TH8698), pp. 289–292. Institute of Electrical and Electronics Engineers, New York (2003). https://doi.org/10.1109/ICME.2003.1221610

8. Azure Kinect body tracking joints. https://learn.microsoft.com/en-us/azure/kinect-dk/body-joints. Accessed 09 Mar 2024

9. Jamiroquai - Virtual Insanity (Live in Verona). https://www.youtube.com/watch?v=qT41uNtvmmA. Accessed 13 Mar 2024

10. GOOVIS Pro - GOOVIS IS GOOD VISION. https://www.goovis.jp/goovis-pro. Accessed 10 Mar 2024

11. Oculus Quest 2 Specifications - Studio X. https://studiox.lib.rochester.edu/oculus-quest-2-specifications/. Accessed 10 Mar 2024

Prediction of a Musical Show Liking Using Bio-signals of an Audience

Chang-Gyu Lee[(✉)] and Ohung Kwon

Korea Institute of Industrial Technology, Gyeonggi-do, South Korea
{cglee,ohung}@kitech.re.kr

Abstract. This paper measured the bio-signals and liking of the audience watching a musical show, and then conducted machine learning training using this data. Subsequently, the trained machine learning model was utilized to predict the audience's liking for a musical show. As a result, it was possible to achieve a prediction accuracy of 74.38%. Through additional analysis, it was confirmed that the highest prediction accuracy could be achieved when predicting the audience's liking for the musical show using support vector machine (SVM) and utilizing pupil and facial expression data.

Keywords: Musical show · Liking · Bio-signal · Machine learning · Prediction

1 Introduction

Audience liking is crucial information for musical show officials as it directly impacts the success of the show. According to interviews conducted with musical show officials, the most common method used to gauge audience liking is through surveys. However, this method has the disadvantage of relying on audiences willingly taking the time to participate in the survey. Another approach involves observing reviews left by audience members who have attended musical shows. Nevertheless, this method suffers from the drawback of not being able to accurately predict the liking of the entire audience since only a fraction of the total audience tends to leave reviews. Therefore, studies have been conducted to predict liking based on the bio-signals of audiences consuming audiovisual media.

Koelstra et al. [12] presented 40 one-minute music videos to participants and collected their feedback regarding liking/disliking for each video. While watching the videos, the participants' electroencephalography (EEG), electrooculography (EOG), electromyography (EMG), electrodermal activity (EDA), blood volume pressure (BVP), temperature, and respiration were measured. By analyzing the measured bio-signals to predict the audience's liking, an F1 score of 0.538 (prediction accuracy of 59.1%) was achieved. Since then, various prediction models have been developed using this dataset. Zhuang et al. [17] achieved a prediction

C. Stephanidis et al. (Eds.): HCII 2024, CCIS 2116, pp. 245–250, 2024.
https://doi.org/10.1007/978-3-031-61950-2_27

accuracy of 70.5% using an unsupervised generative model, Gupta et al. [10] achieved an F1 score of 0.65 (67% prediction accuracy) using graph-theoretic features, Xu and Plataniotis [16] achieved an F1 score of 0.867 (89.2% prediction accuracy) using a deep belief network (DBN)-based model, Amjadzadeh and Ansari-Asl [6] obtained a prediction accuracy of 66.41% using k-nearest neighbor (kNN), Alhagry et al. [5] achieved a prediction accuracy of 87.99% using long short-term memory models (LSTM), and Moon et al. [13] obtained an F1 score of 0.969 using a deep neural network (DNN). However, because the bio-signals of liking for a one-minute music video and the bio-signals of liking for an hour-long musical show are different, the existing data [12] cannot be applied to the one-hour-long musical show. Therefore, this paper conducted a study to measure the bio-signals and liking of people watching an hour-long musical show and then predict liking.

The following section is organized as follows: Sect. 2 provides the configuration and procedure of the experiment, along with the application of signal processing, feature extraction, and classification techniques to analyze the measured data. Section 3 presents the experimental results and discussions, while Sect. 4 concludes this paper with a summary and suggestions for future research.

2   Experiment

2.1   Configuration and Procedure

As depicted in Fig. 1, participants wore three pieces of equipment capable of measuring EEG (Epoc X [2]), heart rate, temperature, EDA (E4 wristband [3]), and pupil (Pupil Core [11]). Additionally, their facial expressions were recorded by a front webcam. The captured facial expressions were utilized to estimate eight types of emotions (anger, contempt, disgust, fear, joy, sadness, surprise, and neutral) through Affectiva [1]. Participants were seated comfortably while wearing the bio-signal sensors, with a 75-inch television and 5.1-channel speakers positioned opposite for audiovisual display.

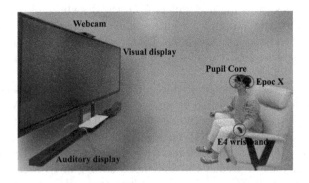

Fig. 1. Experimental configuration

The participants expressed their liking for the musical shows on a scale from 1 to 10 after watching "You&it," a drama genre with a running time of about 1 h and 40 min, and "Doodle pop," a family drama genre with a running time of about 50 min. Ratings from 1 to 5 were considered as indicating dislike, while ratings from 6 to 10 indicated liking. During the viewing, participants were instructed to remain as still as possible to prevent distortion of biosignals caused by movement [7]. To minimize bias based on viewing order, half of the participants watched "You&it" first, while the other half watched "Doodle pop" first. Additionally, a 20-minute break was provided between the musical show viewing sessions.

Thirty participants took part in the experiment, with ages ranging from 22 to 53 (mean: 33.73, standard deviation: 8.35). Nine were male and 21 were female. Among these 30 participants, 20 expressed liking for "You&it," while 16 expressed liking for "Doodle pop." As each participant provided data for both musical shows, a total of 60 sets of data were collected.

2.2   Signal Processing and Feature Extraction

Normalization, noise reduction, feature extraction, and dimensionality reduction techniques were applied to the measured bio-signals. Normalization was performed to scale the biosignal data, with the maximum value set to 1 and the minimum value to 0, considering the varying ranges of biosignals among participants. For noise reduction, a Savitzky-Golay filter with a window length of 81 and an order of 2 was utilized [14]. Subsequently, features listed in Table 1 were extracted. A total of 516 features were created, comprising 434 from Epoc X (EEG), 42 from E4 wristband (heart rate, temperature, EDA), 32 from Pupil Core (pupil), and 8 from the webcam (emotion), selected based on previous studies [4] [9]. Finally, principal component analysis (PCA) with a radial basis function (RBF) kernel, a dimensionality reduction technique, was employed. This step aimed to prevent issues such as overfitting or decreased prediction accuracy due to the curse of dimensionality [15]. Additionally, the kernel method was applied to facilitate classification on nonlinear data [8].

2.3   Classification

For classification, SVM and kNN, which are machine learning techniques, were utilized. These methods are widely employed for biosignal-based classification [4]. The analysis determined which methodology demonstrated higher prediction accuracy.

Furthermore, utilizing the four sensors employed in the experiment, a total of 15 sensor combinations were generated. Through an analysis of the prediction accuracy associated with each sensor combination, we identified the sensor playing a predominant role in predicting musical show liking.

Of the total data, 80% was randomly selected for training the prediction model, while the remaining 20% was used for testing. Likings for the test data were predicted using the prediction model, and prediction accuracy was calculated by comparing the predictions with the correct answers. To minimize the

Table 1. Biosignal features

Biosignals	Features
EEG	Mean, standard deviation, root mean square, min/max difference, number of zero crossings, histogram distribution, skewness, kurtosis
	First 10 auto correlation coefficients, entropy, average energy in the five frequency domains
Heart rate	Mean, median, min/max difference, variance, skewness, kurtosis, mean difference
	First 5 auto correlation coefficients
Temperature	Mean, median, min/max difference, variance, skewness, kurtosis
	First 5 auto correlation coefficients
EDA	Mean, median, min/max difference, standard deviation, skewness, kurtosis, activity, mobility, complexity, mean difference, mean difference of decreasing
	First 5 auto correlations, average of decreasing changes, ratio of decreasing time to total time, number of zero crossings
Pupil	Diameter - mean, median, min/max difference, variance, skewness, kurtosis
	Position - mean, variance
	Fixed time - mean, median, min/max difference, variance, skewness, kurtosis
	Blink time - mean, median, min/max difference, variance, skewness, kurtosis
Emotion	Percentage of each emotion's time to total time

potential impact of data selection on prediction accuracy, both training and test data were randomly selected. Learning and prediction were iterated a total of 10,000 times, and the prediction accuracy for each iteration was averaged to derive the final prediction accuracy.

3   Results and Discussions

As depicted in Fig. 2, the highest prediction accuracy of 74.38% was achieved when predicting musical show liking through SVM using the feature combination of pupil and emotion. This suggests that audience liking can be predicted by installing a camera and pupil tracking device on the audience.

Among SVM and kNN, it was confirmed that SVM was more suitable for predicting musical show liking. Specifically, when using data extracted from four biosignal sensors (Band, Pupil, EEG, and Emotion), SVM yielded the higher prediction accuracy. Similarly, when using data from three biosignal sensors

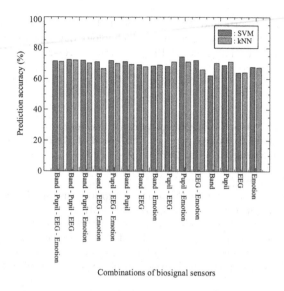

Combinations of biosignal sensors

Fig. 2. Prediction accuracy of musical liking with respect to sensor combinations

(Band, Pupil, and EEG), SVM achieved the higher prediction accuracy. Furthermore, when utilizing data from two biosignal sensors (Pupil and Emotion), SVM resulted in the higher prediction accuracy. Lastly, when employing data from only one biosignal sensor (Pupil), kNN led to the higher prediction accuracy. Based on this analysis, it can be concluded that SVM is more suitable for predicting musical show liking than kNN. Additionally, the analysis of these combinations reveals that pupil is included in all sensor combinations, regardless of whether four, three, two, or one sensor is used. Therefore, it can be observed that pupil features play a crucial role in predicting musical show liking.

4   Conclusion and Future Work

In this paper, a biosignal-based system for predicting musical show liking was developed by analyzing the biosignals and liking surveys of audiences watching musical shows. Through experiments involving 30 participants and subsequent analysis, the highest prediction accuracy of 74.38% was achieved when employing SVM with pupil and emotion features. It was observed that prediction using SVM resulted in higher accuracy than kNN, with pupil features playing a crucial role in predicting musical show liking. In future work, we plan to validate our dataset by comparing it with the Database for Emotion Analysis using Physiological Signals (DEAP) dataset [12] and further validate the developed methodology through live musical shows.

Acknowledgment. This research was supported by Culture, Sports and Tourism R&D Program through the Korea Creative Content Agency grant funded by the

Ministry of Culture, Sports and Tourism in 2024 (Project Name: Real-time feedback visualization and multisensory performance technology development using performer-audience emotional state information, Project Number: RS-2023-00219678, Contribution Rate: 100%).

References

1. Affectiva (2024). https://www.affectiva.com/. Accessed 15 Mar 2024
2. Emotiv epoc x - 14 channel wireless EEG headset (2024). https://www.emotiv.com/epoc-x/. Accessed 15 Mar 2024
3. Empatica e4 wristband (2024). https://www.empatica.com/en-int/research/e4/. Accessed 15 Mar 2024
4. Alarcao, S.M., Fonseca, M.J.: Emotions recognition using EEG signals: a survey. IEEE Trans. Affect. Comput. **10**(3), 374–393 (2017)
5. Alhagry, S., Fahmy, A.A., El-Khoribi, R.A.: Emotion recognition based on EEG using LSTM recurrent neural network. Int. J. Adv. Comput. Sci. Appl. **8**(10) (2017)
6. Amjadzadeh, M., Ansari-Asl, K.: An innovative emotion assessment using physiological signals based on the combination mechanism. Sci. Iranica **24**(6), 3157–3170 (2017)
7. Chen, W., Jaques, N., Taylor, S., Sano, A., Fedor, S., Picard, R.W.: Wavelet-based motion artifact removal for electrodermal activity. In: 2015 37th Annual International Conference of the IEEE Engineering in Medicine and Biology Society (EMBC), pp. 6223–6226. IEEE (2015)
8. Choi, S.W., Lee, C., Lee, J.M., Park, J.H., Lee, I.B.: Fault detection and identification of nonlinear processes based on kernel PCA. Chemom. Intell. Lab. Syst. **75**(1), 55–67 (2005)
9. Egger, M., Ley, M., Hanke, S.: Emotion recognition from physiological signal analysis: a review. Electron. Notes Theor. Comput. Sci. **343**, 35–55 (2019)
10. Gupta, R., Falk, T.H., et al.: Relevance vector classifier decision fusion and EEG graph-theoretic features for automatic affective state characterization. Neurocomputing **174**, 875–884 (2016)
11. Kassner, M., Patera, W., Bulling, A.: Pupil: an open source platform for pervasive eye tracking and mobile gaze-based interaction. In: Proceedings of the 2014 ACM International Joint Conference on Pervasive and Ubiquitous Computing: Adjunct Publication, pp. 1151–1160 (2014)
12. Koelstra, S., et al.: DEAP: a database for emotion analysis; using physiological signals. IEEE Trans. Affect. Comput. **3**(1), 18–31 (2011)
13. Moon, S.E., Jang, S., Lee, J.S.: Evaluation of preference of multimedia content using deep neural networks for electroencephalography. In: 2018 Tenth International Conference on Quality of Multimedia Experience (QoMEX), pp. 1–6. IEEE (2018)
14. Savitzky, A., Golay, M.J.: Smoothing and differentiation of data by simplified least squares procedures. Anal. Chem. **36**(8), 1627–1639 (1964)
15. Schittenkopf, C., Deco, G., Brauer, W.: Two strategies to avoid overfitting in feedforward networks. Neural Netw. **10**(3), 505–516 (1997)
16. Xu, H., Plataniotis, K.N.: Affective states classification using EEG and semi-supervised deep learning approaches. In: 2016 IEEE 18th International Workshop on Multimedia Signal Processing (MMSP), pp. 1–6. IEEE (2016)
17. Zhuang, X., Rozgić, V., Crystal, M.: Compact unsupervised eeg response representation for emotion recognition. In: IEEE-EMBS international conference on Biomedical and Health Informatics (BHI). pp. 736–739. IEEE (2014)

RAR (Reality-Augmented Reality) Experience Awakening Urban Influence - "Fu Metaverse" in Fuzhou, China

Jing Liang, Yiheng Zhong, Yancheng Cao, and Fan Chen[✉]

Tongji University, Siping Road 1230, Shanghai, China
chenfantj@foxmail.com

Abstract. The "Fu Metaverse" project pioneers urban extended reality (XR) within Fuzhou city's rich historical backdrop, especially along the Minjiang River. This paper explores the technical, creative, and practical aspects of deploying XR in urban spaces. Addressing challenges like large-scale environmental mapping, content creation reflecting local culture, and device coordination, we introduce novel solutions including centimeter-level spatial computing, AI-enhanced scene understanding, and high-fidelity visual integration.

Key element to the project is the interweaving of cultural narratives with the XR experience, allowing for immersive storytelling rooted in Fuzhou's heritage. While focusing on local culture, our findings offer insights into the broader application of XR technologies in urban settings.

The "Fu Metaverse" sets a precedent in urban RAR applications, demonstrating how digital overlays can enrich cityscapes, strengthen cultural identity, and contribute to the digital economy. The paper concludes by highlighting the project's technical successes and its potential to revolutionize urban experiences through XR.

1 Introduction

1.1 Background of "Fu Metaverse"

The digital economy is a new engine for high-quality development and represents the future global direction. On July 22, 2022, the "Fu Metaverse" themed Digital Interaction show lit up the 5th Digital China Construction Summit. The project showcased three distinctive areas along the Minjiang River in Fuzhou and the Convention and Exhibition Island through a live "R (Reality-Augmented Reality) " digital light show.

"Fu Metaverse" is custom-made for Fujian, a coastal province in southeast China, embodying the hopes of generations for a better future. Using digital means, it becomes the "Fu Metaverse." The interactive show combines Chinese culture, technology, dragon and fish imagery, and exhibition mascots to create a new digital world. It upholds the principles of grandeur, excitement, and sustainability, showcasing the technological allure of Digital design.

2 Evaluation About Design Challenge

Given the context of extended reality (XR) design, this domain's design practices pose a unique set of challenges to creators due to its three-dimensional and innovative nature. Previous research has outlined the primary obstacles faced in the XR design process, compared to the development of two-dimensional applications [1, 2], with these challenges being particularly evident in the creation of augmented and virtual reality (AR/VR) content. This study identifies and analyzes these challenges with the aim of providing insights for future design practices and theoretical research.

1. **Misunderstandings within the team about the medium**: Design teams might have overly optimistic expectations about hardware and software performance, overlooking specific technical limitations and the impact of external environmental factors on the robustness of sensory inputs. Furthermore, knowledge extracted from two-dimensional design experiences may not be applicable to three-dimensional media, leading to compatibility issues between design thinking and XR technologies.
2. **Lack of tool support and appropriate methodologies**: The XR design field suffers from a scarcity of tools and spaces specifically designed for designing or testing in AR/VR environments, complicating the prototype design process, especially when trying to achieve working prototypes without relying on coding. Moreover, existing tools and methods often fail to integrate creators' workflows comprehensively, such as a lack of design specifications, making it difficult for creators with diverse skills to collaborate, thereby affecting the quality and reusability of code.
3. **Lack of a common language**: Within XR design teams, there is a lack of a shared, precise language for describing system behaviors and design ideas, limiting effective communication. Inappropriate solution choices (e.g., borrowing from 2D design practices) may result in final products that do not meet intended goals, reducing the satisfaction with design outcomes.

In the following sections, this study will analyze the specific challenges present in the cases under consideration, to further elaborate on the discussion of solution strategies in greater detail.

2.1 Technical and Scale Challenges: Computational Difficulty in Large-Scale Environments

The Minjiang River, one of the largest rivers in Fujian Province, also serves as the mother river of Fuzhou City. With a total length of about 409 km and a basin area of about 26,000 square kilometers, the river's section in the Taijiang District of Fuzhou is approximately 200 m wide. As the urbanization of the Fuzhou metropolitan area has rapidly advanced, the banks of the Minjiang River have seen a blend of traditional architecture, which integrates the region's rich historical and cultural heritage, alongside modern financial and business districts, characterized by skyscrapers that showcase a modern urban landscape. With thousands of buildings of diverse styles and varying heights along its banks, and with its broad expanse, the scale and span of the scene, as well as the multitude of details that need to be addressed, present a significant technical challenge.

To realize RAR experiences, it is first necessary to accurately identify and locate the user's spatial position to correctly overlay virtual content. Ensuring spatial perception and positioning accuracy in such complex scenarios is one of the technical challenges. Secondly, acquiring a vast amount of architectural and scenic data to build maps for RAR experiences involves extensive 3D modeling of buildings, image recognition, and processing technologies, requiring significant data collection and processing efforts, which constitutes the second technical challenge. Lastly, the issue of buildings obscuring each other due to their varied heights, along with the differences in brightness, color, and shadows of virtual content under different lighting conditions, can diminish the realism of the experience. Addressing environmental lighting and occlusion issues, as well as real-time rendering and performance optimization for large-scale buildings, represents the third technical challenge.

2.2 Content and Creative Challenges: Innovative Content in Specialized Environments

Fuzhou boasts a unique landscape with the Minjiang River nurturing a special sentiment among its people. It carries the rich historical and cultural heritage of Fuzhou, witnessing its development and changes. Its beautiful riverside scenery also provides citizens with direct access to nature.

Delivering RAR performances in such a setting, closely connected to local emotions, requires a deep understanding and appreciation of the local culture, alongside innovation in both technology and content. The challenge lies in striking a balance between technology and culture, presenting the local culture's charm without cliché. Selecting the most representative symbols, crafting compelling stories, and leveraging technology to enhance immersion and even enable interactions between the virtual and the real pose significant challenges in creating this experience.

2.3 Real-World and Media Challenges: Device Coordination in Complex Environments

The Minjiang River is tranquil and beautiful by day, transforming with lights and shadows at night. The complex environment along its banks, including sunlight, reflected light, and shadows at different times, affects the RAR experience.

One challenge is optimizing RAR content display and lighting effects to ensure an immersive experience at all times. A second challenge is ensuring smooth transitions of scene angles as users move along the riverbanks, maintaining alignment between virtual content and the actual landscape in such a vast area. Precise arrangement of real scenes to complement virtual art is crucial in RAR experiences. Coordinating real-world scene and lighting setups with virtual content along the vast Minjiang River banks involves considering the placement of physical lighting, lighting effects, and interaction with RAR content, marking the third challenge in real-world settings.

3 Design Approaches

3.1 Technical Approaches: Innovative Fusion Interpretation, Based on Four Core Technologies

The "Fu Metaverse" project covers three distinct areas: the Minjiang River, Fuzhou, and the Convention and Exhibition Island. It has addressed key technological challenges through four core breakthroughs: Centimeter-Level Spatial Computing, Advanced AI for Scene Understanding, High-Fidelity Rendering, Large-Scale 3D Map Construction:

a. **Centimeter-Level Spatial Computing**: Offers all-weather, all-scenario centimeter-level spatial computing, enabling precise positioning and orientation (6DOF) within a degree, supporting high-precision AR navigation, holographic POI signage, and digital screens. This computing capability allows for accurate location identification and virtual content overlay, ensuring precise RAR experiences even in complex and large scenes.

b. **Advanced AI for Scene Understanding**: Utilizes powerful AI to deeply understand objects, structures, and environmental features in various scenes, offering millimeter-level 3D recognition of the surroundings and supporting 3D landmark recognition and tour navigation. This enables more accurate identification, tracking, and analysis of both static and moving elements in scenes, providing smarter interactions and content presentations.

c. **High-Fidelity Rendering**: Optimizes lighting, shadows, and reflections through advanced algorithms, delivering realistic and vivid visual experiences by day and night. This ensures the digital content blends seamlessly with the real world, achieving realistic virtual-real occlusions and enhancing the immersion and realism of virtual content.

d. **Large-Scale 3D Map Construction**: Employs multi-source data collection and processing for large-scale 3D map construction, supporting automated mapping pipelines, satellite mapping, and rapid large-area coverage. This facilitates high-precision positioning and content overlay, making AR experiences more accurate and lifelike in real-world settings.

Additionally, Fuzhou Survey Institute conducted "facial recognition" calculations for 328 building complexes, ensuring stability in challenging environments, contributing to a seamless blend of reality and virtuality in the "Fu Metaverse" experience.

3.2 Experimental Approaches: Passing on the Culture and Creating a Digital Experience

In the RAR presentation of the digital interactive show, the content primarily follows a timeline to depict Fuzhou's journey from its ancient past to the present and into the future digital era. Through iconic Fuzhou elements and flavors of Chinese culture, such as goldfish and banyan trees, the audience is invited to experience the essence of Chinese traditional culture and the ancient charm of Fuzhou in a novel digital format. The following is an introduction to the chapters of the interactive show, comprising three chapters in total.

Chapter 1: The Minjiang River, flowing through Fuzhou, symbolizes the city's enduring history (Fig. 1).

Fig. 1. Chapter 1: "A Millennium Journey: Leaping Over the Dragon Gate" RAR Exhibition Content

Chapter 2: Fuzhou's vibrant present transforms into a digital city, hinting at digital's impact on its future (Fig. 2).

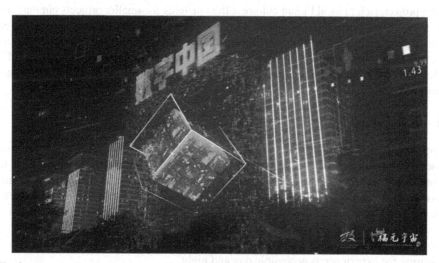

Fig. 2. Chapter 2: "Reflections Across the Banks, Gathering of the Five Blessings" RAR Exhibition Content

Chapter 3: The audience is transported from the real city into a virtual metaverse, where Fuzhou, on the digital Silk Road, aspires to happiness and a cosmic journey towards the future (Fig. 3).

Fig. 3. Chapter 3: "Connecting the World, Changing the Future" RAR Exhibition Content

3.3 Limitations and Future Works

This project, rich in local Fujian culture, offers insights for smaller projects but may not fit all workflows. The fast growth of AR technology, driven by smartphones and web trends, hints at widespread RAR experiences, enriching travel interactions and benefiting local culture and tourism. In conclusion, as tech advances and applications broaden, "Fu Metaverse" can create accessible experiences, shape Fuzhou's image, and boost digital tourism.

4 Conclusion

The "Fu Metaverse" has technically achieved comprehensive point scanning, offering wide coverage that allows audiences on both sides of the Min River viewing area to watch live events. It encompasses 328 buildings, spanning a length of 5,659 m. Content-wise, all aspects of the Fu Metaverse's digital and virtual experience are related to the historical and cultural heritage of Fuzhou. It narrates the local populace's life stories through intangible digital imagery, blending the real with the virtual. In terms of format, it also considers the compatibility with different devices and various application scenarios, ensuring the experience is accessible day and night.

"Fu Metaverse" pioneers urban RAR innovation in China, a milestone in the nation's digital evolution. It seamlessly blends reality and virtual experiences, showcasing key design innovations. Beyond locals, it attracted tourists and professionals, promoting Fuzhou's distinct urban identity as a hub for digital interaction and creativity.

References

1. Krauß, V., Boden, A., Oppermann, L., et al.: Current practices, challenges, and design implications for collaborative AR/VR application development. In: Proceedings of the 2021 CHI
   Conference on Human Factors in Computing Systems, pp. 1–15 (2021)
2. Zuofa, T., Ochieng, E.G.: Working separately but together: appraising virtual project team
   challenges. Team Perform. Manage. Int. J. **23**(5/6), 227–242 (2017)

Research on Interactive Experience Design of Culture-Themed Exhibition Based on Environmental Psychology—Take the "Wu Yun Jiangnan" Theme Exhibition as an Example

Lin Lin[ID] and Lang Lu[✉][ID]

School of Arts, Soochow University, Suzhou, Jiangsu, China
lulang@suda.edu.com

Abstract. With the rapid advancement of digital media technology, museums have gradually transformed from traditional service-oriented spaces to interactive experience-oriented spaces. The focus of museums has also shifted from "objects" to "people". It focuses on the factors affecting people's psychological changes in the environment. It then constantly introduces new exhibition methods and interactive experiences to improve the efficiency of information dissemination.

Based on the theory of environmental psychology, this paper takes the culture-themed exhibition space as the research object. It explores the influence of environmental space and facilities on users' perception from the perspective of interactive experience, and the main research content includes: 1. Explaining the development overview of environmental psychology and analyzing the relationship between environmental elements and users' experience; 2. Exploring the relationship between environmental psychology and culture-themed display space; 3. By constructing narrative spatial sequences and scenes, applying multimedia interactive means, and augmented reality technology to create an immersive experience, users can obtain a richer physical and mental experience.

The design of interactive and experiential cultural-themed exhibition space should synthesize various factors such as artistic design, emerging technology, and user experience and pay attention to realizing the multi-dimensional integration of the user's behavioral mode, emotional change, and interactive experience to create a rich and exciting multi-level, multi-dimensional and diversified culture-themed exhibition experience space.

Keywords: Environmental Psychology · Culture-themed Exhibitions · Interactive Experience

1 Introduction

Exhibition space focuses on the contents of different times and spaces in the same field. It is the medium of communication between exhibits and the public, mainly containing the themes of culture, science, technology and commerce. Among them, culture-themed exhibitions aim to provide information about a particular culture, such as style, conno-tation, history, etc., and often require narrative historical scenes and systematic display contents with rich and diversified exhibition information [1]. Therefore, it is an essen-tial goal of exhibition design to enable visitors to obtain a wholly immersive experi-ence through the conception of an interactive experience in the exhibition space so that they can comprehensively, deeply, and accurately perceive and accept the information. Environmental psychology is committed to the study of the interaction between human psychology, behavior, and environment in a particular field, and the application of its relevant theories to the interactive experience design of culture-themed exhibitions can provide a reference for the contemporary culture-themed exhibition space, which has positive practical value.

2 Perceptual Experience from an Environmental Psychology Perspective

Environmental psychology emerged in the 1950s and 1960s, triggered by issues such as population growth and environmental degradation, and focused on the impact of the environment on human behavior [2]. In 1973 and 1978, Craik and Stokols published a review of research entitled *Environmental Psychology* in *Annual Review of Psychol-ogy*, establishing environmental psychology as a formal branch of psychology [3, 4]. Subsequently, Stokols and others published *Handbook of Environmental Psychology* in 1987, and environmental psychology became a relatively mature theoretical field of view, which aims to analyze the interrelationships between the environment and human behaviors, cognition, and emotions using psychological methods and to explore the psychological changes of human beings under various environmental conditions [5].

In the theoretical field of environmental psychology, the environment is the "sur-rounding situation", which influences human psychological and behavioral activities [6]. For the relationship between the environment and user behavior, American psychologist Gibson proposed that environmental objects should provide users with convenience, have clear meaning, and meet their needs [7]. The environment has a particular order, mode, and structure, directly or indirectly affecting human life, various development factors, and human relations [8]. People and the environment influence each other; peo-ple have a subjective judgment of the environment, and the environmental space can also affect people's perceptions.

3 Analysis of User Requirements for Culture-Themed Exhibition Space

Environmental psychology mainly explores the psychology and behavior of the ontology of "humans" in the object environment, so the change in people's psychological activities and perceptual experience while visiting the exhibition is the primary content of the designer's attention [9]. The psychological changes users produce include awareness, emotion, and will process [10]. In the process of cognition, users are often influenced by the characteristics of the exhibition itself and the environment in which it is located and become interested in the content the exhibition tries to convey. On the other hand, emotion formation passes through a series of insights, comparisons, and analyses of the exhibits, from awareness to gaining experience. Based on the first two stages of psychological activities, which have clear objectives, the dissemination and promotion of the spiritual and cultural connotation of the exhibition is the final process of will. To a certain extent, the user's psychological activity uniquely acts on the exhibition design process.

Combining environmental psychology with Maslow's hierarchy of needs theory, it can be concluded that culture-themed exhibitions have functional, cultural, and experiential needs. The first thing users should satisfy is the functional demand when they enter the culture-themed exhibition space. In addition to the most basic exhibition function, comfort, beauty, reasonableness, and so on are the main elements that constitute its functionality. Secondly, the user's cultural demand and culture determine the quality of this type of exhibition space. The generation of culture has a historical accumulation and precipitation process; forming ideas and habits is a relatively stable psychological need that can meet the user's sense of cultural identity and belonging and draw closer to the user's distance. Finally, experiential demand is the pursuit of self-realization. Experiential exhibition of sensory accessibility, interactive immediacy, and other characteristics have created good conditions for the innovative development of culture-themed exhibition space, which can better meet the spiritual needs of users.

4 Application and Practical Discussion: An Example of Suzhou Bay Museum's "Wu Yun Jiangnan" Theme Exhibition

Located on the shore of East Taihu Lake in Suzhou, Jiangsu Province, China, the Suzhou Bay Museum, to inherit and develop the historical and cultural heritage of Wujiang, combines the functions of display, cultural experience, public education, scientific research, exchange, and cooperation, and is committed to creating a new space for Wujiang culture that connects the ancient and modern worlds. The museum on the 4th-floor set "Wu Yun Jiangnan—Wujiang history and culture display" theme of the permanent exhibition display exhibits 442 pieces, including 130 pieces of cultural relics above the third level. The period of the exhibition is from the Neolithic era to modern times, spanning more than 7,000 years; there are three exhibition areas, respectively, "Prehistory and Pre-Qin Period""Dynasty State Era"and "Into the Modern Society". By combing various cultural heritage resources such as the historical development and significant historical events of Wujiang, the survival and evolution of the people of Wujiang in history, as well as the position of Wujiang in the history of China, it tells about the production and living conditions of the people of Wujiang, displays the splendid culture created by the people of Wujiang, and presents the trajectory of the development of civilization in Wujiang.

4.1 Constructing Narrative Spatial Sequences and Scenes

Space, as the carrier of visitors' behavioral activities, directly affects users' psychological behavior. Environmental psychology research indicates that human behavioral perception and spatial form complement each other, ultimately determining the decision-making and action of human behavior in the environment. The construction of narrative spatial sequences and scenarios is a restoration of the same time and space in the past, recreating historical environments and events that occurred in the past, which can trigger the interactive behavior of users [11]. The exhibition "Wuyun Jiangnan-Wujiang Historical and Cultural Display" of Suzhou Bay Museum contains many restoration scenes with narrative significance. Figure 1 shows the mid- to late-Ming Dynasty when the silk-reeling and textile industries centered on Zhenze and the silk-weaving industries centered on Shengze and Huangjiaxi emerged. Users can quickly immerse themselves in that historical scene and interact with the textile machines, thus understanding the information about the field at that time (see Fig. 1). Figure 2 shows that seven thousand years ago, the ancestors of Wujiang started the road of exploration of history and culture on this land (see Fig. 2). As a typical representative of Liangzhu culture, the Longnan Site in Meiyan, Pingwang Township, is known as "the First Village of Jiangnan". This exhibition restores the production and living scenes of the villagers in the village and realizes narrative scenario reproduction by combining historical photographs, cultural relics, and interactive touch screens with historical scene restoration. At the same time, the efficient integration of exhibits, artifacts, images, fields, explanatory texts, and other elements can make the narrative plot more compact and the historical scenes more emotional impact, thus allowing users to truly feel the historical and cultural information conveyed by the exhibition from the spatial scene. It can be said that scene recovery with narrative significance influences visitors' behavior and perception with its spatial form, optimizes the exhibition space, and promotes the dissemination of history and culture simultaneously, so narrative becomes a critical factor in enhancing the user experience of the exhibition space.

Fig. 1. Textile machinery and equipment, fiber materials, etc., in historical restoration scenes

4.2 Application of Multimedia Interactive Tools

According to the content of visual perception and environmental cognition in environmental psychology, it can be found that for different environmental places, the application

Fig. 2. Restoration of scenes of villagers' production and life at the Longnan Site in Meiyan, Pingwang Township

of multimedia is an essential embodiment of environmental perception and emotional needs to meet the user's functional needs and psychological demands. Multimedia interactive design can enhance the user's visiting experience in visual, auditory, tactile, and even olfactory aspects. In the exhibition, interactive technology makes the screen display system present information about the exhibits, combined with the display of the exhibits in the field, to strengthen the user's understanding of the exhibits [12]. In addition to using multimedia interactive technology to display pictures, text introductions, etc., you can also use holographic projection technology to present the evolution of the exhibits in the form of a form and sound to the audience [13]. Figure 3 shows that the people of Wujiang embrace the ideal of "science and technology to save the country" and constantly create the course of progress (see Fig. 3). The viewer sees the story from the perspective of a character of his or her choice, which provides a stronger sense of immersion and meets individual needs. Figure 4 shows the movie screening scene of Shengze Grand Cinema, the first town cinema in Jiangsu Province, China (see Fig. 4). Multimedia technology is used to enhance the user's perception of the environment, which is the basis of the user's cognition of things, and to help the user identify the relationship between things, environments, and people in the space of historical and cultural displays, to satisfy the visitor's psychological and visual sensory needs.

4.3 Augmented Reality Technology Creates an Immersive Experience

According to the perception theory of environmental psychology, the perception formed by an individual in the surrounding environment is formed after subjective digestion and reconstruction of external stimuli. The perception of users in the exhibition space is generated by their subjective processing of external stimuli and related information. The combination of physical and virtual space-time, with sound, light, and electricity technology, is an essential means of historical and cultural exhibition. Chuihong Bridge, "the first long bridge in Jiangnan", was created in the Northern Song Dynasty in the eighth year of the Qingli (1048 AD). Since then, merchants and literati have gathered here. Using augmented reality technology, the poem and the literati boat tour of Wujiang scenic spots, enjoying the night scene presented in the form of animation, constituting a stimulus to

Fig. 3. Application of multimedia technology

Fig. 4. Shengze Grand Cinema Movie Launch Scene

the perceptual system of the visitor's brain, thus affecting the visitor's psychological activities and behavior, such as attracting users to produce the virtual strings to play music, to participate in the creation of spatial ambiance, and at the same time to increase the interest of the exhibition, attracting more visitors to experience(see Fig. 5). Through the combination of "sound" "painting" and "scenery", as well as accurate ships and running water, users can mentally perceive the scene at that time. Countless vital figures and events in the history of human development can be supported by augmented reality technology to reproduce the scenarios in a dynamic and virtual fusion method, placing the natural display objects and virtual image art in the exhibition space, which enhances the visual effect of users, guides their line of sight and flow to obtain a more continuous experience, and enhances their interest, sense of immersion and sense of immersion in the exhibition [14].

Fig. 5. Spatial and temporal recreation of the virtual scene at the Chuihong Bridge

5   Conclusions and Outlook

This paper discusses the practical application of environmental psychology theory in the interactive experience design of culture-themed exhibition space. It proposes a design strategy that breaks traditional design limitations, adopts multi-perspective and multi-disciplinary research methods, and integrates modern technology to enhance spatial experience and interaction. Meanwhile, the Suzhou Bay Museum's "Wu Yun Jiangnan" thematic exhibition is taken as a case study to analyze how to effectively promote the emotional resonance and communication between the exhibition content and the audience through the construction of narrative spatial sequences, the use of multimedia interactive means and augmented reality technology. In the subsequent research, the following aspects will also be explored in depth: firstly, strengthening user participation, allowing users to explore in depth according to their interests and preferences through the design of interactive exhibits and customized experience paths; secondly, developing an intelligent guiding system, guiding users to learn and explore in depth through the question-and-answer mechanism supported by natural language processing and machine learning technologies, and enhancing the interactivity and knowledge dissemination efficiency of the exhibition; and thirdly, using data analysis and artificial intelligence technologies to optimize the exhibition content and the communication between the audience and the exhibition and using data analysis and artificial intelligence technology to optimize the personalized recommendation of exhibition content, to achieve more efficient information transmission and more profound educational significance[15]. In future research on exhibition space design, an interdisciplinary collaborative approach will be adopted, integrating knowledge and technology from multiple fields, such as visual arts, digital technology, and psychology, to enrich the exhibition space's interactivity and educational function.

In conclusion, by combining the application of environmental psychology in practice, we can effectively enhance the interactive experience of users in culture-themed exhibition space, strengthen the depth and breadth of cultural communication and education, and play a better service and cultural value.

References

1. Jijun, Z., Sheng, Z., Jin, F.: The design of exhibition center with regional cultural symbol. Agro Food Ind. Hi-Tech **28**(1), 3257–3261 (2017)
2. Parathian, H.E., Frazão-Moreira, A., Hockings, K.J.: Environmental psychology must better integrate local cultural and sociodemographic context to inform conservation (2018)
3. Craik, K.H.: Environmental psychology. Annu. Rev. Psychol. **24**(1), 403–422 (1973)
4. Stokols, D.: Environmental psychology. Annu. Rev. Psychol. **29**(1), 253–295 (1978)
5. Altman, I., Stokols, D. (Eds.): Handbook of environmental psychology. Wiley & Sons (1987)
6. Nielsen, K.S., Cologna, V., Lange, F., Brick, C., Stern, P.C.: The case for impact-focused environmental psychology. J. Environ. Psychol. 74 (2021)
7. Gibson, E.J.: Has psychology a future? Psychol. Sci. **5**(2), 69–76 (1994)
8. Blok, V.: The human glance, the experience of environmental distress and the "affordance" of nature: toward a phenomenology of the ecological crisis. J. Agric. Environ. Ethics **28**, 925–938 (2015)
9. Mei, X., Zou, C.: The influence of traditional village landscape design on tourists' tourism psychology under environmental psychology. Psychiatria Danubina, **34**(suppl 1), 829–830 (2022)
10. Daae, J., Boks, C.: A classification of user research methods for design for sustainable behaviour. J. Clean. Prod. **106**, 680–689 (2015)
11. Benson, P.: Space in narrative inquiry on second language learning. System **102**, 102602 (2021)
12. Jeong, S., Hashimoto, N., Sato, M.: Immersive multi-projector display on hybrid screens with human-scale haptic interface. IEICE Trans. Inf. Syst. **88**(5), 888–893 (2005)
13. Li, Y., Yu, Q., Wu, Y., Wei, C.: Research on hologram based on holographic projection technology. Math. Probl. Eng. (2022)
14. Carmigniani, J., Furht, B., Anisetti, M., Ceravolo, P., Damiani, E., Ivkovic, M.: Augmented reality technologies, systems and applications. Multimedia Tools Appl. **51**, 341–377 (2011)
15. Mühlhoff, R.: Human-aided artificial intelligence: or, how to run large computations in human brains? Toward a media sociology of machine learning. New Media Soc. **22**(10), 1868–1884 (2020)

Suzhou Garden Dynamic Image Design Based on Digital Media Programming and Sound Visualization

Muqing Liu, Zhuxuan Chen, Qingyi Li, and Xinlin Li[✉]

Soochow University, Suzhou 215000, Jiangsu, China
xlli1227@suda.edu.cn

Abstract. As an outstanding representative of traditional Chinese garden art, Suzhou gardens are treasures of human culture. However, its interaction width and depth of dissemination in the international arena still need to be improved. As a medium widely accepted by the public, digital media can help global cross-cultural audiences understand and appreciate the deep aesthetic and cultural values of gardens and become a link between different cultures. Currently, the integration and innovation of digital media in traditional garden art still need further development, and this revolutionary technology has yet to realize its full potential. Therefore, the main purpose of this paper is to generate artworks such as interactive installations and dynamic images using programming and sound visualization in digital media to address the shortcomings and challenges faced by interactive and generative digital technologies in the application of traditional garden art. This project began with the field trip research method. Initially, we conducted extensive fieldwork in Suzhou gardens, including taking photos and collecting data on different elements within the gardens to capture the gardens' natural landscapes and culture lag in the application of digital media in the culture of classical Chinese gardens and fully utilizing the carrying capacity and dissemination capacity of information technology to breathe new life into the precious cultural heritage of Suzhou garden art.

Keywords: Suzhou Garden · Dynamic Images · Digital Media · Programming · Sound Visualization

1 Introduction

As an outstanding representative of traditional Chinese garden art, Suzhou Garden not only is famous in China but also has an important historical position and value in the history of gardens worldwide and is a treasure of human culture. The conservation of Suzhou garden landscapes has always been highly valued in China, and the Suzhou municipal government and the garden management department have invested a great deal of manpower and material resources in conservation and restoration every year, but its focus still focuses on the shape and structure of the buildings, and its interactive breadth and depth of dissemination still need to be improved.

With the current rapid development of computer technology and information technology, digital means have also provided technical support for the protection and inheritance of Suzhou Garden. The main research direction of similar related fields is dominated by interior design, garden digital assets, restoration and preservation, etc., in the form of text, photographs, mapping, three-dimensional scanning, visualization technology, interactive and generative digital technology in traditional garden art. On the other hand, most of the existing Suzhou garden digitization achievements are led by the government and enterprises, with the collaborative participation of professional teams, while public participation is insufficient.

Art programming, which is the combination of algorithms, data, and art, allows for the processing of images and graphics, sound information, video information, and so on. It has been tapped for application in more fields as an emerging audiovisual form in the art field to generate various forms of art design, such as moving images. This makes works have a stronger visual impact through the use of modern technology, breaks the boundaries between people and traditional art, closely connects technology, art and people, and reveals the trend of art development in the new era. Digital cultural and creative products are new products that have developed rapidly in recent years due to digital technology. In the digital environment, digital cultural and creative products create and disseminate creative content and provide users with novel and interesting cultural experiences through interactivity, personalization and cross-platform features.

Therefore, we propose the use of modern technological means such as programming, sound visualization, and intuitive moving images, supplemented by digital cultural creations with a wide audience, a high degree of personalization and participation, and easy sharing and dissemination, to combine digital media technology with cultural and creative products and to use digital technology and creative design to create moving images with emotional experience and interactivity, which enhances the attractiveness and infectiousness of the culture of Suzhou gardens and helps traditional garden aesthetics and culture resonate with people in contemporary society.

2 Literature Review

Light, shadow, wind, sound and other similar intangible elements in the garden landscape play important roles in shaping the reality, color and mood of the garden space, but it is often difficult to describe, compare and carry out practical research with specific vocabulary.

Since ancient times, in garden landscape design, the application of light and shadow has become more common, and the garden landscape has become more vibrant and dynamic; thus, the landscape level has become more dynamic and varied. In terms of spatial light and shadow in gardens, existing studies on space creation, flower window construction and light landscapes have focused on color, covering spatial color, static color and dynamic color, etc. In terms of sound, research has been carried out in terms of the symbolic meaning of sound, aesthetics, aesthetics, design introduction and landscaping. There are relatively few studies in the field of sound visualization and interaction, but research on music visualization and spectrum transformation can provide guidance and a reference for this topic.

2.1 Light and Shadow

Table 1. Analysis of the role of light and shadow in gardens [1].

	Effect	Affect	Give an Example
light source	The fundamental source of light in traditional gardens is natural light, and the ancient people's life and labor in the gardens relied mainly on sunlight and moonlight	Different light sources produce different visual effects of warm and cold, light and darkness	Sunlight, moonlight, and light are all different in warmth, coldness, and intensity
missile	Light itself does not have a fixed form, but by modeling the projected objects, light can be made to have a form. The projected objects in the garden are rich in variety, the type of projected objects, the scene itself will have an impact on the formation of the visual effect of static and dynamic state	The regular layout of the projected object itself can form a regular projection or shape, making the space more interesting and rhythmic, giving a sense of spatial dynamics; some of the scenery itself is in the midst of dynamic changes, which will form a dynamic object shadow, bringing the space to the light, dynamic feeling	Static projected objects such as continuous windows and equidistant columns; dynamic projected objects such as plants swaying in the wind, and when the wind blows the water, the reflection in the water ripples
receiving surface	In the garden, the physical environment of the entity is the bearer of light and shadow, and they work together with the light source to form a perceivable visual image of the entity	They work together with the light source to form a perceivable physical visual image. The shapes, interfaces, materials, and colors of these elements affect the light and shadow effects they form	Walls, bodies of water, plants, and rocks all have different textures, which can be projected to produce different effects

2.2 Color

Color plays a very important role in the artistic value system of Suzhou gardens and conveys many cultural messages to people. With the deepening of garden research, color as an abstract form has been emphasized.

Citation 1 Garden colors are divided into dynamic and static. Dynamic color changes with time, such as daylight and plant color, and the dynamic color in gardens is affected by changes in daylight color temperature, early morning warm tones, middle tones during the day, and cold tones at dusk. This color change in the garden landscape provides a rich level of emotion so that people experience different visual experiences at different times and under different atmospheres (see Fig. 1).

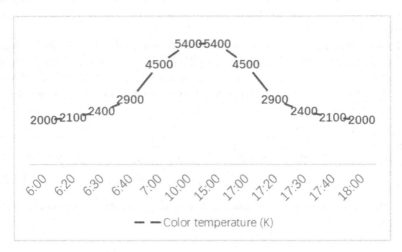

Fig. 1. Graph of time vs. color temperature [2].

Plant color accounts for a large proportion of the color system of the Suzhou classical garden; not only is the inherent color very rich but also, with the change of seasons, it will present different shades, showing the dynamic beauty of color. In addition, under different light intensities, the different transmittances of plant leaves and flowers make the color presentation more diverse. In "A Study on the Rationality of Planting Density of Colorful Shrubs in the Lower Levels of Landscaping", the types of shrubs in some areas of the garden were counted [3].

Table 2. Statistics for some shrubs in the garden [4].

Shrub Species	Specific Shrub Name
Evergreen Shrub	June Snow, Moon Season, Palm Bamboo, Fenghuang Bamboo, Camellia, Camellia sinensis, Hypericum, Red Stepsprings, Ferns
Deciduous Shrub	Lilac, Patagonian, Begonia, Show Residue Chrysanthemum, Red Raspberry, Bauhinia, Wood Hibiscus, Green Maple, French Holly, Bear Paw Wood, Yellow Poplar, Waxberry
Long Green Shrubs	French holly, bearberry, boxwood

According to the above statistics, the garden, by reasonably matching different types of plants, especially deciduous shrubs and evergreen shrubs, makes the overall landscape colorful and diverse, showing seasonal changes and rich visual effects (Tables 1 and 2).

2.3 Sound

Natural sounds in the landscape mainly include natural phenomena, including wind, thunder and lightning, rain, and water, as well as sounds produced by plants and animal chirping.

The following data use water sounds as an example. Water is the main object of soundscape design in garden landscapes. In Wang Yaping's "Research on Sound Preference of Garden Water Features", the sounds of water features with different flow rates and people's preferences for different sounds were counted (Figs. 2, 3, 4 and 5).

Sampling stream number	1	2	3	4	5	6	7	8	9	10	11	12
A sound level/dB	87.1	81.8	81.9	76.3	75.9	66.6	74.9	80.4	77.9	76.6	66.1	71.8
People's preferences	-0.96	-0.68	-0.68	-0.08	-0.38	1.5	1.46	-0.42	-0.38	-0.3	1.8	0.38

Fig. 2. The sounds of water feature different flow rates and people's preferences for different sounds [5].

2.4 Subjective Human Perception of the Above Data

In the interactive relationship between people and gardens, people who are conscious, perceptive, thinking about the ability to exist, with the subject position and initiative, can take the initiative to appreciate, experience, and perceive the beauty of the garden and, through their own behavior and attitudes toward the garden, to have an impact; thus, people's perceptions and reactions are particularly important.

According to the data collected, among the natural sounds of gardens, the people who like the sound of water the most account for 49% of the total number of people surveyed, ranking first, followed by the sounds of rain and wind, ranking second and third, with 18% and 11%, respectively. These natural sounds have a unique attraction and soothing effect on people's minds and can bring people a pleasant feeling and relaxing experience.

The survey data in "Research on the Optimization of Suzhou Garden Scenic Area Operation and Management Mode" show that the comfort level of Suzhou Garden visitors is high during nonholiday seasons [6].

2.5 Programming Combined with Sound Visualization Product Examples

In the case of a physical installation interactive sound visualization product, Ryoji Ikeda's Transfinite utilizes projection technology, various frequencies, and the visual effect of light and shadow beams transforming to create a special interactive sound visualization installation that visualizes frequencies at the edge of the human auditory range.

Neil Mendoza's work "Robotic Voice Activated Word Kicking Machine" combines projection and robotics to explore areas of interaction between the virtual and the physical, programmatically transforming language into visual text.

Fig. 3. Robotic Voice Activated Word Kicking Machine https://m.manamana.net/video/detail/ 1248

3 Overview of Digital Creative Product Design

3.1 Design Concepts

Product Name: WonderLog.

Product Concept: In a certain year and a certain month, you took a tour in a garden in Suzhou. This product, as a cultural creation accompanying the tour, converts tourists' tour data into an interesting and watchable moving image in an artistic form.

Product Composition: The product consists of two parts: a hardware setup and a motion picture.

Hardware Setup and Material Selection: This product is divided into two layers: the first layer consists of a wood composite board replica garden window, a window for hollow design, and the second part consists of a transparent LED display, which is used to project the generated image. The product is connected to a computer for use, and the image data are in the form of a file with the body of the device.

Motion Picture Generation: Garden Elements Comprising the Moving Picture.

a. Changes in light and shadow patterns:

Changes in light and shadow patterns affect the design of device structures and the choice of materials.

We chose to use a wooden shell structure and an LED transparent screen to simulate a flower window precisely because such a structure can better show changes in light and shadow. The wooden shell can create a natural, warm atmosphere, echoing the garden environment, while the transparent LED screen can display dynamic images of light and shadow changes in real time, enabling the audience to more intuitively feel the beauty of the garden.

b. Color:

Color is an important part of the visual effect of the moving image, and the color in the garden will produce dynamic fluctuations according to the change in season. This feature can be effectively used in the expression of the moving image: a digital way to quickly change the color of the wonderful image is more intuitively displayed, and rich color data can make the content of the moving image more three-dimensional and vivid. According to our research results, in the time period of 10:00–15:00, the color temperature is above 5500, and the color temperature is blue in the color table; in the time periods of 7:00–10:00 and 15:00–17:20, the color temperature is between 3000–5500, and the color temperature is white in the color table; in the time period of 17:20–10:00 the next day, the color temperature is less than 3000, and the color temperature is white in the color table; and in the time period of 17:20 to the next day, the color temperature is less than 3000, and the color temperature is white in the color table. Values are less than 3000 and appear red in the color table. We extracted the results of these data and entered them into the moving image code to represent parts of the image.

c. Tourists:

Understanding and fully utilizing the importance of human involvement in moving images in creative design can make the image work more attractive and deeper. Therefore, we investigated people's emotional response to the gardens, and the data are summarized as follows: more than half of the respondents had a high level of comfort in the gardens during nonholiday periods, and more than 90% of the tourists provided positive feedback on their visit to Suzhou Gardens.

This positive feedback can also increase viewers' trust and credibility in images, making them more inclined to accept the information and emotions conveyed by the images. Finally, based on the positive feedback from visitors, images can also show the beauty and atmosphere of the garden more vividly.

3.2 Product Design Program

The generation of moving images is controlled by a series of variables within the code. These variables use real garden data, including environmental data such as temperature, light conditions and vegetation distribution in the garden where the tourists are visiting, and at the same time, a section of sound samples from the garden is selected. These data are input into processing and introduced into the minim library, which controls the changes in the moving images by means of sound visualization and other means.

This approach not only makes the generation of moving images more random and flexible but also enables us to more intuitively perceive the changes and evolution of the internal garden environment.

Fig. 4. Abstract moving image drawn in processing controlled by several sets of variables Still frame presentation.

Fig. 5. Conceptual graph.

This interactive design allows visitors to perceive and understand the environmental characteristics of the place they are visiting, thus deepening their impressions and emotional experiences.

Through this sound visualization, we not only provide visitors with a novel experience but also a more intuitive and dynamic way of perceiving the site. The program aims to stimulate visitors to think and feel about the environment and art and to promote an emotional connection to the places they visit.

4   Conclusion

This study revealed that there is insufficient application in the excavation and dissemination of historical and cultural connotations, as well as insufficient application of the current interactive and generative digital technology for garden culture dissemination.

To address the above problems, this paper proposes the use of modern technical means such as programming, sound visualization and intuitive moving images to deconstruct classical oriental aesthetics and traditional culture supplemented by digital cultural creations and to create content with emotional experience and interactivity by using digital technology and creative design so that cultural and creative products can be interactive and participatory to enhance the attractiveness and infectiousness of the Suzhou Garden culture and to improve the effectiveness of dissemination.

This is an innovative approach to alleviating the relative lag in the application of digital media in the culture of classical Chinese gardens, breaking through traditional modes of thinking, enabling research on the digitization of Suzhou gardens to be carried out from a new perspective, filling the research gaps in the application of programming and sound visualization in Suzhou gardens, and shedding light on the digitization of other traditional cultures. The combination of technology and art promotes the dissemination of traditional Chinese garden culture in multiple contexts and helps global cross-cultural audiences better understand and appreciate the deep aesthetic and cultural connotations of gardens. At the same time, showcasing the innovative application of digital and interactive technologies in the field of art enriches the sensory experience of gardens, explores new ways for technology to capture and reproduce the beauty of nature, and injects new vitality into the invaluable cultural heritage of Suzhou garden art.

Second, the field of garden culture integration with science and technology is a cutting-edge field, with challenges such as rapidly updating technology and imperfect theories, and our research may not be able to cover the latest developments and theoretical advances.

Future research can further expand the sample size, broaden the scope of collaboration, strengthen interdisciplinary cooperation with other organizations and professionals, dig deeper into the theoretical framework of gardening technology integration, focus on the field of science and technology, and keep abreast of the development and application trends of the latest technologies to explore the development of this field in a more comprehensive and in-depth manner.

Disclosure of Interests.   The authors have no competing interests to declare that are relevant to the content of this article.

References

1. Mengxin, R.: Research on the Application of Music Visualization Dynamic Design on Mobile Terminals. Jiangnan University, Wuxi (2020). (in Chinese)
2. Jie, Y.: Color analysis of Suzhou gardens. J. Shanghai Arts Crafts, 93–95 (2010). (in Chinese)
3. Aihua, X.: Research on Plant Configuration in Suzhou Classical Gardens. Suzhou University, Suzhou (2011). (in Chinese)

4. Bijuan, W.: Research on the rationality of planting density of color-block shrubs in the lower layer of landscaping. J. Eng. Technol. Res. **7**(04), 215–217 (2022). (in Chinese)
5. Yaping, W., Xiaolei, X., Mingxia. S.: Research on sound preference of garden waterscapes. Archit. Sci. **31**(04), 79–83+101 (2015). (in Chinese)
6. Yide, G.: Preliminary Study on Garden Acoustic Landscape Design. Nanjing Forestry University, Nanjing (2011). (in Chinese)

Research on the Digital Exploration and Inheritance of Tibetan Cultural Landscapes—Take the Mani Heap as an Example

Zhiming Liu[✉], Han Sun, and Zhijun Peng

Tianjin University, Tianjin, People's Republic of China
1966196246@qq.com, pengzhiju@tju.edu.cn

Abstract. As a ubiquitous cultural landscape in the Tibetan region, Mani heap, adorned with the sacred mantra and various Buddhist scriptures, as well as a myriad of Buddha images and meaningful patterns, stand as not just unique cultural landmarks of the Tibetan people but also as a testament to the intricate interplay of Tibetan art, rituals, daily life, and nature. These stone piles, integral to the region's living cultural heritage and landscape, are currently facing threats from insufficient preservation efforts and the relentless march of industrial urbanization, leading to their dismantlement and damage. In response to this crisis, this study advocates for the digital preservation of Mani heap. Through 34 days of intensive fieldwork and visual ethnography, we aim to explore a comprehensive set of evaluation metrics including coordinates, altitude, scale, color, shape, arrangement, condition, and interactivity. This approach allows for a rescue-oriented digital preservation of existing Mani heap through digital archiving. Moreover, building upon current digital technologies, we propose a structured strategic model for the digital transmission of Mani stone pile heritage. This model encompasses various facets of digital interaction including storage, retrieval, dissemination, display, communication, and innovation, offering suggestions and concepts for the digitization of Mani heap, thus safeguarding and perpetuating this vital aspect of Tibetan cultural heritage.

Keywords: Intangible Heritage Protection · Mani heap · Digitalization · Cultural Preservation and Inheritance

1 Introduction

Mani heaps consist of stones or slates carved with Buddhist figures, mantras, scriptures, and expressions of daily life, prayers, and confessions of the Tibetan people, forming a living landscape adorned with religious cultural structures such as wind-horse flags, white stupas, making each Mani heap uniquely morphological and culturally valuable, as shown in Fig. 1. Mani heaps are prevalent in Tibetan areas, located near temples, villages, mountains, and rivers, accompanied by interactive activities such as prayer and circumambulation, embodying significant dynamic and interactive cultural value [1].

© The Author(s), under exclusive license to Springer Nature Switzerland AG 2024
C. Stephanidis et al. (Eds.): HCII 2024, CCIS 2116, pp. 276–284, 2024.
https://doi.org/10.1007/978-3-031-61950-2_31

As a cultural landscape formed over a long period, Mani heaps play an important role in religion, history, social interaction, and handicrafts [2].

Fig. 1. Diversity of Mani heap Forms

Currently, there is no clear definition in the academic circle regarding whether they belong to cultural heritage or intangible cultural heritage. However, according to UNESCO's definitions of cultural heritage and intangible cultural heritage, Mani stone piles not only encompass the "objects of symbolic, historical, artistic, or scientific importance" found in the definition of cultural heritage but also meet the characteristics of "inheritance expressions, rituals, festive events, and traditional crafts" found in the definition of intangible heritage, possessing high cultural and research value.

However, with the development of modernization and industrialization, the traditional social structure and production methods of ethnic minorities have been significantly changed, and Mani stone piles face severe situations of damage and abandonment. The urgent rescue and inheritance of Mani stone piles need relevant attention and response.

As the digital landscape rapidly evolves, the use of digital means to inherit and protect intangible cultural heritage (ICH) and cultural heritage has become a practical necessity of our times. This approach not only bridges the gap between traditional and modern worlds, igniting the contemporary relevance and value of traditional cultures but also serves as a crucial method for integrating ICH and cultural heritage into everyday life, enhancing cultural creativity and outreach. The digitization process supports the three-phase development of ICH and cultural heritage, including digital archiving, creation, and utilization. Among these, digital archives, 3D scanning models, and photography stand as essential tools for the digital preservation of ICH [3]. The application of digitalization and Information and Communication Technology (ICT) has been considered an effective means of protecting cultural heritage, producing a large amount of beneficial results and achievements. In previous research on digitalization of cultural heritage and intangible heritage, scholar HOU discussed the importance of digitalization of intangible heritage. The paper also emphasized the development of interactive narrative and educational purposes of intangible heritage through a comprehensive digital archive including multi-sensory aspects [4]. Scholar FONI provided a classification of various visualization technologies used in cultural heritage and introduced a 4D classification model based on visual consistency, accuracy, interactivity, and virtual dimensions to help protect and present cultural heritage [5]".

This study focuses on the living cultural landscape of Tibetan Mani heaps as its primary subject, covering geographic areas including Gannan Tibetan Autonomous Prefecture, Golog Tibetan Autonomous Prefecture in Qinghai, Ganzi Tibetan Autonomous

Prefecture in Sichuan, Tibet Autonomous Region, and Diqing Tibetan Autonomous Prefecture in Yunnan, spanning across 32 counties and cities. From 2016 to 2023, our research team conducted annual field investigations for two to three months each year and documented 1708 Mani heaps sites through visual ethnography, as shown in Fig. 2. By constructing a comprehensive digital archive, including visual ethnography, digital archives, digital maps, and digital experiences, this study aims to advance the digital preservation and inheritance of Mani heap.

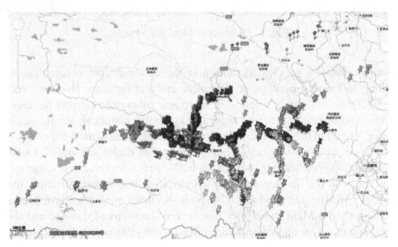

Fig. 2. Display of Survey Mani heap Digital Points from 2016 to 2024

2   The Dilemma Faced by Mani Heap

2.1   Changes in Ecology and Environment

The advancement of technology has altered the relationship between humans and the environment, facilitating our lives and enhancing production efficiency, but it has also had significant, and sometimes irreversible, impacts on natural resources and the environment.

One of the factors contributing to the challenges faced by Mani stone piles is changes in the natural environment and ecology. As economic and tourism development progresses, road construction in Tibet is continuously evolving and being repaired, as shown in Fig. 3. This development can lead to the removal or relocation of some Mani stone piles located along the roadsides during construction. Moreover, the alteration of travel routes due to road development changes the traditional pathways of the Tibetan people, leading to decreased contact and accessibility for some original Mani stone piles. Consequently, the connectivity between Mani stone piles and traditional communities is gradually diminishing.

Fig. 3. Road Construction in the Tibetan Mountainous Region

2.2 Industrialization-Induced Industrial Transformation and Commercialization

Following the China's Western Campaign, national policies of interconnectedness have broken the original isolation of traditional Tibetan communities, bringing significant changes.

Firstly, the economic structural changes brought about by industrialization have led some traditional Tibetan farmers and herders to opt for urban employment. This symbolizes the gradual loss of cohesion in traditional communal environments, as villagers leaving their villages also reduce their contact frequency and time with Mani stone piles due to increased absences.

Secondly, the commercial development from industrialization has changed the traditional Tibetan community's habit of seeking craftsmen for hand-carving. Now, there are machines that print scriptures on slates and stones, as shown in Fig. 4. Additionally, the choice of stone material has shifted from original irregular natural stones to manufactured slabs.

2.3 Modernization and the Evolution of Social Relationship Structures

The rapid development of modernization has altered not only social structures but also the ways in which people access information and carry out their daily activities. The prevalence of social media and electronic devices has led to a decrease in communal activities and traditional religious events and rituals among the Tibetan people. Modernization has significantly transformed the social relational structure from both physical and spiritual perspectives. In the physical realm, in some modernized cities in the Tibetan area, excessive tourism and modern housing construction have squeezed the developmental space for cultural landscapes. On the spiritual level, the rapid advance of modernization has altered people's living situations and aesthetic choices, leading to a gradual reduction and fading of the demand for traditional culture.

Fig. 4. A machine for printing scriptures on stone slabs

3 Methods and Approaches for Digitizing Mani Heap

3.1 Field Investigation and Visual Anthropology Collection

Field investigation and visual anthropology methods are among the crucial approaches for preserving and documenting intangible cultural heritage and cultural heritage. In the process of field investigations, we employed graphic and textual scanning techniques to translate the inscriptions on Mani heaps, while also acquiring three-dimensional data of the Mani heaps through 3D scanning models and drone technology.

Beyond merely recording the original locations and environments of the Mani heaps through photography and video, we utilized ethnographic methods such as direct observation, participant observation, in-depth interviews, and focus groups to understand the interactive modes and frequency between residents of the original Tibetan communities and the Mani heaps from a scenographic perspective. These methods allow for more effective collection of contextual folk content related to the Mani heaps and contribute to a comprehensive understanding of them, thereby constructing a multi-dimensional cultural context of the Mani heaps.

3.2 Digital Archive Construction and Evaluation Methods

In the digital preservation and inheritance of Mani heaps, the construction and evaluation of digital archives play crucial roles. Scholar Hardeberg has proposed methods for assessing the changes in cultural heritage objects in previous studies. These methods enable better monitoring and understanding of the degradation processes of cultural heritage artifacts, thereby facilitating the preservation process with more effective protection strategies [6]. Currently, the process of digital archiving involves diverse methods including electronic records, photography, and 3D scanning. However, there are few instances where digital archives have been further structured and encoded, presenting significant challenges in conducting a unified assessment of Mani heaps, which are characterized by their urgent need for rescue, difficulty in capture, and the coexistence of tangible and intangible cultural content.

3.3 Digital Design Construction and Presentation Methods

The construction of digital design encompasses digital restoration and digital presentation of intangible cultural heritage (ICH) and cultural heritage content. In the digital replication part, through field investigation, relevant data are collected and processed with image processing, 3D modeling, etc., to restore and repair the original style and scene of Mani heaps when facing abandonment and damage, using 3D scenes, virtual reality, and special effects rendering.

The development of digital presentation has broken the barriers of time and space, expanding the pathways and methods through which people recognize and experience ICH and cultural heritage. In terms of digital presentation, virtual reality and multimodal sensing methods can be used to present the restored cultural scenes comprehensively and completely to the audience. Moreover, employing animation, cultural creativity, and interactive gaming as construction methods can help promote the dissemination of Mani heaps, enhance people's perception and interaction with them, and thus promote the better inheritance and development of Mani heaps.

4 Strategies for the Digital Preservation and Inheritance of Mani Heap

4.1 Database Collection, Storage, and Retrieval Methods

Facing the endangered living cultural landscape of Mani heaps, we urgently need to establish relevant assessments and unified standards to coordinate and collect years of research data to ensure uniformity of standardized units and presentation methods throughout longitudinal studies.

During field investigations, through the comparison and coordination of data collected over many years, we have gradually established a multi-index digital archive assessment standard. This includes twelve parts: serial number, investigation time information, location information of the Mani heaps, basic attributes of the heaps, degree of damage, associated landscapes, affiliated sects, source of production materials, stone carving content, type of stone material, color, and interview content, as shown in Fig. 5. This facilitates the visualization and comparison of the developmental status and relevant protection and inheritance strategies of Mani heaps from different dimensions, and allows for rapid browsing based on the content of basic information, greatly improving search efficiency. It is more conducive to the systematic and comprehensive protection and inheritance of the Mani heaps, solidifying the academic field's understanding and recognition of them.

4.2 Digital Map and GIS Preservation and Display System

Based on the locations of Mani heaps from 2016 to 2024, we have constructed a longitudinal digital map network, aimed at generating trends related to the historical development and changes of the Mani heaps through comparative observation, as shown in Fig. 6.

This approach allows for the estimation and timely prevention of potential future disasters and unknown risks using large-scale models. Additionally, this digital network

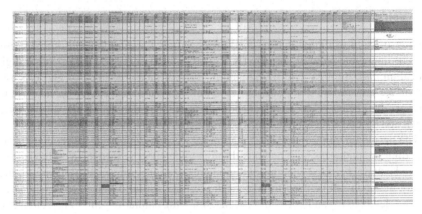

Fig. 5. An information data archive for Mani heap

map also possesses functionalities for communication, dissemination, and presentation. This digital map can be linked with other digital resources to achieve a diversified integration and sharing of digital resources, enhancing the public's understanding and accessibility of Mani heaps.

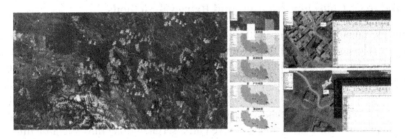

Fig. 6. Mani heap Digital Map

4.3 Digital Navigation and Contextual Virtual Experiences Enhance Interaction and Innovation

Based on the Mani heap cultural landscape database, we have developed an interactive application and gaming experience utilizing Unreal Engine 4, aimed at enhancing public awareness and understanding of Mani heaps, as shown in Fig. 7. This virtual experience program includes an interactive visualization of the distribution of Mani heaps and a virtual tour of the complex cultural landscape of Mani heaps. The project aims to promote cultural exchange and innovation regarding Mani heaps. For those unfamiliar with Mani heaps, this project provides a foundational understanding and popularizes knowledge, encouraging visitors to explore, discuss, and exchange ideas about this cultural feature.

This project represents the transition of scene-specific cultural landscapes from the real world to the virtual realm, intending to foster situational and multisensory cultural understanding for a more comprehensive and complete experiential representation of cultural diversity.

Fig. 7. Mani heap Virtual Experience Exhibition

Besides aiming to enhance the public's cultural recognition of Mani heaps, in the face of industrial and modern impacts on traditional communities, traditional Tibetan communities have gradually dispersed, with Mani heaps no longer serving as sites for rituals and communal activities. Older Tibetans may still keep the tradition of circumambulating and praying at these heaps, a practice rarely found among the younger generation. In future communication and innovation systems, while spreading public awareness, we hope to reinforce traditional communities and folk activities, re-establish local connections, and mitigate the disintegration of community relations caused by modernization, thereby promoting the diversified development of culture.

5 Conclusion

The rapid development of digitalization has provided technical support and new ways of living for the Mani heap cultural landscape, which is facing developmental challenges, ensuring its heritage and continuity. This paper proposes three digital preservation methods based on field survey data collection, evaluation methods, and the establishment of digital archives, along with strategies for digital preservation based on storage, retrieval, dissemination, display, communication, and innovation. It aims to enhance the preservation, dissemination, and inheritance methods of the Mani heaps, continuously increasing their public awareness. This will encourage more entities to participate in the digital preservation and construction of the Mani heaps, allowing them to establish new connections and a sustainable, living development force in the digital and diverse era.

References

1. Peng, Z., et al.: The use of quantitative methods to study the colours of Mani heaps in Tibet: a Dêngqên county case study. Int. J. Humanit. Arts Comput. **15**(1–2), 152–169 (2021). https://doi.org/10.3366/ijhac.2021.0267
2. Peng, Z., et al.: Research, representation, and conservation of Mani heaps: the digitalization projects. Leonardo **56**(3), 272–278 (2023). https://doi.org/10.1162/leon_a_02356
3. Wen, W., Zhao, M.: Digitalization scenarios and construction paths of china's intangible cultural heritage. Theory Mon., **10**, 89–99 (2022). https://doi.org/10.14180/j.cnki.1004-0544.2022.10.011
4. Hou, Y., Kenderdine, S., Picca, D., Egloff, M., Adamou, A.: Digitizing intangible cultural heritage embodied: state of the art. J. Comput. Cult. Heritage **15**(3), 1–20 (2022). https://doi.org/10.1145/3494837
5. Foni, A.E., Papagiannakis, G., Magnenat-Thalmann, N.: A taxonomy of visualization strategies for cultural heritage applications. J. Comput. Cult. Heritage **3**(1), 1–21 (2010). https://doi.org/10.1145/1805961.1805962
6. Hardeberg, J.Y.: Analyzing CHANGE in cultural heritage objects through images. In: Proceedings of the 3rd Workshop on Structuring and Understanding of Multimedia Heritage Contents, pp. 3–4 (2021). https://doi.org/10.1145/3475720.3476878

The Information Visualization Design Research on Turquoise Along the Silk Road

Xiaolei Mi[✉], Bailu Guo, and Xiang Li

Beijing City University, Beijing, China
mx1326563468@163.com

Abstract. The aim of this study is to delve into the multi-dimensional nature of turquoise as a gemstone through visualization techniques, highlighting its unique geological attributes and cultural symbolism. We use advanced computer graphics and data visualization techniques to uniquely present the distribution of turquoise on Earth, its color variation, and its historical pathways. The Silk Road is a typical historical and cultural information, as an extremely important trade route in history, the significance of the Silk Road is not only in the route itself, it is more like a thread through the development history of human civilization. China's turquoise mines are mainly distributed in the Qinling Mountains, Qilian Mountains and Tianshan Mountains, connecting the mining areas and coincident with the Chinese section of the ancient Northwest Silk Road. The development of turquoise on the Han Silk Road is accurately conveyed through the interactive visual design scheme of information to accurately convey the knowledge context of the land Silk Road. It showcases the historical and cultural value of the Silk Road as a model of exchange, mutual learning and coexistence among civilizations in human history. From the perspective of interactive information visualization, it provides more intuitive information visualization for the development of turquoise, increases the artistry of the historical performance of the Silk Road in the Han Dynasty, and allows users to get a better visual experience.

Keyword: Turquoise · interactive information · information visualization

1 Introduction

As a precious gem, turquoise played an important role in the trade of the ancient Silk Road. This gem is often seen as a symbol of wealth, power and status, and is therefore highly sought after in the commerce of the Silk Road.

Turquoise, also known as "turquoise", is named for its "shape like a pine ball, colonearly pine green". The English name is Turquoise, meaning Turkish stone. Turkey does not produce turquoise, and it is said that the ancient Persian turquoise was transported to Europe through Turkey and named. There are huge turquoise reserves, not only China, Egypt, Iran, the United States, Russia, Chile, Australia, Peru, South Africa, India, Pakistan, Kashmir and other regions have abundant mineral reserves."ShiYa" explained: "(turquoise) looks like a pine ball, the color is nearly pine and green, so it is its name".

C. Stephanidis et al. (Eds.): HCII 2024, CCIS 2116, pp. 285–291, 2024.
https://doi.org/10.1007/978-3-031-61950-2_32

The turquoise is mainly found in Central Asia, now in Iran, Afghanistan and China's Xinjiang province. Merchants on the ancient Silk Road shipped turquoise from these areas to the west to aristocrats and wealthy merchants in the Middle East, the Mediterranean coast and Europe. This trade not only brings economic benefits, but also promotes the exchange and integration of Eastern and Western cultures. Its circulation path also reflects the complex network of the Silk Road. Intermiddleman trade from mineral to final consumption, long-distance transportation across deserts and mountains, as well as exchanges and cooperation under different cultural backgrounds all constitute an important part of the turquoise trade.

Turquoise mine, in ancient times, should be a special national resources. During the period of Erlitou culture, turquoise workshops only existed in the core settlement of Erlitou culture, reflecting that turquoise had become the core symbol of the national ritual system, and was a precious jade variety flaunting the aristocratic status. The mining and utilization of turquoise mines should be in the hands of the rulers [2]. The investigation and research of turquoise mining sites can not only provide important clues for the study of the formation of early national civilization in China, but also provide important directional evidence for exploring the driving force of cultural interaction between different regions in ancient times. Therefore, the ancient turquoise mining remains is particularly important. In the Yangshao Culture period, the excavation of turquoise was not only limited to some special sites, but also more than 50 places, the number of which was far beyond the early period, indicating that turquoise ornaments began to be widely distributed in the region. However, a large number of turquoise jewelry concentrated unearthed site is still relatively limited, such as shaanxi south zheng longgang temple site unearthed 75, Henan xichuan wang site unearthed about 33, Shandong big mouth cultural sites and stream cultural sites also found, especially focal site and large paddy field site unearthed more considerable, while other sites are only scattered findings, but widely distributed in the region [3].

In the period of Longshan Culture, the distribution of turquoise was mainly concentrated in the Yellow River basin, especially in the middle and upper reaches of the Yellow River, such as Qijia culture, Siba culture, Tao temple culture and Shimao culture were frequently unearthed. (Fig. 1) In contrast, turquoise ornaments are scarce in general sites. In the pottery Temple culture of the middle and lower reaches of the Yellow River and Shandong province, turquoise jewelry is mainly found in some large cemeteries, while the Yangtze River basin and northeast China are relatively rare, showing significant imbalance in regional distribution.

In terms of turquoise types, the Neolithic age was dominated by decorative ornaments. Early turquoise ornaments are mostly sheet-shaped single holes, suitable for hanging earrings and hanging pendant ornaments, and tube bead class string ornaments are relatively rare. In the middle and late period, the variety of turquoise ornaments increased, first, the increase of tube bead string ornaments, followed by the appearance of wrist ornaments and headdress inlaid with embedded and other materials, showing the significant changes in the production process and product types. The emergence of inlay technology and the special cutting and grinding of turquoise inlay laid the foundation for the development of turquoise in the Erlitou culture period, and became an indispensable link in the selection of objects in the ruler's sacrificial etiquette system.

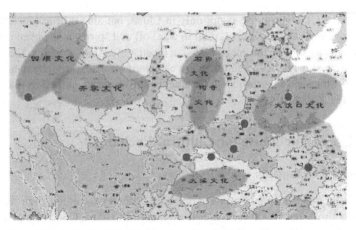

Fig. 1. Map of the distribution of turquoise excavated sites

2 Distribution and Trade Routes of Turquoise on the Silk Road

The heishan Mountain site is only 10 km away from the famous "Great Sea Road" of the Silk Road, which may extend the opening date of the "Great Sea Road" of the Silk Road back to the Spring and Autumn Period and the Warring States Period (Fig. 6). Most of the sites on the Silk Road are ancient cities, pass passes, religious relics, tombs or palace sites, and no ancient mining sites have been found yet. Turquoise mining site is a new type of the Silk Road World Cultural Heritage.

China's central China is the world's earliest use of turquoise area, as early as 8600 to 9000 years ago jia issue, turquoise appeared in the central plains, until the end of the neolithic age, the central plains and grassland frontier, almost all of the archaeological culture has turquoise, the turquoise as a status, status, a symbol of power and wealth. China's turquoise mines are mainly distributed in the Qinling Mountains, Qilian Mountains and Tianshan Mountains, connecting the mining area, which coincides with the Chinese section of the ancient Northwest Silk Road.

During the period of Erlitou culture, turquoise workshops only existed in the core settlement of Erlitou culture, reflecting that turquoise had become the core symbol of the national ritual system, and was a precious jade variety flaunting the aristocratic status. The mining and utilization of turquoise mines should be in the hands of the rulers. The investigation and research of turquoise mining sites can not only provide important clues for the study of the formation of early national civilization in China, but also provide important directional evidence for exploring the driving force of cultural interaction between different regions in ancient times. Therefore, the ancient turquoise mining remains is particularly important. As one of the most important commercial and cultural exchange channels in ancient times, the Silk Road connected the eastern and western civilizations. In addition to commodities such as silk, tea and spices, gems were also an important trade in this ancient trade route. Among them, turquoise, as a precious gem, not only has an important position in business, but also contains rich cultural connotation. The Silk Road runs through Asia, Europe and Africa, covering many countries in East Asia, West Asia, South Asia, Central Asia, Central and Eastern

Europe and the CIS. Turquoise is not only in China, but also in Iran (ancient Persia), Egypt, Turkey, and other countries, used to ward off evil spirits, some even reached the extent of blind worship. In the ancient Persian language, turquoise means "the invincible victor". The Persians believe that turquoise can ward off evil spirits, treat epilepsy and mental confusion, and that turquoise ornaments have been unearthed in many ancient Persian tombs.

3   The Use of Turquoise for Cultural Exchange

3.1   Turquoise Ornaments

The ancient Egyptians carved turquoise into a gods of love to protect their treasure car. For example, more than 5,000 years ago, the mummy arm of the Queen of ancient Egypt, and the gold mask of King Tutankamen was also inlaid with turquoise. Ancient Egyptians also used turquoise to treat eye and respiratory diseases, believing that the discoloration or rupture of turquoise was the result of blocking the damage for the wearer.

In Subai's book "Archaeological Discovery and Cultural Exchange between China and the West", during the Shang and Zhou dynasties, there was a "western spread of silk, soft jade, turquoise and glass beads". Among them, the raw materials of turquoise were likely to come to the west of Cong Lingling, but we did not discuss it in detail. Turquoise jewelry is a common ceremonial item in the ancient civilization of the world. In the ancient civilizations of Central Asia, West Asia, North America and South and Central America, there is a tradition of using turquoise ornaments and ceremonial sacrifices [5].

Scholars have made many mature studies on the ancient turquoise trade and trade path here, and these research results can provide some useful experience for the study of turquoise trade in ancient China. In Persia (Persia), turquoise was a de facto national gem for more than 1,000 years. It is not only decorative, but also used for harness, Mosaic decoration, but also in some important buildings decoration turquoise, the application range is quite wide. Ancient Egypt used turquoise long, dating roughly back to the 1st Dynasty in the 4th century BC. They used to use turquoise in gold rings, chest ornaments and necklaces, its practice is to first process turquoise into beads and other forms, and then inlaid on ornaments, sometimes with agate and other gems, later with glass inlaid examples. Most of the turquoise used in ancient Egypt was found in six mines on the west coast of the Sinai Peninsula (The Sinai Peninsula), which archaeological excavations prove were mined roughly 5,000 years ago. Words were also found on the pillars of the Goddess temple near the mine, which, according to which the ancient Egyptians called the site the "Green Minerals Land". According to the literature records, the dynasties from the early dynasty period of 3200 BC to the Thutmose dynasty of the mid-15th century BC) had mined in these mines, and have been abandoned since. Until these mine sites were discovered again in the 19th century. Archaeologists excavating Egyptian tombs have found that the King of Egypt had worn turquoise beads more than 5,000 years ago. The most precious turquoise ornament is the mummy of the Queen of Egypt (Empress Zer) wearing four gold bracelets inlaid in turquoise. A large number of turquoise inlay was also used on the gold mask of the famous King Tutankamun in ancient Egypt.

3.2 The Transmission and Processing of Turquoise

The Mayan civilization located in Central and South America is an ancient civilization distributed in today's southeastern Mexico, Guatemala, Honduras, El Salvador and Belize. Although its society has always been in the Neolithic Age without metal, it has a developed writing system and has made very high achievements in astronomy, mathematics, agriculture and art. According to the research of archaeologists, the ancient civilizations in Central and South America may be closely related to the thousands of miles of information network formed by the circulation of turquoise and the development of the trade network. According to archaeological excavations, turquoise excavated in southwest America concentrated preferentially in New Mexico and Cheek Valley, and formed grinding processing sites in the 9th century, and then circulated to China and South America respectively, because a large number of rough tools for making production were found in this area [5].

There are also signs that they not only beat the mother rock to get turquoise, but also heated the mother rock and added water to break the turquoise. About 100,000 tons of debris and related items were found in this turquoise processing site, and you can imagine the huge labor force consumed at that time. More than 56,000 pieces of turquoise and semi-finished products were found in Chako Canyon. Chaco Canyon and the surrounding areas do not produce turquoise, so it may be related to long-distance trade, and its main social function is the necessity of various ritual activities in the regional culture. These turquoise are found in the early sites of the Chaco cultural sequence and are also used in some ritual activities. For example, in the southwest of America, the ancient Pueblo people used specially designated caves to perform rituals related to specific seasons and activities. The ors found in the ceremonial cave include prayer sticks and spears besides turquoise, shells and obsidian ornaments.

3.3 The Use Function of Turquoise

Investigate the world's ancient civilization decoration and etiquette, if the use of jade region and groups mainly east Asian ancient Chinese civilization, the ancient Indian and New Zealand Maori so form the Pacific rim famous three jade culture plate, so turquoise and the distribution of inlaid jewelry across east Asia, China, North America and central America, in the world multiple ancient civilization birthplace. In Central and South America, turquoise began to be made in the middle of the preclassical period, and flourished in central and South America throughout the postclassical period.

Maya culture also popular jade jade ornaments, and since then together with turquoise became a popular decorative instrument in the whole Mayan upper society. Maya culture using jade and turquoise decorations, compared with China 9000 years ago found in jia lake site turquoise, a lot of late, and compared with Egypt 5500 BC using turquoise s, jia lake ruins of turquoise also early 1500 years, so the ancient Chinese civilization is the earliest turquoise decoration. From the functional point of view, at the beginning of Chinese turquoise, with simple ornaments, flat round beads and other decorations, but then not only in the regional changes, its functions and production technology also become complex and diverse. First, turquoise inlaid products began to appear from the northeast and the Yellow River basin, and then prevailed in the middle and lower reaches of the Yellow River and the lower reaches of the Yangtze Rivern [3]. In the early Bronze Age, with the bronze smelting technology and bronze containers favored by the upper class of the Central Plains Dynasty, the development and smelting technology of the ceremonial products used in the upper class were changed from traditional jade ritual instruments to bronze containers and turquoise inlaid products with copper, bone teeth and jade as the main materials [4]. This is the original creation of Chinese civilization, and it is also the difference between the turquoise inlaid in the main material and gold and silver in Europe, Central Asia and ancient Egypt, and the shellfish and stone in Central and South America as the main material (Fig. 2).

Fig. 2. Tang inlaid turquoise mother-of-pearl flower mirror

4   Visualization of the Turquoise Material

Through the information visualization technology, we can clearly show the distribution and trade path of turquoise on the Silk Road. Using tools such as geographic information systems (GIS), we can mark turquoise origin, transit stations, and final consumption sites on a map, and indicate trade paths by lines or arrows. Such a visual design can help us to more intuitively understand the circulation of turquoise on the Silk Road, and reveal the complexity and global scope of its trade network (Fig. 3).

The historical evolution of the turquoise trade can be presented using the timeline and dynamic chart approach. By showing the turquoise trade data of different periods and regions, it can reveal the regularity and trend of its occurrence with time and region.

Using network analysis methods, the connections and relationships between different cities and trade centers on the Silk Road can be studied. Building the source, transfer station and final destination of turquoise into a network, and analyzing the connection of nodes and edges can reveal the structure and characteristics of the ancient trade network.

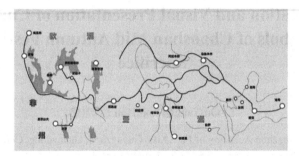

Fig. 3. The possible turquoise circulation route on the Silk Road

5 Conclusion

Information visualization design can also help us to trace the historical evolution of the turquoise trade. Through the combing of the historical documents and archaeological data, combined with the visualization technology, we can present the changing trend of the turquoise trade in different historical periods. These changes may be influenced by political, economic, and cultural factors, such as war, dynastic change, and cultural exchange. The visual analysis of turquoise trade can not only help scholars to deeply study the ancient trade network and gem industry, but also promote the inheritance and development of ancient culture and history. Through visual methods, academic research results can be presented to a wider audience to promote academic exchanges and cooperation in related fields. Through the visualization of these historical changes, we can have a deeper understanding of the development context and influencing factors of the turquoise trade on the Silk Road.

References

1. Qin, X.-L., Li, X.-T., Yang, L.-P., et al.: Comprehensive study on turquoise tools unearthed in Banpo cemetery of Longgang Temple Shaanxi Province. South. Cult. Relics **06**, 216–231 (2023)
2. Guo, D.Y., Li, G.: The aesthetic characteristics of Erlitou turquoise ware and its enlightenment on Zhushan turquoise jewelry design. Chinese Treasure Jade (06):36–43 (2023)
3. Zhao, Y.: From the Erlitou cultural site unearthed inlaid turquoise bronze brand ornaments to see the early Chinese stone inlaid technology overlapping. Art and Design (Theory) **2**(07), 127–130 (2023). https://doi.org/10.16824/j.cnki.issn10082832.2023.07.012
4. Xiao, W., Xian, Y.H., Yu, C., Wang, Y., Sun, L.J., Li, Y.F.: Microinvasive analysis of textile relics from an ancient Silk Road turquoise mining site. Sci. China Technol. Sci. **66**(8), 2286–2296 (2023). https://doi.org/10.1007/s11431-022-2448-1
5. Pang, X.X.: Preliminary study on turquoise wrist ornaments unearthed in pottery temple culture. Central Plains Cult. Relics (02), 76–86 (2023)

Translation and Visual Presentation of Cultural Symbols of Chaoshan Mid Autumn Festival Sacrifice

Li Ou Yang and Han Li[✉]

Guangzhou Academy of Fine Arts, Guangzhou, Guangdong, China
2605078755@qq.com

Abstract. Chaoshan Mid Autumn Festival sacrificial symbols not only reflect the unique festival customs and core values of the region, but also reflect the profound traditional spirit and local characteristics. These symbols not only contain the deep affection of Chaoshan people for local culture, but also provide a window for the outside world to understand Chaoshan society. Nevertheless, the regional culture of Chaoshan has not been fully utilized in modern visual design and communication.

This study analyzes the cultural connotation of Chaoshan Mid Autumn Festival celebration through semiotic method, literature review and field investigation. The study systematically classifies the symbols of Chaoshan Mid Autumn Festival celebration, explores their cultural roots, and reveals the core significance of these symbols. The study successfully constructed a Chaoshan Mid Autumn Festival sacrificial symbol system, and discussed how to combine these symbols with modern design. Through the analysis of design cases, the application and translation skills of Regional Symbols in modern design were put forward.

This study proposes an innovative translation strategy of visual design based on prototype image and cognitive transformation, aiming at reconstructing Chaoshan Mid Autumn Festival sacrificial symbols. This strategy focuses on the four elements of context, image, concept and behavior, provides a new translation path for visual design, and points out its limitations and development direction. Through in-depth study of objects, meanings, environments and characters, this path aims to innovate the content and provide design methods and empirical analysis for the translation of regional symbols.

Through this study, Chaoshan Mid Autumn Festival sacrificial symbol system can be established and applied to visual design, which not only avoids the simple imitation of Chaoshan cultural symbols, but also provides a new perspective for understanding and updating the visual image of Chaoshan festival culture.

Keywords: Chaoshan Mid Autumn Festival sacrifice · culture · symbols · translation

C. Stephanidis et al. (Eds.): HCII 2024, CCIS 2116, pp. 292–302, 2024.
https://doi.org/10.1007/978-3-031-61950-2_33

1 Cultural Characteristics of Chaoshan Mid Autumn Festival Sacrificial Ceremony

1.1 Cultural Harmony and Display of Regional Characteristics

After more than eight centuries of development, Chaoshan Mid Autumn Festival sacrificial ceremony has not only achieved harmony and unity in material and spiritual levels, but also deeply displayed the strong regional cultural characteristics of Chaoshan area. This celebration not only reflects the thinking orientation of society, but also reflects the resonance and uniqueness of culture. In the sacrificial ceremony, the vitality and novelty of cultural symbols, as well as the rich images and profound metaphors they contain, jointly reveal the core values of Chaoshan culture and meet people's spiritual needs.

1.2 Integration of Traditional Etiquette and Modern Design Industry

The traditional rituals and symbols of mid autumn festival celebration in Chaoshan area show a certain monotony in design, and have visual similarities with other areas. This problem of superficial understanding of Chaoshan sacrificial ritual culture and its totem meaning leads to the fixed and rigid design of cultural symbols. The excessive use of cultural totem, which only stays at the visual presentation of the surface, and the mechanical combination of totem elements exacerbate this problem, leading to the loss of cultural vitality and value.

1.3 Modern Embodiment and Design Remodeling of Cultural Symbols

This study focuses on how to reflect the symbolic elements and their deep meaning in the Chaoshan Mid Autumn Festival sacrificial ceremony, and redefine the symbolic meaning of these symbols of Chaoshan culture. At the same time, it discusses how to deeply tap the culture and genes of Chaoshan Mid Autumn Festival sacrificial ceremony in the field of art and design, reshape its unique cultural characteristics in terms of vision and art design, and avoid blind imitation of cultural forms and unreasonable interpretation of the deep meaning of culture, so as to prevent the fuzzy accumulation of local symbols into information.

2 The Modern Challenge of Chaoshan Mid Autumn Festival Sacrificial Symbols

2.1 The Richness of Chaoshan Cultural Resources and Research Needs

Chaoshan area has more than 400000 ancient documents and unwritten Cultural Heritage related to sacrificial ceremonies, as well as precious cultural relics in the museum. These resources provide valuable academic materials for the study of Chaoshan ritual culture. The guiding principle on boosting the development of tourism throughout the country emphasizes the importance of giving full play to cultural advantages and strengthening regional cultural uniqueness. However, under the background of confusion of consumer cultural symbols, the research on the cultural symbols of Chaoshan Mid Autumn Festival sacrificial ceremony is often limited to unilateral qualitative description.

2.2 The Combination of Visual Design and Cultural Heritage

Although studies from the historical and sociological perspectives have discussed the mid autumn festival celebration culture in Chaoshan in detail, there is relatively little research on visual design. The purpose of this study is to explore the core meaning of cultural symbols behind the Mid Autumn Festival sacrificial ceremony in Chaoshan, and to design an appropriate symbolic framework. Through the interpretation and transformation of visual art and design, the visual uniqueness of Chaoshan culture is re displayed, and the deep integration of Chaoshan culture and modern visual design is promoted.

2.3 Interdisciplinary Research and the Theoretical System Construction of Cultural Symbols

The research focuses on some key issues in the academic field. From the perspective of semiotics and design, through the interdisciplinary cooperation strategy, the Chaoshan sacrificial ceremony and its cultural symbols are deeply discussed, classified and sorted out. The research aims to understand the unique nature and cultural meaning of symbols, and provide theoretical support for the practical application of design. Multidisciplinary integration provides knowledge support for local cultural brand building and tourism industry development. Under the background of globalization and the change of urban and rural structure, the combing of the core of Chaoshan traditional culture and the integration of cultural identity are helpful to deeply understand and show the connotation of Chaoshan culture. At the same time, it creatively constructs the theoretical system of cultural symbol transformation, which is of positive significance to promote the dissemination of Chaoshan sacrificial culture and the transformation of tourism industry.

3 Visual Translation Strategies of Chaoshan Mid Autumn Festival Sacrificial Symbols

This symposium mainly focused on the worship tradition of Mid Autumn Festival in Chaoshan area, aiming to study and clarify how to translate and display the unique cultural signs in the area of visual design. Regional culture reflects people's in-depth cultural insights accumulated in daily life and production activities. When this culture and the natural environment of a specific region blend with each other, it will form a unique and historical cultural imprint. The sacrificial activities of the Mid Autumn Festival are not only deeply rooted in the natural and social systems of Chaoshan area, but also integrate many philosophical thoughts, belief activities and other cultural heritage. As a symbol of the traditional culture in Chaoshan area, this festival integrates cultural elements from many aspects, such as physical culture, organizational structure, rituals and beliefs, and has become a classic case and benchmark for in-depth study of folk custom culture in Chaoshan area. Therefore, this study mainly focuses on the folk culture in Chaoshan area and the symbolic significance with the Mid Autumn Festival worship custom as the core, aiming to build a comprehensive cultural symbol system of the Mid Autumn Festival worship custom in Chaoshan.

The word "transliteration" originated from linguistic theory. It was first mentioned in the appendix "Zhengming Zayi" of Zhang Binglin's book "Yushu Dingwen". This article makes it clear that the task of translation is highly complex and challenging, mainly because there are differences in the systems and laws of different countries, which makes it difficult for translation work to be used as a reference. This word was originally used to describe the interpretation or behavior of one language or text to another. However, in situations involving many fields, this word reflects the deep understanding of the target and the construction of new ideas in the process of translation.

Cultural translation is a method of translating cultural content from different regions into information that readers can perceive and accept through translation skills, which includes the whole evolution process of understanding, absorbing and identifying with this culture. Ankapulan's view is that this cultural transformation is essentially a kind of civilization interaction beyond the limits of time and space, but also has the characteristics of self-generation. In other words, in this interaction across cultural boundaries, new cultural entities are born and expanded. Therefore, we can regard the whole process of cultural translation as a continuous process, covering many aspects, such as integration, absorption, revision and recreation. The perspective of translation is mainly divided into the following aspects:

3.1 Confusion and Misplacement

The visual presentation of Chaoshan Mid Autumn Festival sacrificial symbols is characterized by confusion and misplacement. The main performance is: across the boundaries of different materials and organizational structure of misappropriation. This kind of mixing is not only for aesthetics, but also for the needs of service objects. For example, the comprehensive use of materials in the yueniang robe and the organic changes in the form of sacrificial objects all show this feature. This fusion technique often brings unexpected visual effects, and can be flexibly adjusted according to needs.

From the end of the 19th century to the beginning of the 20th century, Shantou commercial buildings began to be influenced by Baroque style and integrated into the local climate design. This marks the beginning of the impact of foreign civilization on the Chaoshan region. The Mid Autumn Festival musical column is an example of the integration of various cultural elements, which shows the inheritance and response to traditional culture in the context of changing real life.

The most impressive is the incense canister decoration, which combines western paintings, eight immortals patterns and seasonal flowers, creates an atmosphere through electronic music, and shows the exchange and collision between Chinese and Western cultures.

3.2 Coding and Communication

Chaoshan Mid Autumn Festival sacrificial symbols realize the visual communication of information through graphic design, and successfully integrate the use of representational images and symbols. Geometric, plant and animal patterns are common in sacrificial objects, showing a wealth of decorative beauty.

Chaoshan Mid Autumn Festival sacrificial symbols present specific visual images according to the theme strategy, which are often divided into three categories of symbols: geometry, plants and animals. Among them, geometric symbols play a key role in the design, such as short line, long line, dragon fish scale, etc. Handicrafts dominate the market, but some products lack creativity and high imitation. Due to the high price and inconvenience of carrying, the selection of sacrificial ritual items is reduced, and the uneven quality of goods in the market weakens the symbolic significance of sacrificial ritual.

In recent years, the value of the cultural and creative industry has been more widely recognized, and with the gradual promotion of the rural revitalization plan, the cultural industry in Chaoshan area has received more in-depth attention under this background. As a source of inspiration for the design, Chaoshan Mid Autumn Festival sacrificial ceremony tradition is committed to displaying the unique cultural characteristics and customs of the region. However, from a broader perspective, the application of cultural symbols still has some imperfections, and most designs are still in the primary stage of imitation (Table 1).

Table 1. Product Cases of Chaoshan Mid Autumn Festival Sacrifice Ceremony Elements.

Product Cases of Chaoshan Mid Autumn Festival Sacrifice Ceremony Elements						
Sample 1	Sample 2	Sample 3	Sample 4	Sample 5	Sample 6	Sample 7
(Jinfuqian)	(Regular eight foil)	(Yue Niang Robe)	(Lotus basket)	(Fuqian Pagoda)	(Eight Immortal Coins)	(Divine Hat)
Sample 8	Sample 9	Sample 10	Sample 11	Sample 12	Sample 13	Sample 14
(Octagonal Pavilion)	(Rubia cordata)	(Phoenix enterprise flower)	(Rose)	(Pineapple peach tower)	(Jelly tower)	(Floral peach)
Sample 15	Sample 16	Sample 17	Sample 18	Sample 19	Sample 20	Sample 21
(Floral peach)	(Floral peach)	(Paper pomegranate)	(Flower tower)	(Flower tower)	(Jingong)	(Musical fragrance)
Sample 22	Sample 23	Sample 24	Sample 25	Sample 26	Sample 27	Sample 28
(Safflower primrose)	(Flos canadensis)	(Happiness red plate)	(Eight Immortals)	(Eight Immortals)	(Eight treasures)	(大曲龙彩丝)

4   The Visual Translation Strategy of Chaoshan Mid Autumn Festival Ritual Symbols

4.1   Creating an Environment with Objects: Field Shifting and Reorganization

Digital Conversion of Content. With the change of social structure, the traditional symbols of Chaoshan Mid Autumn Festival sacrificial ceremony are undergoing digital transformation to meet the needs of modern society. Through digital means, the cultural scene can be reproduced in the virtual space, which expands the boundary of traditional rituals and realizes the continuous inheritance of culture.

The Intertwined Influence of Urbanization and Consumer Culture. In the process of urbanization, the acceleration of information dissemination and the increase of cultural diversity make the traditional festival symbols reinterpreted in the new cultural context. The popularity of digital technology enables these symbols to spread around the world, and also reflects the impact of consumer culture on traditional values.

Conceptual Reorganization of Cognition. The transfer of cultural symbols in new application fields not only stimulates people's cognitive reorganization of tradition and modernity, but also promotes cross-cultural communication and understanding. The use of digital tools makes the self interpretation and reproduction of cultural symbols possible, and promotes the dissemination and renewal of regional culture.

4.2   From Meaning to Form: Literal Translation and Free Translation

Refining of Image Symbols. Through the optimization and innovation of traditional symbol forms, combined with modern technology and artistic techniques, the visual symbols of Chaoshan Mid Autumn Festival sacrificial ceremony can be presented in a new form. This refining not only retains the original cultural connotation, but also enhances the aesthetic value and sense of the times of symbols.

Preservation of Aesthetic Interest. In the process of free translation, attention should be paid to maintaining the aesthetic characteristics and cultural significance of symbols to ensure harmony between form and content. This transformation not only enhances the artistic value of cultural symbols, but also makes them more attractive and influential in modern society.

4.3   Narrative by Field: Activation and Inheritance

Multi Media Participation and Reproduction. Reshape real objects, reproduce the relationship between the action of works of art and the visual symbols of Chaoshan Mid Autumn Festival sacrificial ceremony. The reproduction of symbols needs to dig deep into the theme concept. Digital media has expanded the mode of communication. Chaoshan Mid Autumn Festival sacrifice ceremony may turn to electronic, and digital display will stimulate user participation. Virtual reality technology can realize the integration of online and offline emotions. The sci-fi dramas trisomy II and meet Juliet and Romeo show the application of multimedia technology in stage art. Virtual reality technology provides immersion and changes the traditional narrative mode.

Storytelling and Interesting Experience. Chaoshan Mid Autumn Festival sacrificial ceremony inherits profound cultural heritage through rich historical and cultural symbols. The dissemination of cultural stories is important, and multiple media platforms are used to enhance the attraction. The game "100 sceneries in the south of the Yangtze River" successfully combines regional culture, innovates visual symbols, and stimulates user interaction. Cultural stories have the advantages of simplicity and clarity, innovation promotion and community cohesion.

The translation of Chaoshan mid autumn festival symbols has three core issues: rigid cultural symbol structure, lack of consensus and insufficient digital application. This paper proposes regional norms centered on regional culture to ensure the stability of translation; The harmonious integration of artistic aesthetics and practical application, adhering to the double criteria of aesthetics and practicality; Keep up with the progress of the times and constantly accumulate knowledge. These guidelines constitute three core strategies for the translation of cultural symbols of the Mid Autumn Festival ritual in Chaoshan area.

The translation of cultural symbols of festivals and ceremonies in Chaoshan needs to closely follow the unique cultural characteristics of the region, and build a clear translation path through in-depth analysis of four key aspects: context transfer, image display, concept interpretation and behavior interpretation. The purpose is to redefine the deep meaning of the environment, create new forms, narrate new stories, and promote innovation and renewal. This process aims to deeply understand and reshape the symbols of Chaoshan Mid Autumn Festival sacrificial ceremony, and realize the symbol translation and regeneration of Chaoshan Festival sacrificial culture (Table 2).

Table 2. Translation and regeneration path map of sacrificial symbols in Chaoshan festivals.

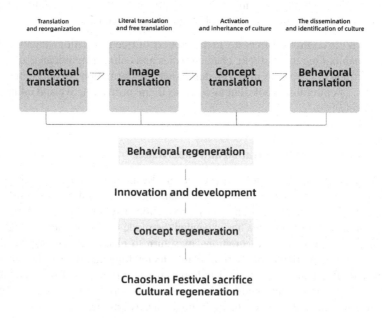

5 Practice: Construction of Chaoshan Mid Autumn Festival Sacrificial Symbols Translation System

5.1 A Deduction Based on Context Translation

Through the literal and in-depth interpretation of the symbols of Chaoshan Mid Autumn Festival sacrificial ceremony, the author reveals its cultural meaning. Special attention is paid to the symbolic characteristics and spiritual value of guizhengshan village in Puning City, Jieyang City, and the research results are organically integrated with cultural theory.

In the design process, attention should be paid to the visual expression of context, form, concept and action. Through the deep integration of design ideas, we can find innovative communication methods for cultural symbols. This design method brings innovative interpretation and expansion to the symbols of Chaoshan Mid Autumn Festival sacrificial ceremony, which is consistent with the traditional painting style (Table 3).

Table 3. Tanslation and deduction of Chaoshan Mid Autumn Festival sacrificial symbols in illustration application

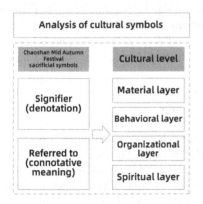
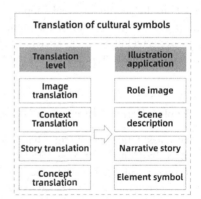

5.2 Element Sorting Based on Image Translation

When studying the symbol translation of Chaoshan Mid Autumn Festival sacrificial ceremony, we made a field investigation, especially visited guizhengshan village in Jieyang. Through this investigation, we screened out some cultural symbols and pattern prototypes with local culture, historical background and aesthetic value. These prototype designs need to meet the selection criteria of accuracy, practicality and easy to remember, and match the symbols of Chaoshan Mid Autumn Festival sacrificial ceremony, and create a new visual image after visual reproduction. In this process, we classified the basic elements collected, summarized and drawn the image elements in traditional cultural symbols and rituals, and finally realized the innovation of visual design (Table 4).

Table 4. Color extraction of Chaoshan Mid Autumn Festival sacrificial symbols

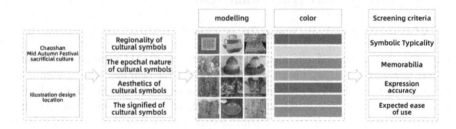

5.3 Morphological Refinement of Visual Elements

In terms of the choice of visual elements, the color transmission of image elements is not only based on the single tone of planar images, but also needs to have a deep understanding and accurate grasp of the unique Mid Autumn festival atmosphere in Chaoshan area. After an in-depth field visit to the region, we noticed that the praying elements in the sacrificial ritual supplies were constantly integrated into it. Therefore, in the process of processing the symbol translation of visual images, we recommend using various technical means such as rendering and stippling, so as to comprehensively display the unique texture features of the Mid Autumn Festival design style in Chaoshan area.

5.4 Exploration and Innovation of Aesthetic Style

The basic aesthetic style of Chaoshan Mid Autumn Festival ritual symbols was mainly influenced by Confucianism and Taoism. In the late Qing Dynasty, this culture gradually showed a folk aesthetic tendency. The symbols of Chaoshan Mid Autumn Festival sacrificial ceremony are influenced by the different preferences and pursuits of the business community and bureaucrats for aesthetics, which makes them show rich and varied meanings in visual elements. The author chose guizhengshan village as the main object of the field survey, and discussed the unique features and styles in the shape, internal design, layout skills and decorative details of the items of the Mid Autumn Festival sacrifice ceremony in Chaoshan area.

In the process of field research, the author specially studied those elegant and detailed design elements in the symbols of the Mid Autumn Festival. These elements generally reflect a kind of design philosophy, that is, "things must decorate the picture, and the picture must be intentional". After carefully combing and summarizing this system, the author hopes to deeply understand the symbolic meaning and internal relations contained in it, and to realize the unity of the connotation and extension of these symbols in the current visual communication process.

Through a detailed examination of the appearance characteristics of the sacrificial images mentioned earlier, this study explores and analyzes the deep spiritual connotation behind these sacrificial symbols, and considers its value in modern society, and believes that this spiritual core still has reference significance in contemporary society. On this basis, we conceived a series of visual art works, aiming to create auspicious visual symbols that match the aesthetic orientation of contemporary young people and integrate unique regional characteristics.

5.5 Modern Visual Display of Sacrificial Symbols

After in-depth study and interpretation of the decorative patterns, the author also made a detailed analysis and summary of the sacrificial symbols of the Mid Autumn Festival in guizhengshan village. He tried to use the visual method to classify the sacrificial groups, including "flowers", "money", "grass", "Pavilion" and "robes". Through the in-depth study of the original functions of these items and the precise restoration of the visual image, the visual perception ability of the audience has been successfully improved. In the process of design, we refer to the texture and visual effect of paper sacrifice in Chaoshan Mid Autumn Festival, which makes the color block show a profound historical background and vicissitudes of aesthetic charm.

As for the unique ritual symbols used in the folk Mid Autumn Festival sacrificial ceremony in guizheng mountain, we have carried out in-depth analysis and integration, and plan to carry out more detailed visual design and processing. This process skillfully combines the historical and cultural background behind the symbol, and completely presents its unique visual style and various activities, thus vividly showing the cultural significance of the Mid Autumn Festival sacrifice ceremony in Chaoshan area and the traditional folk cultural activities of local residents. After adopting this strategy, we hope to make these traditional cultural elements reappear their unique attraction in contemporary society through modern visual presentation.

6 Conclusion

In the process of in-depth study of design practice, the author interprets and reproduces the symbolic elements in the Mid Autumn Festival sacrificial ceremony in Chaoshan area from three aspects: context, image and behavior. This method not only shows the depth of Chaoshan Mid Autumn Festival etiquette and custom culture in an all-round way, but also highlights the close relationship between regional culture and artistic illustrations, ensuring that the cultural symbols of Mid Autumn Festival sacrificial ceremony can be deeply transmitted in symbolic meaning and content. As designers, we have the responsibility to guard our cultural heritage wholeheartedly, and expect to inject new attraction and lasting vitality into them in continuous innovation. We hope that the vast number of user groups can not only show the core value of art, but also reflect the profound significance of culture when participating in the innovation and inheritance of traditional culture, so as to obtain their own cultural identity and cultural confidence.

Acknowledgments. The project originates from Guangdong Province's First-Class Course "Fundamentals of Design (Three-Dimensional Space)". The project is the interim results of the ideological and political demonstration course "Fundamentals of Design (Three-Dimensional Space)" at Guangzhou Academy of Fine Arts in 2021 (Project Number: 6040321061); and Guangzhou Academy of Fine Arts Graduate Program "Cultural Elements and Creative Design Education" (Project Number: 6040122027SFJD).

References

1. He, L.: Research on the extraction and translation of symbols in regional culture. Design **34**(04), 76–79 (2021)
2. Xu, S.: A Study on the Vocabulary of Zhuzi Yulei. Shanghai Ancient Books Publishing House, Shanghai (2013)
3. Lei, T.: Folklore image research in the visual turn -- a case study of the Northern Song Dynasty genre painting "jinmingchi vies for the standard picture". J. Nanjing Inst. Art (Art Des.) (01), 112–118+214 (2018)
4. Ren, X.: Innovative application of folk pattern culture in modern visual design -- a case study of Zhuxian Town woodcut New Year pictures. Art Educ. Res. (13), 84–85 (2021)
5. Yu, T.: Research on the Cultural Attribute and Reconstruction Path of the Cultural and Creative Design of the Longevity Palace Based on the Principle of Design Semiotics. Nanchang University, Fuxiaolong (2021)
6. Wang, C.: Application of Regional Cultural Symbols in Interior Design of Resort Hotels. Inner Mongolia Normal University, Hohhot (2018)
7. Gao, J.: Applied Research on Majiayao Painted Pottery Theme Packaging Design Based on Semiotics. Lanzhou University of technology, Lanzhou (2018)
8. Yang, L.: The Construction and Dissemination of National Cultural Symbols. Yunnan University, Kunming (2015)
9. Xu, Y., Zhou, Z.: Research on Extraction and translation of semantic symbols in flower tourism commodity design. Decoration (04), 38–42 (2019)
10. Li, M., Meng, L.: Research on cultural translation design strategy in landscape digital navigation system. Art Educ. Res. (19), 55–57 (2021)

The Cross-Cultural Application of Cantonese Opera Costume Elements in 3D Pop-Up Card Design: Focusing on Youth and Intangible Cultural Heritage Elements

Li Ou Yang[1] 🆔, Ying Guo[1] 🆔, Jinrong Liu[1] 🆔, and Jie Ling[2(✉)] 🆔

[1] The Guangzhou Academy of Fine Arts, Guangzhou 510261, Guangdong, China
[2] Zhongkai University of Agriculture and Engineering, Guangzhou 510220, Guangdong, China
47219382@qq.com

Abstract. Study aims to explore the role of three-dimensional greeting cards in disseminating the non-heritage culture of Cantonese Opera. Three-dimensional greeting cards have crossed cultural barriers with their intuitive appeal and exquisite craftsmanship, becoming a global form of artistic expression. This study designed three-dimensional greeting cards featuring Cantonese opera costume elements - phoenix crown, leaning, official coat, open cloak, cape wind and python robe - with the aim of enhancing viewers' appreciation of Cantonese opera costumes, stimulating non-local youths' interest in Cantonese opera and traditional Chinese culture, and promoting cultural heritage and innovation. In this study, a quantitative questionnaire survey was conducted among adolescents aged 13 to 17 to assess their understanding of the cultural elements of Cantonese opera and their preference for visual representation. The results of the study showed that the respondents generally demonstrated a strong interest in NLCs and a preference for sharing three-dimensional greeting cards, although there were differences in their understanding of different cultural elements. This study emphasises the importance of in-depth understanding of non-heritage cultural elements for innovative communication, and concludes that three-dimensional greeting cards, as an innovative communication medium, significantly enhance the enthusiasm for exploring non-heritage culture and effectively promote the wide dissemination of Cantonese opera non-heritage culture.

Keyword: cross-cultural design · non-heritage culture · Cantonese opera

1 Introduction

1.1 Background

Traditional Chinese culture, as the valuable spiritual heritage of the Chinese nation, not only constitutes an important part of human civilisation, but also carries profound historical and cultural values. However, in the wave of modernisation and globalisation, these traditional cultures are facing unprecedented challenges. How to effectively pass on and innovate them to meet the needs of the new era has become an urgent task to safeguard the country's cultural self-confidence and satisfy the spiritual needs of the people. In recent years, attention to intangible cultural heritage has increased significantly.2021 In May 2021, the Chinese government promulgated the "14th Five-Year Plan for the Safeguarding of Intangible Cultural Heritage," which put forward a series of measures and policies aimed at strengthening education on intangible cultural heritage, incorporating intangible cultural heritage into the national education system, and advancing a series of activities such as introducing intangible cultural heritage into campuses, communities, and enterprises, in order to cultivate young people's interests and hobbies in non-heritage and enhance cultural confidence and national pride [1]. The plan emphasises the importance of intangible cultural heritage as a living culture passed down from generation to generation, and as an important carrier of cultural inheritance and development.

Intangible cultural heritage, as a core component of traditional culture, is the crystallisation of national wisdom and emotion, and represents the cultural memory and heritage of a country or nation. Its preservation is not only the maintenance of cultural diversity, but also the respect for the common spiritual wealth of mankind. This study focuses on Cantonese opera as a non-heritage item. Cantonese Opera, as an art form with a long history that incorporates a variety of musical and dramatic elements, is not only an important part of Lingnan culture, but also plays an important role in cultural transmission and exchange at home and abroad. However, Cantonese Opera is currently facing inheritance difficulties and innovation challenges, and it has become an urgent problem to adapt it to the changes in modern society and to expand its audience base, especially to attract the interest of young people and international audiences. This study proposes the use of three-dimensional greeting cards as a communication medium to explore its potential role in the inheritance and innovation of Cantonese opera culture. Not only are three-dimensional greeting cards artistic and innovative, they can also cross cultural boundaries and become a bridge to connect audiences from different cultural backgrounds. By designing three-dimensional greeting cards that reflect the characteristics of Cantonese opera costumes, this study aims to enhance the audience's appreciation of the art of Cantonese opera, stimulate the younger generation's interest in traditional culture, and thus promote cultural inheritance and innovation.

1.2 Purpose and Significance of the Study

This study aims to delve into the important value of Cantonese opera as an intangible cultural heritage and explore the potential of three-dimensional greeting cards in disseminating the culture of Cantonese opera. In addition, the study also aims to enhance the audience's appreciation of the costumes of Cantonese opera by presenting them in the form of three-dimensional greeting cards. Cantonese opera is an important branch of traditional Chinese opera with a rich historical background and deep cultural heritage. As an intangible cultural heritage, Cantonese opera carries a unique theatre tradition, which is of great significance in maintaining cultural diversity, preserving historical and social memory, enhancing national cultural identity, promoting social harmony, facilitating local tourism and economic development, and supporting the healthy growth of youth. Through in-depth study and active dissemination of Cantonese Opera culture, we can not only promote its inheritance and innovation, but also open up new paths for social and cultural enhancement and progress.

This study also pays special attention to the role of three-dimensional greeting cards in the dissemination of Cantonese opera culture. The three-dimensional greeting card is an innovative and cross-cultural communication tool, which opens up new ways for the enhancement of the contagiousness and dissemination of the art of Cantonese Opera with its multiple advantages, such as its unique cultural carrying capacity, creative display and educational value. In addition, the integration of Cantonese opera elements into the design of three-dimensional greeting cards can not only provide a new impetus for the industrial development of Cantonese opera, but also provide valuable theoretical and practical experience for the innovative communication of intangible cultural heritage.

This paper argues that displaying Cantonese opera costumes through three-dimensional greeting cards not only enhances the public's aesthetic appreciation, but also has far-reaching cultural dissemination significance. Through its detailed presentation, artistic display and transmission of cultural symbols, the three-dimensional greeting card can enable the audience to have a more comprehensive and deeper understanding of the unique charm of Cantonese opera costumes. This form of communication helps to stimulate the audience's emotional resonance with history and tradition, promote cultural education, and at the same time facilitate non-local youth audience to actively explore and understand the history and characteristics of Cantonese opera costumes and their traditional significance. In this way, this study expects to build an effective bridge for the innovative dissemination of Cantonese opera culture as well as the cultural identity of the younger generation.

2 Literature Review

2.1 Cross-Cultural Design Research

With the continuous evolution of the design discipline, cross-cultural design has become a research field that has attracted widespread attention and a large number of scholars' in-depth discussions. In the context of globalisation, scholars have adopted a cross-cultural product design model based on Hofstede's theory of cultural dimensions to carry out their research, which provides a new frame of reference for the cultural transformation of design thinking (Lu, Chunfu and Qiao, Xiaoling [2]). By studying the social innovation service design cases in Wuxi and Milan, constructive suggestions for social innovation services were made by combining Hofstede's cultural dimension theory and hierarchy of needs theory (Linghao Zhang [3]). In addition, scholars respectively use the theory to conduct comparative analyses of website design cases in Malaysia and other countries, and summarise the experience of cross-cultural digital interactive product design, as well as the analysis of Chinese cultural product styling and design measures. These research results not only promote the promotion of Chinese cultural products in the international market, but also facilitate the global dissemination of cultural elements (Chen Jiajia [4], Zhou Jian [5]). In addition, scholars have explored in-depth the design of ice play games using digital media technology, emphasising the importance of immersive experiences and participatory cultural interactions in cross-cultural communication (Li Jiao-long, Si Zheng-ming et al. [6]). Scholars have raised crucial questions about cultural respect and the balance between tradition and modernity in design, and emphasised the design concepts of "seeking common ground while reserving differences" and "harmony and difference", which provide new perspectives and approaches to cross-cultural design (Lan Zhang [7]).

2.2 Research on Cantonese Opera Costume Design

As a highly influential traditional opera art form in southern China, Cantonese opera not only has a profound heritage in performing arts, but its costume design also contains rich cultural connotation and artistic value. In recent years, with the increasing awareness of the protection and inheritance of traditional culture, the research on the applied design of Cantonese Opera costumes has gradually been paid attention to, and it has become an important bridge connecting tradition and modernity, art and life. Cantonese opera costumes are famous for their unique colour combinations, cutting styles and decorative techniques. The design of costumes not only reflects the character traits and social status of the characters, but also incorporates the folk culture and aesthetic interests of the Guangdong region. The patterns, motifs and colours of Cantonese opera costumes have specific symbolic meanings, such as the dragon and phoenix motifs for good luck, and the fish motifs for wealth.

The researcher extracts the classical elements through in-depth excavation of the culture of Cantonese Opera costumes and creates innovative designs by combining them with modern design concepts. For example, traditional patterns such as cloud patterns and phoenix patterns in Cantonese opera costumes are integrated into modern costume design in a simplified or abstracted form, which not only preserves the essence of traditional culture, but also meets the modern aesthetic needs (Fan Yinghui [8]). Some other scholars have investigated, for example, the craft of Cantonese embroidery and found that it has a strong visual impact and can be constantly innovated to meet the needs of social development (Chen Jinyi and Ke Huiming [9]). Although the research on the applied design of Cantonese opera costumes has achieved certain results, it still faces many challenges, such as how to maintain the traditional characteristics and at the same time make effective innovations, and how to balance the artistic value and market demand. In addition, the accelerated pace of modern life and the diversification of entertainment forms also pose challenges to the inheritance of Cantonese opera culture.

3 Application of Cross-Cultural Design in the Dissemination of Non-heritage Culture

The aim of this study is to design a unique three-dimensional greeting card featuring the cultural characteristics of Cantonese Opera through cross-cultural design by transforming the costume elements of non-heritage Cantonese Opera into visual symbols and combining them with the creative craftsmanship of the three-dimensional greeting card. The purpose of this design is to let the youth and non-local audience intuitively feel the charm of non-heritage culture through the specific design work of greeting card, so as to stimulate their interest in non-heritage culture.

3.1   Organic Integration of Cultural Elements

In this study, we applied a cross-cultural design approach by subtly integrating the typical costume elements of Cantonese Opera - such as the phoenix crown, leaning, open cloak, and official coat - into the design of a three-dimensional greeting card. By simplifying these cultural symbols into modern, abstract visual images, we have preserved their essential characteristics while transcending geographical and cultural boundaries, making them more widely universal. Considering the aesthetic preferences of young people aged 13 to 17, we adopted abstract art and geometric design styles to make the cultural symbols easily recognisable and memorable, which will help to enhance the young audience's understanding and memory of the non-heritage Cantonese opera culture.

3.2   Abstract Refinement of Visual Symbols

In our design practice, we put special emphasis on transforming the characteristics of the Cantonese opera costume elements into simple visual symbols that are easily recognisable (see Fig. 1). This process involves not only an in-depth excavation of the cultural elements themselves, but also the abstraction and symbolisation of the elements to ensure that these cultural icons are universally recognisable in different cultural contexts. In addition, by adopting a distinctive colour scheme, we have enhanced the visual impact of the cultural elements, which further enhances their prominence and recognition in the design, enabling the audience to quickly identify and associate them with the Cantonese Opera culture.

Fig. 1.   Intangible Cultural Heritage Cantonese Opera Three-dimensional Greeting Card

3.3   Unique Presentation of Three-Dimensional Greeting Cards

In our study, we put special emphasis on the presentation of three-dimensional greeting cards in order to fully demonstrate the three-dimensionality and artistry of the cultural elements of Cantonese Opera. Through clever folding and unfolding techniques, the greeting card presents a unique three-dimensional effect visually, making the cultural elements vivid and distinct. This unique way of presentation not only makes the cultural symbols more vivid and concrete, but also provides a brand new perspective, enabling the audience to appreciate and experience the non-heritage culture from multiple dimensions. The design of the three-dimensional greeting card not only attracts the audience visually, but also provides a participatory viewing experience through the interactive process of unfolding and folding, which enhances the audience's cultural perception and memory.

In conclusion, by applying cross-cultural design concepts to the dissemination of non-heritage culture, especially through the unique medium of three-dimensional greeting cards, we have not only given a new life to the cultural elements of Cantonese Opera, but also provided a new path for the innovative dissemination of non-heritage culture, promoting cross-border dissemination and international presentation of culture.

4   Research Methodology

4.1   Analysis of Subjects' Characteristics

The age group of the subjects in this study was centred on 13 to 17 year olds, an age group that exhibits unique characteristics in terms of cultural perception and acceptance among adolescents. This age group is more likely to be exposed to information and experiences from around the globe, demonstrating an openness to multiculturalism. Social media has a profound impact on their cultural perceptions, leading them to pay attention to trendy culture. As their identities develop, they are interested in unique and personalised cultural expressions. The youth group actively participates in cultural creations, including music and videos, showing a spirit of innovation and accepting new things more easily. With a high level of concern for social issues, they tend to support cultural content that conveys positive values. In terms of cultural perception and acceptance, the youth group is more willing to challenge traditional concepts and hold values of openness, tolerance, equality and pluralism. On the whole, 13–17 year olds are characterised by openness, pluralism and innovation, and three-dimensional greeting cards as a relatively new form are easily accepted by young people and are conducive to the dissemination of non-heritage culture. In order to make the research data more scientific, the author will conduct a quantitative questionnaire research on the subjects.

4.2   Quantitative Questionnaire Research Design

The questionnaire was divided into a pre-test and a post-test, and the number of respondents was 40. The pre-test was designed to gain a comprehensive understanding of the awareness of three-dimensional greeting cards among teenagers aged between 13 and 17, as well as their aesthetic and visual preferences for greeting cards, and their role in spreading the non-heritage culture of Cantonese Opera. By investigating whether the audience has known and used three-dimensional greeting cards, we can assess the popularity of this cultural product among the target age group and provide reference for future design and promotion. The main purpose of the post-test is to understand the experience of the subjects after using the non-heritage Cantonese Opera three-dimensional greeting cards, to understand their suggestions and to further improve the original design. In addition, the questionnaire will delve into the audience's understanding of the costume elements of Cantonese opera to assess the accuracy and effectiveness of the three-dimensional greeting card in cultural communication. By understanding the audience's interest and participation in NCS, we are able to reveal the potential of three-dimensional greeting cards in generating cultural interest and stimulating participation. A mixed-methods approach was adopted throughout the study, combining quantitative data with personal experience, with the aim of gaining a more comprehensive understanding of youths' acceptance and perception of NRM culture and the potential of three-dimensional greeting cards as a communication medium. Such a study has important implications for designing more effective cultural communication strategies and promoting the transmission of cultural heritage.

5 Findings and Analyses

5.1 Analysis of Adolescents' Perceptions

In our preliminary survey, we found that 70% of non-local youths have limited understanding of Cantonese opera culture, revealing the distance between them and this intangible cultural heritage. This phenomenon may stem from the fact that they grew up in a cultural environment different from the traditional context of Cantonese opera, resulting in a lack of direct experience and understanding of this traditional art form. However, through subsequent studies, especially the in-depth understanding of the costume elements of Cantonese opera, we noticed a significant cognitive enhancement. This change proved the effectiveness of the research strategy and intervention method we adopted.

We set a benchmark for the study by analysing the participants' basic perceptions when they first encountered Cantonese opera. This helped us to focus the study and develop an effective intervention strategy. In particular, we chose a three-dimensional greeting card design centred on the elements of Cantonese Opera costumes and used a quantitative questionnaire to prompt participants to explore and understand these cultural elements in greater depth. The intervention strategies included displaying visual images of Cantonese opera costumes, explaining the cultural connotations, and engaging the subjects more personally through the design and sharing of the three-dimensional greeting card, so that a deeper understanding of the elements of Cantonese opera costumes could be observed in the follow-up test. In summary, by comparing the results of the pre- and post-tests, we conclude that the intervention method effectively enhanced the subjects' understanding of Cantonese opera culture and strongly contributed to the deepening of their cultural cognition.

5.2 Analysis of Visual Representation Preferences

In our preliminary survey, we found that over 80% of the teenagers interviewed preferred modern fashion and abstract art styles. This trend reflects that teenagers in this age group tend to pursue uniqueness and avant-garde, and they can easily empathise with designs with a modern feel. Modern fashion is associated with hipness, individuality and innovation, while abstract art inspires imagination and creativity with its openness, which is in line with their values of diversity and independent thinking.

Three-dimensional greeting cards, combining traditional media with modern and abstract elements, not only retain cultural uniqueness, but also cater for the aesthetic preferences of teenagers. Therefore, the preference of non-local 13–17 year olds for three-dimensional greeting cards reflects their pursuit of unique, innovative and personalised designs, and is also in line with their integration with modern culture.

5.3 Analysis of Interest and Willingness to Share

The follow-up survey showed that most of the adolescents showed strong interest in Cantonese opera-themed three-dimensional greeting cards and were willing to share these cards. This phenomenon can be attributed to a number of factors. Firstly, the unique and attractive design of these greeting cards, incorporating traditional elements of Cantonese opera such as phoenix crowns, leans, and official clothes, has successfully attracted the attention of teenagers and aroused their interest in traditional Chinese culture. Secondly, the three-dimensional design of the greeting card satisfies the modern teenagers' demand for visual experience and makes them more inclined to explore the cultural details of Cantonese opera. Furthermore, as a modern communication medium, the three-dimensional greeting cards offer the convenience of sharing through channels such as digital social platforms, which fits in with the familiar interaction methods of teenagers. Most importantly, these greeting cards are not only artefacts, but also a vehicle for expressing cultural identity and heritage. Through sharing, teenagers not only demonstrate their understanding of and respect for traditional Chinese culture, but also deepen their sense of cultural identity, turning cultural heritage into a meaningful social activity. All in all, the interest of non-local youths in Cantonese Opera three-dimensional greeting cards and their willingness to share them reflect the intertwining of multicultural factors, presenting traditional culture through innovative ways, which effectively promotes their recognition of and enthusiasm for cultural diversity.

6 Conclusion of the Experiment

Summing up the results and analyses of the above studies, three-dimensional greeting cards show considerable potential in the field of cultural communication of non-heritage Cantonese opera. This medium not only crosses cultural barriers through its intuitive charm and exquisite craftsmanship, but also succeeds in becoming a globally resonant artistic language. Particularly among non-local youths aged between 13 and 17, the high level of interest in non-heritage Cantonese Opera and their willingness to disseminate this culture through the sharing of three-dimensional greeting cards demonstrated the great potential of three-dimensional greeting cards in cultural transmission and innovation. However, the study also reveals areas for further improvement in design practice. We need to gain a deeper understanding of how different cultural elements are perceived and accepted by the youth population in order to better meet the needs of multiculturalism. At the same time, exploring the integration of different art styles and modern fashion elements can enhance the appeal of three-dimensional greeting cards among young audiences. In terms of design, more flexible interactivity and personalisation options need to be considered to bring the three-dimensional greeting cards closer to the aesthetic and cultural preferences of the audience.

In order to further promote the heritage and innovation of the non-heritage Cantonese opera culture, it is suggested that more emphasis be placed on user feedback and participation in the design practice so as to continuously improve the product. In addition, combining three-dimensional greeting cards with modern technologies such as digital media can create a more diversified and interactive mode of dissemination. In promotion, co-operation with schools, communities and other organisations should be strengthened to carry out cultural and educational activities to increase the visibility and influence of non-heritage Cantonese opera.

Through this paper, we focus on the role of three-dimensional greeting cards in disseminating the non-heritage culture of Cantonese opera, and explore their dissemination effects among youths and non-local audiences by designing three-dimensional greeting cards featuring elements of Cantonese opera costumes. The results show that three-dimensional greeting cards are an innovative communication medium that is particularly suitable for the transmission and innovation of non-heritage Cantonese opera culture. To better realise its potential, we suggest focusing on the integration of multiple cultures and enhancing the artistic appeal and attractiveness of the product. At the same time, by strengthening the integration with modern technology and expanding the communication channels, we can further promote the dissemination and awareness of the non-heritage Cantonese opera culture among the younger generation.

Acknowledgments. The project originates from Guangdong Province's First-ClassCourse "Fundamentals of Design (Three-Dimensional Space) (Project Number: 6040324137)". The project is the interim results of the ideo- logical and political demonstration course "Fundamentals of Design (Three-Dimensional Space)" at Guangzhou Academy of Fine Arts in 2021 (Project Number: 6040321061); and Guangzhou Academy of Fine Arts Graduate Program "Cultural Elements and Creative Design Education" (Project Number: 6040122027SFJD).

References

1. Circular of the Ministry of Culture and Tourism on the Issuance of the 14th Five-Year Plan for the Safeguarding of the Intangible Cultural Heritage (2021). Accessed 10 Dec 2022. http://www.gov.ch/zhenccelzhenaceku/2021-06/09/content_5616511.htm
2. Lu, C., Qiao, X., Jie, D., Wu, J.: Research on cross-cultural product design based on Hofstede's cultural dimension theory. Packa. Eng. **41**(12), 117–124 (2020)
3. Zhang, L., Yang, G.: Cross-cultural thinking of sustainable social innovation service design - a case study of Milan and Wuxi. Creat. Des. (03), 66–70 (2015)
4. Chen, J.: The application of cross-cultural design in digital interactive product design in the post-industrial era. J. Nanjing Art Inst. (Art Des. Ed.) (02), 168–173 (2012)
5. Zhou, J., Li, B.: Cross-cultural theory analysis and product design. Art Des. (Theory) **2**(09), 248–250 (2009). https://doi.org/10.16824/j.cnki.issn10082832.2009.09.088
6. Li, J., Si, Z.: Immersive ice game design for overseas audiences in cross-cultural communication perspective. Packa. Eng. **44**(10), 213–220 (2023)
7. Zhang, L.: Cross-cultural design. J. Nanjing Art Inst. (Art Des. Ed.) (03), 147–149 (2012)
8. Fan, Y.: Innovative application of cantonese opera cultural elements in modern garment design. Print. Dyeing **50**(01), 92–94 (2024)
9. Chen, J., Ke, H.: Artistic embodiment of canton embroidery in traditional cantonese opera costumes. Silk **57**(05), 109–114 (2020)

Research on Public Identification and Influencing Factors of Public Art in Urban Subway: A Case Study of Shenzhen Subway

Ke Qian[1] and Yuanfang Zhao[2][(✉)] [iD]

[1] College of Architecture and Urban Planning, Shenzhen University, Shenzhen 518060, China
[2] College of Art and Design, Shenzhen University, Shenzhen 518060, China
zhaoyuanfang@szu.edu.cn

Abstract. Research on public identification of subway public art contributes to the integration of urban subway public art with urban life and the creation of a pleasant riding experience. To reveal the public identification of urban subway public art and its influencing factors, this study builds a logistic theoretical model of subway public art public identification based on field research and questionnaire survey data of Shenzhen subway public art, and explores the key factors affecting public identification. The research results show that: 1) the public's preference for Shenzhen subway public art is relatively low, with only 2 stations expressing "like" and "very like," accounting for 7.41% of the total number of surveyed stations. 2) Compared to personal attributes, the characteristics of public art have a greater impact on public identification. Among personal attributes, only cultural level has a significant impact on public identification; among the characteristics of public art, artistic quality, reflection of regional culture, spatial location, color, and materials have a significant effect on public identification. Artistic quality and reflection of regional culture have a greater impact on subway public art public identification; compared to color and materials, the spatial location of public art has a greater influence on public identification. Based on these conclusions, the study proposes recommendations for urban subway public art creation, such as integrating art into life, highlighting regional cultural characteristics, setting up public art works based on visual focus, and innovating, being inclusive, and collaborating in terms of color and materials.

Keywords: Subway · Public Art · Public Identification · Logistic Regression Model · Shenzhen Subway

1 Introduction

Since January 1883, the British Pearson constructed the "Metropolitan District Railway" by utilizing steam locomotives to pull trains, marking the birth of the subway system. Although the development of China's subways began relatively late, its growth rate has attracted worldwide attention. As early as 2015, Beijing's subway system recorded an average of 8.46 million passenger trips per month, becoming one of the busiest subways

C. Stephanidis et al. (Eds.): HCII 2024, CCIS 2116, pp. 312–324, 2024.
https://doi.org/10.1007/978-3-031-61950-2_35

in the world (Li 2016a). As a new aspect of social and urban development, subways demonstrate their vigorous vitality. Subways have evolved from merely being public transportation tools and urban infrastructure to becoming windows showcasing urban features, playing an increasingly significant role in the dissemination and inheritance of urban culture.

In recent years, public art in subway stations in international cities such as Paris, London, Moscow, and Stockholm have increasingly appeared in the public's view, becoming a means for these cities to "re-promote" themselves in a global context (Hao and Yao 2018). Urban subway public art is an essential way for the public to experience and connect with urban culture personally. Similar to other urban landscape elements such as parks, buildings, and streets, they serve as crucial windows to showcase urban features. With the openness and inclusiveness of contemporary society, China's subway public art has gained significant development momentum. The public not only takes subways but also experiences the new atmosphere of social development and urban life, subtly appreciating the city's humanistic and historical cultural atmosphere during daily commuting.

Existing research on urban subway public art mainly focuses on the development history, construction elements, regional culture, and design methods (Yang and Zhang 2017; Xiong and Chen 2018; Hou 2007; Mo et al. 2015), as well as the analysis of classic cases of domestic and foreign subway public art (Wu and Su 2015; Zhang 2016). However, from the public's perspective, there has been no reported research on the public's sense of identification with subway public art. In the relationship between humans and public art, people are the subjects of public art. A complete public art piece requires the joint participation of designers and the public. The public should have the power to decide and speak out whether a public art piece can become genuine public art. Many current public art pieces not only deviate from the public's aesthetic orientation and pursuit but also lack social value guidance and fail to arouse public interest and interaction. With the development of social civilization, the public has ample freedom and opportunities to express opinions in public art activities. Designers of public art need to maintain effective communication with the public and accurately grasp the public's concerns and interests (Li and Zang 2017). As subways transition from purely public transportation services to carriers of urban culture, subway public art aims to integrate art and public life more closely while creating better riding experiences. However, from the practical perspective of today's subway public art, creators have yet to clarify the logical relationship between public art creation and public recognition. Moreover, academia lacks systematic theoretical support for enhancing the public's sense of identification with subway public art. Public identification is crucial for the creation of subway public art, the integration of art and urban life, and the improvement of urban features. Public identification is a multidimensional concept characterized by various independent indicators, easily influenced by public personal attributes, artwork features, and environmental factors. This paper takes Shenzhen subway public art as the research object, explores the public's sense of identification with subway public art, and its key influencing factors from the public's perspective, aiming to provide scientific references for the creation and development of urban subway public art.

2   Research Methodology

Based on the existing research findings of public art (Li and Zang 2017; Wang 2010; Zhang and Lu 2018) and combining field research on subway public art, this paper classifies the influencing factors of subway public art public identification into two dimensions and 13 factors to be verified, including personal characteristics of the public and characteristics of public art works, as shown in Fig. 1.

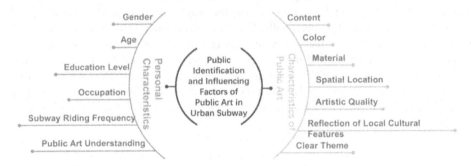

Fig. 1. Influencing Factors of Public Identification for Urban Subway Public Art

Based on this theoretical framework, a questionnaire was designed with Shenzhen subway public art as the research object. The public was randomly selected within subway stations, and an on-site questionnaire survey was conducted.

2.1   Questionnaire

The questionnaire consists of two parts: 1) personal characteristics of the public, such as the respondent's gender, age, education level, occupation, frequency of subway travel, and degree of understanding of public art; 2) the respondent's identification with the characteristics of public art works, such as whether the content is easy to understand, whether the color and material are appropriate, whether the spatial location is suitable, whether it has artistic quality, whether it has a clear theme, and whether it reflects the regional culture of the surrounding area of the station. Public identification can be measured by public preferences, so the questionnaire finally sets a scoring question on the public's preference for subway station public art works, described using the Likert 5-point scale. The variables set in the questionnaire are described and assigned, as shown in Table 1.

2.2   Field Survey

The survey was conducted at stations with representative public art works on Shenzhen subway lines 7, 9, and 11, covering a total of 27 stations. The geographic locations of these stations are shown in Fig. 2. A total of 1,120 questionnaires were distributed, and after excluding questionnaires filled out randomly or with missing information, 1,025 valid questionnaires were obtained, with a recovery rate of 91.52%.

Table 1. Relevant Variables and Descriptive Assignments for Public Identification of Subway Public Art

Variables	Variable Name	Assigned Definition
X1	Gender	Male = 1; Female = 2
X2	Age	Below 18 = 1; 18–30 years = 2; 30–50 years = 3; Above 50 years = 4
X3	Education Level	Junior high school or below = 1; High school = 2; Undergraduate or diploma = 3; Masters or above = 4
X4	Occupation	State-owned enterprises = 1; Private enterprises = 2; Student = 3; Other = 4
X5	Frequency of Riding Subway	Almost never = 1; Occasionally = 2; Sometimes = 3; Frequently = 4; Almost every day = 5
X6	Understanding of Public Art	Completely do not understand = 1; Roughly understand = 2; Average = 3; Quite understand = 4; Very well understand = 5
X7	Understandability of the Conten	Completely do not understand = 1; Roughly understand = 2; Average = 3; Quite understand = 4; Very well understand = 5
X8	Appropriateness of Color	Very inappropriate = 1; Inappropriate = 2; Average = 3; Quite appropriate = 4; Very appropriate = 5
X9	Appropriateness of Material	Very inappropriate = 1; Inappropriate = 2; Average = 3; Quite appropriate = 4; Very appropriate = 5
X10	Appropriateness of Spatial Position	Very inappropriate = 1; Inappropriate = 2; Average = 3; Quite appropriate = 4; Very appropriate = 5
X11	Artistic Quality	Yes = 1; No = 2
X12	Representation of Regional Culture	Yes = 1; No = 2
X13	Presence of Clear Theme	Yes = 1; No = 2
Y	Public Preference	Very like = 5; Like = 4; Neutral = 3; Dislike = 2; Strongly dislike = 1

2.3 Questionnaire Reliability Analysis

The purpose of the questionnaire on public identification of subway public art is to measure the public's subjective attitude towards subway public art. Therefore, this paper adopts the Cronbach's alpha coefficient to evaluate the reliability of the questionnaire. This coefficient is the most commonly used reliability analysis tool in current empirical

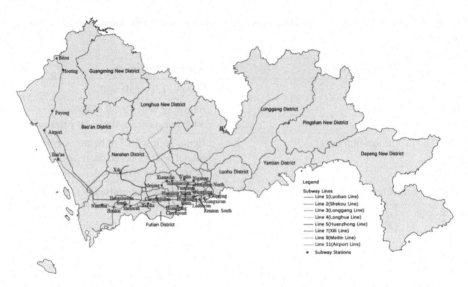

Fig. 2. Spatial Distribution of the 27 Subway Stations

research. The Cronbach's alpha coefficient of the survey questionnaire is 0.719, which is greater than 0.7. Therefore, the questionnaire data used in this paper is reliable.

3 Data Analysis

3.1 Collinearity Diagnosis

The collinearity test is performed on the independent variables. The maximum value of the condition index in the diagnostic results is 27.948, which is still below the generally accepted 30. The highest variance inflation factor among the 13 variables is 2.081, which is also below 3. Based on the above analysis combined with the correlation analysis results among the 13 variables, it can be considered that there is no significant collinearity problem among the variables.

3.2 Logistic Regression Analysis

In this paper, the public's identification with subway public art is considered as a binary classification variable, that is, the evaluation results of "subway public art public preference" as "very like" and "like" are collectively classified as "identification", with a value of "1"; the evaluation results of "neutral", "dislike", and "strongly dislike" are collectively classified as "non-identification", with a value of "0". This paper adopts a binary logistic regression model to analyze the influencing factors of subway public art public identification.

3.3 Overview of the Research Object

In order to transform Shenzhen's subway from a simple transportation service function to an urban cultural radiation function, to truly integrate art with regional culture and the lives of citizens, and to create a better riding experience for passengers, Shenzhen has carried out public art projects on subway lines 7, 9, and 11 in recent years. This study selects 27 stations with relatively large passenger flow out of the 50 stations on lines 7, 9, and 11 to conduct research on urban subway public art public identification and its influencing factors. The summary of the spatial location, scene pictures, and characteristics of public art works at the 27 stations is shown in Table 2. It was found through field research that the public art works at subway stations were all placed in the subway station halls, with mural decorations as the main form, belonging to more traditional forms of public art. Among the 27 subway stations, only Huanggang Port Station adopted the design form of ceiling hanging installations. The materials used are mainly metal, ceramics, and glass, as well as less commonly used materials in public art works, such as silk threads and cement.

Table 2. Overview of Subway Station Public Art

4   Analysis of Public Preferences for Subway Public Art

4.1 Overview of Personal Characteristics of Respondents

Among the 1,025 respondents, there were more males than females; the majority were aged 18–30, accounting for 64.68% of the total, with fewer respondents under 18 and over 50; 62.24% of the respondents had a college or associate degree education; 43.71% of the respondents were private or self-employed workers; 44.29% of the respondents often took the subway, and 11.41% of the respondents took the subway almost every day; 10.44% of the respondents had no understanding of public art, while 30.15% and 1.76% of the respondents had a relatively good and very good understanding of public art, respectively (Table 3).

Table 3. Descriptive Statistics of Respondents' Personal Characteristics

Personal Characteristics	Parameter	Number of Instances	Percentage
Gender	Male	621	60.59%
	Female	404	39.41%
Age	<18 years old	76	7.41%
	18–30 years old	663	64.68%
	31–50 years old	255	24.88%
	>50 years old	31	3.02%
Education Level	Junior high school or below	57	5.56%
	High school	245	23.09%
	Undergraduate or diploma	638	62.24%
	Masters or above	85	8.29%
Occupation	State-owned enterprises	119	11.61%
	Private enterprises	448	43.71%
	Student	344	33.56%
	Other	114	11.12%
Frequency of Riding Subway	Almost never	23	10.44%
	Occasionally	157	15.32%
	Sometimes	274	26.73%
	Frequently	454	44.29%
	Almost every day	117	11.41%
Understanding of Public Art	Completely do not understand	107	10.44%
	Roughly understand	287	28.00%
	Average understanding	304	29.66%
	Quite understand	309	30.15%
	Professionally understand	18	1.76%

4.2 Respondents' Degree of Identification with Artwork Features

The public preferences statistics for the public art works at 27 subway stations are shown in Fig. 3. There are two subway stations with an average public preference score of more than 4 points, "like." The highest average score is for the public artwork "Southern Splendor" at Xili Station, followed by the public artwork "Water and Milk Blend as One Family" at Shenwan Station. The average scores for the public art works at the remaining 25 subway stations are between 3 points, "average," and 4 points, "like."

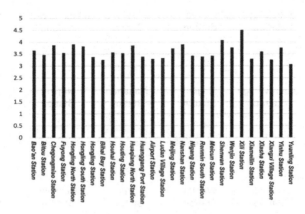

Fig. 3. Overall Satisfaction with Public Art Works at 27 Subway Stations

The identification statistics for the 7 features of the public art works at 27 subway stations are shown in Fig. 4. The public artwork "Southern Splendor" at Xili Station has received relatively high public recognition in terms of color, material, spatial location, artistic quality, station cultural manifestation, and content, with only a lower score in highlighting the theme. Its public identification is relatively good. The public artwork "Hometown Flavors" at Yuanling Station has low public recognition scores in all six aspects: material, color, spatial location, artistic quality, station culture, and theme highlighting. Its overall public recognition is relatively low. The public artwork "Connection" at Huanggang Port Station has received relatively high public recognition in terms of artistic quality, but its scores in other aspects are extremely low. The public artwork "Urban Stories" at Nigang Station has gained some public recognition in terms of content, but its scores in other aspects are low.

5 Influencing Factors Analysis of Public Recognition of Subway Public Art Based on Binary Logistic Regression

In this study, SPSS 22.0 software was used to conduct a binary logistic regression analysis on the public recognition of urban subway public art, using the forward conditional selection method. As shown in the model (Table 4), six variables have significant explanatory power for the model, and their contributions to the model's explanatory

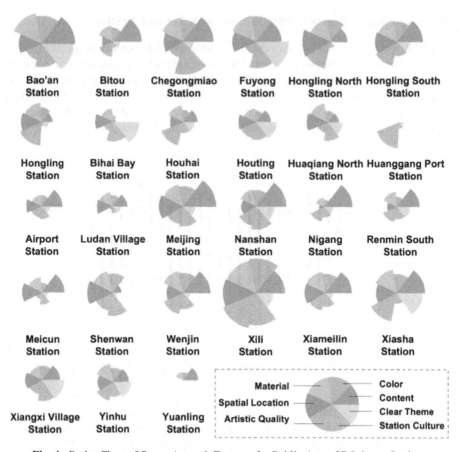

Fig. 4. Radar Chart of Seven Artwork Features for Public Art at 27 Subway Stations

power are, in descending order: artistic quality, reflection of regional culture, appropriateness of spatial location, appropriateness of color, appropriateness of material, and level of education. The fitted equation is:

$$\text{Logit Y} = -5.446 - 0.192 \times 3 + 0.436 \times 8 + 0.398 \times 9 + 0.619 \times 10 \\ + 1.707 \times 11 + 1.404 \times 12 \tag{1}$$

In the individual characteristics of the public, the variable "level of education" has a significant impact on the public recognition of urban subway public art at the 0.05 level; the variables "gender," "age," "occupation," "frequency of taking the subway," and "understanding of public art" do not have a significant impact on the public recognition of urban subway public art, and do not appear in the model. Compared with the other five variables of individual characteristics, the level of education has a significant impact on the public recognition of urban subway public art, and a higher level of education is associated with lower recognition of subway public art. This indicates that people with higher levels of education have more rigorous assessments of public art works.

Table 4. Logistic Model Estimation Results of Influencing Factors of Public Recognition of Urban Subway Public Art

Variable	Estimate B	Standard Error S.E.	Wald Statistic Wald	Degrees of Freedom df	Significance Sig.	Odds Ratio Exp(B)
Education Level (X3)	−0.192	0.119	4.630	1	0.035	0.825
Color Appropriateness (X8)	0.436	0.136	10.260	1	0.001	1.547
Material Appropriateness (X9)	0.398	0.155	6.585	1	0.010	1.488
Spatial Location Appropriateness (X10)	0.619	0.141	19.252	1	0.000	1.857
Presence of Artistic Quality (X11)	1.707	0.167	103.978	1	0.000	5.511
Representation of Local Culture (X12)	1.404	0.171	67.473	1	0.000	4.071
Constant	−5.446	0.604	81.326	1	0.000	0.004

Among the features of subway public art, the variables "artistic quality," "reflection of regional culture," "appropriateness of spatial location," "appropriateness of color," and "appropriateness of material" have significant impacts on the public recognition of subway public art, and all have passed the test at the 0.01 or 0.05 significance level. Among these variables, the absolute value of the estimated value B for "artistic quality" reaches 1.707, with the highest contribution rate to the model. This indicates that the stronger the artistic quality of subway public art works, the higher the public recognition. It was found in field interviews that the public consistently values the artistic quality of public art works, with high demands, which should be taken seriously by designers and builders of subway public art. The absolute value of the estimated value B for "reflection of regional culture" ranks second among the six variables with significant explanatory power, with a relatively high contribution rate to the model. This suggests that the public places importance on the function of public art works in reflecting regional culture, which is consistent with existing theoretical research on the regional cultural characteristics of a large number of public art works (Zhang 2013; Yang and Li 2018; Qiu and Zhang 2016). Through field interviews, it was found that the public has higher recognition of public art works that reflect the regional culture of the surrounding area or Shenzhen. If a public art work does not contain regional cultural connotations, even if its artistic quality is strong, the public's recognition will be reduced, such as the public art work "Connection" at Huanggang Port Station. Compared to "appropriateness of material" and "appropriateness of color," the absolute value of the estimated value B for "appropriateness of spatial location" is larger, indicating that the spatial location factor has a greater impact on the public recognition of subway public art than material and color factors. Since the public is in a continuous moving state after entering the subway, the visual focus is constantly changing, and the appreciation of public art works in the station hall is a state of walking and looking. Interested parties will stop and linger (Hou 2007). Therefore, the spatial location of public art works within subway stations is very important and should meet the needs of mobile visual appreciation. Vision is the most developed sense in the human sensory system, and color is an excellent element to attract human visual attention. In the underground subway station space, the oppressive and uncomfortable feeling brought by the subway station architecture itself can be changed through the color design of public art (Li 2016b). Material is the most direct expression of public art works, the foundation of public art, and directly relates to the expression of public art in space, color, texture, and form. Materials can enable the public to obtain intuitive tactile and visual feelings, thereby attracting public interaction with public art (Li 2016c). Therefore, spatial location, color, and material, as the most basic features of public art works, have a significant impact on public recognition. The variables "ease of understanding of content" and "presence of a clear theme" do not have a significant impact on the public recognition of urban subway public art.

6   Conclusion

This study is based on the field research and public questionnaire survey data of Shenzhen subway public art, from the perspective of the public, to explore the public's sense of identity with urban subway public art. The results show that: 1) the overall satisfaction of the public with Shenzhen subway public art is relatively low, with only 2 stations rated as "satisfied" and "very satisfied," accounting for 7.41% of the total surveyed stations. 2) Compared to individual public attributes, the characteristics of public art have a greater impact on the public's sense of identity. Among the individual attributes of the public, only the level of education has a significant impact on the public's sense of identity with subway public art; among the characteristics of public art, artistry, reflection of regional culture, spatial location, color, and material have a significant impact on the public's sense of identity. Among them, artistry and reflection of regional culture have a greater impact on the public's sense of identity with subway public art, and compared to color and material, the spatial location of public art has a greater impact on the public's sense of identity. Based on this, the following suggestions are proposed for subway public art design and construction:

6.1   Integrating Art into Life, Highlighting Regional Cultural Characteristics

Subway public art should be derived from urban daily life, utilizing familiar public images combined with artistic means to bridge the gap between art and urban life, conveying positive energy and warmth, disseminating the message of truth, goodness, and beauty, interacting with people's hearts, guiding social values, and promoting social harmony and stability. Regional culture is a unique cultural label of a place, carrying a long history and cultural accumulation. In the process of rapid urbanization, public art needs to bear the responsibility of commemorating and inheriting regional culture, using diverse art forms to showcase history and evoke urban memory.

6.2 Establishing Public Art Based on Visual Focus

The placement of public art in subway spaces should consider the visual characteristics of the public during subway travel behavior, striving for reasonable locations and diverse forms. On the basis of meeting the public's physiological and psychological needs, enhancing visual impact to improve public attention and participation, and achieving the maximum exchange between art and the public. When the public enters the subway, the sensory focus is more concentrated in the hall, platform, and escalator areas. The hall is a must-pass place for people coming and going, an overlapping space for entering, leaving, and passing through. In this space, people move quickly and there is a large flow of people, often absorbing information quickly while walking and stopping to watch if interested. The visual focus in the platform space is usually on the wall directly in front of the platform. At this time, people are relatively stationary and in a better state to absorb information. On escalators, the public's visual focus often moves within the range of down, left, and right. People are in a moving state, so dynamic effects can be set on both sides of the escalator or on the ceiling to enliven the sense of oppression brought by the narrow and enclosed space.

6.3 Innovation, Inclusiveness, and Collaboration in Color and Material

Color can evoke emotions, express feelings, and affect people's psychological experiences. In the subway space, the oppressive and uncomfortable sensations caused by underground construction can be alleviated through color design. By using low-brightness, low-purity receding colors, the sense of spatial narrowness can be mitigated, creating a more open and bright psychological experience. High-brightness, high-purity colors can be employed to embellish long and narrow passageways, reducing the public's sense of oppression and anxiety. Rapid technological advancements have brought forth numerous new materials and technologies, such as light and shadow that create novel visual experiences, providing infinite possibilities for the creation of subway public art. Nowadays, people's aesthetic tastes are becoming more diversified, and design is also evolving in a more diverse direction. In the application of materials and colors, inclusiveness and collaboration should be fully considered, and unique artistic effects can be created by coordinating contrasts between light, color, texture, and tactile sensations according to the design requirements.

In conclusion, the design and construction of subway public art should focus on integrating art into daily life, highlighting regional cultural characteristics, considering visual focus, and promoting innovation, inclusiveness, and collaboration in the use of color and materials. By doing so, subway public art can not only enhance the public's sense of identity but also enrich the urban environment and contribute to the cultural development of the city.

References

Hao, X., Yao, S.: A study of the degree of thematic integration of the subway public art and the urban tourism image in Shanghai. J. Yunnan Univ. (Soc. Sci.) **50**(02), 148–156 (2018)

Hou, N.: Look at the public art position and form setup of subway from the sensory focus of passengers. Art Des. **03**, 3–14 (2007)

Li, H., Zang, X.: What Kind of Subway Public Art We Need. Art Observation **09**, 26–27 (2017)

Li, L.: The application of color visual perception research in metro public art. Art Obs. **08**, 129–130 (2016)

Li, X.: The aesthetic value of integrated materials in the creation of metro public art - an example of public art design for beijing urban rail transit. Creat. Crit. **24**, 96–99 (2016)

Li, Z.: Exploration of the development of public art in subway service. Art Eval. **04**, 168–169 (2016)

Mo, F., Li, X., Xia, H.: Study on function and aesthetic of public art material in subway. J. Shenyang Jianzhu Univ. (Soc. Sci.) **17**(03), 243–250 (2015)

Qiu, B., Zhang, F.: Public art planning based on collective memory: art involved environment planning. Planners **32**(08), 12–17 (2016)

Wang, F.: The Research on the Interactive Design of City Public Art under the Background of Digital Art. Jiangnan University, Wuxi (2010)

Wu, D., Su, C.: From art decoration space to art activation space: public art development and evolvement of Beijing metroin past 30 year. Urban Mass Transit **18**(04), 1–4+8 (2015)

Xiong, C., Chen, J.: Regional culture characteristics of subway public art design-a case study of Wuhan metro line 2. J. Hubei Univ. Technol. **33**(07), 71–74 (2018)

Yang, L., Li, X.: On the effect of public art based on the inheritance of collective memory: a case study of Nanqili heritage park in Hefei. Urban. Arch. **05**, 30–32 (2018)

Yang, X., Zhang, T.: Development and evolution of contemporary public art in the metro. J. Beijing Univ. Civil Eng. Arch. **33**(02), 6–10 (2017)

Zhang, A.: The application of regional culture in the public space design of Tianjin metro. Packa. Eng. **34**(10), 1–3 (2013)

Zhang, B., Lu, H.: On the interaction of urban public art facility. J. Huzhou Univ. **40**(05), 100–105 (2018)

Zhang, Q.: The development and management mechanism of London underground public arts. Arch. Cult. **03**, 253–255 (2016)

Enhancing Digital Interaction with Intangible Cultural Heritage: A Study on User Experience and Acceptance of the Zhuhai Intangible Cultural Heritage Database

Yudan Shen[1,2] , Zhihong Wu[3]([⊠]) , Xiawei Fang[1] , and Wei Yue[4]

[1] Beijing Institute of Technology, No. 6 Jinfeng Road, Zhuhai 519088, China
[2] National Yang Ming Chiao Tung University, Hsinchu City 300, Taiwan
[3] Guangdong Polytechnic of Science and Technology, No. 65 South Zhuhai Avenue, Zhuhai 519090, China
278200388@qq.com
[4] Anhui University, No. 111 Jiulong Road, Hefei 230601, China

Abstract. As a coastal city in southern China, Zhuhai has undergone rapid transformation within just a few decades. However, due to shifts in economic production and living conditions, a substantial portion of the local intangible cultural heritage has gradually lost physical space for preservation and presentation. In recent years, the application of digital technologies has created extensive digital exhibition platforms and diverse display modalities for the preservation, revitalization, and dissemination of this intangible cultural heritage. Nevertheless, there remains a need for further research into the user experience of digital repositories of intangible cultural heritage and the factors influencing public acceptance of digital technologies in the preservation of such heritage. This paper, adopting a perspective of digital humanities and utilizing the Zhuhai Intangible Cultural Heritage Database as a case study, employs a combined qualitative and quantitative research approach to investigate the user experience and factors impacting the acceptance of this digital repository for intangible cultural heritage. The initial stage of this study involved interviews with intangible cultural heritage custodians and users to gauge their satisfaction and willingness to use the Zhuhai database. The subsequent stage utilized the Technology Acceptance Model (TAM) theory to probe the factors affecting user satisfaction and their intention to sustain usage of the Zhuhai Intangible Cultural Heritage Database. Based on the research results, this study offers optimization strategies for the Zhuhai Intangible Cultural Heritage Database, thereby providing a sustainable solution for the safeguarding and presentation of Zhuhai's intangible heritage.

Keywords: Zhuhai Intangible Cultural Heritage Database · Technology Acceptance Model · User Satisfaction · Continued Usage Intention

C. Stephanidis et al. (Eds.): HCII 2024, CCIS 2116, pp. 325–334, 2024.
https://doi.org/10.1007/978-3-031-61950-2_36

1 Research Background

1.1 A Subsection Sample

Zhuhai is a coastal city in southern China, known for its rich intangible cultural heritage comprising numerous traditional crafts, performing arts, oral traditions, social practices, customs, and rituals. These intangible cultural heritage elements serve not only as carriers of cultural inheritance across generations but also as significant sources of identity and national cohesion. Within just a few decades, Zhuhai has transformed from a small fishing village into a thriving urban center, resulting in significant shifts in economic production and living conditions. Consequently, a substantial portion of the local intangible cultural heritage has gradually lost physical space for survival and presentation. In recent years, the rapid development and application of digital technologies have provided promising digital exhibition spaces and diversified display formats for the preservation, revitalization, and dissemination of these intangible cultural heritage elements.

Currently, there are more systematic digital collection and display of Zhuhai's intangible cultural heritage are primarily concentrated in the Zhuhai Intangible Cultural Heritage Database, a specialized website featuring sections such as the Zhuhai intangible heritage list, heritage map, heritage inheritors, heritage albums, heritage videos, heritage news, and heritage regulations. The content system is relatively comprehensive, providing a wealth of textual, pictorial, and video materials for the preservation of Zhuhai's intangible cultural heritage data. The target audience for this digital heritage dissemination primarily consists of young people. However, based on the website's usage records, the number of page views is low, the database utilization rate is minimal, and the dissemination effect is unsatisfactory.

How do young people perceive the user experience of the Zhuhai Intangible Cultural Heritage Database? What are the factors influencing user satisfaction? How can we increase public, especially the younger generation's interest and satisfaction in using the database? How can we enhance their intention to continue usage? These series of questions have become important directions for exploration in this study.

2 Literature Review

The Technology Acceptance Model (TAM) is widely used to predict users' attitudes and behaviors towards the use of new technological systems. Originating from the psychological Theory of Reasoned Action and the Theory of Planned Behavior, TAM has evolved into a key model for understanding factors that potentially influence the acceptance or rejection of new technology.

TAM consists of two core factors: perceived usefulness and perceived ease of use. In subsequent studies, researchers have expanded the TAM theory from various perspectives, exploring additional factors influencing technology acceptance, such as content quality, user habits [1], computer self-efficacy, and perceived enjoyment [2]. The application scope of TAM theory has also been continuously broadened, including areas such as e-learning, digital libraries, and mobile database applications, to study the behavior of using new information systems and technologies in different digital environments.

Being the cultural presentation of Zhuhai's intangible cultural heritage transitions from physical spaces to online displays and digital collections, digital technology, as a new tool for cultural dissemination, has brought new possibilities for the preservation, revitalization, and dissemination of Zhuhai's intangible heritage. How to enhance the audience's acceptance of the digital transformation of Zhuhai's intangible cultural heritage dissemination is a question worthy of further consideration.

Previous studies have extensively utilized the TAM theory model to investigate digital collection databases. Miller and Khera (2010) identified factors influencing the use of digital libraries by applying TAM [3]. Their research found perceived usefulness to be a key predictor of intent to use digital libraries. Another study examined factors influencing user acceptance and willingness to use digital library systems in emerging countries (Botswana, Ghana, Indonesia, and Nepal). The results showed that perceived ease of use significantly influenced perceived usefulness, affecting user acceptance and usage intention [4].

Perceived ease of use is defined as the degree to which a person believes that using a particular system would be free from effort [5]. In this study, it is understood as the ease with which users can use the Zhuhai Intangible Cultural Heritage Database. Perceived usefulness is defined as the degree to which a person believes that using a particular system would enhance their job performance, specifically referring to the extent to which the public perceives the Zhuhai Intangible Cultural Heritage Database as useful.

Previous research has demonstrated the significant impact of perceived usefulness on the intention to use a specific system. Yoon (2016) identified a positive correlation between perceived usefulness and the intention to use mobile library services [6]. Similarly, Xu, Gan, and Yan (2010) found that perceived usefulness has a constructive impact on the intention to use digital library services [7].

Currently, there is a significant gap in research on how external factors such as technology application and user experience influence the acceptance and usage of the Zhuhai Intangible Cultural Heritage Database by the public. Therefore, through leveraging the TAM theoretical framework, this study aims to explore the factors influencing user satisfaction and intention to continue usage of the Zhuhai Intangible Cultural Heritage Database, with the goal of providing practical and effective recommendations for optimizing the Zhuhai Intangible Cultural Heritage Database. Building upon previous studies, this research poses the following research questions regarding the use of the Zhuhai Intangible Cultural Heritage Database:

RQ1: What factors influence user satisfaction with the Zhuhai Intangible Cultural Heritage Database?
RQ2: What factors predict the continued usage intention of the Zhuhai Intangible Cultural Heritage Database?

3 Research Methodology

This study adopts a digital humanities perspective and focuses on the Zhuhai Intangible Cultural Heritage Database as the research subject. A combined qualitative and quantitative research approach is employed to investigate the user experience and factors influencing acceptance of the Zhuhai Intangible Cultural Heritage Database. The first phase of the study involves in-depth interviews with users and inheritors of intangible cultural heritage to understand the public's satisfaction with and willingness to use the database, as well as potential influencing factors. In the second phase, the study utilizes the Technology Acceptance Model (TAM) theory and collects data through questionnaire surveys to measure whether these factors positively influence user satisfaction and intention to continue using the database. By combining qualitative and quantitative research methods, the researchers aim to delve deeper into the reasons for the low utilization rate of the database and provide practical and effective recommendations for its optimization.

3.1 In-Depth Interviews

In the first phase of the study, interviews were conducted with 5 university students and 3 inheritors of intangible cultural heritage from Zhuhai. These university students all have experience using the Zhuhai Intangible Cultural Heritage Database, and the inheritors are also familiar with it to some extent. Each interview, focusing on aspects such as digital intangible cultural heritage exposure, experiences with using the heritage database, and suggestions for optimization, lasted approximately 30 min per participant. With the consent of the interviewees, the interviews were partially recorded, and key points were later transcribed into text for analysis.

3.2 Questionnaire Survey

In the second phase of the study, a quantitative research method was primarily employed. A total of 448 valid questionnaires were collected through offline recruitment and online surveying. Among the participants, 32.4% were male and 67.6% were female. The majority of participants (97.8%) were under the age of 25, and 95.1% had education levels ranging from high school to university (or vocational college). Regarding the participants' locations, 33.5% were from Zhuhai, 60.7% were from other cities in Guangdong province (including Zhongshan, Dongguan, Shantou, Shenzhen, Qingyuan, Foshan, etc.), and 5.8% were from cities outside Guangdong province (including Beijing, Hunan, Shandong, Zhejiang, etc.). Among them, 35.9% of the participants had produced works related to Zhuhai's intangible cultural heritage, while 64.1% had not.

The questionnaire survey was divided into two sections. In the first section, participants were asked to browse and familiarize themselves with the Zhuhai Intangible Cultural Heritage Database. The second section consisted of questions for participants who had already browsed and used the database.

The questionnaire items were primarily designed based on the Technology Acceptance Model (TAM) theory and tailored to the specific context of the database. Drawing from previous research [7, 8] the following measurement variables were included:

1. **Perceived Ease of Use.** This variable was measured using three items to assess participants' perception of the ease of use of the database. Specific items included "Browsing information on the Zhuhai database is simple and easy," "Interactions with the Zhuhai database are clear and understandable," and "Finding information on the Zhuhai database is easy and convenient." The Cronbach's alpha for perceived ease of use was .926.

2. **Perceived Usefulness.** This variable was measured using three items to assess participants' perception of the usefulness of the database. Specific items included "I can obtain the knowledge or information I want from the Zhuhai database," "Using the Zhuhai database improves my efficiency in accessing relevant resources," and "The Zhuhai database is useful to me." The Cronbach's alpha for perceived usefulness was .903.

3. **Perceived Enjoyment.** This variable was measured using three items to assess participants' perceived enjoyment of the database. Specific items included "The Zhuhai database is very interesting," "When browsing the Zhuhai database, I forget how much time has passed," and "When browsing the Zhuhai database, I am not easily distracted by other things." The Cronbach's alpha for perceived enjoyment was .918.

4. **Media Richness.** This variable was measured using three items to assess the media richness of the database. Specific items included "The Zhuhai database can provide me with instant feedback according to my requests," "The Zhuhai database presents information about intangible cultural heritage in different formats (e.g., text, images, videos, audio, animations, and 3D virtual environments)," and "The Zhuhai database has rich interactive features." The Cronbach's alpha for media richness was .924.

5. **Self-efficacy.** Three items were used to measure the self-efficacy of users of the database. The specific items included: "I am confident in mastering how to use the Zhuhai Intangible Cultural Heritage Database without being told how to use it," "I can master how to use the Zhuhai Intangible Cultural Heritage Database well," and "I believe that using the Zhuhai Intangible Cultural Heritage Database is not difficult for me even without experience." The Cronbach's alpha for the self-efficacy scale was .914.

6. **User Satisfaction.** Three items were used to measure users' satisfaction with the database. The specific items included: "I am very satisfied with the performance of the Zhuhai Intangible Cultural Heritage Database," "The experience of using the Zhuhai Intangible Cultural Heritage Database is enjoyable to me," and "The Zhuhai Intangible Cultural Heritage Database gives a good impression." The Cronbach's alpha for the user satisfaction scale was .926.

7. **Continued Usage Intention.** Three items were used to measure users' continued usage intention of the database. The specific items included: "I will continue to use the Zhuhai Intangible Cultural Heritage Database in the future," "I do not plan to replace the use of the Zhuhai Intangible Cultural Heritage Database with other methods," and "I intend to increase my use of the Zhuhai Intangible Cultural Heritage Database in the future to gain knowledge." The Cronbach's alpha for the continuance intention scale was .913.

The questionnaire used a 5-point Likert scale, with 1 indicating strong disagreement and 5 indicating strong agreement.

4 Research Findings

4.1 Analysis of Interview Data

Through the interviews, this study found that most of the interviewees believed that the Zhuhai Intangible Cultural Heritage Database covers a wide variety of intangible cultural heritage projects, and the preserved data are very useful and valuable, unanimously affirming the usefulness of the database. However, several problems still exist in the current database:

Low Media Richness. Most of the intangible cultural heritage presented in the database remains in traditional display formats, predominantly static with minimal dynamic elements. The main media formats include images, text, and recorded videos, with a relatively traditional approach to digitization and a lack of interactive features such as commenting, liking, or quick secondary dissemination. Additionally, there is a lack of new technologies (such as AR, VR, etc.) for interactive experiences, and the information is not visualized, the dissemination is not interactive, and the experience is not immersive. Interviewees expressed that these media forms are "old-fashioned" and "not easily engaging."

Low Perceived Enjoyment. Several interviewees mentioned that the content and form of the database are "lacking in creativity" and "not fun." There is a lack of technical forms suitable for the aesthetic taste of young people, making it difficult to strike a balance between preserving traditional cultural essence and innovating modern media. Some interviewees stated, "If it could be designed to be more interesting, maybe I would visit the website more often," suggesting a possible correlation between interest and intention to continue usage. The conservative and non-innovative digitized content and forms have contributed to the low-key, disjointed, and backward digitized dissemination of intangible cultural heritage, hindering the promotion and dissemination of heritage information.

Useful But Not Easy to Use for Some People. Almost all of the college students believed that the database is easy to operate. However, for older intangible cultural heritage inheritors, they found it "difficult to find some information we want," possibly due to their limited familiarity with computers and mobile phones. There is a digital gap in the perception of the usability of the intangible cultural heritage database between heritage inheritors and young people. One of the intangible cultural heritage inheritors believed that the unfamiliarity with digital technology would make people "want to use it but not know how to use it," and even "not want to use it and not know how to use it."

Based on these interview results, this study believes that further clarifying the relationships between perceived ease of use, perceived usefulness, perceived enjoyment, media richness, self-efficacy, user satisfaction, and continued usage intention will help to propose more precise and effective optimization suggestions for the database.

4.2 Analysis of Questionnaire Survey Data

In this study, SPSS software was used to conduct statistical analysis of the questionnaire data. Based on the research questions, the study explored the factors influencing user satisfaction and continued usage intention in the Zhuhai Intangible Cultural Heritage Database.

Hierarchical regression analysis was first conducted, with demographic variables such as gender, age, education level, city of residence, and whether the respondent had created Zhuhai intangible cultural heritage works entered into the first block of independent variables, and perceived ease of use, perceived usefulness, perceived enjoyment, media richness, and self-efficacy entered sequentially into the second block. This was done to analyze the factors influencing user satisfaction. The data showed that perceived usefulness ($\beta = .245$, $p < .001$), media richness ($\beta = .351$, $p < .001$), and self-efficacy ($\beta = .249$, $p < .001$) positively influenced user satisfaction, while perceived usefulness ($\beta = .046$, $p > .05$) and perceived enjoyment ($\beta = .05$, $p > .05$) did not significantly affect user satisfaction (see Table 1).

Table 1. Hierarchical regression analysis of user satisfaction

Variables	User Satisfaction	
	β	p
Gender (Male = 1)	.124**	.004
Age group	$-.238$***	.000
Education level	$-.058$	.323
City (Is from Zhuhai = 1)	.186**	.001
Experience related to ICH (Yes = 1)	.087	.057
Perceived ease of use	.046	.297
Perceived usefulness	.245***	.000
Perceived enjoyment	.050	.306
Media richness	.351***	.000
Self-efficacy	.249***	.000

$^{*}p < .05; ^{**}p < .01; ^{***}p < .001$, n = 448

Next, hierarchical regression analysis was conducted to identify the predictive factors of users' continued usage intention towards the database. The data revealed that perceived ease of use ($\beta = .143$, $p < .01$), perceived usefulness ($\beta = .209$, $p < .001$), perceived enjoyment ($\beta = .251$, $p < .001$), media richness ($\beta = .145$, $p < .05$), and self-efficacy ($\beta = .172$, $p < .001$) were all positive predictors of users' continued usage intention (see Table 2).

The data results indicate that perceived usefulness ($\beta = .245$, $p < .001$), media richness ($\beta = .351$, $p < .001$), and self-efficacy ($\beta = .249$, $p < .001$) positively influence user satisfaction with the database. However, perceived ease of use ($\beta = .046$, $p > .05$) and perceived enjoyment ($\beta = .05$, $p > .05$) do not significantly affect user satisfaction. Additionally, perceived ease of use, perceived usefulness, perceived enjoyment,

Table 2. Hierarchical regression analysis of continued usage intention.

Variables	Continued Usage Intention	
	β	p
Gender (Male = 1)	.126**	.004
Age group	−.192***	.000
Education level	−.059	.323
City (Is from Zhuhai = 1)	.201***	.000
Experience related to ICH (Yes = 1)	.068	.139
Perceived ease of use	.143**	.005
Perceived usefulness	.209***	.000
Perceived enjoyment	.251***	.000
Media richness	.145*	.016
Self-efficacy	.172***	.000

*p < .05;**p < .01;***p < .001, n = 448

media richness, and self-efficacy are all positive predictors of user continuance intention, positively influencing users' continued usage intention.

5   Conclusion and Recommendations

Through interviews and questionnaire surveys, this study found that factors influencing user satisfaction with the Zhuhai Intangible Cultural Heritage Database include perceived usefulness, media richness, and self-efficacy. Further analysis revealed that perceived ease of use, perceived usefulness, perceived enjoyment, media richness, and self-efficacy are all positive predictors of continued usage intention.

Regarding the basic demographics of the respondents, females exhibited higher satisfaction and continued usage intention compared to males. Additionally, age and education level showed negative correlations with satisfaction and continued usage intention. This result might indicate varying expectations of users from different age and educational backgrounds towards the database. With higher age and education levels, the demand for accessing ICH information and related database experiences also increases.

Moreover, compared to non-Zhuhai users and individuals who haven't experience related to ICH, residents in Zhuhai and those who have experience may have higher expectations or demands, resulting in lower satisfaction and continued usage intention.

Based on the research findings above, this study proposes the following optimization suggestions for the Zhuhai Intangible Cultural Heritage Digital Database:

From both a technological and user experience perspective, enhancing the usefulness and media richness of the database can increase user satisfaction. Therefore, the optimization strategies for the database include:

1. Enhancing the information capacity of the database to improve access efficiency, thereby increasing its usefulness to users.
2. Many interviewees felt that the current digital format of the database is too monotonous, and the "media richness" score in the questionnaire survey was not high. For future technical updates and media usage of the database, it is suggested to consider enriching the database's interactive forms. In addition to traditional text, images, and audio-video formats, consider adopting more diverse forms such as multimedia, animation, information visualization, and 3D virtual presentations of intangible cultural heritage information. Providing users with bidirectional interactive instant feedback can improve user satisfaction.

From a psychological perspective, the data indicates that establishing user self-efficacy can help improve user satisfaction with the database. The research results suggest that for the technological application and cultural promotion of Zhuhai intangible cultural heritage digital collections, it is necessary to promote user confidence in some way, eliminate users' unfamiliarity and fear of using digital technology, and reduce the digital gap among different age groups, which can promote higher user satisfaction.

Perceived ease of use, perceived usefulness, perceived enjoyment, media richness, and self-efficacy have a significant positive impact on users' continued usage intention. Therefore, the construction of the Zhuhai Intangible Cultural Heritage Database should consider the following aspects:

1. Reduce the difficulty of user access and the technical threshold, making information browsing simple and easy to use, with clear and understandable interactive operations, and convenient data retrieval.
2. Improve the efficiency of accessing related intangible cultural heritage resources, allowing users to quickly obtain useful information and enhance perceived usefulness.
3. Enhance the entertainment value through creative content and formats. By providing more expressive audiovisual experiences, users can enjoy accessing Zhuhai intangible cultural heritage information and find pleasure in it.
4. Enhance media richness by expanding diverse media presentation approaches. In addition to traditional text and image introductions and visual recording formats, incorporate popular new media forms such as short videos of intangible cultural heritage, motion graphics animations, information visualization, 3D modeling, interactive devices, augmented reality, and virtual reality. Showcase the essence of Zhuhai intangible cultural heritage and transform the one-way information dissemination mode into a two-way interactive mode to enhance users' willingness to continue using it.
5. User self-efficacy is a positive predictor of users' continued usage intention. This suggests that the enhancement of usefulness, entertainment value, and media richness needs to be balanced with users' self-efficacy. While improving usefulness, enjoyment, and media richness, complexity should be avoided to prevent a decrease in users' confidence due to excessive technical difficulty. Enhancing users' sense of autonomy can effectively increase their willingness to continue using the Zhuhai Intangible Cultural Heritage Database.

It is recommended that the Zhuhai Intangible Cultural Heritage Database carry out customized design for user segmentation in the future. Statistical results show that factors such as user gender, age, education level, whether they live in Zhuhai, and previous exposure to intangible heritage information can affect user satisfaction and continued usage intention. In the future, the database can integrate user information and browsing records to provide intelligent intangible heritage information push, or conduct zone design based on user identity, allowing Zhuhai intangible cultural heritage professionals and the general public to more efficiently access the required information, achieving precise promotion effects.

Acknowledgments. This study was funded by Philosophy and Social Science Planning Project of Zhuhai City, "Research on Digital Collection, Digital Creative Design, and Dissemination of ICH in Zhuhai" (2021YBA048).

Disclosure of Interests. The authors have no competing interests to declare that are relevant to the content of this article.

References

1. Rafique, H., Almagrabi, A.O., Shamim, A., Anwar, F., Bashir, A.K.: Investigating the acceptance of mobile library applications with an extended technology acceptance model (TAM). Comput. Educ. **145**, 103732 (2020)
2. Venkatesh, V., Davis, F.D.: A theoretical extension of the technology acceptance model: four longitudinal field studies. Manage. Sci. **46**(2), 186–204 (2000)
3. Miller, J., Khera, O.: Digital library adoption and the technology acceptance model: a cross-country analysis. Electron. J. Inf. Syst. Dev. Count. **40**(1), 1–19 (2010)
4. Park, S.Y.: An analysis of the technology acceptance model in understanding university students' behavioral intention to use e-learning. J. Educ. Technol. Soc. **12**(3), 150–162 (2009)
5. Davis, F.D., Bagozzi, R.P., Warshaw, P.R.: User acceptance of computer technology: a comparison of two theoretical models. Manag. Sci. **35**(8), 982–1003 (1989)
6. Yoon, H.Y.: User acceptance of mobile library applications in academic libraries: an application of the technology acceptance model. J. Acad. Librariansh. **42**(6), 687–693 (2016)
7. Xu, Y., Gan, L., Yan, D.: Study on influence factors model of technology acceptance in digital library based on user cognition and TAM. In: 2010 International Conference on Management and Service Science, pp. 1–3. IEEE (2010)
8. Wu, Y., et al.: Critical factors for predicting users' acceptance of digital museums for experience-influenced environments. Information **12**(10), 426 (2021)
9. Wang, Z.: "Self-Cognition" in the construction of digital museums—a study based on the "Collection of Famous Paintings in the Palace Museum". Open J. Soc. Sci. **6**(11), 293–300 (2018)

Reviving He Xiangning's Artistry in the Digital Age: An Exploration of Music Visualization and Interactive Design Techniques

Weilin Su🄳, Jie Ling(✉)🄳, ZhongCheng Luo🄳, and QiShan Ye🄳

Zhongkai University of Agriculture and Engineering, Guangdong 510220, China
47219382@qq.com

Abstract. He Xiangning, an illustrious figure in Chinese revolutionary history and the artistic domain, employed metaphorical techniques in her Chinese paintings to convey the indomitable spirit of the nation. Yet, with evolving times and shifts in aesthetic preferences, He Xiangning's artistry began to fade, relegating traditional Chinese paintings to a specialized status. This study endeavors to rejuvenate appreciation for He's work by leveraging music visualization and interactive design technologies, aiming to augment public recognition and value attribution to her oeuvre. The research experimentally utilizes three distinct categories of He's artwork, namely, floral and avian, fauna, and landscape, as representative samples. Within each category, three interactive experiments were designed using Touchdesign software and music visualization. The objective was to evaluate audience cognizance and preference for different interactive modalities paired with He's paintings. Ten experts in relevant fields and fifty general audience members were invited to engage with these designs. Feedback was captured through structured interviews, with key statements subsequently extracted and coded using Nvivo software. The findings show that after people experience He Xiangning's digital works, viewers feel the unique charm of traditional art in the process of digital presentation, and their knowledge and preference of He Xiangning's culture are enhanced. What's more, the universality of music and graphic interaction promotes the cross-cultural dissemination and value enhancement of He Xiangning's art.

Keywords: He Xiangning · Music Visualization · Interactive Design · Traditional Chinese Painting · Cross-Cultural Dissemination

1 Introduction

He Xiangning, as an outstanding artist and revolutionary, occupies an important position in the history of Chinese art. Her art works not only show diverse subjects and unique styles, but also through her paintings, we can get a glimpse of the development trajectory of traditional Chinese painting in modern times. [1].

With the rise of the digital age, the art field is also facing profound changes. The traditional art represented by He Xiangning has encountered new challenges in the digital

C. Stephanidis et al. (Eds.): HCII 2024, CCIS 2116, pp. 335–342, 2024.
https://doi.org/10.1007/978-3-031-61950-2_37

age, but it has also spawned a series of revitalization attempts, forming an organic combination of tradition and modernity. The impact of the digital age on traditional art is reflected in several aspects. The rise of digital media has changed the way art is disseminated. While traditional paintings are limited to physical exhibition spaces, digital platforms allow artists to market their works globally through the Internet, expanding the audience for traditional art. In addition, digital technology has provided new possibilities for artistic creation, including generative art, virtual reality art and other forms, allowing traditional art to be presented in richer and more diverse ways. The digital age has also given rise to new concepts such as digital collection and digital copyright, which present new challenges and opportunities for the protection and management of works of art.

2 Research Methodology

2.1 Interview Questionnaire Survey

Invite 10 experts in related fields and 50 general audience members who have the same research in the preliminary stage to experience He Xiangning's digitized artworks. The purpose of this exercise is to obtain professional opinions and overall feedback from the general audience, and to test the actual effect of the attempt to revitalize traditional art in the digital era.

Detailed feedback was obtained using structured interviews with experts and audience members. Getting their in-depth feedback on the digitized artworks. The process was recorded in audio throughout and the audio was subsequently converted into text form and the text was organized. Key statements were then extracted and coded using Nvivo software, which should be used to process and analyze unstructured data, including text, audio, video, images, etc., which can be easily organized and managed to ensure that all the information needed for the study is included in the analysis.

The interviews focused on the users' feelings about the digital artworks, changes in their perception of He Xiangning, their views on music visualization and interactive design, and suggestions for subsequent works. This step was used to gain an in-depth understanding of how users felt during the actual experience. to discover the users' main points of view, emotional feedback, and possible suggestions in the experiment. [2].

2.2 Experimental Design

Flowers and Birds

Painting Analysis. He Xiangning's works demonstrate her sensitive insight into plant forms and colors. She is adept at expressing the delicate textures and layers of flowers through fine lines and unique ink colors, making the viewer feel as if he or she can smell the fragrance of the flowers. He Xiangning's flower paintings often reflect her inheritance and development of traditional Chinese literati paintings, demonstrating a delicate taste for nature through elegant compositions and meticulous depictions. [3].

Visualization Design. The overall picture adopts particle deconstruction of the painting, triggering changes in the particles in the painting through the audience's interactive actions, thus revealing the scene of the original flower and bird painting. The audience's interaction becomes the key to reveal the complete painting. Through waving movements, the audience is able to change the direction and speed of the particles, gradually revealing the full picture of the original painting. This interactive exploration process allows the viewer to go beyond mere viewing and actively participate in the artistic process. The original abstraction is gradually restored to the detailed textures and vivid scenes of He Xiangning's bird and flower paintings. Particle changes echo the blooming of flowers and the fluttering of birds, a dynamic expression that gives new life to a traditional work of art (Fig. 1).

Fig. 1. Effect display

This work focuses on the interactive exploration part, the interactive action greatly affects the output of the screen, in order to avoid the confusion of the screen, so in the music visualization is relatively weakened on the impact of the screen. The music is a traditional Chinese folk music ensemble, and the rhythm and melody complement the fresh and elegant mood of He Xiangning's bird and flower paintings. The ambience of the music, with its melodious melody and clear sound like a mountain spring, introduces the audience to a peaceful and vibrant natural scene. Under the background of such music, the elegance of the flowers and the spirit of the birds in He Xiangning's bird and flower paintings seem to dance among the notes. The dynamics of the plucked instruments in the music are extracted to vary the localized particles of the picture with brightness, blurring and delay.

Animals

Painting Analysis. The Lion is a representative work of Chinese painter He Xiangning, painted in 1914. The painting shows a lion reclining on a slope, with glaring eyes and a thick, powerful mane. In this painting, He Xiangning demonstrated excellent painting skills and also incorporated some elements of Western painting, injecting new concepts into Chinese painting at the time. [4].

Visualization Design. Based on He Xiangning's paintings "Lion" and "Tiger", it aims to create a more vivid art experience through dynamic design and interactive experience. Ripple and fluctuation effects are added to the whole picture in the picture design to give the picture a dynamic sense of fluctuation. This effect can be realized through techniques such as floodlighting and ripple diffusion. Especially around the lion, the ripple effect can be strengthened, as if a breeze comes from the picture, making the environment around the lion fluctuate. Make the lion more vivid and alive. Through the clever use of shadows and light, to strengthen the three-dimensional sense of the lion. The projected shadows can vividly present the bulge of the lion's head and the texture of its body. At the same time, the changes in light and shadow make the lion more three-dimensional under the ripple effect (Fig. 2).

Fig. 2. Effect display

The interaction with the viewer utilizes a camera to capture the viewer's movements. As the viewer moves in front of the painting, the ripple effect and the lion's dynamics change accordingly. The audience's gestures are captured in real time by the LeapMotion sensor, and the interaction of the movements can change the intensity and direction of the ripple effect, making the interaction more flexible and creating a more vivid art experience.

In terms of sound mapping, selected ethnic tribal percussion music can emphasize the majesty of the lion, and even more in the sound rhythm to show a primitive, wild atmosphere. The change in the strength of the drum beat will directly echo the diffusion speed of the ripples in the picture, forming a vivid synchronized effect. For the long line sounds, we chose flute, string and gourd tones, which will be mapped onto the dynamic curvature of the picture. Each line will undulate and sway like a musical note, guided by the sound. Other percussion sounds will be mapped to show tiny ripples on the screen. The formation and dissipation of these small ripples will be closely related to the changes in the notes of the percussion. The audience will feel the subtle interaction between the music and the image, as if the lion in the image is dancing uniquely under the guidance of the music, playing a dynamic audio-visual feast together with the audience.

Landscapes

Painting Analysis. In her early landscape paintings, He Xiangning utilized the basic elements of traditional landscape painting, such as green mountains, green water, meandering hills, and pine trees. These elements are painted in a vivid and layered manner, demonstrating her deep understanding of traditional Chinese landscape painting. The undulating mountains and lush trees in the paintings evoke a serene and grand natural scene. He Xiangning focuses on the creation of mood in her landscape paintings, creating poetic and lyrical images through delicate brushstrokes and skillful color combinations. Her works are not only reproductions of natural scenery, but also expressions of emotions and thoughts. This emotional expression gives her landscape paintings a deeper connotation, allowing the viewer to immerse themselves in the artist's emotional world while enjoying the picture. [5].

Visualization. By deconstructing and cutting the design of He Xiangning's landscape paintings, a new sense of hierarchy and artistic expression can be given to the picture. By recombining the layered mood of the mountains through cutting, the basic elements of traditional landscape painting are retained, while giving the picture a more modern and abstract expression. The cutting design can emphasize the layering of the mountains, making each piece of the picture a unique scene. This treatment not only increases the dynamism of the picture, but also enables the viewer to feel the grandeur and magnificence of the landscape more deeply. By skillfully arranging and combining the images, it creates varied and interesting images, giving the work more of a contemporary art langu.

In terms of interaction, users can use the IPAD devices provided on site or download the ZIG SIM software by themselves, and connect to the WiFi on site, and enter the corresponding IP address and PORT number in the software to interact with the works. On the mobile side, four interactive interfaces are open: gravity sensor, 2D touch, touch radius and microphone level. Gravity sensing can control the rotation and distance of the screen; 2D touch control controls the moving position of several cutting screens; touch radius controls the size of a single cutting screen, which further enhances the experience of viewing the details of the screen and deepens the understanding of the structure of the screen; and the microphone level controls the speed of the overall dynamic movement (Fig. 3).

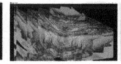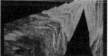

Fig. 3. Effect display

In terms of sound, Glitch electronic music style is chosen, Glitch music usually uses digital distortion, displacement and broken sound effects, Glitch music is known for its digital slicing characteristics, this slicing technique makes the music appear intermittent, subverting the traditional structure of the effect, and echoing with the picture of the slicing effect. The irregular use of these acoustic elements echoes the innovative and groundbreaking nature of modern art, further emphasizing the modernity of the images. Extracting the rhythmic signals in the music mapped onto the flickering effect of the picture can create an audio-visual resonance.

3   Interview Questionnaire Survey Data Collection

3.1   Interview Text Coding

The post-interview phase delved into users' feelings about digital artworks, changes in their perceptions of He Xiangning, and their views on music visualization and interactive design. By collecting 60 interview texts and importing them into NVivo for analysis, we gained a deeper understanding of how users felt during the actual experience, in order to discover their main opinions, emotional feedback, and possible suggestions during the experiment.

During the analysis process, the content was organized in detail around the four areas of experience emotions, art integration, cognitive feedback and suggestions for improvement. This phase resulted in 366 reference points that were based on user responses covering all aspects of perception and opinion. These data will provide enrichment for further analysis and help to fully understand users' feelings and perceptions of He Xiangning's digital artworks (Table 1).

Table 1. Node Hierarchy and Coding Statistics of New Media Art Cognition Differences in He Xiangning

Primary node	Secondary nodes	Number of interview materials	General audience reference points	Domain expert reference points	Total reference points	percentage
Experiencing emotions	pleasure	23	26	5	31	34%
	Sense of wonder	34	31	7	38	
	Curiosity	12	18	6	24	
	Empathy	24	24	9	33	
Artistic integration	Cross-Border Convergence	11	11	3	14	32%
	Fusion of content and form	21	22	3	25	
	Fusion of abstraction and figuration	13	20	6	26	
	Fusion of tradition and modernity	42	42	9	51	
Cognitive Feedback	Cognitive Enlightenment	36	36	5	41	31%
	Cognitive deepening	34	35	4	39	
	Cognitive linking	21	28	4	32	
Suggestions for Improvement	Display Scene Innovation	4	4	1	5	3%
	Social interaction function	2	3	1	4	
	Personalization	3	2	1	3	

3.2 Analysis of Four First Node

Experiencing Emotion. The audience feels pleasant emotions from the work through the colors, lines and dynamics brought by digitization in the work. Amazement and curiosity mainly stem from the visual effects of the physical interaction design and unexpected musical counterparts incorporated in the work. The sense of resonance is reflected in the fact that the audience can often find elements related to their own lives and emotions, causing memories and emotional resonance through the scenes or abstract forms in the works.

Art Integration. Cross-border fusion attracts the attention of audiences and experts, especially through the integration of various art forms such as painting, music and interactive design through digital media, resulting in a novel art experience. Audiences pay attention to the fusion of content and form, emphasizing the expression of the theme by the elements of the picture, as well as the diversity of artistic language. In the fusion of abstract and figurative, the audience felt the emotional expression of the abstract elements, while the experts paid more attention to the storytelling expression of the figurative elements. The fusion of tradition and modernity aroused widespread interest, with both audiences and experts focusing on the combination of modern technology and traditional craftsmanship, as well as the interpretation of traditional elements by digital expression.

Cognitive Feedback. The audience was cognitively inspired through metaphors and emotional resonance, deepening their understanding of He Xiangning's work. Cognitive deepening enables viewers to experience He Xiangning's art more profoundly through multi-sensory experience, repetition and enhanced memory. Identity linking is reflected in the audience's identification with the cultural symbols and shared values in the works, which brings the distance between the audience and the artist closer and makes the artworks more intimate and interesting.

Suggestions for Improvement. The audience suggests innovative display scenarios, such as virtual reality experiences and multi-dimensional interactions, to deepen the audience's experience of the work. Suggestions for social interaction features include social sharing and real-time feedback and interaction to facilitate communication and interaction among audiences. For personalization, the audience emphasizes personalized artwork generation so that everyone can find elements in the work that are relevant to them, enhancing audience engagement and empathy. These suggestions provide an innovative direction for the development of traditional digitally combined art to enhance audience engagement and the presentation of works.

4   Experimental Results

The experimental results show that the audience's cognition and preference for different categories of interactive artworks in the actual experience are significantly improved and enhanced. This suggests that the digital artworks successfully aroused the interest and attention of the audience, and had a positive impact on the cognitive level. Through the actual experience, they gained a deeper understanding of the characteristics, interactive design and artistic expression of the works, thus deepening their understanding of He Xiangning's art and digital art. This cognitive enhancement may come from the innovative elements, interactive nature of the works and the use of digital technology, which enable the audience to perceive the artworks more comprehensively and deeply.

5 Conclusion

Through an in-depth study of the impact of digital art on audience experience, a series of findings were harvested in terms of emotional experience. Audiences show a variety of emotions such as pleasure, surprise, curiosity and empathy when experiencing digital art. These emotions mainly stem from the rich colors, dynamic effects, digital breakthroughs and interactive elements in the works.

The digital art successfully conveys the characteristics of He Xiangning's traditional art and makes the audience feel the unique charm of traditional art in the process of digital presentation. The experts considered the digital artworks to have highlights in terms of technical application and artistic expression, and also put forward some suggestions for improvement, which provided useful guidance for He Xiangning's digital art.

Through the display and communication of digital artworks, the art of He Xiangning's paintings can be more vividly presented, and a continuous feedback mechanism is established to listen to the audience's voices and better meet their expectations and needs. It helps to promote the innovation and development of art, lead the revival of He Xiangning's art, and demonstrate the unique charm of traditional art in the digital age.

Acknowledgments. I want to thank zhongkai university of agriculture and engineering University Student Innovation Fund for its science and engineering project "Synapse, a visual device for real-time performance of electronic music based on immersion theory" (2023CX07); Zhongkai university of agriculture and engineering University Student Entrepreneurship Fund Project "Huimin Art and Art Entrepreneurship Training Program" (2023CY05); Supported by the Guangdong Science and Technology Innovation Strategy Special Fund "Music Visualization Device for Reviving He Xiangning Art in the Digital Age" (pdjh2024b206).

Disclosure of Interests. The authors have no competing interests to declare that are relevant to the content of this article.

References

1. Le, Z., He, X.: Pioneer of modern revolution and fine arts. China Natl. Expo (19), 1–18+229 (2021)
2. Pan, H., Tang, L.: The application of qualitative data analysis tools in social science research in China-taking Nvivo as an example. Data Anal. Knowl. discovery **37**(01), 51–62 (2020)
3. Zhu, W., He, X.: Lingnan School Paint. J. Fine Arts (5), 58–62 (2014)
4. Shang, H., He, X.: artistic conception and aesthetic characteristics of painting composition. J. Fine Arts (6), 110–116 (2013)
5. Zhou, J.: Spreading, path and reputation of He Xiangning lion and tiger works in the first half of the 20th century. J. Fine Arts (4), 84–92 (2023)

Constructing a New Interactive Visual Narrative of Contemporary Digital Wooden Carving Window Decorations

Linxi Xu⬧, Haoyuan Yang⬧, and Lin Lin⁽⊠⁾⬧

Institute of Creativity and Innovation, Xiamen University, Xiamen, Fujian, China
linlinxiamen@xmu.edu.cn

Abstract. Traditional Wooden Carving in Quanzhou, China is a National Intangible Cultural Heritage (ICH), which was established in Tang Dynasty (AD 686), and has a history of more than a thousand years. It is a narrative presentation of the life, culture and other daily respects of the people in southern Fujian province. The project focuses on the Wooden Carving Window Decoration in Southern Fujian Ancient Building, by using AI technology to extract features of the landscape, figures and various types of rare, exotic creatures in wooden carvings, their digital 3D models can be generated and presented, a comprehensive database of elements of wooden window carving can also be built. Furthermore, the human–computer interaction is supported by hand gesture recognition technology, allowing participants creatively design their own contemporary digitalized wood window carving. This project expects the interactive and narrative features of the digital wooden window carving model can trigger a deeper sense of identification with the traditional southern Fujian culture among the young generation and erase the distant feeling towards traditional ICH culture spatially and temporally. Moreover, it could also provide a new way of thinking for the innovative inheritance of ICH.

Keywords: Digital wooden carving window · ICH · Interaction design · Interactive visual narrative

1 Introduction

The United Nations Educational, Scientific and Cultural Organization (UNESCO) promulgated the Convention for the Safeguarding of the Intangible Cultural Heritage in 2003 [1] to save ICH from "McDonaldization" [2] and reduce the negative impact on cultural diversity.

Many scholars have explored different perspectives on the preservation, dissemination and innovative transmission of ICH digitized by combining digital technology. For example, by adopting Gesture mapping technology and Real-time sand simulation technology [3], the work, Sand Canvas, simplified the creation process of sand painting ICH. Additionally, the work, 4D viewer, on the other hand, by abstracting performance data into multi-dimensional symbols [4], improved the capture and analysis of ICH in three-dimensional and temporal respects. Furthermore, the work, Terpsichore,

C. Stephanidis et al. (Eds.): HCII 2024, CCIS 2116, pp. 343–353, 2024.
https://doi.org/10.1007/978-3-031-61950-2_38

employed photogrammetry and Computer Vision technology to digitally model and further choreograph folk dance, such visualization of folk dance enables the preservation and presentation of ICH [5].

These works provided inspiration for our project. The project followed the workflow of "Digital archiving and preservation - Database creation - Participant-oriented transformation". Firstly, the traditional wooden carving window narrative themes in the ancient building in southern Fujian was categorized. Secondly, feature extraction and generation of a database of new wooden carving window patterns was created by AI technology. On this basis, by closely participating the interaction between technology, participants can design wooden carving window personally with a new visual narrative in the form of autonomous interactive creation, thus, the sense of distance and disconnection from the participants for the ICH can be erased spatially and temporally [6].

2   Relevant Information: Background and Motivation

Wooden Carving Window Decoration in Southern Fujian Ancient Building is a highly narrative condensation of local cultural life, religion and other daily respects, which delicately combined the practicality and aesthetics, and carries the local customs and historical memories of people in southern Fujian. In the early stage of the project, we conducted field research on several ancient building in southern Fujian province and took a vast number of pictures, which provided samples for the characterization of the wooden carving window patterns. At the same time, we found that the wooden carving window decorations in the ancient building are strongly characterized locally, and the folk artists in different periods reflected the local life scenes through this form of visualized narratives. As a result, this special art forms, which have been forgotten by modern people, have attracted our attention.

The protection of traditional wooden carving ICH, not only need to inherit, but also need to keep pace with the times of innovation. Consequently, we propose that, in order to preserve its unique cultural genetic characteristics [7], by feature extraction and evolutionary analysis, the big data model, mid journey, became a qualified choice to create digital wooden carvings with different contemporary living contexts.

I   II   III

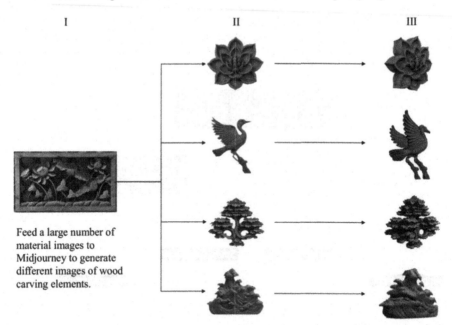

Feed a large number of
material images to
Midjourney to generate
different images of wood
carving elements.

Using AI to turn images into 3D models.

Fig. 1. Flowchart for digitizing ICH Wooden Carving Window Decoration.

3 Our Approach

3.1 Design Concept and Technical Realisation

Under the guiding principle of "Preservation, Inheritance and Innovation", the project aims to effectively preserve and disseminate ICH by digitally constructing a contemporary interactive visual narrative with the aesthetics of traditional intangible cultural heritage. The project is committed to maximising the innovative inheritance of traditional Chinese wooden carvings by digital means through the efforts of multiple parties (wood carvers, wood carving businessmen, and the general public).

During the process of design, a large number of existing traditional wooden carvings are used to provide raw materials for the AI big data model; virtual 3D digitised wooden carving materials of different styles and contents are generated through the training of the AI model, and all kinds of wooden carving data are structurally annotated; a relational wooden carving database is formed by the accumulation of virtual wooden carving materials as shown in Fig. 1.

The database also contains a large number of photos of wooden carving objects, design drawings, process descriptions, etc. In the management of the database, image recognition, natural language processing and other technologies are used to achieve intelligence, which provided support for querying, analysing and restoring wooden carving data. Based on the big data model, the quantitative analysis of wooden carving window techniques is carried out to explore its inherent cultural characteristics and evolutionary laws, and to formulate protection and inheritance strategies based on the data.

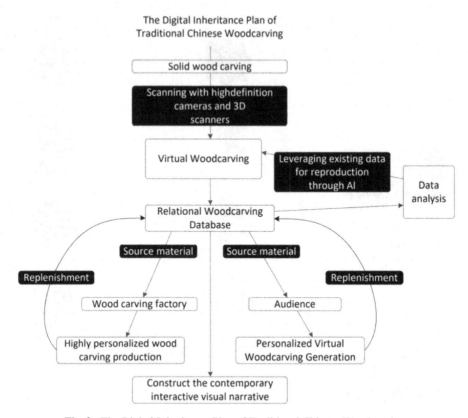

The Digital Inheritance Plan of
Traditional Chinese Woodcarving

Solid wood carving

Scanning with highdefinition
cameras and 3D
scanners

Virtual Woodcarving

Leveraging existing data
for reproduction
through AI

Data
analysis

Relational Woodcarving
Database

Source material   Source material

Replenishment   Replenishment

Wood carving factory   Audience

Highly personalized wood
carving production

Personalized Virtual
Woodcarving Generation

Construct the contemporary
interactive visual narrative

Fig. 2. The Digital Inheritance Plan of Traditional Chinese Woodcarving.

The project encouraged participants to upload images of contemporary life, and based on the cultural characteristics of the wooden carving window flowers extracted from the existing samples, the style transformation is achieved by relying on the big data model. Participants can creatively design their own contemporary digital wooden carvings based on their own life experiences. Thereby, elements that combine both traditional wooden carving cultural features and contemporary visual narratives are continuously inputted into the database.

The database is the basis of the project, providing material for the wooden carving factory and the gesture interaction system for the general public. With the help of the database, the wooden carving factory will be able to design and produce highly personalised wooden carvings; the richness and playfulness of the gesture-based interactive system will be increased; and users will be guided to enrich the database with elements of contemporary life scenes. Ultimately, a contemporary interactive visual narrative is constructed to make the project design concept a reality. Figure 2 illustrates the full flow of the project programme.

3.2 Interaction Design Forms

The gesture interaction system developed in this project allows the user to select the style and pattern of the wooden carving from the database through gesture operation as shown in Fig. 3, and generate personalised designs in real time, as shown in Fig. 4. The interactive approach breaks the threshold of wooden carving creation, enables the public to deeply experience and participate in the creation of ICH culture, transforms the user into a designer, and stimulates their enthusiasm for participation.

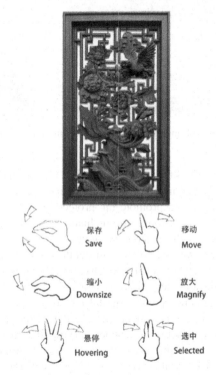

Fig. 3. Gesture maps for interactive installation.

In the study of traditional Chinese wooden carvings, we have noticed that the wooden carvings of each period were characterised by the era in which they were made. For example, the wooden carvings of the Ming Dynasty were renowned for their grandeur and magnificence, fine carving, and mostly used for the decoration of palaces, temples and monasteries, etc.; In the Qing Dynasty, wooden carving placed more attention to the delicate performance and exquisite carving skills, often used storyline and characters as themes to express a strong traditional cultural atmosphere; and modern wooden carvings are integrated with modern aesthetics and innovative elements on the basis of the traditional skills, which present more diversified and personalised characteristics.

Based on this discovery, we can use digital means to simulate and reproduce wooden carvings from different periods, and generate virtual wooden carving materials with

Fig. 4. A user experiencing real-time generation of a personalised design.

specific epochal characteristics through training of AI big data models. Such an initiative can enable the public to better understand and appreciate the art of wooden carving from different historical periods, and promote the protection and inheritance of traditional wooden carving. In addition, through the inclusion and intelligent management of a large number of data such as physical photographs of wooden carvings, design drawings and process descriptions, we can conduct in-depth research on the intrinsic cultural characteristics and evolutionary laws of wooden carving window techniques, and provide scientific basis for the development of protection and inheritance strategies.

In short, through the application of digital means, we can better protect, pass on and innovate traditional Chinese wooden carving ICH. From providing materials and supporting personalised production in wooden carving factories, to enriching the functionality of the gesture-based interactive system, to guiding participants to construct interactive visual narratives on their own, this project will inject new vitality into the dissemination and development of wooden carving culture (Figs. 5 and 6).

Fig. 5. Exhibition process: participants' interaction with the interactive installation.

Fig. 6. Exhibition process: participants' interaction with the interactive installation.

4 Results

4.1 Assessment Collection by Visitors

During the exhibition, we conducted an on-site questionnaire survey to participants who were willing to be accept observation and interviews to better evaluate the innovative aspects of the project and the results of the interactive translation. The survey questionnaire used an ordinal scale, and respondents chose among the following five options based on their level of agreement with each statement: strongly disagree, disagree, neutral, agree, and strongly agree. Based on the choices of the respondents, we transformed each of these five values into five standardised values of 0, 1, 2, 3, and 4 in turn. Respondents were authorised to comment on the statements or provide additional information. We eventually collected 52 responses to the questionnaire. Questions included:

1. Do you agree that the gesture interaction of the installation does not require additional knowledge and skills?
2. Do you think you can quickly learn how to interact with this installation?
3. Were the instructions for the interactive installation easy to understand?
4. Did the interactive installation provide enough feedback and guidance during the interaction so that you understood how to interact effectively?
5. Can the ICH + Interactive model of the project generate revenue or value-added services for commercial activities?
6. Can the project reduce costs and increase the commercial profitability of the wooden carving industry?
7. Is the installation innovative in combining wooden carving Window Decoration with interactive installation?
8. Does the installation introduce new technologies, designs and concepts, or bring new experiences to the user?
9. Does the project have traditional aesthetics in the wooden carving Window Decoration pattern, and is it able to better pass on and protect the Wooden Carving Window Decoration Intangible Cultural Heritage?
10. Does the project focus on the unique cultural value of Wooden Carving Window Decorations in terms of design and functionality, and inject new ways of expression and experience into it?

4.2 Results and Discussion

We visually documented the questionnaire results with mean bar charts to illustrate the perceptions of different respondents on the interactive experience of the project and the value of the project. Higher mean values of the questions indicate a higher level of recognition by participants.

The questions were arranged in a sequential order, with every two questions being an assessment dimension, and were divided into five groups: I. Ease of interaction assessment, II. Interaction guidance assessment, III. Business value assessment, IV. Innovation value assessment, V. Cultural value assessment (Table 1).

Table 1. Bar charts: statistics on the average number of answers to each question in the questionnaire results.

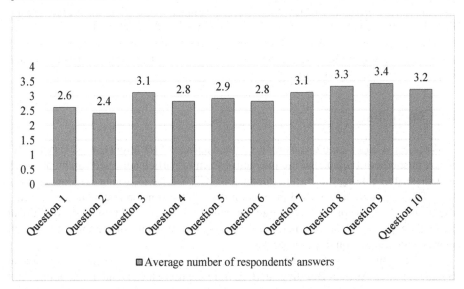

Firstly, in the three groups of data on the assessment of value, the mean value of all questions did not fall below 2.8 (above the middle of the "neutral" and "agree" ranges), and the group of respondents was generally positive about the three values of the project. Groups V and IV have higher mean values, while Groups II and III have medium mean values. In descending order of general agreement among the respondent groups, the values were: cultural value, innovation value, interaction description, and commercial value. Group I, which represents the ease of interaction, has the lowest mean value, but its mean value is 2.5, which is in the middle of the range between "Neutral" and "Agree". Question 2 received the lowest mean score of all the questions, with some viewers adding that the interactive installation was limited by light intensity, distance, and other factors. Respondents' ratings of the ease of interaction tended to be slightly in favour overall, but there is still more room for improvement.

Collectively, the respondent population fell into four categories: ICH researchers, business people, children and parents. The majority of respondents felt that the project had a very positive effect. For example, ICH researchers believed that the database format is conducive to ICH restoration and research; Business people were concerned about the project's strong commercial conversion value, as the personalised Wooden Carving Window Decoration can be used for customised services; Parents accompanying their children to visit the project recognised the educational value of the interactive installation for ICH; A number of children were interested in the interactive and fun aspects of the project.

In addition, a small number of interviewees suggested that the light and darkness of the light affected the speed of gesture recognition; while some of the younger children had difficulty in recognition due to their skeleton being much smaller than the recognition model, and the sensitivity of gesture recognition needs to be improved.

Overall, respondents gave positive feedback in terms of digital archiving and narrative translation of wooden carving motifs of contemporary life scenes. Further technical improvements will be made to address the issue of gesture recognition sensitivity.

5   Conclusion

This project is based on the construction of a database of traditional wood carving elements in southern Fujian, and the interactive form of participants' self-creation, which is dedicated to solving the current dilemma of ICH Wooden Carving Window Decoration. The intervention of virtual interaction reduces the time and economic cost of the experience. In terms of interactive transformation for the general public, the traditional aesthetic experience, the fun, narrative and easy-to-use nature of the interaction, well enhance the immersion of participants.

In the future, we will further focus on Wooden Carving Window Decoration in Southern Fujian Ancient Building, starting from the user side and adopting online APP development to improve the project, in order to attract more young people to take the initiative to participate in the inheritance of ICH and extend the vitality of Wooden Carving Window Decoration ICH.

References

1. UNESCO Intangible Cultural Heritage. Text of the Convention for the Safeguarding of the Intangible Cultural Heritage. https://ich.unesco.org/en/convention. Accessed 10 July 2023
2. George, R.: McDonaldization of Society. SAGE Publications, Carytown (2020)
3. Kazi, R.H., Chua, K.C., Zhao, S., Davis, R., Low, K.L.: SandCanvas: a multi-touch art medium inspired by sand animation. In: CHI 2011: CHI Conference on Human Factors in Computing Systems, SIGCHI, p. 483. Association for Computing Machinery, New York (2011). https://doi.org/10.1145/1979742.1979562. Accessed 15 July 2023
4. Doulamis, N., Doulamis, A., Ioannidis, C., Klein, M., Ioannides, M.: Modelling of static and moving objects: digitizing tangible and intangible cultural heritage. In: Ioannides, M., Magnenat-Thalmann, N., Papagiannakis, G. (eds.) Mixed Reality and Gamification for Cultural Heritage. Springer, Cham (2017). https://doi.org/10.1007/978-3-319-49607-8_23. Accessed 18 July 2023
5. Doulamis, A.D., Voulodimos, A., Doulamis, N.D., Soile, S., & Lampropoulos, A.: transforming intangible folkloric performing arts into tangible choreographic digital objects: the terpsichore approach. In: Imai, F., Tremeau, A., Braz, J. (eds.) Proceedings of the 12th International Joint Conference on Computer Vision, Imaging and Computer Graphics Theory and Applications, VISIGRAPP, vol. 5, pp.451–460. SCITEPRESS, Porto (2017). https://doi.org/10.5220/000634 7304510460. Accessed 22 July 2023

6. Wang, K., Chen, H.: Media use and thinking in the context of globalization. J. News Res. **10**(22), 144–145 (2019)
7. Li, M., Wang, Y., Xu, Y.-Q.: Computing for Chinese cultural heritage. Vis. Inf. **6**(01), 1–13 (2022)

Research on the Application of Shangri-La Regional Color Extraction in the Design of Cultural and Creative Products

Xingqiao Yang, Ren Long[⊠], Tianyue Zhang, Xiaoran Yang, and Wanlin Yang

Huazhong University of Science and Technology, Wuhan 430074, Hubei, China
longren@hust.edu.cn

Abstract. The regional colors of Shangri-La in China have high representativeness and research value. This study aims to explore the regional color extraction method using the K-means++ clustering algorithm for the extraction of Shangri-La regional colors and apply the extracted colors to the design practice of Shangri-La cultural and creative products.

The study includes: selecting representative pictures as data samples; using the K-means++ clustering algorithm to carry out scientific color extraction, outputting a network model of Shangri-La's regional colors, a standard master color card, and a color matching design guideline, etc., and completing the design practice; and collecting users' evaluations through questionnaire surveys and quantifying the results by using a five-level Likert scale. The results show that the color extracted based on the K-means++ algorithm is very characteristic, and its application to cultural and creative product design can reflect the cultural characteristics of Shangri-La and have a good color-matching effect.

Keywords: Shangri-La regional color extraction · K-means++ algorithm · cultural and creative product design

1 Introduction

Regional color refers to the relatively stable color style and aesthetic concepts that have been formed over a long period in a certain region under the joint effect of natural climate, geographic environment, and cultural traditions [1]. A region from food, clothing, housing, and transportation, to folklore, all show differences in color and uniqueness so that the color has accumulated as a sign and symbol of regional culture. Regional color fusion of regional history, folk culture, and human characteristics of the typical color, can intuitively represent the regional characteristics, reflecting the regional culture. French colorist Jean-Philippe Lenclose first confirmed through a large number of field investigations, the geographical environment will directly affect the human race, race, customs, culture, art, and other aspects of the shaping and development of a regional color, and local geography, history, culture, customs and other inextricably linked to the complexity of the link [2].

C. Stephanidis et al. (Eds.): HCII 2024, CCIS 2116, pp. 354–364, 2024.
https://doi.org/10.1007/978-3-031-61950-2_39

Cultural and creative products highlight cultural confidence and cultural soft power, although there are many cultural and creative products in the market that are loved by consumers, there is still the blind pursuit of economic benefits when developing and designing cultural and creative products, lack of excavation of regional culture, and copying of design innovation points, which leads to the lack of cultural connotation of some cultural and creative products, and the problems of homogenization, symbolization, and blindness.

Designers can extract the corresponding regional cultural elements from the abstract culture with regional characteristics and apply them to the shape, material, and process, to design cultural and creative products reflecting the local regional culture. Regional cultural and creative products using regional colors are richer in regional character-istics and regional cultural connotations, and extracting regional colors and applying them to regional cultural and creative products can be a solution to the problems of homogenization and low connotations of regional cultural and creative products.

2 Overview of Color Extraction Methods

2.1 Primary Color Extraction Algorithm

The primary color system of an image reflects the distribution of the main colors in the image, which directly affects the overall impression that the image brings to people. Several methods have been proposed for primary color extraction, such as the color histogram method, which calculates the proportion of colors in an image to find the main color of the image. Zhu Zhenyang et al. proposed a histogram peak screening and rejection algorithm for main color extraction based on the analysis of the meaning of the main color features for the problems of misdetection and omission as well as the requirement of a fixed number of main colors in the color histogram method; Tian Shaoxu et al. [3] proposed the method of color image coordinates, which summarizes the hue and color imagery of the image through the construction of the color spatial coordinate system; the clustering algorithm is a method for a statistical analysis method to study the classification problem (of samples or indicators), and also an important algorithm for data mining [4], which can quickly and automatically extract the characteristic colors of an image, and has a natural advantage in the extraction of the main color of an image. Wang Fen et al. [5] based on mean drift clustering algorithm to extract the main color of Chinese traditional dress images, and obtained a more accurate main color.

The current mainstream clustering algorithms are K-means, DBSCAN, mean drift clustering, and hierarchical clustering algorithms. Among them, K-means is a classic and widely cited clustering algorithm, simple and efficient, fast convergence; DBSCAN and mean drift clustering are density-based clustering algorithms, which do not need to define the number of categories in advance, and at the same time can adapt to clusters of different shapes and sizes [6], but do not apply to high-dimensional data, and are com-putationally large and time-consuming for larger feature spaces; hierarchical clustering algorithms have distances and similarity of rules are easy to define, less restrictive, can find the hierarchical relationship of categories, but easy to cluster into chains, and the computational complexity is high. In summary, this paper chooses the K-means cluster-ing algorithm, and to reduce the sensitivity of the clustering results to the selection of the initial clustering center [7], the K-means++ algorithm that improves the initialization of the clustering center is used for the extraction of the main color of the image.

2.2 K-means++ Algorithmic Principle

means++ is calculated as follows:

Determine the Initial Clustering Centre

1. One sample is randomly selected from the dataset X (with a total of N samples) as the first initial clustering centre C1.
2. Calculate the shortest distance D(x) between the remaining samples and the currently existing cluster centers, calculate the probability P(x) that each sample point will be selected as the next cluster center, and finally select the sample point corresponding to the maximum probability value as the next cluster center:

$$P(x) = \frac{D(x)^2}{\sum_{x \in X} D(x)^2} \tag{1}$$

3. Repeat 2) until K clustering centers Ci are selected (i = 1,2...K).

Iterative Updates

1. The Euclidean distance of the remaining N-K sample points from each initial cluster center is calculated and they are assigned to the category in which the nearest cluster center is located. The distance is calculated using the following formula:

   Displayed equations are centered and set on a separate line.

$$d(x_i, g_K) = \sum_{j=1}^{n} \left(x_i^j - g_k^j \right)^2 \tag{2}$$

where denotes the clustering centre and j denotes the data dimension

2. Calculate the mean of all the data in each category on each dimension and then use these K means as new cluster centers.
2. Repeat 1) - 2) until the newly generated cluster centers no longer change or are smaller than a specific threshold.

3 Shangri-La Regional Colour Extraction and Application Guide

3.1 Establishment of the Shangri-La Regional Colour Atlas

Shangri-La, formerly known as Zhongdian County, is known by the Tibetan name "Jie Tang", which first appeared in the Tang Dynasty in Fan Chuo's "Yunnan Zhi-Name Class" as "Jian Yan". The natural geography of Shangri-La brings together snowy peaks, glaciers, canyons, lakes, waterfalls, rivers, etc., and the humanistic features include the ancient city, temples, villages, and other buildings, as well as the Tibetan and Buddhist cultures with a long history and rich heritage. Photo collection of Shangri-La. The natural landscape and humanistic architectural landscape are selected from different attractions in Shangri-La, while the humanistic features are based on the Tangka of Shangri-La.

To ensure the objectivity of the picture selection, the attractions were selected concerning the popularity ranking of Shangri-La tourist attractions on the official website of Ctrip Travel, and the top 10 natural attractions and the top 6 humanistic attractions were selected. We screened and removed images that did not meet the requirements, such as overly cluttered scenes, obvious traces of post-processing, unclear color intention, and rich light and shadow effects, and finally selected 68 natural landscape images, 45 humanities landscape images, and 45 Shangri-La thangkas, for a total of 158 images as the source of data analysis. To ensure the authenticity and clarity of the images, necessary adjustments are made to the images, such as removing watermarks, adjusting the clarity, and restoring the real colors. See Fig. 1 for the color gallery of the Shangri-La region.

Fig. 1. Shangri-La Regional Colour Gallery.

3.2 Color Clustering Extraction for Single Images

Firstly the single image is clustered using the K-means++ algorithm to get the extracted colour. Usually, available spatial models are RGB color space, HIS color space, HSV color space Lab color space, etc. Different color spaces have their advantages and disadvantages. Except for the RGB space, all the other spaces require spatial conversion calculations, which are more complicated. HIS color space and HSV color space cannot directly perform K-means clustering, and need to coordinate the relationship between the three components, i.e., redefine the distance function; Lab space is also complicated in the conversion process [8], and is generally applicable as a judgment condition for image segmentation.RGB color space is the most The RGB color space is the most commonly used color space, which has the advantages of uniform distribution, easy calculate of the distance, and effectively and intuitively reflecting the degree of similarity of the colors, therefore, this paper adopts the RGB color space for clustering analysis.

For the extraction of the main color of a single image, through several experiments and comparisons, when the number of clusters is 8, the extracted color is close to the best effect and the degree of differentiation is high, so the number of clustering categories set in the process of single-image color extraction is K = 8. Taking the image of the Yila Grassland in the natural landscape of Shangri-La as an example, the results of the color extraction of a single image are shown in Fig. 2.

Fig. 2. Single image color clustering extraction results

3.3 Colour Clustering Extraction for Batch Images

After separate color extraction for each image in the color gallery, color block fusion is performed to obtain the fused image, and the K-means++ algorithm is again used for the final primary color extraction. The schematic diagram of color block fusion for the natural landscape, humanistic landscape, and Tangka of Shangri-La is shown in Fig. 3. Through many experimental comparisons when the final number of extracted primary colors is 12, the results obtained have a better representation and can well reflect the color imagery of different landscapes, so the number of clustering categories set by the secondary K-means++ algorithm is K = 12, and the final results of the primary color extraction of the different landscapes and the accounted for as shown in Fig. 4.

Fig. 3. Schematic diagram of color block integration (a) Natural landscape (b) Human landscape (c) Thangka.

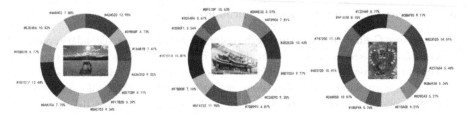

Fig. 4. Extraction results and percentage of different landscape (Nature, Humanities, Thangka) dominant colors.

3.4 Construction of Shangri-La Regional Colour Network Model

After extracting the main colors of different landscapes, it is also necessary to obtain the collocation relationship between different main colors, i.e. which main colors often appear in the same image at the same time. Therefore, it is necessary to draw a color network model to show the collocation relationship between different primary colors in a concrete image, to assist designers in color matching and application.

The color network model constructed for different landscapes is shown in Fig. 5, in which the 12 dots indicate the 12 main colors extracted, the size of the dots indicates the size of the proportion of the main colors, and the connecting lines between the different dots indicate that there is a high-frequency co-occurrence relationship between the two colors in a single image. The method of determining the co-occurrence relationship is as follows: count the frequency of any two colors appearing in all the images of the color gallery, set the co-occurrence threshold, when the co-occurrence frequency of the two colors is higher than the threshold, determine that the two colors are co-occurring, and connect the corresponding dots two by two. At the same time, the set threshold can not be too high or too low, the threshold is too high will make the number of co-linear colors small, the color matching is single, and the threshold is too low will make the co-occurring colors complicated, and it is difficult to get a representative color matching scheme. After several experiments and comparisons, when the co-occurrence threshold of Shangri-La's natural and humanistic landscapes is set to 0.25, and the co-occurrence threshold of Shangri-La's Thangka landscape is set to 0.2, the structure of the color network model is more optimal.

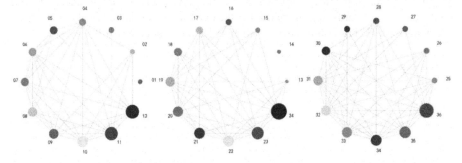

Fig. 5. Network model of different landscapes (Nature, Humanities, Thangka) colors

3.5   Shangri-La Regional Colour Application Strategy

Color Design Guide.   When designing the color, the primary color, secondary color, and accent color are used as the most basic division of the color function [9]. To reproduce Shangri-La's regional color intention as much as possible, the development of the color scheme was carried out based on the color network model and HSB color analysis, and the color network model mainly assisted the color scheme design in the selection of primary and secondary colors [10].

The guidelines for constructing the color scheme design are as follows: ① Primary color selection. The main color is the iconic color and the main color of the picture, which determines the style and cultural direction of the whole work as well as the first sensory impression. The color with the largest proportion and the highest frequency is the best choice for the main color, and the selection of the main color can be based on the priority of proportion or the frequency of occurrence [11]. Secondary color selection. Auxiliary colors are mainly used as secondary colors or background colors of the screen. In the color network model, auxiliary color selection is generally determined after the primary color, auxiliary color should have a connection with the primary color, and auxiliary color is more than two, the primary color and auxiliary color nodes can form a complete network. (iii) Embellishment color selection. Embellishments are mainly used to highlight the main color, usually jumping colors, small areas, and the number of times. The accent color is usually chosen to be in greater contrast with the primary and secondary colors.

Matching Color Card Construction.   Concerning the above color matching strategies, 6 color schemes were selected from the 3 established color network models, and for each color scheme, 4 interrelated colors were selected as the primary and secondary colors, as well as 1 smaller color as the accent color. The final 6 color schemes selected were: color scheme 1–11, 07, 06, 04, 01 (Fig. 6), color scheme 2–09, 08, 06, 05, 02 (Fig. 6), color scheme 3–23, 22, 19, 18, 13 (Fig. 6), color scheme 4–24, 20, 19, 18, 13 (Fig. 6), color scheme 5–36, 33, 32, 28, 27 (Fig. 6), color scheme 6–35, 32, 31, 26 (Fig. 6).

As the color scheme colors do not have obvious light and dark variations and are not necessarily suitable for picture color matching, the colors are extended by adjusting the color scale variations to form three light and dark dimensions of light, grey, and dark to provide picture light and dark and level variations. The light side extension adjusts the grey scale factor to 1.6, and the dark side extension adjusts the grey scale factor to 0.6, which finally forms the three color scales of light, grey, and dark, and produces a total of six 15-color color cards, which are used as the color cards for the regional color scheme of Shangri-La. Figure 7 shows the six Shangri-La regional color cards.

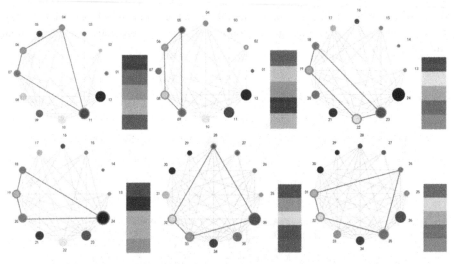

Fig. 6. Color scheme 1–6.

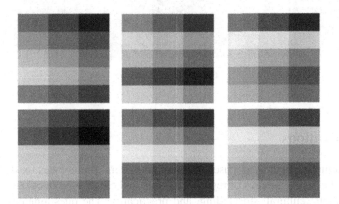

Fig. 7. Shangri-La Regional Color Palette.

4 Shangri-La Regional Cultural and Creative Design Practice Based on Regional Color Extraction

The composition of the main image is based on the "split composition" of Shangri-La's thangka, and the design is based on the concept of combining thangka with trendy elements. In the main visual, the main statue depicted in the center of the thangka is still retained, and the features of the thangka, such as the large earlobes and accessories with Buddhist characteristics, are extracted. Around the main venerable figure, we design patterns and motifs with cultural characteristics, and the motifs are mainly distributed on the left and right sides of the main venerable figure in the form of axial symmetry, to achieve the symmetrical aesthetics of balance and stability in the visual sense. To better reflect the characteristics of Guochao's cultural and creative products, the process of assigning colors to the line drawings is mainly based on solid color block filling. Using the six groups of Shangri-La regional color cards from the previous chapter, the final effect is shown in Fig. 8.

Fig. 8. Color scheme

5   Deliberations

The questionnaire method was used to investigate users' preferences for different color schemes. The characteristics of regional cultural and creative products are summarised as three points: cultural, storytelling, and practicality. The questionnaire is set up to provide three evaluation modules and is quantified using a five-level Likert scale, with five levels corresponding to the scores of "5, 4, 3, 2, 1".

A total of 89 valid questionnaires were received, and the analysis shows that: (1) the basic information of the participants in the questionnaire research: 35 men, accounting for 39.33%; 54 women, accounting for 39.81%. The age of the respondents is mainly distributed 18–40 years old, a total of 80 people, accounting for 89.89%. (2) Distribution of fondness of color schemes: the average score of all color schemes in the cultural module is 3.67, which can better reflect the regional humanities of Shangri-La; in the storytelling module, the average score of all schemes is 3.83, which indicates that the color schemes have commemorative value and have successfully conveyed some cultural information to the consumers; in the practicality, the average score of the six schemes is 3.67, which indicates that the color schemes can be integrated into the life by the consumers. In terms of practicality, the average score of the six schemes is 3.67, indicating that the color schemes can be integrated into life and used by people. Option 3 (Fig. 9) received the highest rating, with an average score of 7.56.

Fig. 9. Top-rated color schemes.

The results show that the regional cultural creations produced through this study have high ratings in terms of culture, storytelling, and practicality, and can conform to a certain extent to the user's impression of the Shangri-La region; the colors extracted based on the clustering algorithm can represent the colors of the majority of the consumers' impression of the Shangri-La region, and they have good results in application. The study provides a methodological reference for the extraction and application of representative colors of regional culture. The color scheme that is more popular among young people, i.e. Scheme III, is used for design application practice. The application effect is shown in Fig. 10.

Fig. 10. Application effect demonstration.

6 Conclude

This paper proposes a regional color extraction method based on the k-means++ clustering algorithm, which extracts the characteristic colors and constructs the color network model for the regional colors of Shangri-La, and discovers the color ratios and neighboring relationships in a scientific way, to assist the designers in designing, improve the efficiency of the designers' work efficiency in matching the colors, and accurately reflect the regional cultural intention of Shangri-La. The regional color extraction scheme and color clustering method proposed in this study can be applied to the extraction and application of other regional cultural color factors, which has a certain degree of universality.

There are still some shortcomings in the study: firstly, there are limitations in the understanding of Shangri-La, and there may be the problem of poor sample representativeness in the Shangri-La color gallery; secondly, the clustering thresholds are mainly set for the subjective assessment and setting of the viewing effect, and there are certain errors, which will have some impact on the stability and authenticity of the color network construction; finally, the five Chinese geographical regions have a close relationship with the five traditional Chinese colors, and the present Finally, the five regions of China have a close relationship with the five traditional Chinese colors, and this study only takes the region of Shangri-La in Yunnan as an example, and fails to conduct a comparative study on the cultures and colors of the five typical regions of China. A follow-up study will be conducted to address the above issues.

References

1. Li, Y., Yan, Q.: Regional color extraction and design application based on visual saliency. Packa. Eng. **42**(16), 219–225+230 (2021).https://doi.org/10.19554/j.cnki.1001-3563.2021. 16.030
2. Yanhui, W., Xinyan, Z., Shuqi, Y.: Color geography theory and its development in China. Tropical Geogr. (2010)
3. Shao-Xu, T., Li-Jun, X.U.: Comparison between China's and Japan's color culture: the color image based on national mentality. J. Shenzhen Univ. (Human. Soc. Sci.) (2015)
4. Wei-Ben, Z., Yue-Xiang, S.: Optimization algorithm of K-means clustering center of selection based on density. Appl. Res. Comput. **29**(5), 1726–1728 (2012)
5. Wang, F., Huang, L.: Application of mean shift clustering method in traditional clothing image extraction. Wool Text. J. **50**(04), 89–95 (2022). https://doi.org/10.19333/j.mfkj.20210703107
6. Jie, Z., Liu, Y.: The improvement and implementation of dBscan clustering algorithm. Microelectron. Comput. (2009). https://doi.org/10.1360/972009-1549
7. Lin, Z., Yan, C., Ye, J.I., et al.: Research on K-means algorithm based on density. Appl. Res. Comput. **28**(11), 4063–4071 (2011). https://doi.org/10.1007/s00466-010-0527-8
8. Ming-Mei, L.: Color image segmentation based on region saliency. Electron. Des. Eng. (2013)
9. Liang, J.: The Color Book for Everyone 1: The Basic Knowledge for Color Matching of Design. Posts & Telecom Press, Beijing (2018)
10. Liu, X., Cao, Y., Zhao, L.: Color networks of traditional cultural patterns and color design aiding technology. Comput. Integr. Manuf. Syst. **22**(04), 899–907 (2016). https://doi.org/10. 13196/j.cims.2016.04.003
11. Qiu, Z., Zhou, C., Zhan, X., Jia, H., Kang, M.: The color design of the Italian sofa based on the HSB color model. Furniture **41**(03), 41–45 (2020). https://doi.org/10.16610/j.cnki.jiaju. 2020.03.010

Design of NiNiGou Cultural and Creative Products Based on KANO-AHP-QFD

LiJia Yun[✉]

Fuzhou University, Fuzhou 361021, Fujian, China
1433808375@qq.com

Abstract. To promote the innovative inheritance of China's national intangible cultural heritage - HuaiYang NiNiGou and improve user satisfaction with NiNiGou cultural and creative products, we design a NiNiGou's cultural and creative product that can meet user needs. Firstly, through research, user's needs for NiNiGou's cultural and creative products are discovered and divided into three latitudes: vision, function, and emotion. The Kano model is used to attribute the user's needs and screen out the key user needs, then use the AHP method to calculate the weight value of each requirement. Finally, use QFD theory combined with expert opinions to map user demand information into specific design elements and sort them according to their importance. According to the design elements, the design practice of an interactive NiNiGou book that meets the needs of users is completed. The research method combined with Kano-AHP-QFD can accurately and effectively obtain user needs, and the designed NiNiGou cultural and creative products are more scientific and reasonable, providing new ideas for the innovative development of NiNiGou. For other intangible cultural heritage products Innovative design research also has certain reference significance.

Keywords: Intangible Heritage Preservation · HuaiYang NiNiGou · Cultural and Creative Product Design · User Need · KANO · AHP · QFD

1 Introduction to KANO-AHP-QFD Method

Huaiyang NiNiGou is China's national intangible cultural heritage and the only oldest artistic variety among mud toys in the world today [1]. However, its material and product presentation are very different from contemporary people's living habits and consumption methods. Through cultural and creative product design, the modern transformation of NiNiGou culture can be realized, giving it greater space for survival and development. Due to the complexity of consumer culture and social life, people's demand for cultural and creative products has shown characteristics such as blurring and diversification. Identifying the structural characteristics of the audience is a necessary path for the success of NiNiGou's cultural and creative product design. Therefore, this study starts from the perspective of user needs and conducts research on the design of NiNiGou's cultural and creative products. KANO model, AHP analytic hierarchy process, and QFD quality function are used to systematically explore the user satisfaction and design element importance of mud dog cultural and creative products and obtain the design scheme of NiNiGou's cultural and creative products.

C. Stephanidis et al. (Eds.): HCII 2024, CCIS 2116, pp. 365–377, 2024.
https://doi.org/10.1007/978-3-031-61950-2_40

The three methods of KANO-AHP-QFD each have their own strengths, but they also have their own limitations. The KANO model is an important method for initially establishing user needs [2], which can effectively find the relationship between various user needs and satisfaction with cultural and creative products but cannot clearly present the weights of these needs. Using the AHP method to calculate the importance of various demand indicators can further improve the accuracy of demand weights [3, 4]. However, KANO and AHP methods cannot provide clear design standards for how user needs can be realized in cultural and creative products. The use of QFD theory characterized by quantitative analysis can output user demand information as design parameters [5]. The combination of KANO-AHP-QFD method can more accurately solve the key needs of users of NiNiGou cultural and creative products compared to traditional design and research methods, making design decisions more efficient.

Zhongyi Lev et al. [6] used the Kano-AHP-QFD method to establish an innovative design scheme for a reasonable and easy-to-use fruit logistics turnover box based on user needs; Shijian Cang et al. [7]. Proposed a hybrid model based on KANO-AHP-TOPSI and completed a design scheme superior to the existing packaging of clay figurine Zhang; Wei Qiang [8] established the KANO model and QFD quality house based on user travel maps, providing methodological guidance for the interaction design of new energy vehicles on the mobile end; Hongyu Zhou et al. [9] used KANO and QFD methods to clarify design requirements, guide design implementation, and combined with PUGH evaluation method to comprehensively evaluate the design scheme to obtain the optimal design scheme. Many scholars in the current academic research of product design have used KANO, AHP, and QFD methods for product development and improvement, which can effectively adapt to market demand and improve user satisfaction. The application of these three methods in the development of NiNiGou's cultural and creative product design has high feasibility. Please note that the first paragraph of a section or subsection is not indented. The first paragraphs that follows a table, figure, equation etc. does not have an indent, either.

2 Construction of Design Process for NiNiGou Cultural and Creative Products Based on Kano-AHP-QFD

Under the user demand driven design pattern of cultural and creative products, the research method of KANO-AHP-QFD integration can accurately obtain the user needs of NiNiGou cultural and creative products, and further quantify them into design requirements. The overall process framework is shown in Fig. 1.

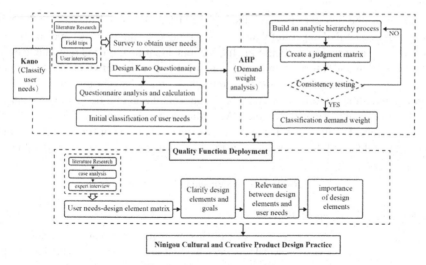

Fig. 1. Research Framework.

3 User Demand Analysis of NiNiGou Cultural and Creative Products Based on KANO

3.1 KANO Model

Consumer demand for products has characteristics such as subjectivity, differentiation, fuzziness, and versatility, and classifying user needs is the core function of the KANO model [6, 10]. The five levels of user demand types are: essential demand M, which refers to the product design elements that users consider essential; Expected demand O refers to the design elements that users hope NiNiGou cultural and creative products can possess; Charm requirement A refers to design elements that exceed user expectations. When these requirements are met, user satisfaction will greatly increase; Undifferentiated demand I, regardless of whether this type of demand has been experienced on the product or not, will not affect user satisfaction; Reverse demand R should not be reflected in the product.

3.2 Research on Demand for NiNiGou Cultural and Creative Products

Based on the distribution characteristics of the production areas of NiNiGou products, we first conducted a field investigation in Huaiyang District, Zhoukou. We surveyed 10 shops selling NiNiGou related tourism souvenirs in the Fuxi Ling Scenic Area of Taihaoto understand the development and innovation inheritance of NiNiGou products.[1] We also randomly selected 20 tourists who have some understanding of NiNiGou cultural and creative products near the scenic area for interviews, and initially obtained 52 user demand text information.

---

[1] It is a large ancient architectural complex built to commemorate the head of the three emperors in ancient China, Taihao Fuxi, and is one of the eighteen famous tombs in China.

Secondly, the literature research method was used to sort and summarize the existing literature on NiNiGou cultural and creative products, and to extract and supplement user demand information. Considering the accurate identification and reasonable differentiation of demand information expression, 5 cultural and creative product designers, 2 university visual communication design teachers, and 1 NiNiGou intangible cultural heritage inheritor were invited to screen, merge, and classify 52 demand items, and 20 key demand vocabulary were obtained. According to expert opinions, they were divided into two levels. The first level is the three experience elements of function A, visual B, and emotional C, and the second level is the 19 user demand indicators (See Table 1.)

Table 1. User demand index system.

experience elements	user needs
Function A	cheap price A_1, easy to carry A_2, rugged and durable A_3, safety and environmental protection A_4, education function A_5, natural materials A_6
Vision B	simple abstract B_1, mysterious color B_2, Local specialty B_3, high-resolution B_4, creative and novel B_5, color jump B_6, fashionable and cool B_7, traditional charm B_8
Emotion C	fun interaction C_1, relaxation and healing C_2, meaning of praying C_3, cultural connotation C_4, lively and cute C_5

3.3 Kano Attribute Classification and Requirement Acquisition

The questionnaire survey was conducted through a combination of online and offline methods. A total of 70 questionnaires were distributed, 70 were collected, and 66 were valid, with an effective response rate of 94.28%. 50 questionnaires were distributed online through Question Star, and 20 were distributed offline at the Huaiyang Taihao Fuxi Mausoleum Scenic Area. The survey population consisted of 43 females and 27 males. The research mainly targets young people, with 73% of the population aged 16–25, including 86% being students and business personnel. The educational level is relatively high, with a bachelor's degree or above accounting for 91%.

Based on the bidirectional questionnaire survey data of user needs and the KANO model measurement evaluation table, as shown in Table 2, the demand attributes of NiNiGou cultural and creative products were determined. The specific results are shown in Table 3. Among them, minimalist and abstract B_1, high recognition B_4, color jumping B_6, traditional charm B_8, and vivid and cute C_5 are essential requirements(M), and these 5 types of needs need to be prioritized in design; Local characteristic B_3, innovative creativity B_5, and cultural connotation C_4 are expected needs(O). Meeting these three types of needs in the design can improve user satisfaction, while the opposite will decrease. Safety and environmental protection A_4, educational function A_5, fun interaction C_1, and relaxation and healing C_2 belong to charm needs(A). NiNiGou cultural and creative products meet these four needs, which can greatly improve consumer satisfaction, and vice versa will not reduce satisfaction.

Table 2. Kano model metrics evaluation table.

meet needs	unmet needs				
	like	It should be	indifferent	can endure	dislike
like	Q	A	A	A	O
It should be	R	I	I	I	M
indifferent	R	I	I	I	M
can endure	R	I	I	I	M
dislike	R	R	R	R	Q

Table 3. Attributes of User Demands of NiNiGou Cultural and Creative Products (%)

type need	A	O	M	I	R	Q	need Attributes
A_1	20	6.8	22	50.8	0	0	I
A_2	10	0	33.9	55.9	0	0	I
A_3	5	11.8	28.8	54.2	0	0	I
A_4	32	23.7	18.6	25.4	0	0	A
A_5	44	22	3.4	30.5	0	0	A
A_6	1.7	5	40.7	52.5	0	0	I
B_1	5	15.2	42.4	32.2	1.7	3.4	M
B_2	0	6.8	37.3	52.5	1.7	1.7	I
B_3	13.6	47.5	30.5	8.5	0	0	O
B_4	16.9	11.8	39	32.2	0	0	M
B_5	8.5	49.2	33.9	8.5	0	0	O
B_6	5.1	22	39	30.5	3.4	0	M
B_7	8.5	8.5	28.8	52.5	1.7	0	I
B_8	3.4	3.3	52.5	40.7	0	0	M
C_1	50.8	15.3	10.2	23.7	0	0	A
C_2	40.6	23.7	5.1	30.5	0	0	A
C_3	1.7	3.4	45.7	49.2	0	0	I
C_4	6.8	42.4	39	11.9	0	0	O
C_5	1.7	16.9	54.2	25.4	0	1.7	M

4   Analysis of User Demand Weights for NiNiGou Cultural and Creative Products Based on AHP

4.1   AHP Analytic Hierarchy Process

After analyzing the KANO model, the AHP method with strong logical decision-making can scientifically analyze complex elements and further calculate the weight values of each requirement in a hierarchical and systematic manner [4] [11], providing a more accurate hierarchy of requirements for cultural and creative product design. The specific operation process is mainly divided into four steps: constructing a hierarchical structure model of NiNiGou cultural and creative products; Compare the elements of the criterion layer and each sub criterion layer pairwise and provide scores and establish the corresponding judgment matrix; Calculate the weights of each element in the sub criterion layer and sort them; Perform consistency checks on the target weight results and analyze them.

4.2   Construction of a Hierarchical Model for the Demand for NiNiGou Cultural and Creative Products

Based on the preliminary classification of user demand types and the principle of AHP method, a hierarchical model of demand for NiNiGou cultural and creative products is established, which includes a target layer (the only element is the optimal solution for NiNiGou cultural and creative product design), a criterion layer (composed of three demand dimensions: functional *A*, visual *B*, and emotional *C*), and a sub criterion layer (composed of 12 essential, expected, and charismatic requirements analyzed by the KANO model)(see Fig. 2).

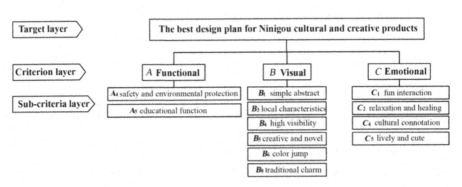

Fig. 2. Attributes of User Demands of NiNiGou Cultural and Creative Products.

4.3   Analysis of User Demand Weights for NiNiGou Cultural and Creative Products

Build an AHP judgment matrix. Using the 1–9 scale method [12], establish an adjacent evaluation index questionnaire, as shown in Table 4. Invite 5 experts in the field of cultural and creative product design and 10 product users to compare and score the elements of the criterion layer and sub criterion layer pairwise. Take the average of the evaluation results and construct a judgment matrix.

$$
M = \begin{bmatrix} b_{11} & b_{12} & \cdots & b_{1j} \\ b_{21} & b_{22} & \cdots & b_{2j} \\ \vdots & \vdots & \ddots & \vdots \\ b_{i1} & b_{i2} & \cdots & b_{ij} \end{bmatrix}
$$

Among them: $b_{ij} \cdot b_{ji} = 1, i \neq j = 1, 2 \cdots, n$.

Using the geometric mean method as the basis for weight calculation to calculate the geometric mean values of each level a_i

$$
a_i = \sqrt[n]{M_i}(i = 1, 2, \cdots, n)
$$

Calculate relative weight values W_i.

$$
W_i = \frac{a_i}{\sum\limits_{i=1}^{n} a_i}
$$

Calculate the maximum eigenvalue of the judgment matrix λ_{max}.

$$
\lambda_{max} = \frac{1}{n} \sum_{i=1}^{n} \frac{B_{w_i}}{W_i}
$$

Among them: B_{w_i} is the i-th component of vector B_w; n is the order.

Calculate the consistency ratio CR value. To ensure the validity of the judgment matrix, consistency check is performed on the judgment matrix based on the CR value. $CR \leq 0.1$ indicates that the consistency check is passed.

$$
CR = \frac{\lambda_{max} - n}{(n - 1) * RI}
$$

By using MATLAB calculation, the CR value of the first level indicator is 0.003 6, and the CR values of the second level indicators A, B, and C are 0, 0.039 6, and 0.005 4, respectively, all less than 0.1. Therefore, the consistency test is passed, and the weight of the judgment matrix is valid.

According to the above steps, calculate the weights and relative weight values of various indicators in the criterion layer and sub criterion layer of the user demand hierarchy of NiNiGou cultural and creative products. Among the three indicators in the criterion layer, emotional demand C has the highest weight proportion. In the sub criterion layer, the relative weight proportion of demand elements in descending order is C_4 cultural connotation, C_1 interesting interaction, B_5 creative novelty, C_5 vivid and lovely, B_3 local characteristics, A_4 safety and environmental protection, B_4 high recognition, C_2 relaxation and healing, A_5 educational function, B_1 simple and abstract, B_6 color jumping, and B8 traditional charm (see Tables. 4, 5 and 6).

Table 4. 1–9 scale method.

Scaling	Demand i is relative to demand j
1	as important
3	slightly important
5	obviously important
7	very important
9	extremely important
2, 4, 6, 8	adjacent judgment intermediate value
reciprocal	the importance of requirement i relative to j is X_{ij},then the importance of requirement j relative to i is $1/X_{ij}$

Table 5. Judgment matrix of first-level indicators.

index	A	B	C	Weights a_i	CR
A	1	1/3	1/5	0.109 5	0.003 6
B	3	1	1/2	0.309 0	
C	5	2	1	0.581 6	

Table 6. Judgment matrix of secondary indicators.

First level indicator	Secondary indicators	Judgment Matrix						Weights a_i	relative weight W_i	CR
A	A_4	1	2	X	X	X	X	0.666 7	0.073 0	0
	A_5	1/2	1	X	X	X	X	0.333 3	0.036 4	
B	B_1	1	1/5	1/4	1/6	1	3	0.061 3	0.018 9	0.039 6
	B_3	5	1	3	1/2	5	7	0.286 8	0.088 6	
	B_4	4	1/3	1	1/3	4	6	0.168 2	0.051 9	
	B_5	6	2	3	1	6	8	0.392 6	0.121 3	
	B_6	1	1/5	1/4	1/6	1	3	0.061 3	0.018 9	
	B_8	1/3	1/7	1/6	1/8	1/3	1	0.029 8	0.009 2	
C	C_1	1	3	1/2	2	X	X	0.271 7	0.158 0	0.005 4
	C_2	1/3	1	1/5	1/2	X	X	0.088 2	0.051 2	
	C_4	2	5	1	3	X	X	0.482 9	0.280 9	
	C_5	1/2	2	1/3	1	X	X	0.157 0	0.091 3	

5   Design of NiNiGou Cultural and Creative Products Based on QFD

5.1   QFD Theory

Quantifying user requirements and determining design functional items are the core of Quality Function Deployment Theory (QFD) [8]. After determining the weights of various user requirements for NiNiGou cultural and creative products through the AHP method, the QFD method is used to transform user requirements into design elements for NiNiGou cultural and creative product design [13]. This can provide evaluation elements for the optimization of design schemes and more accurate technical support and constraint guidance for design [14].

5.2   User Requirements - Design Element Mapping for NiNiGou Cultural and Creative Products

Based on various user demand information, analyze, and expand the design functional indicators of NiNiGou cultural and creative products through literature research, case analysis, and expert interviews. Firstly, by studying relevant literature on NiNiGou and cultural and creative products, analyzing excellent cases of NiNiGou cultural and creative products, and initially transforming user needs into functional requirements, 13 experts were invited to provide opinions on the preliminary design parameters, including 9 cultural and creative product designers and 2 professors in product design and visual communication design. Through three rounds of summary, correction, and re collection, Determine the mapping results from user needs to design element D (see Table 7).

Table 7. Mapping results of user requirements and design elements.

User needs A	Design elements D
safety and environmental protection $A4$	paper material $D1$
education function A_5	book design D_2
simple abstract B_1	geometric design D_3
Local specialty B_3	Local drama, acrobatics, etc. D_4
high-resolution B_4	Various and weird shapes D_5
creative and novel B_5	flat design D_6
color jump B_6	Bright colors D_7
traditional charm B_8	Typical NiNiGou types and patterns D_8
fun interaction C_1	Gamification design $D9$
relaxation and healing C_2	storyline setting D_{10}
cultural connotation C_4	historical legend D_{11}
lively and cute C_5	Anthropomorphic design D_{12}

5.3 Building a QFD Model

The construction of the House of Quality (HOQ) model is the focus of the entire quality function deployment. Based on the Kano model and AHP method, the user demand elements and design parameters are obtained to construct the HOQ. The user demand weights are imported into the left wall of the HOQ, and the design elements form the ceiling of the HOQ. ▲ ● and ★ correspond to the correlation between user needs and design elements, with ▲ = 1.5, ● = 1.2, and ★ = 1. The final calculation of design element weights is the sum of all requirements under the design elements multiplied by the corresponding weight values to form the basement of the quality house. Finally, analyze the positive and negative correlation between the various design elements of NiNiGou cultural and creative products, with "+" representing positive correlation and "–" representing negative correlation, marked on the roof of the HOQ (See Fig. 3). Normalize the weights of the obtained design elements according to their importance and sort them accordingly (See Fig. 4).

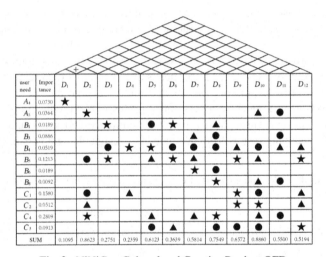

Fig. 3. NiNiGou Cultural and Creative Product QFD.

6 Design of NiNiGou Cultural and Creative Products Based on QFD

According to the results in Fig. 4, the weight of design elements is determined to be $D_{10} > D_2 > D_8 > D_9 > D_5 > D_7 > D_{11} > D_{12} > D_6 > D_3 > D_4 > D_1$. The top 10 main design requirements are selected for the design practice of NiNiGou cultural and creative products. They are storyline setting, book design, typical NiNiGou types and patterns, gamified design, diverse and quirky shapes, bright colors, historical legends, anthropomorphic design, flat design, and geometric graphic design. Based on this, design and practice the NiNiGou cultural and creative products (See Fig. 5).

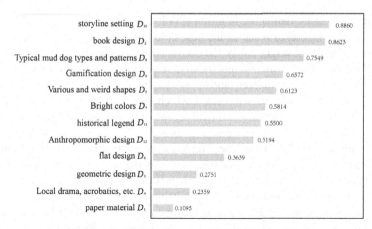

Fig. 4. Design Requirements Weight Priority Chart

Fig. 5. Design practice of interactive NiNiGou book.

The ultimate choice of NiNiGou cultural and creative products is presented in the form of interactive books - "Mud Tan", which mainly revolves around the types of shapes and historical legends of NiNiGous. The size of a book is 38cm * 38cm; Use recyclable paper materials on the material, with a textured wrinkled paper on the cover and a harder white cardboard on the inner page to make the interactive device more durable and not easily damaged; In terms of color, it follows the five color concept of NiNiGou [15], which uses black as the base color and red, yellow, blue, and white as decorative colors, with bright colors; 20 classic NiNiGou designs were selected for the design of the NiNiGou, which geometrically, exaggerates, and anthropomorphizes the original irregular shapes into lively and lively images; The book consists of a total of 12 chapters, which are illustrated with text. Each chapter corresponds to a story plot, and the story content is based on the historical legend of NiNiGou and local folk customs; In terms of interactive form, the design is based on the story content of each page and the corresponding NiNiGou type. The left page is the text description of the story, and the right page is the interactive page, such as the story of "overlapping arhats". Corresponding to the "nine headed birds" shape in the NiNiGou, pulling the first head will gradually appear the nine heads stacked behind.

The design of mud dog cultural and creative products based on books is an innovative inheritance of mud dog intangible cultural heritage, meeting 12 key needs of users for knowledge learning, relaxation, and healing. Users can understand the cultural connotation of mud dogs in an intuitive, relaxed, and enjoyable way [16].

7   Conclusion

With the continuous improvement of people's living standards, consumption concepts and lifestyles are gradually changing, and people's demand for cultural and creative products presents characteristics of ambiguity and diversification. The development of traditional Chinese clay sculpture - NiNiGou cultural and creative products urgently need precise and effective exploration of contemporary needs. Therefore, from the perspective of user needs, this article integrates the Kano/AHP/QFD method to screen the design functions of NiNiGou cultural and creative products, which can to some extent compensate for the lack of single method research on consumer needs. Integrate these three methods into the research of NiNiGou cultural and creative products and complete the design practice of NiNiGou cultural and creative products in the form of interactive book design based on the obtained design elements. The design scheme obtained by this research institute can provide guidance for the development of future NiNiGou cultural and creative products, and its combination research method can also serve as a reference for the development of other intangible cultural heritage products. In the design proposal section of the article, it is only from the perspective of book design. In future research, the design and development of NiNiGou cultural and creative products can be approached from a more diverse perspective.

References

1. Zhao, Y.: Folk art in the discourse field: the social life of NiNiGou as a commodity in different contexts. National Art (06), 59–70 (2019). https://doi.org/10.16564/j.cnki.1003-2568.2019.06.009
2. Cao, M., Yang, C., Zhou, P.-H.: Research on bicycle design decision-making in the post-sharing era based on KANO model——from the perspective of designers and consumers. Packa. Eng. **22**(43), 395–404 (2022). https://doi.org/10.19554/j.cnki.1001-3563.2022.22.045

3. Al-Harbi, K.M.A.-S.: Application of the AHP in project management. Int. J. Project Manag. **1**(19), 19–27 (2001)
4. Khorsandi, A., Li, L.: A multi-analysis of children and adolescents' video gaming addiction with the AHP and TOPSIS methods. Int. J. Environ. Res. Public Health **15**(19): 9680 (2022)
5. Wasserman, G.S.: On how to prioritize design requirements during the QFD planning process. IIE Trans. **3**(25), 59–65 (1993)
6. Lv, Z., Yang, B., Chen, Y.: Research on design of fruit logistics turnover box based on KANO–AHP–QFD. Packa. Eng. **18**(43), 95–103 (2022). https://doi.org/10.19554/j.cnki.1001-3563.2022.18.013
7. Cang, S., Yu, M., Qian, M., et al.: Research on the application of KANO-AHP-TOPSIS hybrid model in the packaging design of clay figurines. Packa. Eng. **18**(43), 169–177 (2022). https://doi.org/10.19554/j.cnki.1001-3563.2022.18.021
8. Qiang, W.: Mobile terminal interaction design for new energy vehicles based on Kano-QFD. Packa. Eng. **20**(43), 212–219 (2022). https://doi.org/10.19554/j.cnki.1001-3563.2022.20.023
9. Zhou, H., Zhu, Q., Wang, J., et al.: Design and research of laser cleaning machine based on Kano-QFD-PUGH. Packa. Eng. 1–9 (2023). https://doi.org/10.19554/j.cnki.1001-3563.2023.10.016
10. Zhao, X., Wei, F., Bai, Y.: Construction and application of product design model driven by user needs. Mech. Des. **S1**(38), 56–61 (2021). https://doi.org/10.13841/j.cnki.jxsj.2021.s1.014
11. Dai, Y., Zhang, Z., Chen, N., et al.: Research on the design of home-friendly seats for the elderly based on AHP, QFD and AD. Packa. Eng. **20**(43), 228–236 (2022). https://doi.org/10.19554/j.cnki.1001-3563.2022.20.025
12. Deng, X., Li, J., Zeng, H., et al.: Analytic hierarchy process weight calculation method analysis and application research. Pract. Understand. Math. **07**(42), 93–100 (2012)
13. Miao, Y., Li, J., Xu, Y.: Design and evaluation of children's infusion area furniture based on Kano-GRA-AHP. Furn. Interior Decorat. **01**(30), 44–49 (2023). https://doi.org/10.16771/j.cn43-1247/ts.2023.01.010
14. Zhang, D., Hou, Z., Huang, L., et al.: Research on product demand configuration method integrating user satisfaction. J. Graph. **04**(41), 649–657 (2020)
15. Jia, H.: The Story Form of NiNiGou Images in Huaiyang, Henan Province and the Aesthetic Potential of Their Images. Fudan University, Shanghai (2012)
16. Xiong, Y., Cheng, J.: The expression of leisure aesthetics in contemporary book design. Packa. Eng. **04**(42), 185–190 (2021). https://doi.org/10.19554/j.cnki.1001-3563.2021.04.026

A Study on the Dissemination of Xiamen's Urban Image Through the BiliBili Platform

Jiayi Zhang[1], Weiqi Li[1(✉)], Kunhe Li[2], and Shichao Zhang[3]

[1] School of Film Television and Communication, Xiamen University of Technology, Xiamen, Fujian, China
liweiqi@t.xmut.edu.cn

[2] Department of Journalism and Visual Communication College of Social Science, Keimyung University, Daegu, South Korea

[3] Department of Media and Communication, Kyungpook National University, Daegu, South Korea

Abstract. This study conducts an in-depth content analysis of videos related to the city of Xiamen on the Bilibili platform. It summarizes the image of Xiamen portrayed in self-media videos with "Xiamen city" as the primary search term. Xiamen is depicted as a city embodying healing power, a romantic atmosphere, vibrant development, and urban scenery. Furthermore, through high-frequency word analysis and sentiment analysis of comments on Xiamen city-related videos on the Bilibili platform, this research summarizes the audience's perception and attitude towards the image of Xiamen city. The high-frequency word analysis results indicate that "housing prices" is the most prominent concern for the audience regarding Xiamen city. The sentiment analysis results reveal that the audience on the Bilibili platform generally holds positive and affirmative emotional tendencies towards the image of Xiamen city. Positive evaluations from the audience primarily focus on aspects such as "beautiful natural scenery," "livability," and "romance," while negative evaluations predominantly revolve around "high housing prices," "tourism services," and "economic livelihood."

Keywords: City Image · Bilibili · Sentiment Analysis

1 Introduction

"City image" concept was first introduced by the American urbanist Kevin Lynch [1]. He believed that the city image is a comprehensive impression of the city as a whole formed by the public, which is the integrated psychological image formed by people's perception of the city's physical environment.

In the context of the increasingly rapid urbanization process and intensifying urban competition, a favorable and widely recognized city image is beneficial externally for attracting high-quality talent, capital, and technological resources, while internally it helps foster a sense of belonging, identity, and cohesion among the citizens towards their own city [2].

C. Stephanidis et al. (Eds.): HCII 2024, CCIS 2116, pp. 378–386, 2024.
https://doi.org/10.1007/978-3-031-61950-2_41

In the era of self-media, the public's perception of urban image is no longer solely influenced by the news agenda set by traditional media. Instead, individuals can autonomously participate in constructing the news agenda and form a more comprehensive and diverse urban image based on their own agenda setting regarding the city image.

Bilibili platform, as a hybrid video social platform combining PGC (professionally generated content) and UGC (user-generated content), provides advantages for urban image dissemination in the era of self-media. With its unique bullet chat interaction feature, verticalized video sections, and predominantly long-form video content, Bilibili offers a platform conducive to the communication of city images.

According to the "2023 Q3 Financial Report" released by the Bilibili platform, as of October 1, 2023, there were an average of 341 million monthly users, with users spending an average of 103 min per day on the platform [3]. Additionally, the number of videos uploaded by content creators (Up主) reached 21 million. Videos published on the Bilibili platform combine various elements such as text, audio, and visual, breaking away from the traditional static symbols of urban image communication. This advancement promotes the transition of urban image communication into a new stage characterized by audiovisual symbolic texts.

Xiamen, located on the southeastern coast of China, boasts beautiful natural scenery. The Gulangyu Island, also known as the "International Architecture Complex", was inscribed on the World Heritage List on July 8, 2017, becoming the 52nd World Heritage Site in China [4]. As a city facing Taiwan across the sea, Xiamen has various cultural forms such as "Overseas Chinese Culture" and "Min Nan Culture". In addition, in recent years, Xiamen has also emerged a variety of "internet-famous" check-in spots. These "internet-famous" elements add a modern and fashionable atmosphere to Xiamen, making the city more attractive and vibrant.

This study focuses on Xiamen city-related videos published on the Bilibili platform as the main research samples, exploring how self-media accounts utilize symbols to construct and disseminate the city image. Additionally, through high-frequency word analysis and sentiment analysis of the comments on these videos, the study investigates the audience's perception and attitude towards the Xiamen city image. Based on these findings, the study aims to analyze the Xiamen city image presented on the Bilibili platform, providing a reference case for the further application of self-media in the dissemination of the Xiamen city image.

2 Methods

2.1 Date Collection

This study utilized the big data scraping tool "Octopus" (website: https://rpa.bazhuayu.com/) to collect data on Bilibili video titles, posting times, and comments. After setting the keyword "Xiamen city," a total of 802 related videos were retrieved. These 802 video titles were then deduplicated, and through manual screening, irrelevant videos and advertisements were excluded, resulting in a final sample size of 702 videos for analysis.

2.2 Research Framework

This study consists of three parts:

1. Count the number of Xiamen city-related videos uploaded to the Bilibili platform by month and year.
2. Select the top 10 videos with the highest view counts from the sample and analyze the language symbols used in their titles.
3. Select the comments from the top 100 videos ranked by comprehensive popularity (comprehensive popularity = clicks + other data) in the sample as the research sample. Adopting a stratified sampling method, crawl the top 20 comments for each video, obtaining a total of 1705 valid comment samples for text analysis, and conduct high-frequency word analysis and sentiment analysis.

3 Results

3.1 Video Quantity Analysis

The earliest Xiamen city-related thematic video appeared on the Bilibili platform in February 2016 (see Fig. 1), with the release of the "2016 China Xiamen City Image Promotional Video" produced by the studio of Fujian documentary director, Teacher Wei Guohai. Since 2020, there has been a notable increase in the number of videos on the Xiamen city theme on the Bilibili platform (see Fig. 2). According to the Bilibili financial report, the daily average views of Bilibili videos increased from 2.125 billion in 2020 to 2.437 billion in 2021, then to 3.996 billion in 2022, and finally reached 4.1 billion in 2023 [5]. This growth trend reflects the platform's significant achievements in attracting users and content creators. More and more content creators and travel enthusiasts are choosing to publish videos on the Bilibili platform, driving the growth in the number of videos related to Xiamen city.

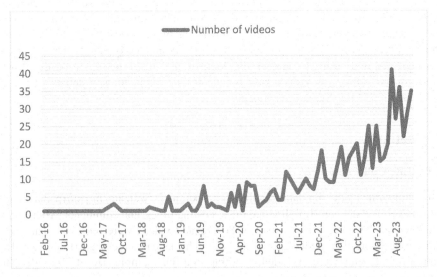

Fig. 1. Xiamen city-related videos published on the Bilibili platform each month.

During the COVID-19 pandemic outbreak from 2020 to 2022, the global tourism industry was severely impacted, leading to many people being unable to travel in person. In such circumstances, individuals turned to online platforms to obtain information and experiences about tourist destinations, satisfying their curiosity and desire for travel experiences. As travel restrictions across regions were gradually lifted, there was a surge in the number of tourists, and Xiamen, as a popular tourist city in China, naturally became one of the choices for travelers. This further inspired more tourists to share their travel experiences, journals, and travel tips about Xiamen, thereby increasing the offline tourism content related to Xiamen city on the Bilibili platform.

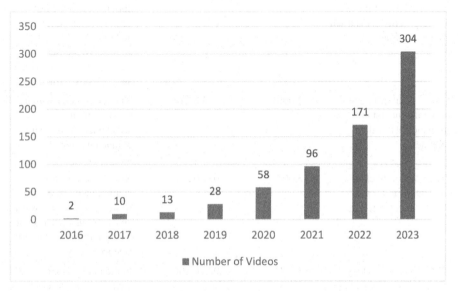

Fig. 2. Xiamen city-related videos published on the Bilibili platform each year.

3.2 Language Symbol Analysis of Popular Video Titles

This study selected the top 10 videos with the highest view counts from the 702 videos as research samples. It analyzed the linguistic symbols reflected in their titles and compiled and summarized the linguistic symbols found in the video titles, view counts, posting times, and titles.

From Table 1, it can be observed that video creators on the Bilibili platform aim to convey a positive image and attractiveness of Xiamen city to the audience through their videos. The video titles emphasize Xiamen as a city embodying healing power, romantic atmosphere, vibrant development, and urban scenery. The content of the videos focuses on presenting the beauty, vitality, and uniqueness of Xiamen city.

Table 1. Analysis of Language Symbols in Popular Video Titles in Xiamen City

Sample video name (signifier)	Number of views	Video upload data	The symbol refers to
Love Story I "Xiamen has always been a city with strong healing abilities, healing in every person and corner of Xiamen."	324,000	2023.2.24	Xiamen is a city with healing power that can provide people with inner comfort and comfort
Xiamen: The Internet celebrity city of the last century "The Sea Garden" is not all of her!	433,000	2022.11.19	Xiamen was highly anticipated in the last century (20th century), and now Xiamen, in addition to its "sea garden", has more diverse and rich urban images
There shouldn't be any city that understands romance better than Xiamen!	183,000	2023.01.14	Xiamen is a city with a highly romantic atmosphere, possessing unique charm and attraction
The counterattack of Xiamen is not just a "internet celebrity" city!	113,000	2021.09.26	Xiamen has been continuously developing from relatively backward areas, not just because of its reputation as a "internet celebrity" city
Xiamen City Strategy! Crazy play all day in the hot summer!	681,000	2023.06.06	In the hot summer, there are also many places to visit in Xiamen for sightseeing
Xiamen - a beautiful garden city, opened for the new year, with beauty always present, and with egrets, you can start the 2023 energetic new year!	51,000	2023.01.19	Xiamen is a beautiful garden city, welcoming the new year with Xiamen's egrets, showcasing the natural beauty and vibrant New Year atmosphere of Xiamen city
Xiamen is a city that once you come, you don't want to leave!	45,000	2021.06.04	Affirming and loving the urban charm of Xiamen, emphasizing the attraction and comfort it brings to people

(continued)

Table 1. (*continued*)

Sample video name (signifier)	Number of views	Video upload data	The symbol refers to
Searching for the Ideal City Stop 7: Xiamen, a place as beautiful as a movie~	35,000	2023.12.29	Xiamen is a beautiful place like a movie, with the beauty and charm of an ideal city
From a regular tea port to one of the busiest cities in the world, Xiamen, China | China City 4K Film and Television	29,000	2022.04.11	The development process of Xiamen is full of vitality, representing the changes and rapid development of Chinese cities
Why do old tourist cities still bring us surprises when we revisit Xiamen after 10 years?	73,000	2023.04.06	Xiamen, as an old tourist city, will still experience new changes or experiences after many years, bringing surprises and freshness to tourists

3.3 Analysis of High-Frequency Words in Comments

Through high-frequency word analysis of comments below the videos, we can identify the most frequently used words by the audience when expressing their opinions or reflecting their emotions. Figure 3 shows the wordcloud of high-frequency words in the comments. "厦门" (Xiamen) and "城市" (city) appeared 910 and 248 times respectively, accurately reflecting the focus of audience comments. Additionally, "房价" (housing price) appeared 161 times, indicating a focal issue sparking discussions among the audience. According to the "National Housing Price Ranking" released in February 2024, the average land price in Xiamen is 47,184 yuan per square meter, ranking fourth nationwide [6]. Similarly, according to the "2023 China 333 Cities (including Hong Kong, Macao, and Taiwan) GDP Ranking" published by the Star Data Pie, Xiamen ranks 32nd [7]. This disparity between housing prices and development level has made "high housing prices" a unique label for the city of Xiamen.

Words like "生活" (life), "宜居" (livable), "养老" (retirement), "舒服" (comfortable), and "适合" (suitable) reflect the audience's focus on the living environment in Xiamen. Through high-frequency words such as "经济" (economy), "消费" (consumption), "工作" (work), "收入" (income), and "工资" (salary), it is evident that the discussions among the video audience about Xiamen revolve around the employment environment and economic level. Words like "鼓浪屿" (Gulangyu Island), "风景" (scenery), and "景点" (tourist attractions) also reflect Xiamen's tourism resources and features.

The domestic cities mentioned in conjunction with Xiamen include "烟台" (Yantai), "大连" (Dalian), and "宁波" (Ningbo). All these cities are coastal cities. This suggests that short video users who are interested in Xiamen also pay attention to other cities of similar type and compare Xiamen with them. The city image presented in short videos will become a reference for short video users when choosing a settlement city or a travel destination.

Fig. 3. Wordcloud of high-frequency words in the comments

3.4 Sentiment Analysis of Comments

This study utilized the SnowNLP library in Python to conduct sentiment analysis on 1705 comments from the top 100 videos ranked by comprehensive sorting related to Xiamen city on the Bilibili platform. Among these, "positive" represents audience comments affirming and identifying with the Xiamen city image presented in self-media communication. "Negative" denotes audience comments criticizing and disapproving of the Xiamen city image presented in self-media communication. "Objective" refers to audience comments providing factual descriptions and constructive suggestions regarding the Xiamen city image presented in self-media communication.

Table 2 shows there are a total of 990 comments with a positive sentiment, accounting for more than half of the total sample size. This indicates that the audience generally agrees with the Xiamen city image presented on the Bilibili platform and resonates with the portrayal of Xiamen in self-media content.

There are a total of 525 comments with a neutral sentiment, accounting for 30.79% of the total. These comments mostly consist of fair evaluations and objective descriptions of the Xiamen city image, as well as supplementary explanations about the city's image and cultural background. Some comments also provide suggestions for improving the

Table 2. Bilibili Platform Xiamen City-Related Video Comments Sentiment Analysis.

Emotional color	Quantity	Frequency
Postive	990	58.06%
Objective	525	30.79%
Negative	190	11.15%

Xiamen city image. These comments contribute to conveying a more objective city image, facilitating a more comprehensive understanding of Xiamen city among the audience.

Negative sentiment comments only accounted for 11.15% of the total comments, indicating a minority. The main content of these comments includes a negative attitude towards the low housing prices in Xiamen, disdain for various "internet-famous" spots in Xiamen, and evaluations from local residents regarding the city's originality. These comments often criticize the drawbacks of Xiamen's urban development perceived by tourists, while also expressing nostalgia from long-time Xiamen residents for the original city.

Negative sentiment comments only accounted for 11.15% of the total comments, indicating a minority. The main content includes a negative attitude towards the high housing prices in Xiamen. Additionally, many netizens believe that the "internet-famous spots" and "internet-famous food" depicted in the videos are not as advertised.

Positive comments frequently mention Xiamen's beautiful coastline and scenery, while also providing suggestions for improvement and pointing out flaws, such as the need to increase the number of shopping and coffee shops, and enrich nightlife activities. Commenters also praise Xiamen's urban culture, its clean and tidy environment, charming natural landscapes, rich culinary culture, and pleasant living atmosphere. They generally believe that Xiamen has made significant achievements in urban development and infrastructure, particularly excelling in public transportation and urban environmental improvement.

Neutral comments do not entirely negate the image of Xiamen city but rather offer "suggestions" in certain aspects. While expressing appreciation and recognition for Xiamen's urban scenery, they also provide different perspectives on some details. For example, comments like "I love Xiamen, but it should not rely solely on tourism and real estate" or "Xiamen is beautiful, but urban development still needs improvement." In fact, it is these objective interpretations, rational suggestions, and fair evaluations that can better expose the areas for improvement in the dissemination of Xiamen's city image, providing more specific and instructive directions for future improvements in the dissemination of Xiamen's city image.

4   Discussions

Several videos on Bilibili showcase Xiamen as a livable city through beautiful scenery and natural landscapes, emphasizing the city's environmental advantages and natural resources. Some tourism promotional videos depict Xiamen as a "hotspot" city with a romantic atmosphere and cultural heritage. In the comment sections of numerous related videos, there remains strong support for the image of Xiamen city, with comments praising the city's scenery and excellent coastal views. Some audiences also highlight the high housing prices in Xiamen and the corresponding lower incomes, expressing sentiments such as "locals find it more livable" and "unable to afford houses due to relatively low wages." Additionally, local residents of Xiamen contemplate the consequences of rapid development, questioning aspects like "Is the 'hotspot economy' a bubble?" and expressing hopes for improvements in transportation. The diverse perspectives of various audiences converge to shape new aspects of the image of Xiamen city.

Through analyzing the content of videos and comments related to Xiamen city on the Bilibili platform, it is evident that the image of Xiamen presented on Bilibili is relatively singular, summarized as "a highly popular tourist city" and "a city with high housing prices," with the city's rich history and diverse culture not being the focal points of short video users. Indeed, this study only selected videos from the Bilibili platform as research objects, and future research could continue to quantitatively analyze the portrayal of Xiamen city image on other video platforms. Additionally, this study did not classify Xiamen city-related videos; in future research, keywords such as "Xiamen history" and "Xiamen culture" could be set to collect relevant videos for analysis.

Acknowledgments. This study was funded by XMUT Graduate Science and Technology Innovation Project (grant number YKJCX2022244) and XMUT Education and Teaching Reform Research Project (grant number JG202346).

References

1. Lynch, K.: The Image of the City. MIT Press, Cambridge (1964)
2. Qi, R.: Research on the dissemination of urban image by food-related self-media [MD, Wuhan Textile University] (2022). https://doi.org/10.27698/d.cnki.gwhxj.2022.000272
3. Bilibili released Q3 2023 financial report: Daily active users exceeded 100 million mark, adjusted net loss significantly narrowed by 51% year-on-year. https://baijiahao.baidu.com/s?id=1783898903753192378&wfr=spider&for=pc
4. UNESCO. Kulangsu: a Historic International Settlement (n.d.). https://whc.unesco.org/en/list/1541/
5. Bilibili Inc. Overview of Bilibili financial statements (n.d.). https://ir.bilibili.com/en/financial-information/?tab=sec-filings#annual-and-interim-reports
6. Ju Hui Data. National House Price Rankings (2024). https://m.gotohui.com/fangjia/
7. Exclusive! 2023 GDP Ranking of 361 Cities in China (including Hong Kong, Macao, and Taiwan) Released (Version 1)]. (n.d.). https://zhuanlan.zhihu.com/p/682709698

Between Mountains and Rivers, Reality and Virtuality: Empowering Traditional Intangible Cultural Heritage Plant-Dye Apparel Design and Display Through Virtual Digital Technology

Xinru Zhang [ID], Lijian Chen, and Yuanfang Zhao[✉] [ID]

College of Art and Design, Shenzhen University, Shenzhen 518060, People's Republic of China
zhaoyuanfang@szu.edu.cn

Abstract. Since 2020, with the rapid development of digital technology and virtual fashion, three-dimensional virtual clothing technology has gradually been applied in the clothing industry with its advantages of high environmental protection, robust simulation, and intuitive output effects. At the same time, with the rapid development and popularization of digital technology, digital conversion, restoration, and innovation of traditional intangible cultural heritage have become a new wave. This study explores the application of three-dimensional virtual technology in designing and performing conventional intangible cultural heritage plant-dyed clothing. Applications. By combining traditional craftsmanship with modern technology, this research aims to improve the accuracy of digital communication of plant-dyed clothing and pattern design, break the inefficiency barriers of conventional intangible cultural heritage communication, and achieve "online + offline" and "virtual" + reality" comprehensive promotion and communication. This study hopes to provide new ideas for greater attention and faster dissemination of intangible cultural heritage and to explore new practical directions for promoting the inheritance and development of traditional intangible cultural heritage handicrafts.

Keywords: Virtual Digital Technology · Traditional Intangible Cultural Heritage · Plant Dyeing · Clothing Design · Clothing Performance

1 Introduction

The 2nd Plant Dye Earth Art Festival in Guilin, Dongli, China, 2023, uses plant dyeing as a medium to explore innovative artistic methods and collectively discuss new trends in the development of the plant dyeing industry. Among them, the virtual digital technology explored by this research institute empowers traditional intangible cultural heritage plant-dyed fashion clothing shows as one of the opening performances of this art festival. For a long time, the conventional fashion show form was limited by the small size of the venue, low communication efficiency, and single viewing form. Since 2020, with the rapid development of digital technology and virtual fashion, three-dimensional virtual clothing technology relies on its high environmental protection, robust simulation, and Advantages such as intuitive output effects, which are gradually being rapidly applied in the clothing industry. At the same time, with the rapid development and popularization of digital technology, digital conversion, restoration, and innovation of traditional intangible cultural heritage have become a new wave, which has also brought more opportunities for rapid sharing, timely preservation, efficient promotion, and adequate inheritance of intangible cultural heritage, possibilities, and development opportunities.

Based on the above research background, the theme of this study is how to empower traditional intangible cultural heritage plant-dyed clothing design through virtual digital technology. The purpose of the research is as follows: Based on the China Plant Dyeing Art Festival, using plant-dyed clothing in the landscape show as a medium to implement the environmental protection concept of plant dyeing from the perspective of combining traditional craftsmanship and modern technology through three-dimensional virtual technology to assist conventional intangible cultural heritage plants Dyed clothing has been promoted in many aspects in "virtual + reality," providing new ideas and methods for the inheritance and effective dissemination of intangible cultural heritage.

2 Literature Review

2.1 The History and Current Situation of Traditional Intangible Cultural Heritage Plant Dyeing

The traditional intangible cultural heritage handicraft plant dyeing technology has a long history in China. Its dyeing materials are derived from nature, have the sustainable advantages of being environmentally friendly and widely sourced, and are of great application value in textile dyeing applications. Since the 21st century, many scholars have begun to conduct in-depth research on traditional intangible cultural heritage plants and natural techniques. They have gradually made in-depth refinements in the dyeing technology itself from aspects such as dyeing technology, dyeing effects of dye materials, performance of dyed fabrics, improvement of dyeing auxiliaries, etc. Research [1, 2]. At the same time, with the continuous advancement and promotion of dyeing technology, researchers have begun to emphasize the importance of inheriting cultural elements of intangible cultural heritage plant dyeing technology, especially the potential application and continuous innovation of plant dyeing in fashion [3]. Especially with the wave of environmental protection concepts and sustainable development, the intangible cultural plant dyeing process has attracted the attention of designers. It has gradually begun to realize industrial production. Therefore, improving the color fastness of plant dyes and achieving standard industrial production of textiles are current and future goals [4].

2.2 Application and Development of Virtual Reality Technology

Today, with the rapid development of innovative technology, virtual reality technology with computer technology as its core has become a research hotspot in various fields due to its conceptual, interactive, and immersive characteristics. It is precisely because of the correlation between virtual reality technology and computer technology that its application status in education, medicine, military, industry, digital media, and other fields is different. Affected by the uncertainty of the effect, the application status of virtual reality technology in education, medicine, military, and other fields is different. The field still has significant challenges but plays a vital role in the industry and digital media. As the country has established a complete support system for virtual reality technology, virtual reality technology is moving towards the realization of dynamic environment modeling technology, real-time three-dimensional graphics generation and display technology, new human-computer interaction equipment research and development, application of VR technology, intelligent technology and speech recognition Technology completes the development direction of virtual reality modeling, network distributed virtual reality technology, and other aspects. Overall, virtual reality technology in various fields provides people with a more realistic experience, requiring researchers to continue to innovate and improve [5].

2.3 Virtual Reality Technology in Clothing Design

The application of virtual reality technology in the clothing industry originated in the 1980s and has shown significant advantages in reducing production time, improving creative efficiency, and realizing interdisciplinary integration. In the book "Clothing Virtual Reality and Implementation," the application of virtual clothing technology is summarized into five sections: technology promotes the development of the clothing industry, related virtual human body realization technology, introduction to the characteristics of virtual clothing design systems and model systems, and implementation of virtual clothing display, Virtual clothing technology application case [6]. Especially in the clothing industry production model, virtual reality technology has promoted the rapid development of clothing customization production models, bringing a new look to the entire clothing industry chain from "design-production-publicity-sales" [7].

3 Research Methods

This study is based on the landscape theme of the China Plant Dyeing Land Art Festival, with the research and exploration goal of digitally empowering the presentation of traditional plant dyeing art (see Fig. 1) to promote the multi-dimensional dissemination of niche traditional intangible cultural heritage handicrafts, the following points are the main points of this study:

1. A realistic simulation of traditional intangible cultural heritage craft plant-dyed clothing.
2. Artistic style simulation creation of realistic scenes.
3. Digitally transform traditional intangible cultural heritage craftsmanship for rapid sharing and efficient dissemination.

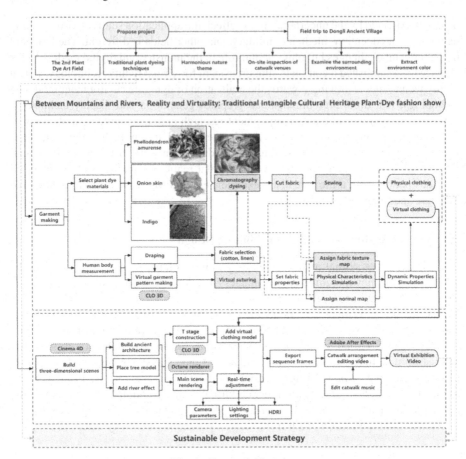

Fig. 1. Research Flowchart

4   Practical Application

4.1   The Specific Process of Simulating the Characteristics of Traditional Plant-Dyed Clothing in Real-Time

The production of three-dimensional virtual digital clothing requires the completion of human body measurements first. The size of the virtual model is used to complete the pattern-making of the virtual clothing style. The fabric properties are set, and the material map and normal map are given to it like plant-dyed fabrics to approximate the texture of natural fabrics—simulation effect. Based on CLO 3D, the physical and dynamic properties of the natural world can be simulated intuitively, virtually, and in real-time, thereby restoring the uncertainty of traditional plant dyeing to the greatest extent and optimizing and adjusting according to the real-time dressing effect (see Fig. 2).

Fig. 2. Three-dimensional virtual digital clothing production simulation process

4.2 Detailed Steps for Creating 3D Scenes Using Digital Tools Such as Cinema 4D and CLO 3D

This study is based on the actual scene of Dongli Ancient Village during the on-site investigation. It cooperates with the surveyed live show, using Cinema 4D to build a three-dimensional virtual simulation of the ancient village scene. It completes the location construction and arrangement of ancient buildings, trees, rivers, and other scenes, giving it a realistic visual effect. Using the Octane renderer as the rendering medium, the camera movement, lighting, and environment setting paths are updated in real-time, restoring the space while giving more potent visual effects and exporting sequence frames to complete virtual scene animation production (see Fig. 3).

Fig. 3. Three-dimensional virtual scene construction simulation process

4.3 Emphasis on Three-Dimensional Virtual Technology to Optimize the Visual Presentation of Traditional Plant-Dyed Clothing

After completing the structure of the main scene, CLO 3D was used to construct the virtual fashion show scene. Based on Cinema 4D, the required element modeling was first completed, and the material model in FBX format was exported and inserted into CLO 3D to give the water wave texture and normal stickers. Then, gradually import scene materials such as trees to complete the configuration of surrounding scenes and continuously update and iterate the background, lighting, and HDR to achieve the best visual presentation effect (see Fig. 4).

Fig. 4. Virtual scene and virtual clothing combination simulation process

Then, we export sequence frames from CLO 3D and Cinema 4D, import them into the AE rendering queue, adjust the model queue, import show music, perform virtual video editing, and finally output the virtual video (see Fig. 5).

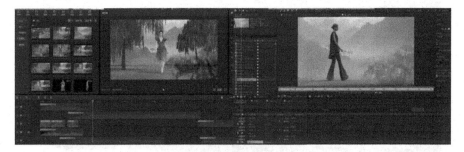

Fig. 5. Video production process

4.4 Live Performances and Virtual Performances

On July 21, 2023, the second Plant Dyeing Land Art Festival opened in Dongli Ancient Village. This study explores the enabling role of virtual digital technology in designing traditional intangible cultural heritage plant-dyed clothing, especially in apparel that incorporates natural landscape elements. The research team displayed a physical Shan-shui fashion clothing series at the opening ceremony. These works are the inheritance of craftsmanship and the fusion of culture and modern aesthetics. At the same time, the static exhibition area also presents a series of virtual clothing displays (see Fig. 6). Traditional art is disseminated digitally through high-fidelity three-dimensional simulation, allowing visitors to experience intangible cultural heritage without being restricted by beauty in the physical space.

This study aims to practice and verify the application potential of virtual digital technology in inheriting and innovating traditional plant-dyed clothing design. By combining traditional craftsmanship with cutting-edge digital technology, this research not only broadens the communication channels of intangible cultural heritage but also provides new perspectives and possibilities for the modern performance of traditional costumes. The research results also reflect the vital value of virtual technology in improving the efficiency of cultural communication, enhancing audience interactive experience, and promoting the innovative development of intangible cultural heritage, providing critical practical cases and theoretical basis for future research on the integration of intangible cultural heritage and digital technology.

Fig. 6. Shanshui Fashion Show – Virtuality and Reality

5   Conclusion and Future Work

Through method application and implementation, this study digitally presented traditional intangible cultural heritage handicrafts and obtained the following results:

1. **Accuracy and visibility of digital communications:** in the research practice, using digital virtual software such as Cinema 4D and CLO 3D, we successfully created a three-dimensional scene with an artistic stylization similar to reality. We realized the real-time simulation of the characteristics of traditional plant-dyed clothing. The results show that with the help of modern digital software, traditional plant dyes' colors and presentation effects can be restored with higher accuracy, making clothing appear more realistic in virtual scenes.

2. **Three-dimensional virtual technology optimizes traditional plant-dyed clothing design effects:** based on detailed research on the live show, Cinema 4D was used to build a simulated three-dimensional scene. Iteratively adjusting the scene, lighting, and decorative elements restored the space and gave a more substantial visual effect. In addition, virtual real-time simulation based on CLO 3D further optimizes the design

of traditional plant-dyed clothing. This means that the impact of clothing in actual wearing can be simulated as accurately as possible, thereby providing designers with more reliable reference ideas for design practice.

3. **Three-dimensional virtual digital technology plays a role in the promotion of traditional intangible cultural heritage:** through these research results, empirical support is provided for the practical application of digital technology in the design of conventional intangible heritage plant-dyed clothing, and, at the same time, an in-depth assessment of the advantages and limitations of its innovative methods is conducted. It helps to provide a more comprehensive understanding of the role of digital technology in the design of traditional intangible heritage plant-dyed clothing.

4. **Reveals the strengths and limitations of innovative approaches:** although digital technology has made significant progress in designing traditional intangible heritage plant-dyed clothing, this study still needs some help. In terms of application, although digital communication can improve the visual effect and promotion effect of traditional intangible cultural heritage, digital technology can only partially replace the conventional artistic value and skill inheritance due to the complexity of traditional crafts and pure handicraft processes.

Due to the intuitive visibility and other advantages of three-dimensional virtual technology, it ensures the accuracy of the conversion of subjective designs of plant dyeing clothing patterns and patterns into digital communication, breaks the inefficient communication barriers of niche intangible cultural heritage processes, and realizes the "line of traditional intangible cultural heritage" The multi-faceted promotion of "online + offline" and "virtual + reality" provides greater attention and faster sharing and dissemination for intangible cultural heritage, and assists the inheritance and development of traditional intangible cultural heritage handicrafts. These research results on The practical application of digital technology in conventional intangible heritage plant-dyed clothing design provide empirical support and, at the same time, provide in-depth thinking on the advantages and limitations of its innovative methods, which helps to more comprehensively understand the application of digital technology in traditional intangible heritage plant dyeing—the role of dyeing in clothing design.

Acknowledgements. The authors acknowledge the funding support by the "High-Level Achievement Cultivation Project" of Shenzhen University's Phase III Construction of High-Level Universities (Project No: 24GSPCG18).

References

1. Zhang, X.: An analysis of domestic plant dyeing research in the past 30 years. Dyeing Finish. Technol. **36**(06), 9–11 (2014)
2. Zhang, W., Huang, P., Yao, J.: Research progress of natural plant dyes for textile dyeing. Print. Dyeing Aux. **35**(11), 5–9 (2018)
3. Chen, X., Song, D., Guo, S.: Inheritance of plant dyeing techniques in clothing design. J. Plant Genetic Resour. **24**(06), 18–23 (2023)
4. Sun, J., et al.: Textile industrial application and development of plant dyes. Chin. J. Text. Eng. **1**(06), 54–70 (2023)

5. Shi, X.: Virtual reality technology's application status and development trends. Digit. Technol. Appl. **41**(06), 77–79 (2023)
6. Xiang, W.: Application and development of virtual reality technology in clothing design - comment on "clothing virtual reality and implementation." Print. Dyeing Aux. **35**(12), 76 (2018)
7. Cong, S., Zhang, W.: Application of digital technology in clothing customization. J. Donghua Univ. (Nat. Sci. Ed.) 125–130 (2006)
8. Sun, Y.: Plant dyeing technology. Silk 24–27+29–0 (2000)
9. Wei, L.: Establishment of plant dyeing color system and production of dyeing color cards. J. Liaodong Univ. (Nat. Sci. Ed.) **27**(03), 197–200 (2020)
10. Guo, R.: Dynamic display of clothing based on virtual reality technology. Western Leather **45**(03), 20–22 (2023)
11. Gao, X.: Interpretation of standards: Analysis of relevant standards for textiles dyed with plant dyes. Silk **60**(12), 162–166 (2023)

Immersive Virtual Reality Embodied Interaction Design for the Ephemeral Monument of Tengwang Pavilion

Yue Zhao and Rui Tang[✉]

Jiangxi University of Finance and Economics, No. 665, Yuping West Street, Xinjian District, Nanchang, China
2603805429@qq.com

Abstract. Built over 1,300 years ago, the Tengwang Pavilion has undergone 29 renovations and witnessed the complex historical trajectory encompassing wars and various other factors. Regrettably, with the passage of time, a portion of its cultural essence and relics has gradually faded, hindering contemporary individuals from fully appreciating its original charm. This study employs virtual reality technology to delve into the profound interactive design and exhibition of the thousand-year-old historical and cultural treasure, the Tengwang Pavilion. Through procedural modeling, geometric optimization, and Level of Detail (LOD) grading, we have successfully constructed a highly realistic and immersive virtual environment of the Tengwang Pavilion. The game design is rooted in the historical narrative and representative elements of the Tengwang Pavilion, integrating a range of interactive features such as ascending heights for panoramic views, composing poems, engaging in rowing activities, and other tasks. The objective is to enable players to gain a deeper understanding of the historical development trajectory and cultural heritage of the Tengwang Pavilion through personal engagement and firsthand experience. The project effectively resurrects the history and culture of the Tengwang Pavilion through the ingenious implementation of virtual reality and interactive design. By providing the public with a novel means of experiencing cultural heritage, it introduces innovative concepts and methodologies that pave the way for future advancements in cultural communication and educational initiatives.

Keywords: Tengwang Pavilion · Virtual reality technology · Interactive design · Cultural heritage experience

1 Introduction

The Tengwang Pavilion, an ancient edifice boasting a history spanning thousands of years, stands prominently as one of the four renowned structures in ancient China. It harmoniously merges the grand architectural style of the Tang Dynasty with the intricate designs of the Song Dynasty. Since its establishment in the 7th century, the Tengwang Pavilion has undergone 29 renovations, standing as a silent witness to wars and the ebb

C. Stephanidis et al. (Eds.): HCII 2024, CCIS 2116, pp. 397–404, 2024.
https://doi.org/10.1007/978-3-031-61950-2_43

and flow of history itself. Beyond its physical form, the Tengwang Pavilion serves as a vessel for Chinese culture, encapsulating a wealth of historical and cultural significance. However, as time has elapsed, a portion of its cultural essence and relics has gradually dissipated, impeding the contemporary populace from fully embracing its original allure.

While the historical and cultural significance of the Tengwang Pavilion has garnered widespread recognition, challenges persist in its preservation and inheritance. Traditional methods of display, such as showcasing cultural relics in museums, often fall short in fully conveying the rich history and cultural heritage encapsulated by the Tengwang Pavilion. Furthermore, current research predominantly focuses on the architectural style and historical context of the pavilion, with less emphasis on leveraging virtual reality and interactive modalities to restore and showcase its historical and cultural legacy. Equally important is the exploration of interactive tasks that effectively convey its cultural value to the public, fostering a deeper understanding of the pavilion's history and culture. Consequently, the need to explore and employ interactive approaches for cultural dissemination has emerged as a pressing research agenda. This entails investigating how culture can be effectively communicated through interactive means, ultimately facilitating a profound comprehension of cultural aspects among the general public.

This paper aims to address crucial aspects pertaining to the precise restoration of cultural heritage using virtual reality technology, as well as the augmentation of public comprehension of cultural content through interaction design. In light of these objectives, the following issues will be thoroughly investigated and analyzed:

How to enable the public to have a deeper understanding of the historical development track and cultural heritage of Tengwang Pavilion through the interactive form of virtual reality?

To address the aforementioned research challenges, this study presents a meticulously designed immersive interactive game utilizing virtual reality technology. Set against the cultural backdrop of the Tengwang Pavilion, the game incorporates a series of interactive tasks aimed at facilitating a profound understanding of its history and culture. Leveraging the Unreal Engine development platform, meticulous attention is given to replicating historical intricacies and seamlessly integrating cultural elements. This meticulous approach enables players to personally experience the historical transformations and cultural allure of the Tengwang Pavilion within the immersive virtual space.

2 Related Work

In recent years, a plethora of scholarly research has explored the application of various technologies in the preservation and exhibition of cultural heritage. Portales et al. (Year) examined the impact of technological advancements on cultural heritage preservation and emphasized the significance of employing ICT, VR, AR, and other technologies to reimagine and exhibit cultural heritage, thereby enhancing user experience and heritage conservation [1]. Pietroni and Ferdani (Year) focused on the digital reproduction and restoration of virtual heritage, emphasizing the need for authenticity, reliability, and a reevaluation of related concepts [2]. Fan, Dandan et al. (Year) showcased the application and challenges of virtual restoration technology in the realm of cultural heritage protection. They proposed the establishment of cultural heritage databases and improvements in software and hardware design to foster technological advancements [3]. Soto-Martin et al. (Year) demonstrated the utilization of VR for the reconstruction and restoration of historical buildings and murals, underscoring the importance of immersive and interactive VR experiences in cultural heritage exhibitions [4]. Chai and Deng (Year) introduced the novel concept of "embodied transformation" to enhance the social interaction of digital art in cultural heritage exhibitions through the transfer of media, experiences, and encounters [5]. These case studies collectively exemplify the wide-ranging applications and potential of technology in the conservation and exhibition of cultural heritage. By surpassing the limitations of traditional approaches, they enhance the effectiveness and display quality of cultural heritage preservation while providing users with more profound and immersive experiences.

Currently, scholars primarily focus on leveraging technology to improve and enhance the preservation and exhibition of cultural heritage. However, there remains a need for further in-depth discussions on how to effectively showcase cultural connotations and provide users with more profound cultural experiences through interactive modalities within the virtual reality-restored environments of cultural sites. Consequently, this study conducts an extensive exploration of the Tengwang Pavilion as a cultural site. Its objective is to delve deeper into the cultural value of the Tengwang Pavilion by harnessing virtual reality technology. Additionally, the study aims to investigate more captivating interaction mechanisms to enhance user experiences and augment their perception and comprehension of the cultural connotations embodied within the Tengwang Pavilion.

3 Related Work

3.1 Model Design

Prior to commencing the development of the virtual reality environment for the Tengwang Pavilion, extensive literature reviews and data collection were conducted. As a historical and cultural heritage site, our primary focus lies in achieving a more precise restoration of the cultural site. Given the numerous restoration and reconstruction efforts undertaken on the Tengwang Pavilion in modern times, particular attention was dedicated to its recent reconstruction period to gather the most accurate information regarding its architectural form and structure. To faithfully restore the historical style of the Tengwang Pavilion, we consulted materials from different periods pertaining to the pavilion, ensuring a comprehensive and accurate representation.

In terms of material design for the Tengwang Pavilion, we employed a combination of historical document descriptions and contemporary modeling techniques. To exemplify, the pillars of the pavilion were crafted using antique wood, with meticulous adjustments made to achieve a simplistic and elegant appearance while capturing the desired light effects. The roof, adorned with antique glazed tiles, was designed to showcase its distinctive and ornate style. Furthermore, we tailored the material combinations according to the spatial layout and functional requirements of the Tengwang Pavilion, aiming to create a virtual environment that harmoniously blends historical authenticity and modern aesthetic sensibilities. During the modeling process, we adopted high-precision modeling technologies and extensively referenced historical photos and documents to ensure the accurate representation of each component of the Tengwang Pavilion. Through meticulous detailing and optimization techniques, including texture enhancements, we enhanced the realism of the model. Additionally, several adjustments and optimizations were implemented to ensure optimal performance of the model within the interactive game environment (Figs. 1 and 2).

Fig. 1. Digital topology model of Tengwang Pavilion

Fig. 2. Construction of virtual environment

3.2 Interactive Program Design

In the design of our interactive program, we place significant emphasis on the seamless integration of technology applications and user experience, aiming to effectively communicate the historical and cultural significance of the Tengwang Pavilion. To achieve this, we leverage state-of-the-art game engine technology to implement a diverse range of interactive tasks for players. These tasks are thoughtfully crafted to not only provide engaging challenges but also serve as a means to progressively guide players towards a deeper understanding of the cultural connotations embedded within the Tengwang Pavilion.

For instance, upon entering the virtual Tengwang Pavilion, players will be prompted to undertake a task that involves ascending to a higher point and gazing into the distance. An example of this is Scene 6, where numerous Tengwang Pavilion-related poems depict the act of climbing to heights and taking in the panoramic vistas. Players can ascend the virtual staircase to the pinnacle of the Tengwang Pavilion and behold the breathtaking scenery of the entire virtual world. Through this experience, players can not only appreciate the grandeur of the pavilion's architecture but also immerse themselves in the sentiments of the ancients.

Additionally, we have incorporated an interactive poetry writing task into the design. In specific areas of the Tengwang Pavilion, such as Scene 10, players can trigger interactions related to composing poetry. The system offers an array of poetic options, allowing players to select verses that align with their preferences and understanding, enabling them to create their own unique poem. This design not only enhances the game's entertainment value but also fosters a deeper comprehension of the cultural connotations of the Tengwang Pavilion during the creative process.

To enrich the player's experience, we have included boating tasks, as exemplified in Scene 12. Near the lakes surrounding the Tengwang Pavilion, players can virtually rent a boat and row across the lake, basking in the reflections of the pavilion and the surrounding natural beauty. This design not only expands the exploration space for players but also evokes a sense of tranquility and relaxation during gameplay.

Furthermore, we offer players the freedom to explore the entire human scene. They can freely navigate through every nook and cranny of the Tengwang Pavilion, savoring the beauty of various scenes. Whether it's the majestic structures of the Tengwang Pavilion or the surrounding lakes, gardens, and other natural landscapes, they will be vividly presented in the virtual world. Through this feature, players can gain a comprehensive understanding of the history, culture, and cultural landscapes associated with the Tengwang Pavilion.

Lastly, we have designed a humanistic tour route for players. Many scenes along this route faithfully recreate historical sites, allowing players to experience the historical transformations and cultural heritage of the Tengwang Pavilion. Through this design, players can develop a profound understanding of the cultural connotations and historical significance of the Tengwang Pavilion.

Through the implementation of these interactive tasks, our goal is to provide players with not only an opportunity to appreciate the beauty of the Tengwang Pavilion within the game but also a chance to personally participate in and experience the history and culture of the pavilion. We aim to deliver a vibrant and immersive gaming experience that engages players on multiple levels (Figs. 3 and 4).

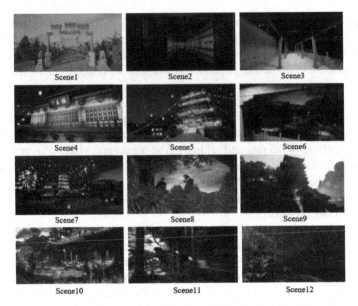

Scene1   Scene2   Scene3

Scene4   Scene5   Scene6

Scene7   Scene8   Scene9

Scene10   Scene11   Scene12

Fig. 3. Restored scene of Tengwang Pavilion cultural site

Fig. 4. Virtual environment rendering

4 Discussion and Limitations

When designing interactive links and scenes for cultural sites using virtual reality, it is crucial to consider technical feasibility and implementation costs to ensure the practicality of the interactive scheme. While showcasing the historical culture of these sites, it is essential to strive for a seamless integration of historical allusions, such as poetic imagery, and interactive scenes. This approach enables users to better appreciate the allure of cultural sites through interactive experiences within the digitally restored cultural environments.

Furthermore, despite the significant advancements in 3D modeling and virtual reality technologies, challenges may persist in acquiring and processing detailed data pertaining to historic buildings. For example, the lack of data may result in inaccuracies when attempting to restore certain historical details. Additionally, the rendering quality of virtual environments and the real-time nature of user interactions can be limited by hardware capabilities and device constraints. These factors should be carefully considered to strike a balance between achieving a high level of realism and ensuring smooth user interactions within the virtual environment.

By addressing these considerations, we can create interactive experiences that effectively convey the historical and cultural significance of cultural sites while taking into account technological constraints and cost-effectiveness.

Hence, due to the passage of time, ancient buildings inevitably undergo aging and damage. Alongside physical protection measures, it is imperative to employ digital means to permanently preserve these cultural heritages, thereby safeguarding the imprints of human civilization for posterity. By leveraging digital technologies, we can ensure the enduring preservation of these invaluable cultural artifacts, transcending the constraints of physical decay.

5   Conclusion

This research endeavors to employ virtual reality technology to faithfully recreate the rich history and culture of the Tengwang Pavilion. We have designed an immersive virtual reality interactive game centered around the Tengwang Pavilion. Leveraging key techniques such as programmatic modeling, geometric optimization, and Level of Detail (LOD) grading, we have successfully constructed a highly realistic and immersive virtual environment that faithfully represents the Tengwang Pavilion.

In the game design, we draw upon the historical narratives and significant landmarks associated with the Tengwang Pavilion as references. By integrating a series of interactive links, we provide users with a diverse range of immersive experiences, granting them access to a wealth of information and enabling them to actively engage with the history and culture of the Tengwang Pavilion. Through these interactive links, users can personally participate in and experience the rich historical tapestry and cultural heritage of the Tengwang Pavilion, fostering a deeper understanding of its historical development trajectory and cultural legacy.

Through the empirical findings of this study, we have substantiated the immense potential of virtual reality technology in the realms of cultural heritage preservation and exhibition. Moving forward, we anticipate an increasing number of researchers and practitioners harnessing the power of virtual reality technology, in conjunction with embodied interaction and gamification design, to deliver to the public an even more immersive, captivating, and profound cultural heritage experience. By leveraging these innovative approaches, we can bridge the gap between traditional cultural heritage and contemporary audiences, fostering a deeper appreciation and engagement with our shared cultural legacy.

References

1. Portalés, C., et al.: Digital cultural heritage. Multimodal Technol. Interact. **2**(3), 58 (2018)
2. Pietroni, E., et al.: Virtual restoration and virtual reconstruction in cultural heritage: terminology, methodologies, visual representation techniques and cognitive models. Information **12**(4), 167 (2021)
3. Dandan, F., et al.: Current status of application of virtual restoration technology in cultural heritage conservation. Front. Soc. Sci. Technol. **4**(4), 83–90 (2022)

4. Soto-Martin, O., et al.: A digital reconstruction of a historical building and virtual reintegration of mural paintings to create an interactive and immersive experience in virtual reality. Appl. Sci. **10**(2), 597 (2020)

5. Qiuxia, C.: A new exploration of virtual reality displays of immovable cultural relics: a case study of digital art special exhibition "Carving Han Rhyme -- A Journey to Find Han Dream". Southeast Cult. **39**(06), 12–19+191–192 (2023)

Visualization and Interactive Design of Cultural Heritage Information

Qinqin Zhao⬤ and Shisi Wang(✉)⬤

Wuhan University of Technology, No. 122 Luoshi Road, Hongshan District, Wuhan, China
sunnywang@whut.edu.cn

Abstract. Tibetan medicine, as a valuable achievement, encompasses rich medical knowledge and unique cultural traditions. Among them, the "*Medical Canon in Four Sections*" stands as a representative classic work of Tibetan medicine, containing invaluable medical wisdom. However, there are several challenges in the dissemination and application of the "*Medical Canon in Four Sections*". Firstly, for non-medical professionals, its medical content may be overly specialized and difficult to understand. Additionally, difficulties in preservation, scattered content, inconsistent versions, outdated information, and accessibility issues often hinder people from quickly and accurately finding the information they need. To address these challenges, this study collected, organized, summarized, and analyzed information from different versions of the "*Medical Canon in Four Sections*". Using the metaphor of "three trees of life", we interpreted its content, establishing a logical framework of "tree-branch-leaf". Simultaneously, we developed a visual dynamic interactive software that allows users to swiftly search medical content, understand visual information, and interact with relevant knowledge points, thereby enhancing users' efficiency and experience in acquiring Tibetan medicine knowledge. By combining digital dissemination methods, this paper provides users with a comprehensive and agile platform for learning Tibetan medicine knowledge, which facilitates the dissemination and application of the valuable information within the "*Medical Canon in Four Sections*" and promotes the inheritance and development of Tibetan medicine culture.

Keyword: Tibetan Medicine · Information Visualization · Interaction Design

1 Introduction

Tibetan medicine, as a cultural heritage, carries rich medical knowledge and unique cultural traditions, exerting significant influence on the development of human medicine and culture, and thus is regarded as a valuable asset for all humanity [1]. The *Medical Canon in Four Sections*, as a treasure of traditional Chinese medicine, has inscribed a brilliant chapter in the cultural history of traditional Chinese medicine [2]. In order to better disseminate and teach the knowledge of the *Medical Canon in Four Sections*, Tibetans have compiled a large number of medicinal charts and medical hanging scrolls. These hanging scrolls, based on the medical work *Medical Canon in Four Sections*, are divided into 80 pieces, and vividly depict the content of Tibetan medicine through Tangka paintings, presenting it in a lifelike and realistic manner.

C. Stephanidis et al. (Eds.): HCII 2024, CCIS 2116, pp. 405–414, 2024.
https://doi.org/10.1007/978-3-031-61950-2_44

As a classic in ancient medicine, the Medical Canon in Four Sections contains rich medical wisdom, but also faces some challenges [3]. First, for non-medical professionals, the medical content of the Medical Canon in Four Sections may be too specialized and difficult to understand. Additionally, due to difficulties in preservation, scattered content, inconsistent versions, outdated information, and limited accessibility, people often struggle to quickly and accurately find the information they need. To overcome these challenges, it is necessary to digitize and organize the Medical Canon in Four Sections, and utilize modern technology to establish a comprehensive database. At the same time, leveraging digital dissemination methods is crucial to better integrate it into the modern medical system and ensure its enduring value.

Therefore, in response to the challenges of digital dissemination posed by the *Medical Canon in Four Sections* and its scroll content, we have developed a visualization dynamic interactive software named "*Medical Canon in Four Sections*". Drawing inspiration from 80 scrolls, the software constructs a "tree-branch-leaf" knowledge framework, aiming to assist users in easily accessing and understanding the medical knowledge and visual information in the *Medical Canon in Four Sections*. Through this software, users can quickly search the content of the *Medical Canon in Four Sections* and interact with the production process of Thangka art and related knowledge points. The results of this research not only enhance the efficiency of knowledge acquisition in the field of Tibetan medicine, but also stimulate people's interest in the content of the *Medical Canon in Four Sections*, promoting the digital dissemination and popularization of Tibetan culture.

2   Related Work

2.1   Study of the Content of the Medical Canon in Sections

The *Medical Canon in Four Sections*, as a classic of Tibetan medicine covering multiple domains, has drawn widespread attention and deep exploration from researchers. Scholars are committed to delving into the rich knowledge contained within the *Medical Canon in Four Sections*, analyzing its medical theories, diagnostic and treatment methods, and pharmaceutical applications, while also considering its close associations with Tibetan culture and religious beliefs [4]. Research also includes literary studies on the history, versions, and compilation characteristics of the *Medical Canon in Four Sections*, as well as discussions on its position and influence in the development of Tibetan medicine.

Wüntrang Dhondrup et al. analyzed the disease classifications listed in the "Oral Instructions Treatise" of the Medical Canon in Four Sections (Manngagrgyud), exploring the causal relationships between five diseases among the fifteen major disease categories [5]. Cairang Nanjia, combining the content of the Medical Canon in Four Sections, studied the inherent effective rules in the compatibility of prescriptions for treating heart diseases [6]. Wen Cheng Danzhi conducted a scientific analysis of the theory of "taste transformation" based on the medication laws in the Medical Canon in Four Sections [7]. Ren Zeng Duo Jie analyzed the content of the Medical Canon in Four Sections, focusing on bloodletting therapy, which treats 63 diseases based on the "cold and heat differentiation" fundamental principle, particularly suitable for diseases with heat syndromes such as those involving fever, lumps, and swellings [8].

2.2 Digitalization Research in Tibetan Medicine

Wüntrang Dhondrup and colleagues conducted the first analysis of the database, development, and methodology of Tibetan medicine informatics, quantitatively evaluating Tibetan medical works and disease categories within these data sources [9]. Christine McCarthy Madsen from the University of Oxford shed light on the role of academic libraries in Tibetan medicine development, providing normative inspiration for future research and discussions on their online presence [10]. T. Shan et al. utilized Neo4j in conjunction with Py2neo knowledge graph technology to construct a knowledge graph of the *Medical Canon in Four Sections* [11]. Yong Cuo et al. studied a method combining deep learning text line detection with rule-based layout analysis to achieve layout analysis of Tibetan historical documents, promoting the digitization of Tibetan classical texts [12]. Ravi Krishna et al. digitized Tibetan documents using a text analysis tool based on machine learning technology, combining optical character recognition with manual input [13]. Wen Cheng Dangzhi et al. delved into the study of prescriptions in the *Medical Canon in Four Sections*, proposing the construction of a prescription database based on Visual FoxPro and complex networks to explore medication rules in the classics [7]. Shen Wang et al. conducted structural visualization analysis based on the content of the *Medical Canon in Four Sections*, exploring the relationship between Tibetan medical symptoms, etiology, medication rules, and the discovery path of new prescriptions [14]. Liu Xiaotong from Yunnan University of China utilized artistic design to assist in the popularization and dissemination of Tibetan medicine knowledge, focusing on information visualization design centered around Tibetan medicinal plants. Xin Nie et al. applied spatial analysis technology using ArcGIS to express the spatiotemporal development of Chinese medicine intangible cultural heritage, analyzing factors influencing the spatial distribution of Chinese medicine intangible cultural heritage [15].

The *Medical Canon in Four Sections*, as a traditional medical application book, holds tremendous potential for application. Its system is extensive, particularly detailed in the fields of pathology and pharmacology. However, this specialized content might appear overly complex for ordinary users. Current research mainly focuses on the digitalization and visualization aspects, leaving gaps in user experience and application scenarios. Therefore, this paper emphasizes the integration of digital technology and interactive design to visualize the content of the *Medical Canon in Four Sections* and develop more intuitive and user-friendly applications. This will help better disseminate and utilize the valuable information in the *Medical Canon in Four Sections*, promoting the inheritance and development of Tibetan medicine culture.

3 Design

3.1 Design Methodology

During the material collection phase, we conducted thorough searches and analyses of different versions of the *Medical Canon in Four Sections* and related pictorial materials, and categorized the literature based on the principles of knowledge visualization. The *Medical Canon in Four Sections* exists in various versions, including the Zatang version, the Loroke version, the Ereguochaga version, the Dege second edition, and the Beijing edition, among others, (see Fig. 1) [16, 17]. By examining the relationships and contexts among these versions, we found that the Zatang version serves as the prototype for all woodblock versions of the *Medical Canon in Four Sections*, with the earliest carving and the highest version value. Therefore, our research focuses on a detailed exploration of the Zatang version of the *Medical Canon in Four Sections*.

The content of the *Medical Canon in Four Sections* is classified according to different medical themes, such as disease diagnosis, treatment methods, medication formulations, anatomical knowledge, etc. It is also classified based on historical periods, schools of thought, and regions, such as divisions according to different historical periods or medical schools. Combining the content of the Medical Canon in Four Sections with the pictorial materials, our work interprets them in the form of three trees of life, corresponding to the three parts of the canon: physiology and pathology, disease diagnosis, and disease treatment. This vivid interpretive approach provides a unique perspective and context for understanding and exploring Tibetan medicine. Through this method, users can gain a deeper understanding of the medical knowledge contained in the *Medical Canon in Four Sections*, from physiology to pathology, from diagnosis to treatment, thus establishing a systematic and vivid cognitive framework. This research not only contributes to a deeper understanding of Tibetan medicine but also provides important references and support for subsequent research and visualization presentations.

Fig. 1. Different versions of *Medical Canon in Four Sections*

3.2 Prototype Design

When designing the interface and visual specifications, we focused on utilizing modern color translation to cater to contemporary aesthetics. Firstly, we addressed the issues of overly complex shapes and overly vibrant colors in the hanging scroll images, adopting a concept of simplification. By reducing the complexity of the graphics and the saturation of colors, visual information becomes clearer and easier to understand, (see Fig. 2). In interface design, colors were referenced from the original thangka palette, attempting to lower color saturation to retain the unique style of thangka while ensuring overall color harmony, (see Fig. 3). This design approach can maintain traditional historical features while emphasizing modern application transformation. Through carefully selecting primary and complementary colors, we can preserve the traditional characteristics of thangka while aligning with modern aesthetic trends. This allows users to experience the charm of traditional culture while conveniently accessing knowledge through interactive means, (see Fig. 4). Additionally, we can utilize principles of color psychology to choose appropriate color schemes based on the characteristics of different functions and content, enhancing user comfort and attractiveness to the interface.

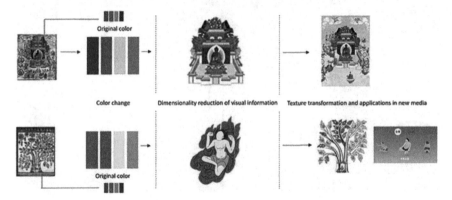

Fig. 2. Interface elements, color matching and visual scheme design process

Fig. 3. Digital translation of thangka production process

Fig. 4. The medical Thangka images, exhibiting significant signs of wear, underwent a meticulous redesign

Furthermore, in terms of interface layout and element design, the design avoids excessive decoration and redundant information. By organizing the content of the *Medical Canon in Four Sections* into a logical framework of "tree-branch-leaf," the relationship between interface elements becomes clear and adheres to the principles of human-computer interaction, (see Fig. 5). Moreover, to enhance user convenience, the interface undergoes iterative refinement, employing intuitive icons and interactive elements. Users can quickly and accurately access the desired information by clicking on the branch graphics they are interested in. The interface material has been transformed from traditional fabric to a style suitable for modern app media, such as flat design and minimalist style. This transformation aims to improve the user experience, aligning the application more closely with contemporary aesthetics and user habits. By adopting flat design and minimalist style, we simplify interface elements, reduce visual complexity, and make it easier for users to understand and navigate the application, thereby enhancing overall user satisfaction and experience quality.

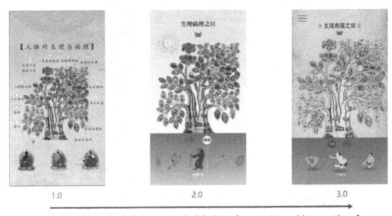

Iterate repeatedly to find the most suitable interface style and interaction format.

Fig. 5. Interface elements, color matching and visual scheme design process

3.3   Ineractive Program Design

The Interactive Program for the *Medical Canon in Four Sections* is based on Unity and C#. Its graphics are presented in a two-dimensional plane, and it achieves a 3D visual experience through layered processing of the screen and the development of parallax scrolling technology. The program is designed and developed from three aspects: animation effects, interaction logic, and image text rendering, (see Fig. 6).

In terms of animation effects, the SceneManager.LoadSceneAsync method is called to asynchronously load specified scenes, and a while loop is used to wait for the completion of scene loading. Within the loop, the asyncLoad.isDone property is checked to determine if asynchronous loading has been completed, avoiding blocking the main thread and thereby improving game performance and user experience. The image rendering achieves various materials such as flow, transparency, glow, and blur, combined with Gaussian blur algorithm, providing users with diverse visual experiences.

Moreover, the program implements various complex text rendering effects, including distance fields, masks, font text filling, outlines, shadows, reflections, and glowing effects, utilizing techniques such as color interpolation and cube map reflection. The overall implementation achieves smooth animation effects and intricate interaction logic, meeting users' needs for information exchange and interaction. Additionally, it can be published to multiple platforms through Unity's cross-platform capabilities.

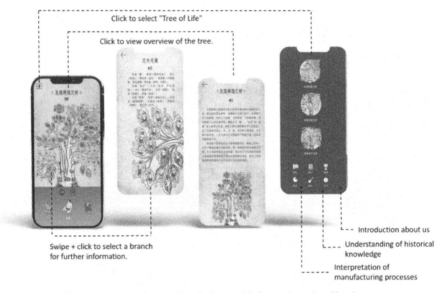

Fig. 6. Interface interaction design and information visualization

4   Discussion and Limitation

Through in-depth analysis and exploration of the *Medical Canon in Four Sections*, this paper transforms its important information into visual forms vividly through the App, such as the "Three Trees of Life," and adopts a logical framework of "tree-branch-leaf," which helps users intuitively understand the key content and structure of medical knowledge. Utilizing interactive design techniques, we provide users with diverse browsing and querying methods, such as interactive navigation systems and search functions, enhancing user convenience and experience. In terms of interaction, we have designed engaging animation effects and gamified experiences, such as the "branch swing" animation effect, to attract users' attention and increase their engagement.

However, despite our efforts to overcome some obstacles in the design, there are still some shortcomings. The completeness and accuracy of the data may affect the visualization effect and user experience of the software. As the medical knowledge contained in the *Medical Canon in Four Sections* has a profound background in Tibetan medicine culture, users may need a certain level of cultural literacy and background knowledge to fully understand and apply the content in the software. Additionally, for Tibetan medicine professionals, the software may lack specialized analysis tools, limited functionality for in-depth research, and insufficient interactivity.

5   Conclusion and Future Work

This software demonstrates significant advantages in both functionality and user experience. By integrating digital dissemination methods, it provides users with a comprehensive, rich, and convenient platform for learning Tibetan medical knowledge, thus facilitating the inheritance and development of Tibetan medicine culture. The contributions of this study are as follows:

1. Visual design tailored to the vast medical system and knowledge points of the *Medical Canon in Four Sections*, making it more accessible for practical use.
2. Development of an app allowing users to easily search for knowledge and access educational materials.
3. Effective dissemination of the history and culture of the *Medical Canon in Four Sections* through interactive features.

In future work, the app will need further improvement in data acquisition and processing techniques to enhance accuracy and comprehensiveness. Additionally, providing explanations and guidance on user cultural backgrounds can help users better understand Tibetan medical knowledge, thereby improving their learning experience and satisfaction.

References

1. Cheng, Y., et al.: Analysis on the english translation of the four medical codes of tibetan medical classics. Chin. J. Integr. Med. **43**(10), 1261–1267 (2013)
2. Dejitzom, et al.: The four medical codes: an encyclopedia of tibetan medicine from national to international perspective. Arch. China (07), 16–18 (2023)
3. Cairang, W.M., Jia, L., et al.: Research on the literature inheritance and development based on the ancient Tibetan medical classic "Four Medical Codes". Basic Chin. Med. **1**(05), 74–80 (2022)
4. Zhaxi, D., et al.: Basic Chinese: Theory of "the four medical" in the Tibetan ethical thoughts. Chin. Med. Guide **25**(20), 1261–1267 (2019)
5. Dhondrup, W., et al.: Dataset of illness classifications in sowa rigpa: compilations from the oral instructions treatise of the Tibetan medical classic. Chengdu Univ. Tradit. Chin. Med. **250**(29), 2352–3409 (2020)

6. Nanjia, C., et al.: A study of the patterns of prescriptions for heart diseases in The Four Tantras**05**(01n04), 39–41 (2022)
7. Wen-Cheng, D., et al.: The law of drug use in the four medical codes – an analysis of the scientific connotation of the theory of "flavor characteristics transforming flavor". J. Chin. Exp. Formulae **25**(05), 201–207 (2019)
8. Ren, Z., et al.: Analysis on bloodletting methods in Huangdi's internal classic and four medical codes. Shanghai J. Acupunct.**34**(07), 0686 (2015)
9. Dhondrup, W., et al.: Tibetan medical informatics: an emerging field in sowa rigpa pharmacological & clinical research. J. Ethnopharmacol. **250**(112481), 0378–8741 (2020)
10. Madsen, C.M., et al.:Communities, innovation, and critical mass: understanding the impact of digitization on scholarship in the humanities through the case of tibetan and himalayan studies. J. Ethnopharmacol. **250**(11281), 0378–8741 (2020)
11. Shan, T., et al.: Construction of knowledge graph based on the four treatises of tibetan medicine and its searching system. In: 2023 IEEE 4th International Conference on Pattern Recognition and Machine Learning (PRML), Urumqi, China, pp. 463–469. IEEE (2023)
12. Cuo, Y., et al.: Layout analysis of tibetan historical documents based on deep learning. In: Proceedings of the 2019 the International Conference on Pattern Recognition and Artificial Intelligence, pp. 96–101 .Association for Computing Machinery, New York (2019)
13. Krishna, R., et al.: Applying text analytics to the mind-section literature of the tibetan tradition of the great perfection. ACM Trans. Asian Low-Resour. Lang. Inf. Process. **20**(21), 1–32 (2021)
14. Wang, S., et al.: Research on knowledge discovery of ancient Tibetan medical. Mod. Inf. **43**(11), 21–36 (2019)
15. Nie, X., et al.: The spatial distribution of traditional intangible cultural heritage medicine of China and its influencing factors. Heritage Sci. **11**(1), 90 (2023)
16. Dorje, P., et al.: The origin of the four medical codes. J. Xizang Univ. **37**(04), 116–124 (2022)

Digitization of Cultural Relics: Augmented Reality Display of Ru Ware

Jie Zhou and Xinyue Liu[✉] [ID]

East China University of Science and Technology, Meilong Road 130, Shanghai, China
lxyky1230@163.com

Abstract. Cultural relics are products of human production and life at a certain stage, containing cultural and aesthetic elements that has a reciprocating effect on the development of contemporary humanity. Traditional methods of relic display face numerous challenges in the digital era. Applying digital technology to this field is a method to enhance the visibility of relics, as well as promote their protection and inheritance. Ru ware refers to celadon ceramics produced during the heyday of the Ru kiln in China, which holds significant value. However, outdated and monotonous display methods have rendered them unattractive, and public knowledge about Ru ware is generally limited. This paper analyzes the current exhibition methods of Ru ware relics, and through case studies, field investigations, and questionnaire surveys, the necessity and feasibility of applying AR technology to Ru ware exhibitions are determined. Subsequently, a viable solution is proposed: integrating AR glasses with Ru ware. Practical evidence demonstrates that this solution can enhance public awareness and interest in Ru ware, thereby playing a positive role in the protection and inheritance of cultural heritage.

Keywords: Digitization · Cultural Relics · AR · Ru Ware

1 Introduction

Cultural relics refer to "cultural artifacts of human production and life that exist in society or are buried underground and underwater." [1] Protected relics possess historical, artistic, scientific, and educational value, with their cultural and aesthetic essence playing a significant role in contemporary human development. In recent years, there has been increasing global attention to the conservation and exhibition of cultural relics. However, in the context of the "digital technology" era, research on relic conservation and development faces numerous challenges. These include contradictions between the interactive needs of viewers and the traditional one-way exhibition methods, the demand for systematic learning and the scattered distribution of relics, and the contrast between the diverse entertainment options and the relatively dull museum exhibitions.

The development of digital technology, especially in areas such as digital photography, 3D information acquisition, Virtual Reality, Augmented Reality, multimedia, and networking, has provided a solid technical foundation for the digitization, preservation, and development of cultural relics. Attempts to integrate digital technology into the field

© The Author(s), under exclusive license to Springer Nature Switzerland AG 2024
C. Stephanidis et al. (Eds.): HCII 2024, CCIS 2116, pp. 415–425, 2024.
https://doi.org/10.1007/978-3-031-61950-2_45

of relic conservation and exhibition have demonstrated tremendous potential. Some notable projects include the "American Memory" [2]program initiated by the Library of Congress in 1990, which focused on digitizing collections; "The Digital Michelangelo Project" [3], a large-scale 3D scanning project of sculptures conducted jointly by Stanford University and the University of Washington in 1997; the collaboration between Rokid and Liangzhu Museum in 2020 to create a smart guidance system based on AR glasses; and the "Horizon of Khufu" virtual reality exhibition [4] developed by Excurio in partnership with the Harvard University Giza Project in 2022.

Adapting to the trend of the times, the reasonable application of digital technology in relic preservation and exhibition work establishes a bridge of communication between relics and viewers. This enhances the public accessibility, vitality, and social influence of relics, marking new directions in the field of cultural relic exhibition today.

2   The Demand for the Digitization Exhibition of Ru Ware

Chinese ceramics are renowned worldwide, and the Song Dynasty represents a pinnacle in the history of Chinese ceramic development. Among the many ceramics produced during the Song Dynasty, Ru Ware is particularly favored for its elegant colors and simple designs. However, the current display methods of Song Dynasty Ru Ware in museums are outdated and dull, failing to meet the public's aesthetic needs. Additionally, the craftsmanship of Ru Ware is designated as intangible cultural heritage in China. Despite its cultural importance, public understanding of Ru Ware and its production techniques is limited, raising concerns about the potential loss of this heritage. Introducing digital technology into the conservation and exhibition of Ru Ware can greatly contribute to the dissemination of Ru Ware culture and the inheritance of Ru Ware production techniques.

2.1   The Value and Status of Ru Ware

Ru Kiln, one of the five famous kilns of the Song Dynasty including "Ru, Guan, Jun, Ge, and Ding", derives its name from its location in Ruzhou (now Ruzhou City, Henan Province). Ru Ware refers to celadon ceramics fired in the Ru Kiln during the Song Dynasty. As shown in Fig. 1, Ru-kiln celadon features an ash-grey body with a light azure glaze coating. The coating was usually covered with fine crackles, commonly known as "ice crackles". Typical forms include bowls, brush washers, and zun goblets.

The extremely high value of Ru Ware is primarily reflected in the following aspects:

Looking back at the history of Chinese porcelain making, there are hardly any terms like "Tang porcelain" or "Yuan porcelain" that associate dynasties with porcelain. However, "Song porcelain" exists as an independent term and has gained widespread recognition. Song porcelain has transcended its role as mere daily utensils of ancient people and has become a symbol reflecting various aspects of the Song Dynasty, including politics, economy, and culture.

Secondly, Ru Ware is the most representative type of porcelain in the Song Dynasty, with the saying in Chinese ceramic history that "Ru Kiln ranks first." Ru Kiln not only broke the tradition of "southern celadon and northern white" that had existed since the Tang Dynasty but also elevated the technique of celadon firing to unprecedented heights by drawing on various influences. Additionally, it pioneered new aesthetic realms, transitioning from the grand and majestic aesthetics of the Tang Dynasty to the delicate and restrained aesthetic culture of the Song Dynasty, thereby influencing subsequent national characteristics and aesthetic orientations.

Lastly, due to the short production period of Ru Kiln and the rarity of Ru Ware, Ru Ware is particularly precious.

Fig. 1. Some Ru Kiln porcelain from the Song Dynasty, originating from the Taipei Palace Museum. In clockwise order from the top left in the figure are: Narcissus basin with bluish-green glaze, Brush washer with celadon glaze, Feng-hua mallet vase with greenish-blue glaze, Dish with celadon glaze, Lotus-shaped warming bowl in light bluish-green glaze, Gallbladder-shaped vase with green glaze. [5]

2.2 The Necessity of Combining Ru Ware with Augmented Reality (AR) Technology

The rareness of extant imperial Ru Ware from the Song Dynasty is widely acknowledged. Currently, there are approximately 70 known pieces of Ru Ware worldwide, distributed among institutions such as Taipei Palace Museum (23 pieces), The Palace Museum (17 pieces), Shanghai Museum (8 pieces), Percival David Foundation of Chinese Art (7 pieces), Victoria and Albert Museum, and The Museum of Oriental Ceramics in Osaka.[6] National-level museums primarily showcasing Ru Ware or celadon include the Baofeng Ru Kiln Museum (2nd level), the Celadon Museum (2nd level), and the Ruzhou Ru Ware Museum (3rd level). [7].

The author visited these museums either online or through field visits and found that they primarily employ conventional display cabinets supplemented with textual explanations, which are outdated and lack appeal. Some museums offer online VR or pseudo-holographic digital exhibitions, such as The Palace Museum's online "Palace Museum

Panorama" and the Baofeng Ru Kiln Museum's small-scale pseudo-holographic display of Ru Ware on the third floor. Additionally, many museums have digital collections accessible to the public. However, the display methods are still limited to the digitization of text and images, restricted to one-way transmission of relic information, lacking interactivity and appeal.

The exhibition design of cultural relics is aimed at the general public, therefore it is necessary to determine the user needs of the audience and decide the direction of the design accordingly. The author employed both field research and questionnaire surveys as complementary research methods. The questionnaire targeted the general public who have visited museums, with the aim of understanding their preferences for museum visits and their awareness of the application of digital technology in relic exhibitions. In the questionnaire survey section, a total of 104 questionnaires were collected, of which 99 were valid. The statistical analysis of user demographics revealed a relatively balanced gender ratio, with males accounting for 42.42% and females for 57.58%. The age of respondents ranged from under 18 to over 60, with a concentration between 18 and 25 years old.

The questionnaire was divided into three parts: "Your preferences for visiting museums", "Views on digital relic exhibitions" and "Survey on awareness of Ru Kiln and Ru Ware".

Users' Preferences for Visiting Museums. Research results indicate that people's frequency of visiting museums is concentrated on semi-annual visits (40.4%), annual visits (13.13%), and rarely visiting (27.27%). This suggests that traditional museum exhibitions primarily focused on artifact displays may not be very appealing to visitors. The duration of user visits to museums is concentrated on one to two hours (44.44%), two to three hours (30.3%), and half an hour to one hour (16.16%). Given the typical size of museums, users may find it challenging to fully comprehend and understand the exhibits within such short periods. In terms of visit purposes, 32.32% of users chose "learning knowledge," while 37.37% chose "leisure and entertainment." This indicates that in museum exhibitions, attention should be paid to both knowledge dissemination and the entertainment value of the display methods. Regarding preferred visitation methods, the majority of respondents prefer undisturbed visitation methods such as 30.3% choosing self-guided tours, 22.22% following guidebooks, 21.21% renting audio guides, and 9.09% following online guides. This indicates that in museum exhibition design, people tend to prefer private, undisturbed visitation methods. In terms of preferred forms of artifact exhibitions (this question allowed multiple selections), the most selected option was a mixed exhibition format of "digital technology + artifacts": 71 respondents chose "interactive media + physical artifacts" and 55 chose "audio/video + physical artifacts". Traditional "artifact display with textual explanations" was also chosen by 48 respondents. The least preferred option was a purely virtual display format, chosen by only 5 respondents. Analysis suggests that among various exhibition methods, users prefer physical artifact displays and multimedia interactive exhibitions, and they have little interest in purely online artifact viewing, preferring the "authenticity" of artifacts.

Users' Views on Digital Artifact Exhibitions. In the survey on digital artifact exhibitions, 59.6% of respondents were aware of digital artifact exhibitions, while the rest stated they had not heard of them. However, all of the latter group expressed a positive inclination when asked if they would be willing to experience such exhibitions, indicating a low level of popularity for digital artifact exhibitions at present. Nevertheless, people generally hold a positive attitude towards the integration of digital technology with artifact exhibitions. In terms of avenues for obtaining information about digital artifact exhibitions (this question allowed multiple selections), the majority of respondents relied on online sources, with 64.41% obtaining information through social media promotion and 33.9% through internet searches. Therefore, online advertising placements and social media promotions should be the primary channels for promoting digital artifact exhibitions. Following an initial understanding, further research was conducted on the user group that had experienced digital artifact exhibitions, aiming to gain insights into their views on existing digital artifact exhibitions. The survey results are shown in Table 1.

Table 1. User feedback regarding their impression of digital artifact exhibitions

Title/Options	Strongly Disagree	Disagree	Neutral	Agree	Strongly Agree	Average
Strong publicity	2(3.4%)	15(25.4%)	20(33.9%)	14(23.7%)	8(13.6%)	3.19
Rich content	2(3.4%)	9(15.3%)	22(37.3%)	17(28.8%)	9(15.3%)	3.37
Interesting format	0(0%)	6(10.2%)	9(15.3%)	24(40.7%)	20(33.9%)	3.98
Easy operation	5(8.5%)	14(23.7%)	15(25.4%)	20(33.9%)	5(8.5%)	3.1
Strong immersion	1(1.7%)	8(13.6%)	12(20.3%)	17(28.8%)	21(35.6%)	3.83

From the table, it can be seen that users generally have a slightly above-average impression of digital artifact exhibitions. However, many users believe that these exhibitions do not meet the convenience needs of visitors, and some feel that the existing digital projects lack diversity and attractiveness in terms of content. Therefore, reducing user operations and improving the quality of content have become important factors in enhancing user experience.

Users' Awareness of Ru Kiln and Ru Ware. Ru Kiln and Ru Ware hold a significant position in the world's material cultural heritage, but public understanding of them is inadequate. Among the 99 respondents, only 3 selected "very familiar," 18 selected "quite familiar," and even 10.1% chose "never heard of." The number of people who have visited Song Dynasty Ru Ware relics is even smaller, but 93.22% of those who have not visited express a willingness to do so. In the questionnaire for the group that has visited Ru Ware relics, 50% of respondents feel "neutral" about the current exhibition form of Ru Ware, 25% "quite like it," and 17.5% "not very fond of it." Regarding areas for improvement in the current Ru Ware exhibitions (this question allowed multiple selections), 70% of respondents hope for enhanced interactivity, 65% wish for richer exhibition forms, 57.5% desire more comprehensive introductions, and 42.5% hope for increased historical and substantial senses, while 2.5% believe no improvement is necessary. Based on the above research, it is believed that people's understanding of Ru Ware is low, and the current exhibition forms of Ru Ware lack sufficient attraction. Utilizing digital technology to assist in the display of Ru Ware relics may enhance their visibility and promote the inheritance of Ru Ware production techniques.

Based on the user research and field investigation in this section, the design goal for this project is defined as follows: an easily operable and engaging Ru Ware artifact exhibition, with augmented reality technology as an auxiliary tool.

Augmented Reality (AR) Technology Overview. Augmented Reality (AR) is a technology that cleverly blends virtual information with the real world. The concept was first proposed by Tom Caudell and his colleagues at Boeing in the 1990s. Currently, there are two authoritative definitions of augmented reality: 1. The Reality-Virtuality Continuum proposed by Paul Milgram and Fumio Kishino in 1994, where AR is situated at the mixed reality end closer to the real environment.[8] 2. Ronald Azuma's definition in 1997: AR as a system has the following three characteristics: Combines real and virtual, Interactive in real time, Registered in 3D. [9] Augmented Reality emerged as a branch of Virtual Reality but differs by seamlessly integrating virtual and real worlds, offering more natural interaction capabilities, and providing a new way for people to perceive and experience the objective world, making it a more widely applicable human-computer interaction technology.

In an Augmented Reality system, the real-world environment is first established through analysis and processing of input images. Virtual objects are then generated by the computer and embedded into the real-world space based on geometric consistency, creating an augmented reality environment that combines virtual and real elements. This combined output is then presented to the user through display systems (see Fig. 2).

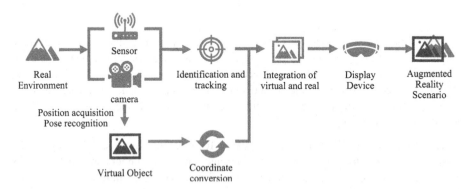

Fig. 2. Workflow of Augmented Reality System

AR technology applied in the exhibition of cultural relics is not uncommon. After reviewing AR exhibition projects in museums both domestically and internationally, it was found that most exhibition halls utilize smartphone applications as the medium for AR displays, while a few use projections and AR glasses within the museum. Some museums in China also employ WeChat mini-programs for this purpose. With a focus on "no-touch" operations, the entire AR exhibition process should minimize user interference. Projection and AR glasses are the preferred media for AR displays, as they require less interaction from the audience. Considering the personalized viewing preferences of users, different viewing options should be provided for different users. Projection displays have a wider range of influence and may cause noise and color interference for non-audience groups during viewing activities. In comparison, wearing AR glasses for viewing provides a more personalized and individualized experience.

One notable example is the AR exhibition project collaborated on by Rokid and over 200 museums in China. The exhibited content includes cultural relics such as the Chime-bells from the Tomb of Marquis Yi of Zeng State and Tang Dynasty figurines, fossils like the Yellow River elephant skull and dinosaur fossils. Users on-site only need to wear Rokid AR glasses to be guided by virtual tour guides. By simply staying in front of the relics and watching, users can automatically identify and play video animations. It's worth mentioning that the exhibition project at the Kaifeng Museum, in cooperation with Rokid, provides personalized display solutions for audiences of different ages. The AR videos in this project not only include professional explanations suitable for adult audiences but also feature more lively hand-drawn animation scenes tailored for younger audiences.

3   Exploration of AR Display Solutions for Ru Ware

According to the preliminary research, it is found that the Augmented Reality (AR) technology using AR glasses as a medium, combining with physical artifacts, has the advantages of high flexibility, personalization, good presentation effects, and simple operation. It is a good choice for displaying Song dynasty Ru ware. For the content design of this "AR + Ru ware" project, the user needs collected through interviews, questionnaires, and other forms should be transformed into functional points for product design. Table 2 shows the user requirements and the corresponding functional points annotated by the author.

To guide users through the overall operation, we have designed a user-centered complete exhibition experience flow. We simulated the user experience flow to better understand the priority sequence and frequency of use of each function, deleting unnecessary functions, and designing an AR experience scheme centered around immersive interactive experiences. Before the visit, the smart guide briefly introduces the history of Ru kiln and Ru ware to the visitors. When the audience stops in front of this artifact, the system tracks the location information and triggers the playback of an animation video depicting the process of making Ru kiln porcelain. Following the instructions of the voice of the elderly gentleman providing the introduction, users can personally participate in the process of making Ru kiln porcelain, including clay preparation, glaze mixing, glazing, and kiln firing. Upon completion of the production, visitors will also receive the "Exemplar of Ru ware craftsmanship inheritance" medal and can take a photo with the AR Ru ware artifact they participated in making.

The Augmented Reality content in this solution utilizes Rokid AR Studio (Rokid Station Pro + Rokid Max Pro) [10], developed jointly using Unity and YodaOS-Master.

Table 2. User Needs and Corresponding Functionality

Stage	User Needs	Functions
Before Visit	Access to exhibition/event information online	Online notification of exhibition/event information
During Visit	Convenient Visiting Diverse Exhibition Formats Strong Interactivity Comprehensive Introduction Personalized Services	Customizable Guided Tours Exhibition Commentary 3D Artifact Animations AR Interactive Games Artifact Production Process
After Visit	Comprehensive Understanding Engaging Experience	Achievement Check-ins Series Activity Follow-up

The hardware components include: Rokid Max Pro, which supports nearsighted adjustment within 600°, has a refresh rate of 120 Hz, weighs 75 g, addressing issues such as inconvenience, excessive weight, and dizziness caused by wearing traditional AR display devices. In terms of interactive functionality, it supports 6 Degrees of Freedom (6DoF), 3D gestures, object recognition, and image recognition. Rokid Station Pro serves as the terminal device for Rokid Max Pro, equipped with Snapdragon XR2 + chipset, 12 GB of Random Access Memory (RAM), and 128 GB of Read Only Memory (ROM), ensuring smooth application performance.

The project production process involves 3D model scanning and modeling, Unity development package creation, SDK importation, application creation, packaging, and file publishing. Specific operational steps are not detailed here, focusing instead on gesture interaction and design specifications.

Gesture Interaction. In the AR Ru ware pottery-making experience, users are required to participate in the virtual process of Ru kiln pottery making, including shaping, glaze preparation, glazing, and kiln firing. Therefore, a program for recognizing and responding to the user's hand gestures needs to be set up. The UXR2.0 SDK provides four hand gesture states: Open Pinch, Pinch, Palm, and Grip. The current gesture type can be obtained using "Ges Event Input. Instance. Get Gesture Type (HandType handType)". Similarly, replacing the content inside the parentheses with "Skeleton Index Flag flag, Hand Type type" can retrieve the skeletal information of the hand represented by Hand Type. Fig 3 shows the correspondence between finger bone nodes and their names. During shaping, the hand needs to be in the "Pinch" state and in contact with the virtual model to change the model's state. In other steps, when the hand touches an object, if the gesture is "Pinch", the "Throwable" parameter of the object is set to 0; if the gesture is "Palm", the "Velocity Estimator" is used to create the effect of the object being put down.

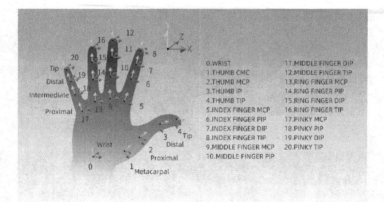

Fig. 3. Correspondence between finger bone nodes and their names in UXR2.0 SDK

Design Guidelines. AR display differs from traditional screens and virtual reality, as it allows simultaneous viewing of virtual imagery and the real world. Therefore, in design, it is necessary to consider the relationship between users, virtual content, and the real environment. Key design principles to consider include:

In AR systems, black represents non-illumination, i.e., transparency, while white represents strong light, similar to staring directly at the sun's brightness. Therefore, in design, it is essential to use black space and avoid large areas of white. Using a black aperture at the edge of the virtual scene can achieve a more realistic and integrated visual effect.

In AR environments, the fixed position of the screen's light-emitting points results in unchanged focal depth of the eye. However, users' eyes require variable focal depths to obtain images of objects at different depths. This creates a conflict and may cause visual discomfort. Through testing, it was found that when the virtual object is 2 m away from the user, the conflict is minimized, and viewing is most comfortable. Therefore, the observation point is set at a distance of 2 m from the display to ensure users have a better visual experience.

Taking the "Feng-hua mallet vase with greenish-blue glaze" currently housed in the Taipei Palace Museum as an example, Fig. 4 depicts a rendered view of the Ru kiln porcelain production process from the perspective of visitors, including the four main steps of Ru kiln production.

After completing the project, the author conducted a user experience survey, which included participants ranging from 5 to 67 years old. Through the process of user experience testing, it was found that people spent 208% more time at the exhibition booth with AR-assisted Ru ware artifacts compared to purely Ru ware exhibitions. When inviting visitors from both environments to participate in a questionnaire survey related to Ru kiln and Ru ware knowledge, the group that accepted the combination of AR and Ru ware exhibition had an average questionnaire score of 87.2/100, while the group that accepted the traditional exhibition format had an average score of only 56.8/100. In subsequent interviews, the majority of respondents found that viewing Chinese Song dynasty Ru ware exhibitions based on AR technology was "interesting", "fun", "inspiring to learn",

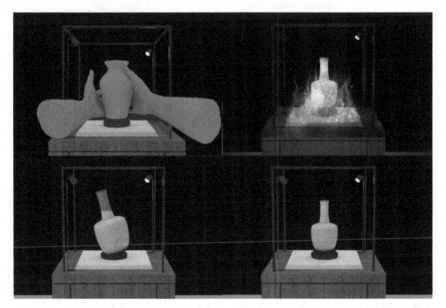

Fig. 4. Partial rendering of the visitor's perspective of the Ru kiln porcelain production process.

and "novel". A few people believed that the projection content interfered with the texture and color of the artifacts. In response, we believe that appropriately increasing the weight of AR virtual videos to give them a sense of history may be a good solution.

4   Conclusion

The study concludes that the collision between digital technology and traditional artifacts presents a new opportunity for both. For artifacts, the use of digital technologies such as Virtual Reality (VR) and Augmented Reality (AR) as aids can recreate the real historical context of artifact production and use, enhancing the viewer's experience and revitalizing artifacts in the digital age. Taking the AR display of Song dynasty Ru ware as an example, a series of processes including intelligent guidance, detailed introduction of artifact history, 3D animation, and interactive mini-games have enhanced user interest during the visit and strengthened the effectiveness of artifact information dissemination. This allows users to truly immerse themselves in the world of Ru ware production, bringing cultural heritage closer to the public and becoming a promotable solution for digital artifact display

References

1. Cihai. https://www.cihai.com.cn/detail?q=%E6%96%87%E7%89%A9&docId=5587382&docLibId=72. Accessed 09 Mar 2024
2. American Memory. https://memory.loc.gov/ammem/about/index.html. Accessed 10 Mar 2024

3. The Digital Michelangelo Project. https://accademia.stanford.edu/mich/. Accessed 10 Mar 2024
4. Horizon of Khufu. https://horizonkheops.com/en/. Accessed 10 Mar 2024
5. Archive Search. https://digitalarchive.npm.gov.tw/List/Index. Accessed 13 Mar 2024
6. Duan, D.B.: Study of the Ru Kiln in the Northern Song Dynasty. Hebei Fine Arts Publishing House, Shijiazhuang (2017)
7. National Museum Directory. https://www.henan.gov.cn/2023/03-15/2707848.html. Accessed 11 Mar 2024
8. Milgram, P., Kishino, F.: A taxonomy of mixed reality visual displays. IEICE Trans. Inform. Syst. **77**(12), 1321–1329 (1994)
9. Azuma, R.T.: A survey of augmented reality. Teleoperators Virtual Environ. **6**(4), 355–385 (1997)
10. Rokid AR Studio. https://arstudio.rokid.com/profile. Accessed 15 Mar 2024

Human-AI Co-creation for Intangible Cultural Heritage Dance: Cultural Genes Retaining and Innovation

Hongtao Zhu[1], Xiaoxuan Zhou[2], and Huiwen Liu[3](✉)

[1] Beijing Institute of Graphic Communication, Beijing 102600, China
[2] Hunan Normal University, Changsha 410081, China
[3] Beyondsoft Corporation, Beijing 100193, China
liuhuiwen02@beyondsoft.com

Abstract. The hand-waving dance, originating from the Tujia family in China, represents an ancient sacrificial ritual and has attained recognition by being included in the national intangible cultural heritage (ICH) list. This study is committed to promoting its continuous development while retaining the cultural genes of hand-waving dance. Our contribution is tripled. First, in order to preserve the inherent cultural lineage of hand-waving dance, the performances of folk inheritors and their interpretation of the meaning of dance movements were carefully recorded through videos, thus forming a dataset of inheritors' performances, which contains dance sequences and corresponding semantic annotations. Secondly, we introduced innovative choreography into the hand-waving dance with the assistance of artificial intelligence (AI), and then transformed the novel dance sequence into an experimental performance. Third, with the power of AI, we produced creative short films based on videos of experimental performances. The author emphasizes that the cooperation of folk inheritors, professional choreographers, designers, artificial intelligence engineers and other stakeholders will play an increasingly important role in the preservation, inheritance and dissemination of intangible cultural heritage dance.

Keywords: Intangible Cultural Heritage · Co-creation · AI-assisted Innovation

1 Introduction

The hand-waving dance, an ancient sacrificial dance, is created by the Tujia people living in the Central Nanshan Mountains. Although the dance was included in the national intangible cultural heritage list in 2006, the migration of the Tujia people to modern lifestyles still has a significant impact on its inheritance. Young people lack the willingness to engage in related jobs because of its reduced cultural appeal and low economic returns. Therefore, how to adapt to new social and cultural environment through sustainable innovation while retaining cultural genes is a core issue that needs to be solved in the protection and inheritance of hand-waving dance.

© The Author(s), under exclusive license to Springer Nature Switzerland AG 2024
C. Stephanidis et al. (Eds.): HCII 2024, CCIS 2116, pp. 426–433, 2024.
https://doi.org/10.1007/978-3-031-61950-2_46

Artificial intelligence opens up new horizons for ICH dance innovation. This research introduces the mechanism of co-creation of human and AI into the work process. Through the joint efforts of folk inheritors, professional choreographers, and AI engineers, we have innovatively choreographed the hand-waving dance, and then transformed it into energetic live-action performances, as well as creative short films suitable for young people's tastes.

This article is structured as follows. Section 1 briefly introduces the objectives of the study and outlines the structure of the paper. Section 2 summarizes related work. Section 3 outlines the methodology for dataset construction. Section 4 delves into innovative choreography for the hand-waving dance. Section 5 details the production process of the creative short film. Finally, Sect. 6 concludes the paper.

2 Related Work

The main technical foundations of this research include pose estimation, semantic segmentation, and artificial intelligence-assisted choreography. The subsequent section provides an overview of the advancements in related research.

2.1 Pose Estimation and Semantic Segmentation

Pose estimation plays a key role in enabling machines to comprehend dance movements captured in images and videos. Cao et al. introduced a real-time approach for detecting 2D human poses in images, associating body parts with individuals, encompassing the body, foot, hand, and face [1]. Building upon pose detection, semantic segmentation assigns labels to each part of the body in an image. Chen et al. presented a model for multi-class semantic segmentation that utilizes an encoder-decoder structure to visualize predictions as RGB segmentation masks, with each label represented by a different color [2].

2.2 AI-Assisted Choreography

In the field of dance sequence generation, Li et al. established dance-music embedding relationships based on a manually annotated database. This learned relationship is incorporated into a choreography-oriented motion synthesis framework to generate dance animations [3]. Huang et al. implemented long-term dance generation with music via curriculum learning [4]. For choreography based on human-computer interaction, Henry and choreographer McGregor released a dataset of 5 million dance poses and trained a model for interactive choreography. Utilizing input poses as seeds, the model quickly generates thirty 10-s McGregor-style dance sequences. Wu et al. explored creative dance performances using a lightweight model [5]. While research has expressed mixed views on the use of AI in dance creation, a prevailing view is that AI serves as a tool to facilitate, rather than replace, human choreographers. In assisting innovative choreography, AI has the capacity to learn and reproduce a dancer's distinctive style, introducing unexpected body movement trajectories that may inspire the dancer to create novel and potentially superior compositions [6–8].

2.3 Demonstration of ICH Dance

Traditionally, displays associated with ICH dances occur during ceremonies, funerals, harvest celebrations, and other significant events. With digitalization and the application of interactive technologies, the digital display and dissemination of ICH has become increasingly crucial. Yo et al. visualized knowledge archives of Thai dance by converting LabanWriter files into 3D animation displays [9]. Taking the Chinese Yao dance as a case, Zhao explored the use of virtual reality for dance teaching [10].

While prior research has made valuable contributions in database construction, computing framework development, and model training, most of the efforts focusd on the application of AI technology in the field of modern dance. Given the absence of systematic research on ICH dance, our study aims to establish a dataset for the hand-waving dance and undertake human-AI collaborative choreography and design.

3   Construction of Inheritors' Performance Dataset

3.1   Field Investigation and Data Acquisition

We visited Zhang Mingguang, a national-level inheritor of the big hand-waving dance, and Fu Qingwen, a provincial-level inheritor and apprentice to Zhang Mingguang. At the hand-waving hall, dating back to the Ming Dynasty, we recorded a video of Zhang Mingguang's eight-member team performing the big hand-waving dance. Additionally, we captured Fu Qingwen elucidating the meanings of various dance sequences. Subsequently, we visited Xiang Peihua, the inheritor of the small hand-waving dance, and documented the main sequences of the small hand-waving dance at the hand-waving hall (see Fig. 1). The field investigations not only afforded us precise insights into the semantic meanings of the hand-waving dance but also provided an understanding of essential tasks in hand-waving dance inheritance, such as the innovative choreography suitable for young people's preferences, and the short films production conducive to network communication.

Fig. 1. Field investigation on the hand-waving dance. The left image shows the scene of the big hand-waving dance performance, and the right image shows a demonstration of the small hand-waving dance.

3.2 Dance Posture Estimation and Annotation

The construction of the inheritor performance dataset involved several key steps: semantic sequence division, keyframe extraction, skeleton image generation, and annotation file creation. Based on the inheritors' demonstration and explanation, we categorized different semantic dance sequences and selected representative sequences from each category (see Table 1).

Table 1. Representative Sequences in the Hand-waving dance.

Dance classification	Semantic meanings of dance sequences
Big hand-waving dance	ancestor worship and altar cleaning, rowing, chopping firewood, sowing millet, selecting millet, drinking
Small hand-waving dance	single sway, shaking lice, wearing straw shoes, chopping firewood, digging soil, throwing seeds, plowing, frog announcing spring, frog embracing egg, sowing seeds, transplanting rice, weeding, picking cotton, spinning yarn, weaving cloth, fish-ing, double sway

Next, keyframe images for each sequence were extracted using Euclidean distance. Keyframes, often containing crucial turning points, changes in facial expression, or climaxes of dance movements, were selected based on thresholds. We adopted a threshold of 0.9 ensuring effective capture of key turning points and climaxes in the dance (see Fig. 2). Following keyframe extraction, skeleton images and keypoint coordinates were obtained using the OpenPose posture estimation algorithm.

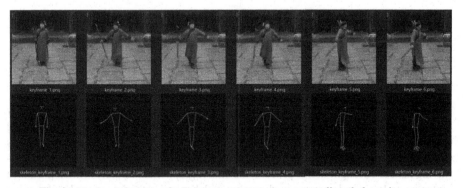

Fig. 2. Keyframe images of a dance sequence and corresponding skeleton images.

Through these processes, we successfully constructed an inheritor performance dataset for the hand-waving dance, comprising 1800 keyframe images along with their corresponding semantic meanings, skeleton images, and keypoints coordinates. To enhance the robustness of our model, we diversified the data by acquiring images in varied environments and scenes; by selecting dancers of different ages, genders, and experiences; by capturing various expressions during performances. These measures collectively contribute to the dataset's scale and diversity, playing a pivotal role in subsequent works.

4 Innovative Choreography

4.1 Co-creation of Innovative Dance Sequences

To facilitate co-creation between humans and AI, the professional choreographer selected some representative dance sequences from the inheritors' performance dataset. Subsequently, the choreographer introduced novel postures infused with the distinctive characteristics of the hand-waving dance to expand the dataset, culminating in the establishment of a dance postures library. Leveraging the library, AI generati dance sequences that transitioned fluidly between each posture (see Fig. 3).

Fig. 3. The process of innovative dance sequences co-creation.

4.2 Experimental Performance

The collaborative efforts of human and AI in crafting dance sequences yielded body movement trajectories that surpassed the bounds of human imagination while retaining the inherent characteristics of the hand-waving dance. To assess the performance effects of these innovative dance sequences, the choreographer executed the experimental hand-waving dance. Throughout this process, the choreographer continually refined the dance sentences and adjusted postures in alignment with her understanding of the hand-waving dance style. The performance was recorded and used as material for subsequent short film creation (see Fig. 4).

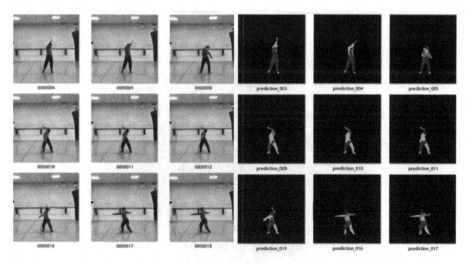

Fig. 4. Translating innovative dance sequences into experimental performance and short film. The left images show the scene of the experimental performance, and the right images show the rendering results of the Fauvism style.

5   Production of Creative Short Film

5.1   Semantic Segmentation and Coloring of Keyframe

Employing the dance posture estimation and annotation techniques, we initiate the production of short films by extracting keyframes from videos of experimental hand-waving dance. Subsequently, we executed semantic segmentation on the extracted keyframes, resulting in a probability distribution of categories corresponding to each pixel, encompassing elements such as the head, hands, and feet. Category labels were assigned based on the probability distribution, and a color map associating segmentation categories with specific colors was applied. This rendered the images with a high level of abstraction and vibrant colors, reminiscent of the Fauvism art style (see Fig. 4).

5.2   Dynamic Images Generation

Building upon the rendered keyframes, dynamic image effects were generated through interpolation. Ultimately, a short film emerged from the rendered keyframes. The creative short film, when compared to the original video, possess distinctive features that captivate attention. Firstly, abstract shapes emerge due to semantic segmentation dividing the human body into geometric facets, accentuating the lines and structure of the dancer's movements. Secondly, the bright colors introduced through color mapping enhances visual impact. Lastly, unique textures result from the segmentation process, introducing noise and irregular edges that contribute to increased variations and details in the images (Fig. 5).

Fig. 5. The dynamic image of the Hand-waving dance.

6   Conclusion

This groundbreaking study marks the inception of a dataset encompassing the fundamental sequences and semantics of the hand-waving dance. Leveraging human-AI co-creation, we successfully achieved innovative choreography for hand-waving dance and produced creative short film aligning with the preferences of youth groups. The innovative dance sequences and creative short film seamlessly blends the characteristics of ICH dance with contemporary visual expressions. This not only showcases the core value and unique spirit of dance but also offers distinct advantages in the realm of new media communication. We anticipate that this work will inspire broader engagement in the innovation of ICH dance, fostering its living inheritance and sustainable development. It is crucial to acknowledge that, presently, AI capabilities are confined to generating dance types existing in the dance database. There is a pressing need for the creation of semantic meaning-embedded datasets for ICH dance, enabling users to construct datasets and programs effortlessly. We assert that these efforts will significantly contribute to redefining technology, aesthetics, and culture in an era where the confluence of the arts and AI plays an increasingly pivotal role in shaping cultural values.

Acknowledgments. Funding from the Beijing Social Science Fund Project (No.19XCB007) is gratefully acknowledged.

References

1. Cao, Z., Hidalgo, G., Simon, T., Wei, S., Sheikh, Y.: OpenPose: realtime multi-person 2D pose estimation using part affinity fields. IEEE Trans. Pattern Anal. Mach. Intell. **43**, 172–186 (2021)

2. Chen, L.-C., Zhu, Y., Papandreou, G., Schroff, F., Adam, H.: Encoder-decoder with atrous separable convolution for semantic image segmentation. In: Ferrari, V., Hebert, M., Sminchisescu, C., Weiss, Y. (eds.) ECCV 2018. LNCS, vol. 11211, pp. 833–851. Springer, Cham (2018). https://doi.org/10.1007/978-3-030-01234-2_49
3. Li, R., Yang, S., Ross, D., Kanazawa, A.: AI choreographer: music conditioned 3D dance generation with AIST++. In: Proceedings of the IEEE/CVF International Conference on Computer Vision, Piscataway, NJ, pp. 13401–13412. IEEE (2021)
4. Huang, R., Hu, H., Wu, W., Sawada, K., Zhang, M., Jiang, D.: Dance revolution: Long-term dance generation with music via curriculum learning. arXiv preprint arXiv:2006.06119 (2020)
5. Wu, Y., Zhang, L., Ding, G., Yan, D., Zhang, F.: TSN: performance creative choreography based on twin sensor network. In: Proceedings of Wireless Communications and Mobile Computing, Hindawi, Cairo, pp. 1–12 (2021)
6. Plone, A.: The influence of artificial intelligence in dance choreography (2019). https://digital.kenyon.edu/dh_iphs_prog/7. Accessed 27 Oct 2022
7. Long, D., Liu, L., Gujrania, S., Naomi, C., Magerko, B.: Visualizing improvisation in Luminai, an AI partner for co-creative dance. In: Proceedings of the 7th International Conference on Movement and Computing, pp. 1–2. Association for Computing Machinery, New York (2020)
8. Pettee, M., Shimmin, C., Duhaime, D., Vidrin, I.: Beyond imitation: Generative and variational choreography via machine learning. arXiv preprint arXiv:1907.05297 (2019)
9. Yo, T., Sureephong, P., Rattanakhum, M., Yu, H.: Thai dance knowledge archive framework based on Labanotation represented in 3D animation. In: Proceedings of the 2017 International Conference on Digital Arts, Media and Technology (ICDAMT), Piscataway, NJ, pp. 66–70. IEEE (2017)
10. Zhao, Y.: Teaching traditional Yao dance in the digital environment: forms of managing subcultural forms of cultural capital in the practice of local creative industries. Technol. Soc. **69**, 101943 (2022)

Immersion in Theatre: The Emergence of Immersive Theatre Spaces

Mengyao Zhu and Kaizhong Cao[✉]

Communication University of China, Beijing 10000, China
526618635@qq.com, ckz.ckz@cuc.edu.cn

Abstract. The interactive design in immersive theatre is diverse for two reasons. On the one hand, the theatre itself is a fusion of space set, lighting, sound, props, actors and many other elements of the art form, these elements themselves will produce a variety of interactive design, and immersive theatre and on this basis, the audience will be placed in the performance space, and around the audience and produce a variety of interactive ways, so immersive theatre in the interactive design contains a variety of types. Large-scale performance theatre and cultural tourism projects are in addition to the storyline, more than with the application of sound and light technology to enrich the scene, to enhance the attractiveness of the project, the small theatre is to choose the plot interaction to enhance the immersive experience. The author will analyse and summarise the travelogues and evaluations of major travel platforms, extract keywords and summarise them, and analyse the ranking of different factors on the immersive experience of tourists in large-scale and small-scale interpretive theatres. And analyse whether the intervention of digital images as well as digital interactive devices can enhance the sense of immersion.

Keywords: Immersion · Theatre · Emotions · Space

1 Introductory

We are familiar with modern immersive entertainment dating as far back as the 1950s and 1960s, and some of the earliest immersive productions have begun to shift entertainment away from the stage and screen and towards an experience-centred approach to engaging audiences. The rise of theme parks such as Disney represents the rise of the immersive entertainment industry. With the booming experience economy, new forms of immersive entertainment are rapidly emerging. Script killing, which has become popular among young groups in recent years, is an immersive entertainment activity originating from abroad and has become widely popular around the world. In this kind of activity, participants play a variety of different roles, reasoning and solving puzzles through simulated plots, and interact socially with other players to achieve an immersive experience. With its strong social attributes, emphasis on intellectual challenges and leisure and relaxation, this form of entertainment is popular among young consumers and has become a new growth point in cultural consumption. Currently immersive experience is mostly used in games, films, performances and other related fields, with the continuous

C. Stephanidis et al. (Eds.): HCII 2024, CCIS 2116, pp. 434–444, 2024.
https://doi.org/10.1007/978-3-031-61950-2_47

emergence of various new digital technologies and new products, immersive experience is constantly enriched, which makes the fantastic symbolic world constructed by digital objects have stronger characteristics, so that the immersive space has the characteristics of big spectacle, super shock, omni-directional experience, and logic force [1]. Advances in technology have provided brand new possibilities in various fields, from script-killing games to large-scale theme parks, and from single performances to immersive theatres, all of which have enhanced the user's sense of participation and interactivity in various aspects.

The intersection of culture and technology is bringing immersive experiences to the forefront of the public's attention. Bai et al. (2021) and Cole and Chancellor (2009) suggest that actors, scenes and performances, have a positive impact on immersive aesthetic experiences [2], the author argues that the number of actors, scene creation, and the form of performances are not the same in different sizes of theatres, and that the three elements that visitors perceive as having a positive experience for themselves are not the same as the number of actors, scene creation, and the form of performances. The influences that visitors perceive as having a positive experience are also different, and the field of immersive experience design is entering a golden age by creating new content and forms using new scenarios, new species, and new media arts. The scope of immersive experiences encompasses immersive theatre, immersive exhibitions, and immersive performing arts, all of which are seeing unprecedented growth.

2 Characteristics of Immersive Theatre

2.1 Immersive Experience

Immersive entertainment environment has been hot in recent years, "immersive experience" and the word "immersion" have the same level of meaning, its English Immersive Experience theory [3], also known as the immersive experience, and the term "immersive experience" has the same level of meaning as the word "immersion". What is important for a well-developed immersive aesthetic experience is that the audience is naturally involved in the process. When unconscious behaviour is transformed into visual effects visible to the naked eye, the aesthetic experience will be more deeply rooted in the mind [4], MSG Sphere was completed and put into use this year, is the world's first spherical immersive top casino, in order to present an immersive entertainment experience, MSG Sphere from the visual, auditory, tactile, taste and so on many aspects of the space together. This also means that the creation of immersive space is moving in a more technological direction. The author believes that unlike traditional viewing entertainment, immersive entertainment environments emphasise interaction with the environment. Participants can influence the storyline, character dynamics or environmental elements, making them part of the story. Immersive entertainment environments provide a more immersive entertainment experience, enabling participants to delve deeper into fictional or real-life scenarios to get closer to the real scene and story. Multiple senses such as sight, sound, touch and smell are used to create an integrated sensory experience. This can include virtual reality (VR) and augmented reality (AR) technologies, 3D sound, haptic feedback devices, etc. In all kinds of cultural and entertainment activities, the presence of theatre is stronger, the characteristics of the theatre itself has a sense of immersion and presence, the current new forms of theatre continue to appear, with the help of all kinds of new digital technology means to strengthen people's sense of presence experience.

Immersive experience is a multi-sensory, instantaneous and controllable industrial form. Immersive experience, called "flow experience", refers to the state of mind in which visitors are completely captivated by an activity and have a high level of enjoyment in it, and affects the satisfaction of the participants mainly by triggering an emotional response (Shisi, 2021). It transcends the traditional mediums of performing arts, film and television, music, and exhibitions to form a service model that includes the full experience of sight, sound, and touch (Hua Jian, 2019). The core of which immersive experience lies in the immediate interaction, which makes the experience and participation both enhanced. The relationship between immersive experience and interactivity is very complex and close. Interactivity is one of the main influencing factors of scene communication mode in immersive experience. The interactivity of immersive experience has game qualities, which are mainly reflected in three aspects, such as digital multimedia, improvisation and play with context, and socialised community (Wu Fan, 2021) [5]. Scholar Mu Chuqiao points out that the three key elements of immersion are mainly location, theme and process, and divides immersive art into three categories, mainly real, virtual, and real-virtual combination approach (Mu Chuqiao, 2020) [6]. Scholar Li Liqing concluded through experiments and data analysis that immersive experience is positively influenced by three characteristics: interactivity, anthropomorphism and entertainment, with anthropomorphism having the most significant effect on immersive experience (Li Liqing, 2023). According to the author, immersive experience refers to the feeling and experience of being in an immersive situation through the involvement of all senses and emotionally, so that the individual is completely immersed in a certain activity or environment. The purpose of this kind of experience is to make the participant fully engaged in a virtual or real situation, forgetting everything around them, in order to obtain a more authentic and rich feeling.

2.2 Distinction from Traditional Theatre

Theatre is a form of art that is intertwined in time and space, it has hypothetical, live and intertwined in time and space, and all three are indispensable. In the book Theatre Ontology Tan Jisheng regards theatre as an independent and self-sufficient existential entity, and through the exploration of the essence and basic characteristics of theatre, he reveals theatre as a dynamic flux of the development process. The essence and basic characteristics of theatre change with the times, influenced by new contexts, norms, technologies, ideologies and other factors. With the combined effect of a variety of factors such as the need for innovation, technological advances, audience demand and cultural innovation, immersive theatre was born, and in the process, the focus of theatre stage performance is also changing somewhat, contemporary Polish director Jerzy Grotowski believes that the core of the theatre actor's individual performance techniques are the core of theatre art. In immersive theatre, however, the performances of the characters need to be 'de-emphasised' so that they become part of the plot rather than the focus. This 'de-centring' can be achieved in a number of ways, for example by reducing the dialogue and actions of the characters and focusing on other elements, such as situation, atmosphere or theme. Multilinear and spatial narratives are two ways in which immersive narrative space can be used to narrate theatre as opposed to traditional linear narratives [7]. "Immersive" theatre goes beyond the single stage setting, with plays taking place in multiple spaces simultaneously. A representative example is the early Sleep No More, a famous immersive theatre work inspired by Shakespeare's classic tragedy Macbeth, but also In Sleep No More, the theatre is designed as a real-life abandoned hotel, where the audience is free to explore the different rooms and corridors and watch the actors perform in a variety of scenes. The audience is not sitting in their seats as traditional spectators, but is invited to wear masks and freely move around the theatre stage environment. Instead of sitting in their seats as traditional spectators, the audience is invited to wear masks and roam freely around the theatre stage environment.

Theatre itself is a multi-element art form, and these elements affect the interaction design in many ways, which makes the interaction design in immersive theatre diverse [8], traditional theatre is completely dependent on literary narrative, emphasizing the space of literary narrative formed under the continuation of time, while contemporary theatre forms represented by immersive theatre focus more on spatial narrative [9], the current npc, video, sound and light interventions so that the theatre also has many projects in the development of immersive interactive theatre, in the process of this experience, many theatre performances try to break the fourth wall, the audience is no longer simply sitting in the seat to watch, but according to the plot of the marching performances, such as the cultural and tourism projects located in Henan: For example, in the Henan Cultural Tourism Project, the audience follows the actors in the theatre in a marching style, or they are an NPC in the plot, so that they are involved in each storyline, and this process deepens the audience's experience of the place. In addition, the project sets up different forms of performance in different sizes of theatre, and in the four large theatres, virtual images are used to assist in the design of immersive theatre scenarios, and sound and light are one of the foundations of immersive scenarios. At the same time, the theatre is also divided into daytime and nighttime tour mode, through the night lighting, digital images, and the creation of light and shadow atmosphere to design the night experience scene, the addition of light scenes to enrich people's visual experience. Immersive theatre with the current scientific and technological improvements, but also in the continuous enrichment of their own scene shaping, and then for example, the fire of the world's projects: "Money World", get the audience unanimous praise, the main selling point is in the original plot settings, the audience is the actor, the audience is involved in the development of the plot throughout the whole process, a virtual identity is their own immersive experience of the key in the play.

2.3 Attributes of Immersive Theatre

Immersive theatre, also known as submerged theatre, is a theatre experience that differs from traditional forms of theatre. It draws on the concept of "environmental theatre" proposed by Richard Schechner [10], and on this basis, it has been extended and developed. Compared with traditional theatre, immersive theatre pays more attention to the autonomy and participation of the audience. Scholar Zhou Ying points out that the characteristics of immersive theatre mainly include four aspects: the combination of space and reality, the integration of the audience into the theatre content, the deep interaction between the audience and the theatre scene, and the enhancement of sensory experience. In the process of participating in the experience the audience can freely explore the spatial environment of the theatre, interact with the actors, and even participate in the development of the plot. This form of theatre breaks down the barrier between the audience and the actors in traditional theatre, making the audience a part of the theatre rather than just passively watching, and enabling the audience to participate more actively in the plot through various interactive methods, such as role-playing, task completion, and object collection. In immersive theatre, story, plot and narration each play different roles and at the same time collaborate with each other to create a personalised and unique journey for the audience, forming an integrative hybrid intermingling, which creates an unpredictable but inevitable immersive experience in its entirety (Wu Fan, 2021) [5]. Immersive theatre focuses on the generation of episodic events, and the audience's actions and choices will directly affect the development and ending of the story, so each performance may present a different outcome and bring different surprises, which enhances the authenticity of the audience in the process of participation.

The breakthrough of immersive theatre is that it redefines the interaction between the audience and the actors, and breaks the traditional mode of theatre viewing. Compared to traditional theatre, immersive theatre is no longer confined to a fixed stage and auditorium, but travels freely throughout the performance space. Actors can interact with or around the audience, and are no longer confined to a fixed position on the stage, but are free to move through the performance space and interact with the audience in close proximity. The audience is also free to choose where they want to watch, which characters they want to participate in, and which storyline they want to follow.

3 Immersive Theatre Space

3.1 Basic Characteristics of Traditional Stage

Set design is one of the most intuitive visual elements in theatre. The set is not only the background for the actors' performance, but also an important environment for the development of the plot and the expression of the scenario. Through set design, various different scenes can be created, thus helping the audience to better understand and experience the plot. Lighting effects play a vital role in theatre, which can regulate the light and colour on the stage and create different emotional atmosphere and dramatic effects. Through the changes and use of lighting, it can highlight the emotions of the characters, emphasise important plots, and guide the audience's attention, thus enhancing the expressiveness and viewability of the play. Costume design is one of the important means to show the image of characters and social background. Costume design can highlight the characteristics and personality of the character, reflect the identity, status and emotional state of the character, so as to enhance the audience's knowledge of the character and emotional resonance. Props are physical symbols in theatre, and props design needs to be coordinated with the stage set, costumes and lighting effects to maintain a unified visual style and artistic effect.

Auditory design in theatre stage is one of the important means to create atmosphere, emphasize emotion, guide audience's attention and enhance the sense of immersion through sound effects and music, which are often used in theatre to strengthen emotion, express the theme, transform the scene and enhance audience's emotional experience. Music can echo the development of the plot and the emotional changes of the characters through different rhythms, melodies and timbres, and music can also become an independent role in the theatre, guiding the expression of emotions.

3.2 The Innovation of Immersive Theatre in the Digital Age

Immersive theatre space is still inseparable from the basic choreographic composition of the traditional theatre space, in the traditional theatre space in the form of visual design and auditory design is more diversified and enriched, the use of all-encompassing theatre space, a strong visual, auditory and other sensory effects reward to guide the audience's attention, attracting them close to the focus of the plot. Under the premise of the development of digital technology, the space of immersive stage is also choosing to add more technological means to make the stage immersive effect better. Immersive theatre in the digital era usually adopts more innovative forms of expression, such as real-time projection, holographic projection, panoramic sound, live interactive, naked-eye 3D technology and other elements are fused together to create a unique theatre scene [11], so that the audience can experience a sense of immersion never before experienced. Through the application of mobile devices or other interactive devices, the audience can choose different directions for the development of the play, interact with the actors, and even participate in the stage performance.

The development of immersive theatre is inextricably linked to its intense sensory stimulation, which to a large extent continues to benefit from the development of digital media technology. In particular, the highly integrated and digitally controlled systems for sound, light, electrical elements and visual effects have provided important support

Fig. 1. Part of the nodes of "Only Henan Theatre Mirage City".

for the formation of immersive theatre. A representative example is the popular "Only Henan Theatre Mirage City" and the series "See You Again", in which surround sound and holographic projection are used to enhance the visual effect in many parts of the theatre (Fig. 1).

Augmented Reality (AR) and Virtual Reality (VR) technologies are key tools for immersion. These technologies can bring users into the virtual world, allow them to interact with the digital environment, and provide realistic audiovisual experiences. Through head-mounted displays, handheld devices, or specialised glasses, users can interact with their surroundings as if they were in an alternate reality, thus deepening the sense of immersion. Most current VR theatre, on the other hand, is an adaptation of a play that has already been performed successfully; Hamlet 360: Thy Father's Spirit, a new play being developed by Commonwealth Shakespeare Company in 2019, is a VR version of the play Hamlet, with a VR space to watch the performance.

3.3 Classification of Immersive Theatre

From the material dimension of immersive theatre to create an atmospheric space is mainly immersive theatre performances, the narrative nature of the architectural layout, and the virtual image of spectacle [12]. This kind of project is mostly a theatre tourism performing arts scenic spot with the premise of cultural and tourism background, the project has a large scale as well as a large spatial scale, and is mostly based on a real historical background, and carries out a real historical story as well as a virtual creation to enrich the historical events, and mainly focuses on the understanding of the theatre theme, and Wang Chiu-go's Only Henan, Theatre Mirage City, which occupies an area of 622 acres, is a theatre with 21 theatres, and features acting as a theatre colony. The theatre colony with 21 theatres, featuring performing arts [13], which "takes the Yellow River civilisation as the background and tells the story about land, grain and inheritance".

Relying on theatre interpretation in the original traditional architectural space, the original Suzhou Neshiyuan's live-action performance "Touring the Garden Today's Dream", Xinanli's immersive performance "Nanjing Joyful Events", and Junyuan's "Jin-ling Dream Seeking Night Zhanyuan" immersive night tour of the smaller scale theatre are in the historical and cultural space already in existence for the plot and stage To enhance the attraction of night play, this kind of project focuses on the creation of the night atmosphere of the actual space, focusing on the exhibition of architectural space and landscape space at night, concentrating on the treatment of lighting, and focusing on the tourists in the process of watching the performance and excursion (Fig. 2).

Another category is the new type of theatre art activities such as environmental reality and script-killing, such as the performance of immersive theatre works like Sleepless Night, Mermaids by the Dead Water, Chengdu Stealing Hearts, etc., which introduces the concept of games into a series of theatre practices, from single-viewing performances to multi-line explorations of narratives, the aim of this type of immersive theatre is to make the audience emotionally invested in the plot and the characters, focusing on the interaction of the tourists with the characters and the plot during the process, and focusing on giving the audience the opportunity to take the initiative in this process plot, with a focus on empowering the audience to take the initiative in order to broaden their

Fig. 2. Part of the nodes of "The Garden of Dreams".

participation and allow them to interact with the stage and the actors, and even to be able to access the same opportunities for improvisation as the actors [14].

4 Analysis of Text-Based Research

The study analysed and aggregated travelogues and reviews from tourism platforms, used ROST CM software to analyse the word frequency of network text data from two different scales of immersive theatre, extracted high-frequency words and keywords and converged them, and, after filtering meaningless words, carried out a co-occurrence analysis of the network text and formed a semantic network graph summary to analyse the connections between the concepts in the different spatial types of immersive theatre and reveal the significance of the concepts connections, and reveal the importance relationship, relevance and hierarchical relationship between concepts.

A total of 300 reviews of "Only Henan, Theatre Mirage City" in Ctrip were selected and summarized.

As shown in Fig. 3, "Henan" is located in the centre of the semantic network and is the absolute central word, connecting almost all the words. In addition to the word "Henan", the words "theatre", "drama" and "culture" are close to the centre of the semantic network and have a close relationship with other words and have a close relationship with other words. It is determined that this type of theatre mainly revolves around stories about the history of Henan, and that the "close association of the words shocking, immersive, and moving" expresses the highly visual and auditory experience on the theatre stage.

A total of 100 reviews of Sleepless Night in Ctrip were selected and summarised.

As shown in Fig. 4, "actor" is located in the centre of the semantic network, which is the absolute central word, connecting almost all the words. In addition to the word "actor", words such as "drama", "performance", "show", etc. are close to the centre of the semantic network and have a close relationship with other words and are closely related to other words. It is determined that this type of theatre focuses mainly on the performance of the actors and the play, and that the close connection of the words

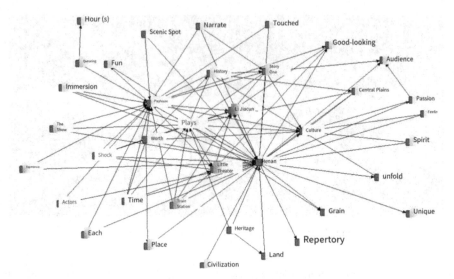

Fig. 3. Semantic Network Diagram of "Only the Dream of the Red Chamber, Theatre Mirage City" (Source: ROST CM6 software)

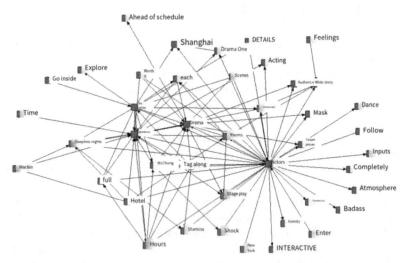

Fig. 4. Semantic network diagram of "Sleepless Night". (Source: ROST CM6 software)

"experience", "follow" and "immerse" is an expression of "the way in which the theatre is viewed". The way of watching this type of theatre is to follow the development of the play, and a high degree of immersion is indispensable for a change in the way of watching the play.

5 Conclusion

This paper discusses the current types of immersive theatre space, and by analysing the definition of immersive theatre, its characteristics, spatial design and the impact of the digital age on it, we find that immersive theatre, as an emerging art form, is influencing the development of various industries, and new forms of performances are appearing, ranging from large-scale cultural tourism to small theatre. The innovative interpretation covers the interaction between actors and audience, the multiple identities and multiple choices of the audience, the multi-dimensional presentation of space, and the multi-linear development of the script [15], through innovative spatial design, diversified forms of expression and the application of digital technology at different spatial scales. The focus of the performance is different at different spatial scales. Large cultural tourism theatre pay more attention to the audience's sensory-emotional experience, using digital technology to enhance the audio-visual effect, providing the audience with a more immersive theatre-going experience, and allowing the audience to feel as if they were in the world of the theatre. Smaller immersive theatre pays more attention to the actors' performances, the logic of the plot, audience interaction and other practical experiences to promote the development and ending of the plot, and this type of theatre emphasis the attractiveness of the plot and the audience's participation. Both enrich the means of expression of theatre art. Although immersive theatre is currently developing rapidly in China, there is a need to consider issues such as the continuous iteration of technology and innovation, the balance between artistry and spectacle, and the relationship between immersive theatre and traditional forms of theatre.

References

1. Jian, H., Chen Q.: Immersive experience: a new business format of the integration of culture and technology. J. Shanghai Univ. Finance Econ. **21**(5), 18–32 (2019)
2. Chen, S.X., Wu, H.-C., Huang, X.: Immersive experiences in digital exhibitions: the application and extension of the service theater model. J. Hosp. Tourism Manag. **54**, 128–138 (2023)
3. Gao, Y.: The Representation and Aesthetics of Digital Media Art in Immersive Theatre. (Master dissertation, Shanghai Conservatory of Music) (2022)
4. Wang, J.: Types and features of Immersion Image under the perspective of experience aesthetics. J. Art Commun. (02), 16–22 (2020)
5. Wu, F., Ma, C.: A study on the scene communication mode of immersive experience drama. Mod. Commun. (J. Commun. Univ. China) **43**(06), 104–109 (2021)
6. Mu, C., Blalack, R.: Self-discovery and redesign of the aesthetic experience of immersive art. Ind. Eng. Des. **2**(06), 67–79 (2020)
7. Hu, Z.: Research on the text characteristics of immersive drama. Drama Lit. (06), 95–99 (2023)
8. Sun, K.: Research on Interactive Design in Immersive Theatre (Master dissertation, Jiangnan University) (2021)
9. Shi, C., Shao, R.: Body, space and presence: the remediated reinvention of theatre online. J. Northeast Normal Univ. (Philos. Soc. Sci.)
10. Shi, H., Lai, Y.: On the aesthetic characteristics of immersive drama: incomplete and unspeakable: a case study of "Chengdu's heart stealing". Playwright (03), 107–112 (2021)

11. Fan, X., Song, C., Wang, Y.: Research on the creative application of immersive audiovisual technology in cultural and tourism projects. China Na. Exhib. (03), 91–93 (2022)
12. Fu, X.: Research on the Communication Practice of Immersion Theater in the Vision of Space Media—Take "Unique Henan Land of Dramas" as an example (Master dissertation, Chengdu University) (2023)
13. Yu, M., Wang, S.: A study on the perceived image of dramatic performance scenic spots based on online text: a case study of "only Henan dramatic city". Manag. Adm. 1–8 (2022)
14. Gao, S.: Application and development of immersive experience. Yi Hai (01), 55–58 (2022)
15. Wang, W.: A Research on the relationship between audience and performers of immersive drama, (Master dissertation, Shanghai Conservatory of Music) (2023)
16. Baía Reis, A., Ashmore, M.: From video streaming to virtual reality worlds: an academic, reflective, and creative study on live theatre and performance in the metaverse. Int. J. Perform. Arts Digit. Media **18**, 1–22 (2022)
17. Hogarth, S., Bramley, E., Howson-Griffiths, T.: Immersive worlds: an exploration into how performers facilitate the three worlds in immersive performance. Theatre Dance Perform. Train. **9**(2), 189–202 (2018)
18. Nakevska, M., van der Sanden, A., Funk, M., Hu, J., Rauterberg, M.: Interactive storytelling in a mixed reality environment: the effects of interactivity on user experiences. Entertain. Comput. **21**, 97–107 (2017)

Author Index

C. Stephanidis et al. (Eds.): HCII 2024, CCIS 2116, pp. 445–447, 2024.
https://doi.org/10.1007/978-3-031-61950-2

Printed in the United States
by Baker & Taylor Publisher Services